Stigma and Prejudice

FIRST EDITION

Edited by Rodolfo Mendoza-Denton
University of California, Berkeley

cognella™
San Diego, CA

Bassim Hamadeh, CEO and Publisher
Christopher Foster, General Vice President
Michael Simpson, Vice President of Acquisitions
Jessica Knott, Managing Editor
Kevin Fahey, Marketing Manager
Jess Busch, Senior Graphic Designer
Melissa Accornero, Acquisitions Editor
Luiz Ferreira, Licensing Associate

First published in the United States of America in 2013 by Cognella, Inc.

Printed in the United States of America

ISBN: 978-1-60927-425-2

www.cognella.com 800.200.3908

Contents

Introduction   v
    Mendoza-Denton, R.

When White Men Can't Do Math:
Necessary and Sufficient Factors in Stereotype Threat   18 pg   1
    Aronson, J., Lustina, M. J., Good, C., Keough, K., Steele, C. M., & Brown, J. (1999)

Status-Based Rejection Sensitivity Among Asian Americans:
Implications for Psychological Distress   24 pg   19
    Chan, W. & Mendoza-Denton, R. (2008)

When Positive Stereotypes Threaten Intellectual Performance:
The Psychological Hazards of "Model Minority" Status   8 pg   43
    Cheryan S. & Bodenhausen, G. (2000)

Field Experiments Examining the Culture of Honor   20 pg   51
    Cohen, D., & Nisbett, R. E. (1997)

The Mentor's Dilemma: Providing Critical Feedback Across the Racial Divide   71
    Cohen, G. L., Steele, C. M., & Ross, L. D. (1999)   28 pg

How Terrorism News Reports Increase Prejudice Against Outgroups:
A Terror Management Account   16 pg   99
    Das, E., Bushman, B. J., Bezemer, M. D., Kerkhof, P., & Vermeulen, I. E. (2009)

On the Nature of Prejudice: Automatic and Controlled Processes   32 pg   115
    Dovidio, J. F., Kawakami, K., Johnson, C., Johnson, B., & Howard, A. (1997)

Why Clever People Believe Stupid Things   10 pg   147
    Goldacre, B. (2010)

It's Not My Fault: When and Why Attributions to Prejudice Protect Self-Esteem   157
    Major, B., Kaiser, C., & McCoy, S. (2003)   18 pg

Personality and Racial/Ethnic Relations:
A Perspective from Cognitive-Affective Personality System (CAPS) Theory   175
    Mendoza-Denton, R., & Goldman-Flythe, M. (2009)

Networks of Meaning: Intergroup Relations, Cultural Worldviews,
and Knowledge Activation Principles   16 pg   193
    Mendoza-Denton, R. & Hansen, N. (2007)

Can Fixed Views of Ability Boost Performance
in the Context of Favorable Stereotypes?   16 pg   209
    Mendoza-Denton, R., Kahn, K., & Chan, W. (2008)

Body Ritual Among the Nacirema   225
    Miner, H. (1956)   4 pg

Confronting Perpetrators of Prejudice: The Inhibitory Effects of Social Costs   229
    Shelton, J. N., & Stewart, R. E. (2004)   16 pg

Concerns About Appearing Prejudiced:
Implications for Anxiety During Daily Interracial Interactions   22 pg   245
    Shelton, J. N., West, T. V., & Trail, T. E. (2010)

Automatic Activation of Stereotypes: The Role of Self-Image Threat   267
    Spencer, S. J., Fein, S., Wolfe, C. T., Fong, C., & Dunn, M. A. (1998)   24 pg

I Thought We Could Be Friends, But … Systematic Miscommunication
and Defensive Distancing as Obstacles to Cross-Group Friendship Formation   8 pg   291
    Vorauer, J. D., & Sakamoto, Y. (2006)

The Nonverbal Mediation of Self-Fulfilling Prophecies
in Interracial Interaction   10 pg   303
    Word, C. O., Zanna, M. P., & Cooper, J. (1974)

Introduction

By Rodolfo Mendoza-Denton

Dear Student/Course Instructor:

The book you are now holding is a flexible pedagogical tool that can be used at both the undergraduate and graduate levels for learning and teaching about the science of stigma and prejudice. It has several key features that differentiate it from other volumes on the topic. One of these features is that the volume is an anthology of original research articles, which have been carefully and systematically selected over the course of a decade of teaching this topic at the University of California, Berkeley. By relying on original research sources, pedagogy around the science of stigma and prejudice can occur at two levels: one toward understanding content and one toward understanding methodology. The empirical selections can help students become increasingly familiar with the approach (e.g., the scientific method, logical deduction), the language (e.g., "main effects," "interactions"), and the tools (e.g., priming methods, control conditions) that social psychologists use to study phenomena of interest. Thus, students learn not only about the concepts and principles associated with the topic, but just as importantly, about the way the science is conducted. The research articles can be digested at various levels of analysis—from a "general message" level appropriate for early undergraduates, to an in-depth, nuanced reading level appropriate for seasoned graduate students. Instructors should decide a priori the amount of scaffolding they will provide their students with.

The second important feature that students and instructors will notice is that the articles are not organized by a pre-defined set of topics. Instead, they are listed in alphabetical order, in much the same way as a list of references would be at the end of a research article. This is done with two objectives in mind: the first, to give students practice in the routine practice of locating references. The second objective is to avoid imposing a single structure or outline on the material at hand, in the hope of giving instructors leeway to formulate an optimal sequence for their course.

Nevertheless, in what follows, I share the sequence that I use in my own course, primarily because it's helpful in illustrating another key feature that makes this compilation unique. This feature is captured in the volume's balance among three areas: processes that result in stereotyping and prejudice (bias); processes that result from being the target of prejudice (stigma); and processes arising from interactions among people of different groups (intergroup processes). Most of the available titles on the psychology of prejudice today reflect the historical emphasis of the field, focusing heavily on bias while devoting only one section or chapter to stigma. By contrast, this text attempts a tripartite view that recognizes both perceiver and target perspectives with respect to prejudice—and how these perspectives play out in intergroup relations. This more balanced emphasis not only reflects the current state of the field, but also appeals to the interests and concerns of an increasingly diverse faculty and student body within psychology.

Beyond exposing students to the psychological literature on prejudice and stigma, this book has two central pedagogical objectives: The first objective is to encourage students to think critically about concepts, ideas, and data. This is an important skill to have when it comes to such an emotionally laden topic as prejudice. The second objective is to empower students by giving them the tools to understand the complex emotions and behavior patterns that are associated with stigmatized identities as well as prejudiced behavior. The material is academically rigorous and often very personal as well.

These goals are achieved, in part, by helping students understand their own biases—and those of others—from a lens that transcends their own points of view. As such, the first reading I like to assign is Goldacre's (2010) "Why Clever People Believe Stupid Things." Written in an accessible, engaging style, this piece lays out a series of "cognitive illusions" or "false beliefs" that everyday perceivers fall prey to in making sense of their world. This reading sets the stage for considering the possibility that the stereotypes and notions around diversity that many students walk into the class with, such as "we are now a post-racial society," "discrimination is no longer a problem in the United States," or "achievement differences between minority and majority groups are inborn," may, in fact, turn out to be false. A similar piece that can be both shocking and amusing is Harold Miner's classic "Body Ritual Among the Nacirema," which masterfully reminds students that the "normalcy" or "weirdness" of a given set of customs, beliefs, and habits is only in the eye of the beholder.

Equipped with a more open mind-set toward accepting cognitive fallacies, students in my own course move to tackling processes related to bias or prejudice from the perspective of the perceiver. I divide research related to bias into two relatively broad traditions: a motivational tradition and an information-processing tradition. The first tradition is covered by "How Terrorism News Reports Increase Prejudice against Outgroups: A Terror Management Account," which provides an overview of the popular and influential Terror Management Theory while also showing students how media coverage can influence what becomes salient in our minds. The information-processing tradition is represented by "On the Nature of Prejudice: Automatic and Controlled Processes," which introduces to students to the critical role of automaticity in social cognition, and more specifically, stereotyping. A third reading, "Automatic Activation of Stereotypes: The Role of Self-Image Threat," combines insights from both the motivational and the information-processing traditions and provides a challenging read for students, both in terms of methodology and the scientific method. This reading is challenging, because it attempts to place (motivational) boundary conditions around the automatic activation of stereotypes, thereby complicating the notion of automaticity and control beyond our traditional understanding of them. As such, instructors may view this particular piece as optional, or as an in-depth assignment for more advanced students.

The reading "Networks of Meaning: Intergroup Relations, Cultural Worldviews, and Knowledge Activation Principles" takes students through a general framework of knowledge activation that allows them to understand social-cognitive principles of knowledge activation, and in particular, the important concepts of availability, accessibility, applicability. These form the foundation for a more general spreading activation model of information processing, which itself provides a basis for understanding modern research on implicit biases. I include the classic reading "The Nonverbal Mediation of Self-Fulfilling Prophecies" as an early classic that laid the groundwork for modern research on implicit attitudes.

Students in my course then transition to "Self-Protection and the Culture of Honor: Explaining Southern Violence," which emphasizes the view that culture, history, and prior experience shape people's interpretations of the events around them. Again, the principal message here is that the same "objective" situation can be viewed, experienced, and reacted to differently depending on one's background and learning history. In contrast to Miner (1956) though, Cohen and Nisbett (1994) demonstrate this insight using an empirical approach. This is a critical point when it comes to understanding—and being open to—how different groups can see the world differently. This recognition lays the foundation for the section on stigma.

Topics covered in the section on stigma, or prejudice from the perspective of the target, include stereotype threat and identity threat, its mediators, stereotype lift, depletion of regulatory resources as a function of threat, status-based rejection sensitivity and threats to belonging, as well as coping and disengagement as coping mechanisms. The selection "It's Not My Fault: When and Why Attributions to Prejudice Protect Self-Esteem" addresses the internalization of stigma hypothesis and introduces students to the foundational concepts of attributional ambiguity and the self-protective properties of stigma. The article "When White Men Can't Do Math: Necessary and Sufficient Factors in Stereotype Threat" introduces the notion of stereotype threat to students, and is chosen specifically for two reasons. The first is that the article outlines two important assumptions about the necessary conditions for stereotype threat to impair performance; the second is that the targets of threat in this case belong to a group that is not often believed to be a target of stigmatization (white men), and thus emphasizes the generalizability of the phenomenon. The article "Can Fixed Views of Ability Boost Performance in the Context of Favorable Stereotypes?" sheds light on the interaction between stereotypes and people's beliefs about the nature of intelligence. With their focus on academic performance, these two articles flow nicely into "The Mentor's Dilemma: Providing Critical Feedback across the Racial Divide," which reinforces insights from stereotype threat, as well as the notion that the same "objective" situation (e.g., feedback from a professor) can have different psychological meanings for different cultural groups. The article "Status-Based Rejection Sensitivity among Asian Americans: Implications for Psychological Distress" introduces the concept of status-based rejection sensitivity and emphasizes how even though different groups may share similar concerns about being the targets of prejudice, both the trigger situations and the outcomes associated with these concerns are different. The piece "Personality and Racial/Ethnic Relations: A Perspective from Cognitive-Affective Personality System (CAPS) Theory" further explores the relationship between stigma, culture, and personality, and can also be conceptualized by the instructor as an "in-depth" supplementary or optional material. The article "When Positive Stereotypes Threaten Intellectual Performance: The Psychological Hazards of 'Model Minority' Status" provides a springboard for linking stereotypes to the concept of cultural/ethnic identity—which can then be further explored and supplemented by the instructor as she or he sees fit.

A third and final section focuses on intergroup processes and threats to getting along across group boundaries. This section covers research on pluralistic ignorance in intergroup relations, intergroup anxiety, signal amplification bias, and concerns about appearing prejudiced (to go along with concerns about being the target of prejudice). This section is anchored by two important pieces from the laboratory of Nicole Shelton: "Confronting Perpetrators of Prejudice: The Inhibitory Effects of Social Costs," and "Concerns about Appearing Prejudiced: Implications for Anxiety during Interracial Interactions." Together, these two articles are intended to stimulate discussion as to why, when talking about intergroup relations, people's often positive intentions (e.g., to speak out against prejudice or to reach out across a group divide) seldom translate into behavior. This idea is further explored in "I Thought We Could Be Friends, but … Systematic Miscommunication and Defensive Distancing as Obstacles to Cross-Group Friendship Formation," which again underlines the difficulty and challenges that diversity and multiculturalism bring. The idea behind these pieces is to alert students (and instructors!) to some of the pitfalls and roadblocks along the way to promoting positive intergroup relations. In this way, we might better understand how to move from numerical diversity to relational or interpersonal diversity—that is, from simply ensuring that different groups are adequately represented in a given environment to making sure that we can get along and reach out across the group boundaries that otherwise divide us.

As the articles in this anthology make clear, getting along is hard, and there are no straightforward, uncomplicated "silver bullets" to simplify the process. The most powerful tools we have in this endeavor are compassion and self-insight, both of which can be achieved through education. My hope is that this anthology can support that education.

—Rodolfo Mendoza-Denton

When White Men Can't Do Math

Necessary and Sufficient Factors in Stereotype Threat

By Joshua Aronson, Michael J. Lustina, Catherine Good, and Kelli Keough, University of Texas, Austin and Claude M. Steele and Joseph Brown, Stanford University

Research on "stereotype threat" (Aronson, Quinn, & Spencer, 1998; Steele, 1997; Steele & Aronson, 1995) suggests that the social stigma of intellectual inferiority borne by certain cultural minorities can undermine the standardized test performance and school outcomes of members of these groups. This research tested two assumptions about the necessary conditions for stereotype threat to impair intellectual test performance. First, we tested the hypothesis that to interfere with performance, stereotype threat requires neither a history of stigmatization nor internalized feelings of intellectual inferiority, but can arise and become disruptive as a result of situational pressures alone. Two experiments tested this notion with participants for whom no stereotype of low ability exists in the domain we tested and who, in fact, we reselected for high ability in that domain (math-proficient white males). In study 1 we induced stereotype threat by invoking a comparison with a minority group stereotyped to excel at math (Asians). As predicted, these stereotype-threatened white males performed worse on a difficult math test than a nonstereotype-threatened control group. Study 2 replicated this effect and further tested the assumption that stereotype threat is in part mediated by domain identification and, therefore, most likely to undermine the performances of individuals who are highly identified with the domain being tested. The results are discussed in terms of their implications for the development of stereotype threat theory as well as for standardized testing. © 1999 Academic Press

One's reputation, whether false or true, cannot be hammered, hammered, hammered into one's head without doing something to one's character.

—Allport (1954, p. 142)

For some reason I didn't score well on tests. Maybe I was just nervous. There's a lot of pressure on you, knowing that if you fail, you fail your race.

—Rodney Ellis, African-American State Senator (Texas) in a 1997 interview

Joshua Aronson, Michael J. Lustina, Catherine Good, Kelli Keough, Claude M. Steele & Joseph Brown, "When White Men Can't Do Math: Necessary and Sufficient Factors in Stereotype Threat," *Journal of Experimental Social Psychology*, vol. 35, no. 1 , pp. 29–46. Copyright © 1999 by Elsevier Science & Technology Journals. Reprinted with permission.

Members of stereotyped groups often feel extra pressure in situations where their behavior can confirm the negative reputation that their group lacks a valued ability (see Aronson, Quinn, & Spencer, 1998b); Steele, 1997, for reviews). We call this pressure "stereotype threat" and argue that in the short term, it can undermine the intellectual performance of virtually anyone whose group is targeted by stereotypes alleging a lack of intellectual ability in some domain (Steele & Aronson, 1995). We have also argued that stereotype threat can prompt a long-term defense against the chronic exposure to ability impugning stereotypes and the low performance that it can provoke—a disengagement or "disidentification" from the threatened domain, a dropping of the domain as a basis of self-esteem (see Steele, 1992, 1997; Steele & Aronson, 1995). The current research focuses on the short-term effects of stereotype threat in an effort to better understand the conditions under which stereotypes impugning intellectual ability are likely to interfere with intellectual test performance.

Empirical support for our contention that stereotype threat can affect the member of nearly any stereotyped social group is now abundant. Steele and Aronson (1995) found, for example, that African-American college students were dramatically affected by stereotype threat conditions; they performed significantly worse than whites on a standardized test when the test was presented as a diagnosis of their intellectual abilities, but about as well as whites when the same test was presented as a nonevaluative problem solving task. When the test was framed as diagnostic, Steele and Aronson hypothesized, the possibility of confirming the well-known stereotype of African-American intellectual inferiority became salient, and thus disruptive. A number of studies have found that women, too, perform less well when the societal stereotype that they face—low math ability—is made relevant by experimental instructions (Aronson, Good, & Harder, 1998a; Shih, Pitinski, & Ambady, in press; Spencer, Steele, & Quinn, 1999). Aronson and Salinas (1997) have found virtually the same results with Latino students, who also face the stereotype that their group lacks scholastic ability, as have Croizet and Claire (1998) in a study involving participants of low socioeconomic status. Finally, Levy (1996) has demonstrated how the cognitive functioning of elderly individuals can be disrupted by stereotype threat. When the elderly participants in her study were subtly primed with the stereotype regarding old age and senility, they performed worse on a test of short-term memory than when they were primed with the more positive "old-people-are-wise" stereotype instead.

That intellectual performance can be spoiled by conditions that make ability stereotypes relevant and improved by conditions that nullify them, and that this occurs across a range of social groups certainly encourages a situationist—or at least person-situation *interactionist*—explanation for the academic underperformance of stereotyped groups (Steele, 1997; Steele & Aronson, 1995). Our analysis, we believe, provides a more hopeful alternative to the standard accounts of minority underachievement, which cite such intractables as poverty (e.g., Bereiter & Engleman, 1966; White, 1982), genetic differences in intelligence (e.g., Benbow & Stanley, 1980; Herrnstein & Murray, 1994; Jensen, 1980), or cultural and societal barriers to skill acquisition (e.g., Hunt, 1969).

Situational Pressure Or Internalized Inferiority?

But an important question remains. Must individuals belong to a minority group—or be chronically targeted by stereotypes—in order to experience stereotype threat and suffer its effects? Undoubtedly, the degree to which a person is exposed to stereotypes about his or her group breeds an awareness of stigma, and such "stigma-consciousness" has been linked with individual differences in responses to stereotype threat (e.g., Lustina & Aronson, 1998; Pinel, in press). Nonetheless, a stigmatized identity may not be necessary to suffer its effects because, in theory, stereotype threat derives its power from a motive common to all individuals, regardless of their race, gender, socioeconomic status, age, and so on—the motive to sustain a self-image of goodness or competence and of being able to secure important outcomes (e.g., Steele, 1988). This motive dramatically influences behavior in performance contexts, where people have been shown to do what they can to make themselves feel that their prospects are good and to project this image of competence to others (e.g., Jones, 1989). This is best accomplished, of course, by performing well, but even when performance is not optimal, individuals enjoy numerous ways of appearing competent or at least appearing not to care (Steele, 1992; Major & Schmader, 1998).

Stereotype threat arises when these performance motives are jeopardized by the awareness of an ability-impugning stereotype in a situation where that stereotype can be confirmed by low performance. Thus, because most people are motivated to feel and to appear competent, nearly anyone, we believe, can experience the pressure of stereotype threat in some situation and thus suffer the short-term consequence of impaired intellectual performance (Crocker, Major, & Steele, 1997).

By showing how subtle situational factors can dramatically affect the performance of minority students, the existing stereotype threat studies make a strong case for the environmental basis of their underperformance. Still, the current body of evidence does not rule out a plausible nonsituational explanation. Specifically, there remains the possibility that there is something special about being Black, Latino, a woman, poor, or old that made these test takers underperform when confronted with stereotypes about their group. Could the performance debilitating effect of stereotypes conceivably depend upon long-term exposure to devaluing stereotypes, real feelings of inferiority that have been "hammered into one's head" by persistent stigmatizing conditions? Various theorists have endorsed such a view, arguing that stigmatizing treatment can result in a stigmatized personality (e.g., Cooley, 1956; Mead, 1934). Indeed, the social scientists whose opinions served as a linchpin in the 1954 Supreme Court case that ended racial segregation in the schools (Brown v. Board of Education) saw internalized inferiority as a necessary consequence of prejudicial treatment (Allport, 1954; Cook, 1979; Gerard, 1983).

Applied to the results of the stereotype threat research, the internalized inferiority interpretation would suggest that in all of these studies, the testing situation merely brings to the surface deep-seated feelings of inferiority or low expectations that have become an unchanging part of the individual whose exposure to devaluing stereotypes has left inferiority as a permanent mark (e.g., Howard & Hammond, 1985; S. Steele, 1990). Thus, although research has shown that stereotypes can undermine the performance of ability-stigmatized groups like African-Americans, Latinos, and women, it is not clear whether belonging to a minority group is a necessary or merely sufficient factor in this underperformance.

The Present Hypothesis

The present research, then, was aimed at testing the situationist hypothesis of stereotype threat phenomena. Specifically, we put to the test our contention that virtually anyone could be made to underperform on a difficult intellectual test if they were exposed to a stereotype that predicted underperformance for their group. In both Studies 1 and 2 we examined the intellectual test performance of the social group we deemed most unlikely to have internalized stereotype-based feelings of intellectual inferiority—white males selected on the basis of their high abilities. If these highly skilled majority-group members could be threatened by a stereotype alleging their relative inferiority, then it seems reasonable to assume that ingrained feelings of inferiority need not be involved in stereotype threat. In Study 2 we sought to replicate this effect, while at the same time testing a second assumption about the short-term effects of stereotype threat—that to underperform as a result of activating a stereotype alleging low ability, the individual must be self-invested in the ability domain being tested.

Study 1

Overview

White males with high scores on the mathematics section of the Scholastic Aptitude Test (SAT) took a very challenging math test. In one condition of this experiment we explicitly confronted them (before the test) with the stereotype that Asian students outperform Caucasian students in mathematical domains. In a control condition no mention of the stereotype was made. The general prediction was that, compared to those not explicitly reminded of the Asian stereotype (control condition), the stereotype threatened test takers would perform less well.[1]

---

[1] This study actually included two additional stereotype threat conditions in which we coupled the Asian Stereotype manipulation with some additional information we thought might moderate the effect of the stereotype on performance. In one condition, we attempted to nullify the stereotype by suggesting that the test at hand was not known to reveal ethnic differences in the past; in the other, we attempted to magnify the effect by presenting the test as having revealed them in the past (see Specer, Steele, & Quinn, this issue). The performance results of these conditions were identical to those of the condition in which only the stereotype was presented. Why these additional statements failed to moderate the effect is unclear, but we suspect the reason may be that the manipulation of stereotype threat (i.e., the news articles) may have been too vivid and powerful to have been modified much by the addition of the more pallid verbal instructions. Because these conditions are not relevant to the central question posed by this study, they will not be further discussed.

Participants

Potential participants, drawn from the Stanford University student body, completed a questionnaire designed to identify students with strong math skills and who attached at least a moderate degree of importance to these skills. Students were eligible for the study if they: (1) indicated that their ethnicity or race was white/Caucasian or Jewish; (2) responded that they were neutral about, agreed with, or strongly agreed with the following two statements: "Math is important to me" and "I am good at math;" and, (3) scored 610 or above (of a possible 800) on the math section of the SAT. The average math SAT score of the participants was 712.17 *(SD = 60.6)*, and the scores ranged from 610 to 800. Twenty-three qualifying male undergraduates participated in this study for pay or for course credit.

Materials and Procedure

Participants were greeted individually by a white female experimenter who explained that the study she was conducting had to do with differences in math ability. Those participants who were randomly assigned to the stereotype condition *(n = 12)* were given 2 min to skim over a packet of articles about the phenomenal math achievement of Asians and were told that the study was specifically concerned with understanding why Asians appear to outperform other students on tests of math ability. Taken from national newspapers and prominent journals, these articles emphasized a "growing gap in academic performance between Asian and white students." The rationale of the experiment, coupled with the articles, we reasoned, would accomplish two things—make the participants feel targeted by a stereotype relevant to their math ability and give some plausibility to the stereotype. The titles strongly suggested that Asians are better at math than Caucasians, though they offered no explanation for the superiority.

At the end of the 2 min interval, the participants in the stereotype condition were further told that there seems to be a growing discrepancy between the academic performance of Asians and whites. "In math," they were told, "it seems to be the case that Asians outperform whites." The experimenter then implied that research findings are inconclusive and that the purpose of the study was to learn more about the nature and scope of these differences. Participants assigned to the "control" condition (n = 11) did not read the articles or hear any mention of Asian-white ability differences; they were told only that the test was a measure of their math ability.

The participants were then given 20 min to take the test, which was administered on a computer. The test was composed of 18 questions derived from the Graduate Record Examination (GRE) mathematics subject test. The computer tracked the time each participant spent on each of the questions and recorded the participant's answers.

At the end of the 20 min time period, participants first completed a measure of state anxiety, a modified form of the state form of the State-Trait Anxiety Inventory (Spielberger, Gorsuch, & Lushene, 1970). They then completed a questionnaire that asked how much effort they expended on the task, how difficult they found the problems, how much pressure they felt, how much confidence they had in their answers, and how many problems they thought they had solved correctly. The participants were then fully debriefed and compensated for their participation.

Results and Discussion

Test performance. The measure of test performance was simply the number of items correctly solved, which we submitted to a one-way analysis of variance (ANOVA). The results revealed the predicted effect of stereotype threat on test performance, $F(1, 21) = 5.51$, $p < .01$.[2] Participants solved fewer of the items in the stereotype threat condition *(M = 6.55)* than in the control condition *(M = 9.58)*.

 Follow-up questionnaire. What processes mediated the underperformance? No condition differences were found on measures of anxiety, time spent on items, or the self-reported difficulty of the items (All *p*'s n.s.). But, the stereotype threat group did report expending more effort on the problems (*p* < .05), suggesting that the stereotype may have boosted their motivation, not undermined it. Thus, the underperformance could stem from trying too hard, rather than not hard enough. This finding is consistent with the analysis provided by Steele and Aronson (1995), who concluded that withdrawal of effort was not the cause of the underperformance of the African-American students in their studies. However, an analysis of covariance (ANCOVA) performed on participants test scores failed to support this reasoning; the difference between means is unchanged when we correct for self-reported effort. Thus, as in many studies of stereotype threat, the mediator between stereotype threat and performance is unclear.

 The performance results are nonetheless quite supportive of our general hypothesis that making salient the Asian stereotype would depress the performance of a group of nonstereotyped, high ability students. Thus, contrary to the prediction derived from the internalized inferiority view of group differences in performance (e.g., Allport, 1954; Howard & Hammond, 1985; S. Steele, 1990), stereotype-related underperformance does not appear to require the existence of doubts drummed in by chronically stigmatizing conditions or by minority status. Study 2 was undertaken to replicate this effect, but also to examine a proposition about what *is* required to induce stereotype threat.

Study 2

As we have noted elsewhere (Aronson et al., 1998b; Steele, 1997) our formulation has assumed from the outset that stereotype threat will have little if any effect on individuals who are not identified with the ability domain in question. To be threatened by the self-evaluative implications of a stereotype that alleges low ability of some kind, a person probably needs to either care about having the ability or at least care about the social consequences of being seen as lacking the ability (Brunstein & Gollwitzer, 1996; Steele, 1992,1997). Thus, in an attempt to find evidence of stereotype threat we have selected students, at least in part, on the basis of their identification with some skill. Although internal analyses of past experiments and pilot studies suggest that stereotype threat has little effect on the unidentified (see Steele, 1997), no research has been conducted that examines domain identification as a factor independent of ability and confidence in that domain. Thus, no satisfactory test of our reasoning exists.

---

[2]An analysis of covariance with participants' quantitative SAT scores used as the covariate was also performed, yielding the same significant pattern of results.

Directly examining the role of identification in stereotype threat processes is important for at least two reasons. First, it may help in making more accurate predictions about which individuals will be likely to most acutely experience stereotype threat, as well as the settings in which they will be at risk. Second, demonstrating the link between domain identification and the experience of stereotype threat will inform and strengthen our reasoning about the longer term self-protective consequences of stereotype threat on the identification process. Specifically, we (Aronson et al., 1998b; Steele, 1992, 1997; Steele & Aronson, 1995) have argued that to protect oneself against the chronic experience of stereotype threat in an academic domain, individuals *disidentify* with the domain, often with serious consequences for their motivation and achievement. In line with this reasoning, there is increasing evidence that ability-stigmatized groups (e.g., African-Americans) are more prone than their nonstigmatized counterparts to disidentify from academics (Aronson & Fried, submitted for publication; Major et al., 1997; Osbourne, 1995). Yet the link between this identification and stereotype threat is unclear. This reasoning would be much strengthened by finding that it is those most identified with a particular academic domain who are most prone to vulnerability to stereotypes alleging limited prospects therein.

Study 2 directly tested this hypothesis by conceptually replicating the previous study with the additional subject factor of students' degree of identification with mathematics. The prediction was straightforward: stereotype threat should be most disruptive to the group selected for having high as opposed to moderate identification with mathematics.

Method

Overview. This experiment took the form of a 2 X 2 factorial design. The factors were math identification of the participant (high vs. moderate) and experimental condition (stereotype threat vs. control). As in Study 1, a math test was presented in the context of the Asian-math-superiority stereotype (stereotype threat condition) or without the stereotype (control condition). Test performance was the primary dependent measure.

Participants. Participants were white male students enrolled in the second semester of a rigorous year-long calculus course at the University of Texas at Austin. This course was selected for its high concentration of math-proficient students. Specifically, no student can enroll in the class with a QSAT score below 550. Furthermore, students are not allowed to enroll in the course's second semester without performing satisfactorily in the first.

Three weeks prior to the experimental session these students filled out a questionnaire during class regarding their math-related attitudes. There were 75 participants who filled out the questionnaire. These students were divided into three groups according to their responses to a question asking them to rate the importance of their math abilities to their self-concept. Scores could range from 1 (not at all important) to 15 (extremely important). Students responses to this item ranged from 4 to 15, (M = 12.49, SD = 2.84). Taking the top and bottom third of students on this measure produced a "high math-identified" group (n = 26, M = 15, SD = 0) and a "moderately identified" group (n = 23, M =

10.27, *SD* = 2.12), who had been randomly assigned to either the stereotype threat condition or the control condition of the experiment.[3]

Procedure. The testing occurred 3 weeks after the initial questionnaire, during students' weekly discussion section meetings, which were run by their calculus teaching assistant. Students were informed that they would receive extra credit on their homework grade for participating in this study, which was described as a national study of mathematics ability. The teacher and an experimenter handed out booklets that provided the manipulation of experimental condition, the test, and the dependent measures. The booklets were constructed so that the participant's experimental condition could not be seen by the teacher or experimenter.

Stereotype threat manipulation. Participants in the stereotype threat condition received an additional description of the study as an attempt to better understand why Asians are superior to other groups in mathematics. Specifically, the participants read the following description:

> As you probably know, math skills are crucial to performance in many important subjects in college. Yet surprisingly little is known about the mental processes underlying math ability. This research is aimed at better understanding what makes some people better at math than others. As you also may know, at some top schools, Asian students outnumber the white students in math majors and majors with math as a prerequisite, and there seems to be a growing gap in academic performance between these groups. A good deal of research indicates that Asians consistently score higher than whites on standardized tests of math. But thus far, there is not a good explanation for this. The research you are participating in is aimed at better understanding these differences. Your performance on the exam will be compared to other students from across the nation. One specific question is whether Asians are superior at all types of math problems or only certain types.

The control (no stereotype) group was run simultaneously. The only difference was in the paragraph that described the reason for the experiment. The control group read the following:

> As you probably know, math skills are crucial to performance in many important subjects in college. Yet surprisingly little is known about the mental processes underlying math ability. This research is aimed at better understanding what makes some people better at math than others. Your performance on the exam will be compared to other students from across the nation.

---

[3]Because the bottom third of this sample was used it might be reasonable to think of the group as "low identified," but only in a relative sense. In absolute terms, both the group mean on the identification measure and the fact that only two of the participants had identification scores below the midpoint of the identification scale make it more appropriate to refer to these students as "moderately identified."

Testing session and measures. We attempted to make the testing session feel similar to an actual standardized test administration such as one might encounter taking the SAT. After allowing participants time to read their test description, the teacher and the experimenter took the class through a sample problem and then allowed the students 20 min for the test.

The math test was developed specifically for use in this experiment by graduate students in the mathematics department. The questions were drawn from the math subject GRE test practice booklets that pilot testing revealed to be at the upper limit of these students' abilities. The test consisted of 15 calculus-related questions.

At the end of the time period, the students were told to stop the test and to proceed with the questionnaire packet. The packet contained the same questionnaire employed in Study 1.[4]

Results and Discussion

Test performance. The primary hypothesis in this experiment was that participants would perform less well when confronted with the stereotype regarding Asian superiority in math, but that this would mainly be the case for those students who cared deeply about their math abilities—the high math-identified students. The ANOVA performed on their test scores offered strong support for this prediction. Only the math identification by experimental condition interaction was significant, $F(1, 45) = 9.66$, $p < .005$. As simple effects tests show, and as may be seen in Fig. 1, high math-identified participants performed less well on the test when the stereotype was mentioned ($M = 2.91$) than when it was not ($M = 4.10$), $t(45) = 2.08$, $p < .05$. Moderately identified participants showed precisely the opposite pattern, performing better when the stereotype was discussed ($M = 4.07$) than when it was not ($M = 2.83$), $t(45) = 2.325$, $p < .05$.

This pattern of data replicated the finding of study 1—and did so with a different procedure, participant population, and a different test—supporting our assumption that stigma is not necessary for stereotype threat to undermine performance. It also provides very clear evidence of the critically important role of domain identification in mediating stereotype threat.

Follow-up questionnaire. The ANOVA performed on participants' responses to the questions in the packet revealed only one significant difference, a significant interaction on the item measuring evaluation apprehension, $F(1, 45) = 4.96$, $p < .05$. Using a scale ranging from 1 ("I never had this thought") to 5 ("I had this thought very often"), high math-identified participants wondered more often what the experimenter would think of them in the stereotype threat condition ($M = 2.46$) than in the control condition ($M = 1.18$), $t(45) = 2.81$, $p < .01$. The stereotype threat manipulation had no apparent effect on evaluation apprehension among the moderately identified participants. They reported equal amounts regardless of whether they were in the stereotype threat condition ($M = 1.64$) or in the control condition ($M = 1.75$), $t < 1$.

---

[4]As in the Study 1, an analysis of covariance was also performed and the pattern of the results and significance are nearly identical—indeed, they are more significant—when participants scores are corrected by their SAT scores.

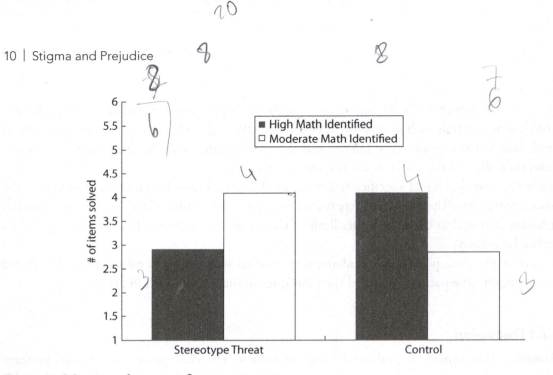

Figure 1. Mean math test performance.

There were no effects on any of the other distraction items, nor on the measures of state anxiety, effort, perceived performance, or confidence (all p's, > .2). Thus, lacking better evidence than participants' own self-reports, the best explanation for the effect of the stereotype on performance appears to be that the underperformance was caused by evaluation apprehension rather than by the withdrawal of effort or by measurable levels of anxiety. This finding is in contrast to that of past stereotype threat research (e.g., Aronson, 1998; Blascovich et al., 1998; Steele & Aronson, 1995), which points to the role of anxiety in undermining performance in stereotype threat conditions.

To further explore this evaluation apprehension interpretation, we submitted participants test scores to analyses of covariance (ANCOVA) using their self-reported evaluation apprehension ratings as the covariate. Although this weakened the effect somewhat, the interaction effect remained significant (p = .02), and the relationship between the adjusted means remained identical to that shown in Fig. 1. Thus, although there appears to be some mediational effect of evaluation apprehension, it does not appear to solely mediate the effect of stereotype threat on test performance.

As in previous studies, it is difficult to determine the precise mediation of stereotype threat effects. The difficulty stems in part from the self-report nature of the measures, but also from the fact that there are undoubtedly multiple mediational pathways through which psychological manipulations can affect performance. Even studies that have used direct measures such as blood pressure to show that anxiety accompanies stereotype threat (Blascovich et al., 1998) cannot confidently rule out the withdrawal of effort as a mediator of underperformance. Anxiety and effort withdrawal are not mutually exclusive. Indeed, they most likely work in tandem to undermine performance.

Looking within the control group, we find what one would reasonably expect on a mathematics test comparing students who are identified with math to students who are markedly less so. At the same level of ability and preparation, the high math-identified participants outperformed their low math-identified counterparts when not confronted with a stereotype alleging relative inferiority. But, the reverse pattern occurred when the stereotype was activated—moderately identified participants actually outscored high math-identified participants. This finding suggests that in stereotype threat testing situations, it may be an advantage to be moderately rather than extremely invested in a domain. The stereotype appeared to challenge these moderately identified students to do their best, but they were not so ego-involved that they were distracted, a finding quite consistent with much research on ego-involvement and performance (see Baumeister & Showers, 1986, for a review).

General Discussion

The existence of negative stereotypes, we have argued, means that in situations where the stereotype is relevant, individuals who are targeted by stereotypes face the unpleasant predicament of confirming those stereotypes. One consequence of this predicament, many studies have shown, is interference with intellectual test performance. Taken together, the results of the present studies strongly suggest that a person need not be chronically targeted by stereotypes to be impaired by them on tests that measure abilities of high personal importance. What appears to be necessary, on the other hand, is that an individual care enough about performing well to be bothered by a stereotype's implication that they may lack the ability to do so.

We can be fairly certain that our participants were not harboring deep-seated feelings of math inferiority—what Allport (1954) referred to as "traits due to victimization." White males of high math ability clearly do not fit the profile of the "target of a stereotype" or "the disadvantaged minority student." They are not normally considered at risk to be stereotyped, looked down upon because of their race, or targeted by low performance expectations. Indeed, in contrast to the cases of women and math, African-Americans and general intelligence, the elderly and forgetfulness, and so on, there is no stereotype directly targeting white males— alleging that "white men can't do math." For example, consider a recent study in which male and female undergraduates (from numerous ethnic groups) were asked to list stereotypes about various groups (Aronson & Disko, 1998a). The study found that whereas 86% of the respondents mentioned the intellectual or academic prowess of Asians, and 30% listed the intellectual weakness of females, not a single participant listed stereotypes regarding the intellectual abilities of whites. Thus, the stereotype either does not exist or it exists only under such narrow circumstances that we would not expect it to be chronically "available" enough to become part of a stigmatized personality (Crocker et al., 1997).

Nonetheless, when placed in a situation where a minority group's relative superiority was made salient and relevant, highly skilled and identified white males experienced a decrement in intellectual performance—much like the members of groups for whom stereotypes regarding their intellectual abilities *do* exist and *are* widely known and cognitively available. Clearly, then, chronic feelings of stigmatization were not a necessary factor in their underperformance. Situational pressures alone—the stereotype about Asians coupled with the strong desire to perform well—were sufficient to interfere with performance.

"Direct" Versus "Indirect" Stereotype Targets

This by no means implies that the white males in these studies experienced the situation in *exactly* the same way or to the same degree as, say, women taking the same math test under stereotype threat conditions. Clearly there must be phenomenological differences that vary as a function of many factors. Otherwise, one would expect to see white males dropping out of math and science graduate programs—which are highly populated by Asian students—with the same frequency as women. According to the most authoritative study of attrition from math and science programs, this is simply not the case. Although white males do complain about the extra pressure engendered by the high concentration of Asian classmates, they are much less likely than women to disidentify and drop out of math and science fields (Seymour & Hewitt, 1997).

What makes the situation different for men than for women—or other stereotype threatened groups? Surely there are many reasons, many of which we believe to stem from the fact that the stereotype directly targets some groups and only indirectly targets others. In the context of math ability, for example, Asians and women are what we could call "direct" targets of a stereotype. The stereotype refers explicitly to them (e.g., "Asians are good at math, women are bad at math") and corresponding expectations (e.g., Asians will perform well on this math test, women will not") may naturally arise whenever they are in a math-relevant situation. It is therefore easier to trigger and more difficult to suppress stereotype threat for them. White males, on the other hand, are "indirect" targets. The stereotype refers to them only by means of a *comparison* with the direct stereotype target. For this reason stereotype-related expectations may only arise in situations—like those of the present studies—where comparisons with direct targets are made explicit. In this, as in many contexts, white males are the implied standard—the norm from which direct stereotype targets are viewed as deviating (e.g., Miller, Taylor, & Buck, 1991).

So while indirect targets are certainly capable of feeling stereotype threatened in some circumstances, they are undoubtedly less likely than direct targets to experience its most pernicious effects (e.g., disidentification), for a number of reasons, a few of which we list here. First, direct targets are likely to have the stereotypes more cognitively available and thus be more easily threatened by them. Pinel (in press) refers to this heightened awareness of stereotypes as "stigma consciousness" and has shown that it predicts underperformance in intellectual testing situations (see also Lustina & Aronson, 1998). Second, in most cases, being a direct target means being distinctive—being readily identified by others as belonging to a particular group. Thus, direct stereotype targets may also tend to feel more identified with their groups (e.g., Brewer, 1991) and therefore more self-threatened than indirect targets by whatever the stereotype alleges. Past research has suggested that people who feel more identified with their group respond differently to stereotypes and prejudice than less identified individuals (e.g., Crocker & Major, 1989; Rosenkrantz, 1994). This greater sense of "groupness" may also make the direct target feel more responsible for representing their group and thus more keenly and chronically apprehensive about representing their group in situations where a group stereotype is relevant. And finally, as suggested by the looking-glass-self models of stigma, chronic exposure to stereotypes could engender self-doubts that are either chronically activated or easily brought to the fore in stereotype-relevant situations, making the direct target more vulnerable to stereotype threat.

It is certainly conceivable that indirect targets, such as white males in a math-intensive environment, could feel like direct targets. But even then, their vulnerability is likely to be mitigated by supports that direct targets do not have—namely, majority status. For instance, although white males pursuing degrees in math or science fields may feel threatened by the reputed superiority of Asians, their belongingness in the domain is nonetheless affirmed by the abundance of similar individuals in their ranks, a luxury that women in these fields do not enjoy (Fulton, 1996). Moreover, as Crocker et al. (1997) point out, members of dominant groups may be stigmatized in one context, but they are buffered from that stigma because of their power position in the larger society. For these, and perhaps additional, reasons, it is understandable that indirect targets are quite capable of experiencing some of the short-term effects of stereotype threat without necessarily feeling the need to disidentify.

An intriguing implication of the direct-indirect distinction is that in performance situations, indirect targets may actually derive a benefit from comparisons with direct targets for whom stereotypes allege *inferior* ability. If stereotypes can cause white males to perform worse when they are made to focus on the abilities of Asians, might they also perform better when led to focus on the abilities of women? Spencer et al. (1999) have found some indirect support for this hypothesis in their studies of men and women taking math tests. The males in their study actually performed worse in conditions where the female stereotype was nullified by experimental instructions. Specifically, males tended to perform worse when told that the test was not expected to show gender differences, suggesting that their performance may be boosted by the implicit stereotype that they are superior to women in math.

Domain Identification and Test Performance

This research adds to the growing body of evidence that domain identification—the degree to which a person stakes their self-image on a given ability—is vitally linked to how people respond to failure (Brunstein & Gollwitzer, 1996) or to stereotypes about their abilities (Steele, 1997). But does this mean that stereotype threat will affect only those students who are highly identified with a domain? Steele (1997) has hinted at such an argument, suggesting that stereotype threat is likely to be felt most keenly among the "vanguard" of students targeted by stereotypes—those at the highest levels of ability and domain identification. The present research is certainly consistent with this reasoning—students who were more domain-identified tended to score less well under stereotype threat. But does this mean that targets who are not in the vanguard are invulnerable?

Not necessarily. It is quite possible that high degrees of domain identification are indeed necessary for stereotypes to become self-threatening in the relatively low stakes setting of the typical laboratory experiment, where the consequences of low performance are primarily self-imposed. After all, psychology experimenters lack "fate control." They do not punish the low performing test taker with low course grades or denied access to college or graduate school. Lacking such consequences, the performance experiment is a high-stakes endeavor for only those participants who are so identified that *any* test of their ability is ego-involving.

In the real world, however, ability tests can be ego-involving even in cases where a person is not particularly identified with a domain because there are self-threatening consequences to underperformance.

For example, a woman seeking an advanced degree in art history may be only marginally identified with her math abilities, yet is nonetheless required to score well on the mathematics portion of the GRE to gain acceptance to graduate school. In such cases, low-identified students may be every bit as debilitated—and perhaps more so—by the relevance of a stereotype alleging low math ability. It therefore may be more correct to say that high motivation—a sense that something important is at stake—is the necessary factor in stereotype threat, not high identification per se. To be sure, the sense of high stakes is undoubtedly greatest among those who are most identified with the domain, but stereotype threat may nonetheless affect the test performances of average students, not just those in the vanguard (Aronson & Disko, 1998b).

The relationship between domain identification and test performance in stereotype threat situations may contribute to the poor predictive validity of college and graduate school admissions tests (e.g., Sternberg & Williams, 1997). Specifically, because extra pressure can cause a person to underperform, it is something of an advantage to be *moderately* identified rather than than to be *extremely* so. But in most academic situations the relationship between domain identification and achievement will be linear; the more one cares, the harder one will study, the more regularly one will attend class, think through ideas, and so on. Thus, scores on high-stakes tests like the SAT may be rendered less accurate because, as in Study 2, test takers can be penalized for their devotion. Thus, we might well question the overreliance on standardized tests as gateways to higher education—certainly in the case of ability-stigmatized minority groups—especially when other measures exist which do not subtract points for caring.

What is Stereotype Threat?

We began this report with a quote from Rodney Ellis, a highly regarded African-American State Senator who "knew he was just as intelligent as the next guy," but attributed his low performance on standardized tests to apprehensions about "failing his race." The current evidence regarding stereotype threat does not allow us to know if Ellis explains or merely describes the process. Is stereotype threat self-threatening because it arouses a fear of being a bad ambassador of one's group to mainstream society? Or is it more simply the apprehension about appearing incompetent—for the sake of one's own reputation? Or alternatively, is it merely the result of worrying that one might lack ability? Or is it some combination of these concerns? These are important questions that will have to await the results of future research for answers.

What these studies do make clear is that, whether the fear is interpersonal or intrapersonal, motivated by staining one's group or merely one's self, it need not arise out of a chronic stigmatization. It is sufficient to be identified enough with a domain to be threatened by the possibility of limited prospects there and unlucky enough to be on the wrong end of a stereotype about an intellectual ability. And, clearly, if stereotype threat can be aroused in highly able, nonstereotyped students merely by making them aware of a stereotype that predicts lower performance for their group relative to another, then it is not some exotic phenomenon felt only by the members of historically stigmatized groups.

As we have elsewhere argued (Aronson, Quinn, & Spencer, 1998; Steele, 1997; Steele & Aronson, 1995), this situationist view of minority underperformance is an encouraging one because it locates the problem not exclusively within the person, but within the social circumstances confronting the person. Stereotype threat research underscores how changing those circumstances, even subtly, can have dramatically positive effects on performance. The present studies carry this message a step further by suggesting that stereotype threat does not uniquely affect members of certain minority groups. Rather, it is a predicament that stems from quite normal responses to the low or demeaning expectations that come to the individual in the form of cultural stereotypes. Moreover, the critical role of domain identification suggests that these responses are based on self-protective processes that can be triggered, and perhaps intensified, by minority status and identity, but which do not depend upon them. This may prove to be useful knowledge because it may point toward ways of reducing stereotype threat that involve self-protective tactics (e.g., Aronson, 1998; Josephs and Scroeder, 1997) rather than the less tractable undertaking of eliminating cultural stereotypes.

References

Allport, G. (1954). *The nature of prejudice.* New York: Addison-Wesley.

Aronson, J. (1998). *The effects of conceiving ability as fixed or improveable on responses to Stereotype Threat.* Manuscript submitted for publication.

Aronson, J., & Disko, D. (1998a). *Frequency of stereotypes about blacks, whites, Asians and Latinos.* Unpublished raw data, Univ. of Texas, Austin.

Aronson, J., & Disko, D. (1998b). *A test of the vanguard hypothesis in stereotype threat.* Unpublished raw data, Univ. of Texas, Austin.

Aronson, J., & Fried, C. (1998). *Belief in the malleability of intellectual ability: An intervention to increase the performance of African-American college students.* Manuscript submitted for publication.

Aronson, J., Good, C., & Harder, J. A. (1998a). *Stereotype threat and women's calculus performance.* Unpublished manuscript, Univ. of Texas, Austin.

Aronson, J., & Salinas, M. F. (1997). *Stereotype threat, attributional ambiguity, and Latino under-performance.* Unpublished manuscript, Univ. of Texas.

Aronson, J., Quinn, D., & Spencer, S. (1998b). *Stereotype threat and the academic under-performance of minorities and women.* In J. Swim and C. Stangor (Eds.), *Prejudice: The target's perspective.* Academic Press.

Baumeister, R. F., & Showers, C. J. (1986). A review of paradoxical performance effects: Choking under pressure in sports and mental tests. *European Journal of Social Psychology,* 16 (4), 361–383.

Benbow, C. P., & Stanley, J. C. (1980). Sex differences in mathematical ability: Fact or artifact? *Science,* 210, 1262–1264.

Bereiter, C., & Engleman, S. (1966). *Teaching disadvantaged children in the preschool.* Englewood Cliffs, NJ. Prentice Hall.

Blascovich, J., Quinn, D. M., Spencer, S. J., & Steele, C. M. (1998). *The effect of stereotype threat on African Americans' blood pressure.* Unpublished manuscript, University of California, Santa Barbara.

Brewer, M. B. (1991). The social self: On being the same and different at the same time. *Personality and Social Psychology Bulletin,* 17 (5), 475–482.

Brunstein, J. C., & Gollwitzer, P. M. (1996). Effects of failure on subsequent performance: The importance of self-defining goals. *Journal of Personality and Social Psychology,* 70 (2), 395–407.

Cook, S. W. (1979). Social science and school desegregation: Did we mislead the Supreme Court? *Personality and Social Psychology Bulletin,* 5 (4), 420–437.

Cooley, C. H. (1956). *Human nature and the social order.* New York: Free Press.

Crocker, J., & Major, B. (1989). Social stigma and self-esteem: The self-protective properties of stigma. *Psychological Review,* 96, 608–630.

Crocker, J., Major, B., & Steele, C. (1997). Social stigma. In D. Gilbert, S. T. Fiske, & G. Lindzey (Eds.), *Handbook of social psychology* (Vol. 4). Boston: McGraw-Hill.

Croizet, J. C., & Claire, T. (1998). Extending the concept of stereotype threat to social class: The intellectual under-performance of students from low socioeconomic backgrounds. *Personality and Social Psychology Bulletin,* 24, 588–594.

Fulton, J. D. (1996). AMS-IMS-MAA Annual Survey (First Report). *Notices of the American Mathematical Society,* 43 (12), 1493–1511.

Gerard, H. (1983). School desegregation: The social science role. *American Psychologist,* 38, 869–878.

Herrnstein, R., & Murray, C. (1994). *The bell curve.* New York: Free Press.

Howard, J., & Hammond, R. (1985, September 9). Rumors of inferiority. *New Republic,* 72, 18–23.

Hunt, J. McV. (1969). *The challenge of incompetence and poverty.* Urbana, IL: Univ. of Illinois Press.

Jensen, A. R. (1980). *Bias in mental testing.* New York: Free Press.

Jones, E. E. (1989). The framing of competence. *Personality and Social Psychology Bulletin,* 15, 477–492.

Josephs, R., & Schroeder, D. (1997). *The self-protective function of the learning curve.* Unpublished manuscript, University of Texas at Austin.

Levy, B. (1996). Improving memory in old age through implicit self-stereotyping. *Journal of Personality and Social Psychology,* 71, 1092–1107.

Lustina, M., & Aronson, J. (1998). *Measuring and predicting stereotype vulnerability.* Unpublished manuscript. Univ. of Texas at Austin.

Major, B., & Schmader, T. (1998). Coping with stigma through psychological disengagement. In J. Swim & C. Stangor (Eds.), *Stigma: The target's perspective.* New York: Academic Press.

Major, B., Spencer, S., Schmader, T., Wolf, C., & Crocker, J. (1997). Coping with negative stereotypes about intellectual performances: The role of psychological disengagement. *Personality and Social Psychology Bulletin,* 24 (1), 34–50.

Mead, G. H. (1934). *Mind, self, and society.* Chicago: Univ. of Chicago Press.

Miller, D. T., Taylor, B., & Buck, M. L. (1991). Gender gaps: Who needs to be explained? *Journal of Personality and Social Psychology,* 61(1), 5–12.

Osbourne, J. W. (1995). Academics, self-esteem, and race: A look at the underlying assumptions of the disidentification hypothesis. *Personality and Social Psychology Bulletin,* 21, 449–455.

Pinel, E. C. (in press). Stigma-consciousness: The psychological legacy of social stereotypes. *Journal of Personality and Social Psychology.*

Rosenkrantz, S. L. (1994). *Attributional ambiguity among Mexican-Americans: The role of ethnic identity.* Unpublished doctoral dissertation, Stanford Univ.

Sarason, I. G. (1980). Introduction to the study of test anxiety. In I. G. Sarason (Ed), *Test anxiety: Theory, research, and applications* (pp. 3–13). Hillsdale, NJ: Erlbaum.

Seymour, E., & Hewitt, N. (1997). *Talking about leaving: Why undergraduates leave the sciences.* Boulder, CO: Westview Press.

Shih, M., Pitinski, T. L., & Ambady, N. (in press). Shifts in women's quantitative performance in response to implicit sociocultural identification. *Psychological Science.*

Speilberger, C. D., Gorsuch, R. L., & Lushene, R. E. (1970). *Manual for the state-trait anxiety inventory.* Palo Alto, CA: Consulting Psychologist Press.

Spencer, S. J., Steele, C. M., & Quinn, D. (1999). Stereotype threat and women's math performance. *Journal of Experimental Social Psychology, 35,* 4–28.

Steele, C. M. (1988). The psychology of self-affirmation: Sustaining the integrity of the self. In L. Berkowitz (Ed.), *Advances in experimental social psychology* (Vol. 21, pp. 261–302). Hillsdale, NJ: Erlbaum.

Steele, C. M. (1992). Race and the schooling of black Americans. *The Atlantic Monthly.* April.

Steele, C. M., & Aronson, J. (1997). A threat in the air: How stereotypes shape intellectual identity and performance. *American Psychologist, 52* (6), 613–629.

Steele, C. M., & Aronson, J. (1995). Stereotype threat and the intellectual test performance of African-Americans. *Journal of Personality and Social Psychology*, 69 (5), 797–811.

Steele, S. (1990). *The content of our character.* New York: St. Martin's Press.

Sternberg, R. J., & Williams, W. W. (1997). Does the Graduate Record Examination predict meaningful success in the graduate training of psychologists? *American Psychologist, 52* (6), 630–641.

White, K. R. (1982). The relation between socioeconomic status and academic achievement. *Psychological Bulletin,* 91(3), 461–481.

Status-Based Rejection Sensitivity Among Asian Americans

Implications for Psychological Distress

By Wayne Chan and Rodolfo Mendoza-Denton

Abstract

We examined whether anxious expectations of discrimination among Asian Americans can help explain this group's elevated levels of internalizing symptomatology, such as lower self-esteem (Twenge & Crocker, 2002) and higher depressive symptoms (Okazaki, 1997, 2002) relative to European Americans. Study 1 reports on the development and validation of a scale measuring status-based rejection sensitivity among Asian Americans (RS-A). In Study 2, scores on the RS-A were related to spontaneous discrimination attributions specifically in situations where discrimination is both applicable and possible for Asian Americans. Study 3 revealed that shame mediated the relationship between RS-A and internalizing symptomatology. Implications for well-being and intergroup interactions are discussed.

A growing body of research documents that Asian Americans may be at heightened risk for anxiety, depression, and low self-esteem (Okazaki, 1997, 2002; Twenge & Crocker, 2002). Such internalizing symptomatology (Nadeem & Graham, 2005) can be differentiated from externalizing symptomatology, which includes aggression and delinquency (Wright, Zakriski, & Drinkwater, 1999). For example, Asian American college students report higher levels of intrapersonal socioemotional maladjustment than European American college students (Abe & Zane, 1990), and Asian American college students have significantly higher levels of depression and social anxiety than do European American college students, even when controlling for generational status and differing response styles (Okazaki, 1997, 2000). In addition, a meta-analysis of 712 American studies comparing levels of self-esteem among American ethnic groups found that, overall, Asian Americans have lower levels of self-esteem than Latino American or African American ethnic groups (Twenge & Crocker, 2002).

Although lower self-esteem among individuals of Asian descent compared to other groups are sometimes interpreted as reflecting cultural differences in the subjective value of high self-esteem rather than

Wayne Chan & Rodolfo Mendonza-Denton, "Status-Based Rejection Sensitivity Among Asian Americans: Implications for Psychological Distress," *Journal of Personality*, vol. 76, no. 5, pp. 1317–1346. Copyright © 2008 by John Wiley & Sons, Inc. Reprinted with permission.

psychological distress (e.g., Heine & Lehman, 1999), converging evidence indicates that this cultural explanation may not necessarily generalize to Asian Americans. The covariation of anxiety, depression, and self-esteem among Asian Americans suggests genuine psychological distress in this group. Asian Americans uniquely experience elevated depression compared to both Asians living in Asia (Chang, 2002) and European Americans (Abe & Zane 1990; Okazaki, 1997), controlling for acculturation. In turn, European Americans and Asians in Asia do not differ on depressive symptomatology (Zhang & Norvilitis, 2002). Furthermore, Asian Americans emphasize the importance of self-esteem as much as European Americans (Heine, Lehman, Markus, & Kitayama, 1999), and the positive relationship between self-esteem and subjective well-being is as robust among Asian Americans as it is among European Americans (Benet-Martinez & Karakitapoglu-Aygun, 2003). Together, these findings suggest that there is something unique about the Asian American experience that contributes to internalizing symptomatology.

In this article, we propose that one of the experiences that distinguishes Asian Americans from Asians living in Asia and European Americans—and which might help account for differences in psychological distress—is that of having to contend with discrimination. Despite their reputation as a model minority (Lee, 1994), various studies confirm that Asian Americans expect and experience at least as much discrimination as other minorities in the United States. (e.g., Crocker & Lawrence, 1999; Oyserman & Sakamoto, 1997; Sue, Bucceri, Lin, Nadal, & Torino, 2007), albeit of a more interpersonal (e.g., being made fun of by peers) and less institutional (e.g., being profiled by police) variety (Greene, Way, & Pahl, 2006). Based on prior research on individual differences in reactions to stigma among African Americans (Mendoza-Denton, Downey, Purdie, Davis, & Pietrzak, 2002), we propose that *status-based rejection sensitivity* (hereafter, status-based RS)—the tendency to anxiously expect, readily perceive, and intensely react to discrimination and prejudice based on membership in a stigmatized social category or status group—can help explain some of the variance in Asian American psychological distress.

The notion that discrimination-related experiences can help account for variance in internalizing symptomatology stands in contrast to a wealth of theory and research on the conceptualization of stigma as a buffer to self-esteem (Crocker & Major, 1989), which proposes that attributions of discrimination can be protective of the self. Specifically, in the face of negative outcomes, blaming negative outcomes on discrimination rather than one's own abilities or effort can be protective against negative self-views (Major et al., 2002). This account has been influential in the literature on stigma from the target's perspective in part because it helps explain the well-replicated finding that African Americans, who have arguably suffered some of the most blatant and severe injustices based on their status group membership in the United States, tend to show significantly higher levels of self-esteem relative to European Americans (Twenge & Crocker, 2002). Given the prototypicality of African Americans as the targets of stigma (Espiritu, 1997), the zeitgeist may have shifted away from efforts to link discrimination to self-esteem and other internalizing symptoms (though see Schmitt & Branscombe 2002; Major, Kaiser, & McCoy, 2003).

Linking Status-Based RS to Asian American Psychological Distress

In contrast to African Americans, there are several theoretical reasons why the self-protective effects of stigma may not apply as readily to Asian Americans. First, the sociopolitical histories of African and Asian Americans have differed importantly (Ogbu & Simons, 1998). The civil rights movement of the 1960s may have served to make the possibility of discounting discriminatory feedback more chronically accessible to African Americans. In support of this idea, data from Twenge and Crocker (2002) show that following the civil rights movement, self-esteem among African Americans has increased linearly. A consciousness-raising movement of such magnitude has not yet occurred among Asian Americans in the United States. Second, the situations where discrimination may occur for Asian Americans differ from those for African Americans. In particular, Asian Americans report being discriminated against in interpersonal situations (Greene et al., 2006) where the typical reaction to status-based rejection has been shown to be self-directed and negative in nature (Dickerson, Gruenewald, & Kemeny, 2004). This may further limit discounting of discriminatory feedback among Asian Americans, leading to negative outcomes in self-esteem. In support of this hypothesis, there is a robust relationship between past experiences of discrimination and lowered self-esteem (Greene et al., 2006) and elevated depressive symptomatology (Liang, Li, & Kim, 2004) among Asian Americans.

Rather than focusing on past experiences of discrimination per se in this research, we examine the psychological legacy of discrimination for Asian Americans by focusing on people's anticipatory threat to such discrimination. We do so because measuring past experiences precludes the possibility that vicarious experiences (e.g., through peer observation, media exposure, or parental communication) may themselves play a role in creating anxiety and threat about stereotyping and prejudice (Mendoza-Denton et al., 2002; Ward, Hansbrough, & Walker, 2005). Further, research has shown that anticipatory threat surrounding discrimination, independent of the materialization of such discrimination, can be a powerful determinant of subsequent behavior and outcomes (Allison, 1998; Blascovich, Spencer, Quinn, & Steele, 2001; Frable, 1993; Lang, 1995; Steele, 1997; Terrell & Terrell, 1981). Together, the above literature suggests that focusing only on past experiences may lead to an underestimation of the effects of discrimination on subsequent outcomes. As such, following prior research on rejection sensitivity (Downey & Feldman, 1996; Mendoza-Denton, Page-Gould, & Pietrzak, 2006), we examine the relationship between discrimination and elevated internalizing symptomatology among Asian Americans by assessing individual differences in anxious expectations of status-based rejection.

The Present Research

In this article, we report three studies that tested the general hypothesis that status-based RS is related to internalizing symptoms among Asian Americans. In Study 1, we report on the development of a measure of anxious expectations of status-based rejection specifically constructed for Asian Americans. In Study 2, we test the predictive utility of the measure by asking whether individual differences in anxious expectations of status-based rejection among Asian Americans predict attributions to racism in negative encounters in a variety of domains. Finally, in Study 3, we test whether individual differences in such anxious expectations help explain differential expressions of internalizing symptomatology following discrimination, and also the emotions that mediate the relationship between anxious expectations and internalizing symptomatology. Together, the studies suggest that individual differences in status-based RS may be related to affective reactions to discrimination and therefore play an important role in helping explain the negative mental health outcomes among Asian Americans.

Study 1

Study 1 describes the development of the status-based RS questionnaire for Asian Americans (RS-A). The measure assesses individual differences in anxious expectations of being discriminated, devalued, or stigmatized on the basis of one's group membership, which we view as being at the core of status-based RS (Mendoza-Denton, in press). In line with our view of anxious expectations as *hot cognitions* in which affect amplifies the impact of a given cognition (Metcalfe & Mischel, 1999; Mischel, Ayduk, & Mendoza-Denton, 2003), people are considered to be high on status-based RS when they both expect rejection based on status and feel anxious or concerned at the possibility of this outcome.

Prior work with African Americans using an individual differences measure of status-based RS specifically designed for this group *(RS-race;* Mendoza-Denton et al., 2002) showed that (a) self-esteem was unrelated to RS-race among African Americans and (b) Asian Americans reported lower levels of RS-race than African Americans on this particular measure. At first glance, these data may argue against the logic of using this construct to explain variability in internalizing symptoms among Asian Americans. However, the measure developed by Mendoza-Denton et al. (2002) specifically targeted African Americans and, as such, does not adequately capture Asian Americans' discrimination concerns (Mendoza-Denton & Mischel, 2007). For example, whereas African Americans may experience anticipatory threat in situations where they may face discrimination from authorities (e.g., when being harassed by security guards, or during a job interview), situations pertinent to athletic inability or language fluency may more readily activate stigma-related threat among Asian Americans (see Cheryan & Monin, 2005; Sue et al., 2007). Thus, situations that are viewed as benign by the one group may pose considerable threat to another, and vice versa (Mendoza-Denton et al., 2002).

Because the antecedents and trigger features that activate anxious expectations of status-based rejection among African Americans and Asian Americans may differ considerably, we developed and validated the RS-A specifically for Asian American populations. The questionnaire is modeled after Mendoza-Denton et al.'s (2002) RS-race questionnaire for African Americans, albeit containing different situational triggers culled from focus group and open-ended interviews. Based on our conceptualization of the dynamics of status-based RS among Asian Americans, we predicted that RS-A scores would be positively related to depression and social anxiety, and negatively related to self-esteem. This prediction differs from one previously made for African Americans (Mendoza-Denton et al., 2002), for whom RS-race has been found to be unrelated to self-esteem.

Importantly, we sought to show that the relationship between RS-A and these outcome variables holds over and above the effect of sensitivity to rejection for personal reasons (RS-personal; Downey & Feldman, 1996), a construct that has also been found to be related to depression and self-esteem (Downey & Feldman, 1996; Ayduk et al., 2000). Partialing out the effects of RS-personal allows us to be more confident that relationships found between RS-A and outcome variables of interest are not resultant from generalized rejection concerns (see Major & O'Brien, 2005). In addition, we included the RS-race questionnaire designed for African Americans to test our key prediction that internalizing symptomatology would be predicted by anxious expectations of discrimination specifically in situations relevant to Asian American discrimination rather than African American discrimination. To the degree that generational status may explain some of the variance in self-esteem among Asian Americans (Heine et al., 1999), we also control for generational status. Finally, because RS-race among African Americans has been shown to be negatively related to academic performance and positively related to ethnic identity (Mendoza-Denton et al., 2002), we measured these two concepts here as well. Although we did not have a straightforward prediction for the relationship between RS-A and ethnic identity, we expected no relationship between RS-A and academic performance, given that low academic competence is not part of the Asian American stereotype (Oyserman & Sakamoto, 1997).

Measure Development and Validation

Participants and Procedure

This study was conducted at the University of California, Berkeley, a large public research university in the United States. Over the course of data collection, the ethnic distribution of the undergraduate population was as follows: 46.8% Asian, 4.3% Black, 12.0% Latino/a, 34.4% White, and 2.5% other.

Study participants were 144 (65% female) self-identified Asian Americans (*M*age = 20.41 years, *SD* = 1.69). Among these, 57 were foreign born and had been in the United States for an average of 10.39 years (*SD* = 6.37), 72 were U.S. born with both parents being foreign born, 6 were U.S. born with one parent being U.S. born, and 6 were U.S. born with both parents being U.S. born. Three participants did not report birthplace information. The pattern of results did not differ when excluding foreign-born individuals, so the final sample retained all participants. Participants completed the study for partial course credit. Participants arrived in the laboratory in groups between 1 and 12 persons in size. They were seated in a large room by an experimenter, who informed the participants that the study was a survey battery that assesses the thoughts and feelings that college students may have in everyday situations. Participants then received the survey packet, completed it, and handed the completed packet in to the experimenter.

Survey Battery—Covariates

RS-personal. The RS-personal (Downey & Feldman, 1996) scale assesses anxious expectations of rejection by significant others due to one's personal, unique characteristics. The questionnaire consists of 18 hypothetical situations in which rejection by a significant other is possible. For each situation, people first indicate their concern or anxiety about the outcome on a 6-point scale ranging from *very unconcerned* (1) to *very concerned* (6). They then indicate the likelihood that the other person would respond in an accepting manner on a 6-point scale ranging from *very unlikely* (1) to *very likely* (6). The score for acceptance expectancy is reversed to index rejection expectancy. The anxiety score is multiplied by the expectation score to generate an anxious expectation score for each situation, and scores for all situations are averaged to compute the total RS-personal score. In this study, we use the RS-personal as a measure of prejudice-irrelevant apprehension in interpersonal interactions (sample a = .81, *M* = 9.57, *SD* = 2.75).

Status-based RS for Asian Americans (RS-A). The questionnaire, modeled after the RS-race measure for African Americans (Mendoza-Denton et al., 2002), assesses participants' anxious expectations of status-based rejection in each situation. The initial step in developing this questionnaire involved conducting focus groups designed to encourage discussion about perceived prejudice. Two 6-person focus groups of Asian American undergraduates were convened in a classroom on campus to generate representative situations in which discrimination could occur. Participants were recruited by announcement in undergraduate classes and by word of mouth; they received free dinner as compensation. All participants in the two focus groups self-identified as being Asian American, with equal distribution of males and females, but participants' specific ethnic identification, age, and socioeconomic status were not collected. An Asian American researcher facilitated each focus group to minimize reluctance to discuss potentially controversial subject matter (cf. Sue et al., 2007). Group participants were prompted to think of situations in which they would anticipate discrimination. Each generated situation was then discussed in the full group, and situations deemed relevant by a majority of group participants were retained. We did not attempt to generate an exhaustive list of status-based rejection situations. Instead, our goal was to collect some representative rejection situations for this group. These focus groups yielded 11 face-valid, nonoverlapping situations in which Asian American students might experience apprehension about being discriminated against on the basis of their being Asian American. Consistent with Greene et al.'s (2006) analysis of discrimination directed at Asian Americans, the situations involve peer interaction with familiar figures (e.g., classmates, possible romantic partners) as well as unfamiliar figures of both the high-investment (e.g., professors) and low-investment (e.g., passers-by) varieties. The situations are also consistent with some of the themes highlighted in Sue et al.'s (2007) qualitative analysis of racial microaggressions against Asian Americans, more specifically, the "Alien in Own Land" theme and the "Ascription of Intelligence" theme. These situations are listed in Table 1 and comprise the RS-A scale.

For each of the 11 situations, people first indicate their concern or anxiety about possible rejection on a 6-point scale ranging from *very unconcerned* (1) to *very concerned* (6). They then indicate the likelihood that the other person would respond in a rejecting manner on a 6-point scale ranging from *very unlikely* (1) to *very likely* (6). The anxiety score is multiplied by the expectation score to generate an anxious expectation score for each situation; scores for all situations are averaged to compute the total RS-A score. In 8 of the 11 generated situations, focus group participants indicated that rejection in those situations would be most likely attributed to discrimination, whereas for the other three situations (Items 7, 10, and 11 in Table 1) there might be multiple bases for rejection concerns (e.g., personal as well as status-based). Therefore, for these three situations we explicitly asked survey participants to indicate how much they expected and were anxious about rejection on the basis of their race or ethnicity.[1] For the other eight situations we asked survey participants to report on their rejection expectations and concerns, without explicitly specifying race or ethnicity. As reported in more detail below, these situations all load onto a single factor, regardless of the exact wording of the prompt, suggesting that they form part of a unitary construct.

RS-Race for African Americans (RS-Race). The RS-race Questionnaire (Mendoza-Denton et al., 2002) assesses status-based RS among African American in situations where discrimination is possible and applicable to African Americans, although some items may be important to non-European Americans in general. The questionnaire consists of 12 hypothetical situations. For each situation, participants first indicate their concern or anxiety about the outcome on a 6-point scale ranging from *very unconcerned* (1) to *very concerned* (6). They then indicate the likelihood that the other person would respond in a rejecting manner on a 6-point scale ranging from *very unlikely* (1) to *very likely* (6). As with other scales within the rejection sensitivity construct, the anxiety score is multiplied by the expectation score to generate an anxious expectation score for each scenario, and scores for all scenarios are averaged to compute the total RS-race score (sample a = .88, M = 5.35, SD = 3.70).

Survey Battery-Outcome Variables

Self-esteem. The Rosenberg (1979) Self-Esteem Questionnaire is a valid, reliable 10-item Likert scale, in which participants indicate on a 6-point scale how much each statement reflects their self-attitudes (e.g., "I take a positive attitude towards myself"). A high score indicates high self-esteem (a = .90, M = 4.40, SD = .87).

Depression. To assess depression, we used the Beck Depression Inventory (BDI; Beck et al., 1979), a widely used 23-item scale that assesses the degree to which participants have experienced symptoms of depression in the past week on a scale from 0 to 3 for each item. Responses are summed across the 23 items, with higher scores indicating more expression of depressive symptoms (a = .90, M = 10.42, SD = 8.85).

Social anxiety. The Social Avoidance and Distress Scale (SADS; Watson & Friend, 1969) is a 28-item true or false scale that assesses the degree to which participants experienced anxiety in social situations, with a subscale assessing the tendency to avoid stressful situations and a subscale assessing felt anxiety.

---

[1] We use the term "race or ethnicity" throughout our survey materials to operationalize the group status of Asian Americans and European Americans for our participants, recognizing nevertheless that differences between these groups may characterized as ethnic, panethnic, racial, cultural, or a mixture of these (Betancourt & Lopez, 1993; Lien, Conway, & Wong, 2004; Phinney, 1996).

Table 1. Factor Loadings for RS-A Questionnaire Items and Psychometric Properties of RS-A Questionnaire for Asian Americans

#	Item	Factor Loading
1.	You are working on a group lab project with several other people from your class. While working, several people mentioned a movie they would like to see afterwards. Someone offers to call people later to organize it.	0.59
2.	Your mother is visiting you this weekend, and she made your favorite home-cooked dish for you to take to school on Monday.	0.53
3.	Imagine that you are in lecture, and the professor poses a difficult question for the class. You happen to know the answer and would like to raise your hand.	0.56
4.	You ask a salesperson at a store about a product, and she mumbles a response that you don't catch. As you ask her to repeat what she just said …	0.62
5.	You are in a shopping mall. Right in front of you is a large group of people your age who are the same ethnicity as you, talking loudly in a foreign language. There are several other shoppers around you.	0.59
6.	You have a big science exam coming up, and some of the students would like to organize their own study group. You are asked to join the group.	0.62
7.	The annual school dance is coming up soon, and there is someone that you know fairly well that you would like to go to the dance with.	0.66
8.	On the first day of your engineering class, your professor asked the students to form groups to work on the class project over the course of the semester. Several other students asked you to join their group.	0.70
9.	You are at a party, and you are introduced to a friend of a friend, who proceeds to ask you where you're from.	0.62
10.	You call an attractive person that you know fairly well, and you leave a message on their answering machine about going to dinner sometime.	0.59
11.	One of your classmates who happen to be of the same ethnicity is having difficulty with a class assignment. You offer your help to the person.	0.63

Note: The anxiety and expectation questions for Items 7, 10 and 11 are asked with "because of your race or ethnicity" appended. A formatted copy of the scale can be found online at http://rascl.berkeley.edu/scales/rs-a.pdf.

Participants either endorse (T) or reject (F) each short description of a felt reaction to a social situation. Responses within each subscale are averaged, with higher scores indicating higher levels of avoidance or anxiety (avoidance a = .88, M = .25, SD = .23; anxiety a = .83, M = .34, SD = .27).

Ethnic identity. The Multigroup Ethnic Identity Measure (MEIM; Phinney, 1992; Roberts et al., 1999) is a 12-item Likert scale measuring the degree to which one is identified with one's own ethnic group, with two factors: the degree to which one is interested to seek out things related to one's own ethnic group (search, $a = .72$, $M = 2.77$, $SD = .61$) and the degree to which one self-identifies with one's own ethnic group (commitment, $a = .89$, $M = 3.11$, $SD = .59$). Sample items include "I have spent time trying to find out more about my own ethnic group, such as history, traditions, and customs" (search subscale) and "I feel a strong attachment towards my ethnic group" (commitment subscale). Participants rate their agreement with each statement on a scale from *strongly disagree* (1) to *strongly agree* (4). Responses are averaged within each subscale, with higher scores indicating higher levels of ethnic identity.

Academic achievement. Participants self-reported their cumulative college grade point average (GPA) on a continuous scale from 0.00 to 4.00, corresponding to the minimum and maximum possible GPA at this institution ($M = 3.23$, $SD = .48$).

Results

Factor Analysis and Psychometric Properties

The RS-A scores for the 11 situations were subjected to a principal component analysis to explore the number of factors that could be extracted from the data. This analysis yielded two factors with eigenvalues greater than 1.00, but only one factor was retained on the basis of the scree test. This factor had an eigenvalue of 4.12 and accounted for 37% of the variance (the next three factors had eigenvalues of 1.34, 0.98, and 0.93, and accounted for 12%, 9%, and 9% of the variance, respectively). The factor loadings of the RS-A are as listed in Table 1. The averaged scores of the 11 scenarios make up the final RS-A score. The resultant measure shows high internal reliability for Asian Americans on the basis of the 11 product scores ($a = .83$). The mean score was 7.20, with a standard deviation of 3.79.

Partial Variables

Unless specifically mentioned, all analyses in this article involving the RS-A scale controlled for RS-personal and RS-race, due to their method and conceptual overlap and to ascertain the unique contributions of RS-A beyond that of the other RS scales. Given consistent gender differences in the incidence of internalizing symptoms (e.g., Hoffmann, Powlishta, & White, 2004), gender was also controlled for in all analyses. Finally, to disentangle the effects of acculturation (Heine et al., 1999) from those of RS-A, generational status was also controlled for. However, consistent with our expectations, generational status was unrelated to RS-A, $F(3, 135) = 1.28$, *ns*.

Criterion Validity

Table 2 provides both zero-order and partial correlations RS-A had with constructs of interest among Asian Americans. RS-A scores were significantly correlated positively with RS-personal, RS-race, depressive symptoms, SADS-avoidance, and SADS-anxiety, and negatively with self-esteem. As expected, the four internalizing symptomatology measures intercorrelated significantly in our sample of Asian Americans (r range = .27 to .66, all ps<.001). Also as expected, the three RS scales intercorrelated significantly due to shared method variance and conceptual overlap (r range = .51 to .61, all ps<.001). Nevertheless, positive correlations with depressive symptoms, SADS-avoidance, and SADS-anxiety, and negative correlations with self-esteem remained significant when we partialed out the effects of RS-personal, RS-race, gender, and generational status. This is initial evidence that RS-A uniquely explains internalizing symptomatology among Asian Americans above and beyond RS-personal (which has been shown to be correlated with self-esteem and other internalizing symptomatology among all American ethnic groups, e.g., Downey & Feldman, 1996) and RS-race (which has not).[2]

Equally important, RS-A did not have the same properties as RS-race. Unlike previous research showing that status-based RS was related to grade point average and ethnic identity among African Americans (Mendoza-Denton et al., 2002), RS-A was not correlated with college cumulative grade-point average, ethnic identity search, nor ethnic identity commitment among Asian Americans. Furthermore, in contrast to RS-A, RS-race was not significantly correlated with any of the dependent variables tested above (all rs <.17, ns) among Asian Americans. This suggests that RS-race was not a relevant outcome predictor for internalizing symptomatology among Asian Americans.

Replication and Test-Retest Reliability

We were interested in demonstrating the test-retest reliability of the RS-A scale as well as to replicate the relationship between RS-A and internalizing symptomatology in a different cohort of undergraduates. Data collection occurred 2.5 years after the administration of the original battery reported above. We selected this time period because the psychology major at the university is a 2-year program, and, as such, the two samples were unlikely to have overlapping participants. Participants were 241 Asian American undergraduates enrolled in psychology classes (Mage = 19.81, SD = 1.47, 68% female) at UC Berkeley. Participants completed an Internet-based survey battery consisting of the RS-personal (α = .78), RS-race (α = .92), RS-A (α = .89), and the Rosenberg Self-Esteem (α = .90) scale at the beginning of the semester for partial course credit. Participants also completed a demographics form containing questions about their race or ethnicity, gender, and generational status. RS-A remained significantly correlated with self-esteem, partial r = — .19, p< .01 in this sample of Asian American participants. A subset of 63 Asian American participants (Mage = 19.94, SD = 1.38, 62% female) also completed the RS-A scale (a = .88) a second time an average of 59.32 days (SD = 24.54) after the first administration. In the new sample, the Pearson correlation coefficient for test-retest reliability of RS-A was high over a 2-month period (r = .58, p<.0001).

---

[2]Supporting the notion that RS-A is less meaningful and does not relate to internalizing symptomatology for European Americans, in a separate sample of European American college students (n = 225), RS-A scores were significantly lower (M = 4.20, SD = 2.69, t = 8.27, p<.0001, d = .91) and had significantly less variability (folded F(143,224) = 1.98, p<.0001) compared to Asian Americans.

Table 2 Zero-Order and Partial Correlations Between RS-A and Outcome Variables Among Asian American Participants in Study 1

Variable	Zero-Order Correlations	Controlling for RS-R, RS-P, Sex, and Generational Status
RS-P	.55***	—
RS-R	.62***	—
Depressive symptoms	37***	.19*
Self-esteem	44***	— .26**
SADS-avoidance	.34 ***	.26**
SADS-anxiety	37***	.21*
Ethnic Identity Search	.00	.03
Ethnic Identity Commitment	— .16 +	— .08
Grade Point Average	— .01	— .03

+p<.10. *p< .05. **p<.01. ***p<.001.

Further, RS-A scores were uncorrelated with self-esteem (r = — .06, ns). A test of differences between correlations showed this relationship to be different than that for Asian Americans, z = 1.88, p(one-tailed) = .03.

Confirmatory Factor Analysis

One concern is the degree to which the one-factor structure derived from the exploratory factor analysis is reliable. To address this question, 463 Asian American undergraduates enrolled in psychology classes 3 years after the conclusion of the first sample (*Mage* = 20.09, *SD* = 2.85, 70% female) at the same university as before completed the RS-A measure (α = .89). The data were submitted to a confirmatory factor analysis, specifying a one-factor structure, using the CALIS procedure in SAS (Hatcher, 1998). The Lagrange Multiplier test revealed that model fit would be improved by allowing some error terms to correlate (E6 & E8, E7 & E10). This is unsurprising, given the thematic overlap across these pairs of items (see Table 1). A subsequent confirmatory factor analysis, modeling the correlated error between item 6 and item 8, and the correlated error between item 7 and item 10, demonstrated adequate fit for the one-factor solution (RMSEA = .08, GFI = .93, CFI = .95; per Brown, 2006).

Discussion

Our aim in Study 1 was to develop a measure of status-based RS among Asian Americans. Consistent with our predictions, this dynamic seems to have a different "footprint," or nomological net, among Asian Americans than among other groups. RS-race among African Americans is related to ethnic identity and academic achievement, yet unrelated to self-esteem (Mendoza-Denton et al., 2002). RS-A, by contrast, is unrelated to ethnic identity and academic achievement, but is negatively correlated with self-esteem and positively correlated with depressive symptoms and social anxiety among Asian Americans. These relationships remain robust even after controlling for theoretically related constructs (RS-personal, RS-race, gender, and generational status).

These findings may provide some insight into explaining the elevated levels of depression and social anxiety among Asian Americans above and beyond cultural factors such as exposure to Western culture (e.g., Heine et al., 1999) or norms and traditions about disclosure of psychological distress (e.g., Okazaki & Kallivayalil, 2002). Rather than being a purely cultural phenomenon, there is some evidence that internalizing symptomatology among Asian Americans may be related to discrimination concerns.

Despite being consistent with predictions, in Study 1 we did not directly assess participants' attributions to the scenarios of the RS-A scale. Study 2 seeks to address this shortcoming by asking participants explicitly to attribute a rejecting outcome to a number of factors, with the prediction that RS-A would be positively related to discrimination attributions only in those situations relevant to the Asian American experience of discrimination.

Study 2

Study 2 addresses the construct validity of the RS-A scale for Asian Americans, asking whether scores on the RS-A scale are indeed related to spontaneous discrimination attributions specifically in the situations described in this questionnaire. We asked Asian American participants to read descriptions of several situations relevant to college students and imagine actually being rejected in them. We selected situations representative of the Asian American experience of discrimination, the African American experience of discrimination, and discrimination-irrelevant interpersonal rejection, hereafter referred to as *As-Am, Af-Am,* and *Irr* situations. These situations were operationalized using situations derived from the RS-A (Study 1), RS-race (Mendoza-Denton et al., 2002), and RS-personal (Downey & Feldman, 1996) questionnaires, respectively. The cause of the rejection was not specified in any of the situations. Participants were asked to report on their attributions for the rejection. We did not expect that participants would make discrimination attributions in the *Irr* situations. We expected participants to recognize discrimination as a possible reason for being rejected in both the *As-Am* and *Af-Am* situations. Nevertheless, without specific applicability, it is likely that *Af-Am* situations do not trigger chronically anxious expectations of discrimination among Asian Americans, and thus RS-A scores should be positively related to spontaneous attributions to discrimination only in the *As-Am* situations.

Procedure

Study 2 was conducted at the same institution as above. Study participants were 184 Asian American undergraduates enrolled in psychology classes (Mage = 19.99, SD = 1.65). Eighty-three of the 184 Asian Americans were foreign born, having been in the United States on average for over a decade (M = 10.15 years, SD = 5.52). The sample was 64% female; 2 participants did not indicate their gender. Participants completed the study for partial course credit.

Rejection Attribution Task

Designed to assess spontaneous attributions in *As-Am, Af-Am,* and *Irr* situations, the rejection attribution task consisted of the two highest-loading situations selected from each of the rejection sensitivity scales, expanded into half-page vignettes by the addition of a short paragraph describing the rejection following the interaction. Participants were first asked to imagine themselves in that situation and were told at the end of the vignette that they had been rejected. Participants were then asked to identify the degree to which they thought each of eight reasons played a role in the rejection on a scale from 1 *(very little)* to 6 *(very much)*. The reasons list included four facets related to self: my personality, my gender, my attractiveness, and my ethnicity; and four facets related to other: their personality, their gender, their attractiveness, and their ethnicity (see Crocker, Cornwell, & Major, 1993). Below the eight reasons, we included a free-response section for participants to indicate any other factors that they felt played a role in the rejection. Participants rarely used the free-response section to indicate other possible factors, and this will not be discussed further.

RS Scales

After the completion of the rejection attribution task, the RS-A scale was administered to participants (M = 9.42, SD = 4.76, a = .75). RS-race (M = 7.33, SD = 5.23, a = .93) and RS-personal (M = 10.78, SD = 2.98, a = .85) were also administered, as in Study 1.

Results

Mean Levels of Discrimination Attribution in Different Situations

In the remaining analyses we will focus on the attribution of rejection to one's own ethnicity. As expected, participants did not attribute rejection to discrimination in *Irr* situations, (M = 1.22, SD = .60) but did attribute rejection to discrimination in *Af-Am* situations, (M = 2.70, SD = 1.42), and in *As-Am* situations, (M = 2.44, SD = 1.18). Paired-samples t-tests revealed that participants attributed rejection to discrimination significantly less in *Irr* situations than in *Af-Am* (t = 13.67, p<.001, *d* = 1.36) or *As-Am* situations (t = 14.25, p<.001, *d* = 1.30). Participants did not differ in the attributions of rejection to discrimination in *Af-Am* situations and *As-Am* situations (t = 1.48, ns).

RS-A and Discrimination Attributions

As predicted, the elevated level of discrimination attribution in the *Af-Am* situations is recognition that discrimination is possible in these situations. Nevertheless, these situations are not as applicable as *As-Am* situations in the experience of discrimination. Consistent with this view, RS-A did not correlate with attributions of rejection to discrimination in *Af-Am* situations, $r = .08$, *ns*, but was positively correlated with attributions of rejection to discrimination in *As-Am* situations, $r = .31$, $p < .0001$. RS-A did not correlate with discrimination attributions in *Irr* situations, $r = .11$, *ns*.

Discussion

RS-A was related to discrimination attributions among Asian Americans only in those situations where status-based rejection is both applicable and possible (cf. Higgins, 1996; Mendoza-Denton et al., 2002). Specifically, even though Asian Americans' mean discrimination attributions in *Af-Am* situations were similar to those in *As-Am* situations, attributions to discrimination in *Af-Am* situations were unrelated to RS-A. The temporal order of the survey administration, with the rejection attribution task completed before the RS scales, reduced the likelihood of discrimination attribution priming by the RS scales as a possible explanation for the results. Together, these findings show converging evidence that the RS-A scale does indeed measure situation-specific status-based RS.

Studies 1 and 2 established the predictive utility and convergent validity of RS-A in that RS-A was correlated with our psychological wellness variables of interest and also related to spontaneous attributions of rejection to discrimination only in relevant situations. In Study 3, we extend and replicate the findings from Study 2 to test possible affective mediators.

Study 3

The typical affective reaction to discrimination is anger among African Americans (Swim, Hyers, Cohen, Fitzgerald, & Bylsma, 2003). Anger is typically seen as an other-directed, externalizing negative emotion (by placing blame on others for injustice; e.g., Lerner & Keltner, 2000). As such, it is unsurprising that exposure to discrimination can lead to hypertension (Blascovich et al., 2001; Harrell, Hall, & Taliaferro, 2003) and externalizing symptomatology among African Americans (Nyborg & Curry, 2003). Indeed, the relationship between subjective experiences of discrimination and externalizing symptomatology in this group is mediated by expressions of anger following discrimination (Nyborg & Curry, 2003).

What would Asian American affective reactions to discrimination be? As Studies 1 and 2 suggest, responses to discrimination among Asian Americans are internalizing rather than externalizing in nature. As such, we might expect a self-directed, negative emotion to mediate the link between perceptions of discrimination and internalizing outcomes among Asian Americans. We specifically hypothesized that *shame,* being a prototypical internalizing negative emotion (Beer & Keltner, 2004), would be the relevant affective reaction to discrimination for Asian Americans. This expectation is consistent with prior research suggesting that shame may be an especially applicable emotion following interpersonally-communicated rejection due to a stigmatizing condition (Dickerson et al., 2004), and especially so given that Asian Americans experience discrimination in interpersonal contexts more than other American ethnic group members (Greene et al., 2006). In sum then, we hypothesized that Asian Americans' self-directed reactions to discrimination would lead to internalizing symptomatology, analogous to the way that other-directed negative emotion following discrimination is related to externalizing symptomatology among African Americans. Not coincidentally, these are also the symptoms on which Asian Americans and European Americans differ (Okazaki, 1997, 2002; Twenge & Crocker, 2002).

In order to assess Asian American college students' emotional reactions to status-based rejection, we asked them to report both on anger and shame reactions after an imagined rejection in the lab. Because the RS construct inherently contains anxiety as the affect of interest, anxiety was also measured. We used happiness as our positive emotion of choice in order to ascertain differentiation between positive and negative emotions. Furthermore, to explore the relationship between RS-A, emotional reactions to discrimination, and internalizing symptomatology, we also measured self-reported change in self-esteem post simulated rejection.

Procedure

Study 3 was conducted at the same institution as Studies 1 and 2. Study participants were 118 Asian American undergraduates enrolled in psychology classes *(Mage* = 19.94, *SD* = 1.34). Forty-two of the 118 Asian Americans were foreign born, having been in the United States for an average of 12.71 years *(SD* = 5.57). The sample was 51% female; 4 participants did not indicate their gender. Participants completed the study for partial course credit.

Rejection Attribution Task

Participants completed a rejection attribution task similar to the measure described in Study 2 but was limited to *As-Am* situations. In Study 3 we included the three highest-loading situations from the RS-A scale, described verbatim to ensure their meanings were not changed by lengthening them. Participants were told that they had been rejected in these situations, to rate their emotions following this event, and to make attributions for the rejection.

Emotion Ratings

Participants were asked to rate their own levels of anxiety, happiness, anger, and shame after the rejection on a scale from 1 *(very little)* to 6 *(very much)*. They were also asked to report their change in self-esteem on a 6-point scale, where 1 is *much worse than before*, and 6 is *much better than before*.

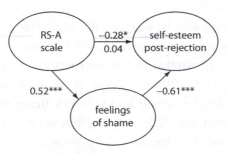

Note: All coefficients are standardized bs. $^{n}p<.05$. $^{nnn}p<.001$.

Figure 1. Mediational analyses with RS-A, shame, and self-esteem in Study 3.

RS Scales

As in Study 2, RS-A (M = 8.12, *SD* = 3.78, a = .83) was administered to participants after the completion of the rejection attribution task. RS-race (M = 6.29, *SD* = 4.15, a = .89) and RS-personal (M = 10.28, *SD* = 2.73, *a* = .83) were also administered to control for the effects of the other two RS scales.

Results

RS-A and Discrimination Attributions

The mean level of discrimination attributions was generally similar to Study 2 (M = 2.28, *SD* = 1.08). Replicating the findings in Study 2 among Asian Americans, RS-A was positively correlated with attributions of rejection to discrimination, $r = .19$, $p< .05$.

Emotion Ratings

RS-A was correlated with feelings of shame, $r = .41$, $p< .0001$, self-esteem, $r = -.22$, $p< .05$, and marginally correlated with feelings of anxiety postsimulated rejection, $r = .18, p = .06$. However, RS-A was not correlated with post-rejection feelings of happiness, $r = -.12$, *ns,* or anger, $r = .12$, *ns.*

Mediational Analyses

To explore the mechanism through which RS-A relates to postrejection self-esteem, we performed a mediational analysis as recommended by Baron and Kenny (1986). The first step confirmed the effect of RS-A on postrejection self-esteem (b = -.28, $p< .05$). The second step confirmed the effect of RS-A on shame (b = .52, $p< .001$). The third step confirmed the effect of shame on postrejection self-esteem, controlling for RS-A (b = -.61, $p< .001$). As predicted, the relationship between RS-A and postrejection self-esteem was mediated by shame, such that, controlling for shame, RS-A was no longer significantly related to postrejection self-esteem (b = .04, ns). The Sobel test revealed this to be a significant mediation (Sobel's $Z = -3.99$, p<.0001). Figure 1 displays this mediational analysis graphically.

Contrary to the externalizing expression of anger towards stigmatizers commonly observed among African Americans as a coping mechanism for discrimination (Swim et al., 2003), Asian Americans internalized the rejection and reported feelings of shame. Furthermore, the internalizing affect reported in this study was related to the internalizing symptomatology measured in the previous studies. This completes the picture: Asian Americans who fear, expect, and perceive discrimination in specific situations interpret negative outcomes as shameful, leading to reduced selfesteem.

General Discussion

The preceding studies establish that status-based rejection sensitivity is useful in understanding Asian Americans' coping with the possibility of discrimination. Status-based RS among Asian Americans was related to internalizing symptomatology, using both correlational and experimental methodology. These findings showed the utility of measuring anxious expectations, in addition to past discrimination experiences per se, as a factor in explaining the elevated risk of internalizing psychological distress among Asian Americans. Unlike for African Americans, the relevant emotion in coping with discrimination among Asian Americans was shame rather than anger. As other-directed anger mediates the relationship between African American perceptions of discrimination and externalizing symtomatology (Nyborg & Curry, 2003), self-directed shame mediates the relationship between Asian American status-based RS and internalizing symptomatology (Study 3). Although our mediational analysis only included change in self-esteem as the outcome measure, broader applicability to internalizing symptoms is suggested by previous research establishing that trait shame may be positively related to depressive symptomatology (e.g., Thompson & Berenbaum, 2006).

Situation-Specific Outcomes of Status-Based RS

The activation of shame as the relevant emotional reaction to discrimination among Asian Americans might be interpreted as an indication of a culturally specific reaction. Zane and Yeh (2002) report that shame is a common response style among those of Asian cultural backgrounds. As such, one might argue that elevated internalizing symptomatology among Asian Americans may be an artifact of differences between "Western" and "Eastern" cultural orientations and may not reflect maladjustment. If this were the case, however, one should not expect to see situational specificity in affective reactions. Preliminary data show that Asian Americans who attribute rejection to discrimination in situations typically provoking status-based RS in African Americans felt more anger postrejection, r(118) = .45, p<.0001. This lends support to our contention that the differences in the negative consequences of status-based RS between Asian Americans and African Americans may be a result of the differing domains where those groups feel stigmatized. It seems prudent to conclude that the differences between Asian American and other American ethnic groups on well-being may not be solely due to cultural differences but to the type of situation the discrimination occurs in as well.

The findings further show that status-based RS among Asian Americans is distinct from both social interaction anxiety and nongroup-specific status-based RS across all situations. While RS-race is uncorrelated with self-esteem in African Americans and Asian Americans, higher RS-A is correlated with lower self-esteem in Asian Americans. This suggests that, although the dynamics of status-based RS (situational triggers → expectations → rejection attributions → affective reactions) may be similar across groups, the nature of the triggers and the psychological sequelae may be group-specific.

Lack of Self-Esteem Protection for Asian Americans

Contrary to the established literature on visible stigma, stigma fails to be a self-protective mechanism for Asian Americans. Because Asian Americans tend to anxiously expect rejection in situations where the prevalent emotional reaction is self-directed and negative in nature, it makes sense that Asian Americans would not be able to credibly discount negative feedback by attributing rejection to the other. There are at least two additional reasons why Asian Americans may be vulnerable to internalizing symptomatology instead of discounting discriminatory feedback. First, interdependence, which tends to be higher among Asian Americans (Markus & Kitayama, 1991; Triandis, 1989), may make it difficult to make discrimination attributions in contexts relevant to stigmatization. Note that this is different from internalization of stigma—theoretically, interdependence should not make a person more likely to believe a given stereotype, but only to feel responsible for not being able to overcome negativity and still have positive social relationships. To the degree that interdependence has been associated with feeling greater responsibility for the smoothness of social interaction, or to maintain positive interpersonal relations, it may be more difficult to blame another person for the negativity of the interaction. On the other hand, Spencer-Rodgers, Peng, Wang, and Hou (2004) found that interdependence alone is insufficient in explaining the lower self-esteem of Asian Americans relative to other American ethnic minority groups, so interdependence may not be adequate in capturing the variance in Asian American psychological distress. Secondly, certain attributes that form part of the Asian American stereotype, such as academic achievement or social ineptitude, may be seen as being malleable, and having a locus of responsibility in the individual. Failure to disconfirm the stereotype, then, is considered a lack of effort on the stigmatized's part or a defect of character (Allport, 1958; Goffman, 1963). In fact, Asian Americans tend to view characteristics such as intelligence as more malleable than fixed (Strage, 1999). As such, Asian Americans may then be blamed for their own plight, not only by society at large but also by themselves. When the responsibility of the stigma is assigned to the target, the target may not be able to credibly claim that a negative event occurred because of discrimination (Crocker et al., 1993; Major et al., 2003). Future studies should examine each of these possible explanations for the lack of self-esteem buffering among Asian Americans.

Limitations

It is worth pointing out that the RS-A in its current form may not capture the situational antecedents that provoke threat to Asian Americans outside of the college context, given that this measure relied on college students in its development. Furthermore, because the RS-A scale was developed at UC Berkeley, where Asian Americans represent the numerical majority ethnic group on campus, the wider applicability of RS-A remains to be tested. On the one hand, this majority context for Asian Americans may have led us to underestimate the effects of institutional discrimination against Asian Americans, such as glass ceiling effects in job settings. On the other hand, because such robust effects of stigma have been found among members of a numerical majority, one might expect status-based rejection effects to be even more robust in contexts where Asian Americans are numerical minorities. Independent of the particular operationalization of RS-A here, however, it is notable that the processes relating to status-based RS may help explain variability in psychological distress among Asian Americans.

Conclusions and Future Directions

Because interpersonal discrimination is such a salient possibility for Asian Americans, whether in academic and professional contexts (Oyserman & Sakamoto, 1997), peer relationship contexts (Greene et al., 2006), or in romantic contexts (Hamamoto, 1998), it may be fruitful to examine the effects of Asian American status-based RS on the quality and type of intergroup interpersonal outcomes. It may be the case that those high in RS-A, when in an intergroup interaction, actively try to reduce the likelihood they may be discriminated against by sacrificing self-authenticity (see, e.g., Shelton, Richeson, & Salvatore, 2005). Another possibility is that those high in RS-A may be less likely to form social bonds with intergroup partners (similar to Mendoza-Denton et al., 2002, Study 3). A reduction in social connections may in turn restrict job advancement opportunities, contributing to the continued wage depression of Asian Americans compared to European Americans controlling for level of education (U.S. Census Bureau, 2000). Together, these findings suggest that reactions to stigma may play a role in explaining some of the variance within Asian American psychological distress and also mean-level differences between Asian Americans and other ethnic Americans on a host of psychological variables. With future studies on the long-term effects of stigma on Asian Americans, it is hoped that this research can lead to interventions to help Asian Americans cope with the detrimental effects of stigma.

References

Abe, J. S., & Zane, N. W. S. (1990). Psychological maladjustment among Asian and White American college students: Controlling for confounds. *Journal of Counseling Psychology, 37*, 437–444.

Allison, K. W. (1998). Stress and oppressed social category membership. In J. K. Swim & C. Stangor (Eds.), *Prejudice: The target's perspective* (pp. 145–170). San Diego, CA: Academic Press.

Allport, G. W. (1958). *The nature of prejudice.* Garden City, NY: Doubleday.

Ayduk, O., Mendoza-Denton, R., Mischel, W., Downey, G., Peake, P. K., & Rodriguez, M. (2000). Regulating the interpersonal self: Strategic self-regulation for coping with rejection sensitivity. *Journal of Personality and Social Psychology,* 79, 776–792.

Baron, R. M., & Kenny, D. A. (1986). The moderator-mediator variable distinction in social psychological research: Conceptual, strategic, and statistical considerations. *Journal of Personality and Social Psychology,* 51, 1173–1182.

Beck, A. T., Rush, A. J., Shaw, B. F., & Emery, G. (1979). *Cognitive therapy of depression.* New York: Guilford Press.

Beer, J. S., & Keltner, D. (2004). What is unique about self-conscious emotions? *Psychological Inquiry,* 15, 126–170.

Benet-Martinez, V., & Karakitapoglu-Aygun, Z. (2003). The interplay of cultural syndromes and personality in predicting life satisfaction: Comparing Asian Americans and European Americans. *Journal of Cross-Cultural Psychology,* 34, 38–60.

Betancourt, H., & Lopez, S. R. (1993). The study of culture, ethnicity, and race in American psychology. *American Psychologist,* 48, 629–637.

Blascovich, J., Spencer, S. J., Quinn, D., & Steele, C. (2001). African Americans and high blood pressure: The role of stereotype threat. *Psychological Science,* 12, 225–229.

Brown, T. A. (2006). Confirmatory factor analysis for applied research. New York: Guilford Press.

Chang, D. F. (2002). Understanding the rates and distribution of mental disorders. In K. S. Kurasaki, S. Okazaki, & S. Sue (Eds.), *Asian American mental health: Assessments theories and methods* (pp. 9–27). New York: Kluwer Academic.

Cheryan, S., & Monin, B. (2005). "Where are you really from?": Asian Americans and identity denial. *Journal of Personality and Social Psychology,* 89, 717–730.

Crocker, J., Cornwell, B., & Major, B. (1993). The stigma of overweight: Affective consequences of attributional ambiguity. *Journal of Personality and Social Psychology,* 64, 60–70.

Crocker, J., & Lawrence, J. S. (1999). Social stigma and self-esteem: The role of contingencies of worth. In D. A. Prentice & D. T. Miller (Eds.), *Cultural divides: Understanding and overcoming group conflict* (pp. 364–392). Thousand Oaks, CA: Sage Publications.

Crocker, J., & Major, B. (1989). Social stigma and self-esteem: The self-protective properties of stigma. *Psychological Review,* 96, 608–630.

Dickerson, S. S., Gruenewald, T. L., & Kemeny, M. E. (2004). When the social self is threatened: Shame, physiology, and health. *Journal of Personality,* 72, 1191–1216.

Downey, G., & Feldman, S. I. (1996). Implications of rejection sensitivity for intimate relationships. *Journal of Personality and Social Psychology,* 70, 1327–1343.

Espiritu, Y. L. (1997). *Asian American women and men.* Thousand Oaks, CA: Sage.

Frable, D. E. S. (1993). Dimensions of marginality: Distinctions among those who are different. *Personality and Social Psychology Bulletin,* 19, 370–380.

Goffman, E. (1963). Stigma: Notes on the management of spoiled identity. New York: Simon & Schuster.

Greene, M. L., Way, N., & Pahl, K. (2006). Trajectories of perceived adult and peer discrimination among Black, Latino, and Asian American adolescents: Patterns and psychological correlates. *Developmental Psychology,* 42, 218–238.

Hamamoto, D. (1998). The Joy Fuck Club: Prolegomenon to an Asian American porno practice. *New Political Science,* 20, 323–345.

Harrell, J. P., Hall, S., & Taliaferro, J. (2003). Physiological responses to racism and discrimination: An assessment of the evidence. *American Journal of Public Health, 93*, 243–248.

Hatcher, L. (1998). A step-by-step approach to using the SAS system for factor analysis and structural equation modeling. *Cary, NC: SAS Institute.*

Heine, S. J., & Lehman, D. R. (1999). Culture, self-discrepancies, and selfsatisfaction. *Personality and Social Psychology Bulletin, 25*, 915–925.

Heine, S. J., Lehman, D. R., Markus, H. R., & Kitayama, S. (1999). Is there a universal need for positive self-regard? *Psychological Review, 106*, 766–794.

Higgins, E. T. (1996). Knowledge activation: Accessibility, applicability, and salience. In E. T. Higgins & A. W. Kruglanski (Eds.), *Social psychology: Handbook of basic principles* (pp. 133–168). New York: Guilford Press.

Hoffmann, M. L., Powlishta, K. K., & White, K. J. (2004). An examination of gender differences in adolescent adjustment: The effect of competence on gender role differences in symptoms of psychopathology. *Sex Roles, 50*, 795–810.

Lang, P. J. (1995). The emotion probe: Studies of motivation and attention. *American Psychologist, 50*, 372–385.

Lee, S. J. (1994). Behind the model minority stereotype: Voices of high- and low-achieving Asian American students. *Anthropology and Education Quarterly, 25*, 413–429.

Lerner, J. S., & Keltner, D. (2000). Beyond valence: Toward a model of emotion specific influences on judgment and choice. *Cognition and Emotion, 14*, 473–493.

Liang, C. T. H., Li, L. C., & Kim, B. S. K. (2004). The Asian American Racism Related Stress Inventory: Development, factor analysis, reliability, and validity. *Journal of Counseling Psychology, 51*, 103–114.

Lien, P., Conway, M. M., & Wong, J. (2004). The contours and sources of ethnic identity choices among Asian Americans. *Social Science Quarterly, 84*, 461–481.

Major, B., Gramzow, R. H., McCoy, S. K., Levin, S., Schmader, T., & Sidanius, J. (2002). Perceiving personal discrimination: The role of group status and legitimizing ideology. *Journal of Personality and Social Psychology, 82*, 269–282.

Major, B., Kaiser, C. R., & McCoy, S. K. (2003). It's not my fault: When and why attributions to discrimination protect self-esteem. *Personality and Social Psychology Bulletin, 29*, 772–781.

Major, B., & O'Brien, L. T. (2005). The social psychology of stigma. *Annual Review of Psychology, 56*, 393–421.

Markus, H. R., & Kitayama, S. (1991). Culture and the self: Implications for cognition, emotion, and motivation. *Psychological Review, 98*, 224–253.

Mendoza-Denton, R. (in press). Stigma. In W. A. Darity (Ed.), *International encyclopedia of the social sciences* (2nd ed.). Thomson Gale.

Mendoza-Denton, R., Downey, G., Purdie, V. J., Davis, A., & Pietrzak, J. (2002). Sensitivity to status-based rejection: Implications for African American students' college experience. *Journal of Personality and Social Psychology, 83*, 896–918.

Mendoza-Denton, R., & Mischel, W. (2007). Integrating system approaches to culture and personality: The Cultural Cognitive-Affective Processing System (C-CAPS). In S. Kitayama & D. Cohen (Eds.), *Handbook of cultural psychology.* New York: Guilford Press.

Mendoza-Denton, R., Page-Gould, E., & Pietrzak, J. (2006). Mechanisms for coping with race-based rejection expectations. In S. Levin & C. Van Laar (Eds.), *Stigma and group inequality: Social psychological approaches* (pp. 151–169). New York: Erlbaum.

Metcalfe, J., & Mischel, W. (1999). A hot/cool-system analysis of delay of gratification: Dynamics of willpower. *Psychological Review,* 106, 3–19.

Mischel, W., Ayduk, O., & Mendoza-Denton, R. (2003). Sustaining delay of gratification over time: A hot-cool systems perspective. In G. Loewenstein, D. Read, & R. Baumeister (Eds.), *Time and decision: Economic and psychological perspectives on intertemporal choice* (pp. 175–200). New York: Russell Sage.

Nadeem, E., & Graham, S. (2005). Early puberty, peer victimization, and internalizing symptoms in ethnic minority adolescents. *Journal of Early Adolescence,* 25, 197–222.

Nyborg, V. M., & Curry, J. F. (2003). The impact of perceived racism: Psychological symptoms among African American boys. *Journal of Clinical Child and Adolescent Psychology,* 32, 258–266.

Ogbu, J. U., & Simons, H. D. (1998). Voluntary and involuntary minorities: A cultural-ecological theory of school performance with some implications for education. *Anthropology & Education Quarterly,* 29, 155–188.

Okazaki, S. (1997). Sources of ethnic differences between Asian American and White American college students on measures of depression and social anxiety. *Journal of Abnormal Psychology,* 106, 52–60.

Okazaki, S. (2000). Asian American and White American differences on affective distress symptoms: Do symptom reports differ across reporting methods? *Journal of Cross-Cultural Psychology,* 31, 603–625.

Okazaki, S. (2002). Self-other agreement on affective distress scales in Asian Americans and White Americans. *Journal of Counseling Psychology,* 49, 428–437.

Okazaki, S., & Kallivayalil, D. (2002). Cultural norms and subjective disability as predictors of symptom reports among Asian Americans and White Americans. *Journal of Cross-Cultural Psychology,* 33, 482–491.

Oyserman, D., & Sakamoto, I. (1997). Being Asian American: Identity, cultural constructs, and stereotype perception. *Journal of Applied Behavioral Science,* 33, 435–453.

Phinney, J. S. (1992). The Multigroup Ethnic Identity Measure: A new scale for use with adolescents and young adults from diverse groups. *Journal of Adolescent Research,* 7, 156–176.

Phinney, J. S. (1996). When we talk about American ethnic groups, what do we mean? *American Psychologist,* 51, 918–927.

Roberts, R., Phinney, J., Masse, L., Chen, Y., Roberts, C., & Romero, A. (1999). The structure of ethnic identity in young adults from diverse ethnocultural groups. *Journal of Early Adolescence,* 19, 301–322.

Rosenberg, M. (1979). *Conceiving the self.* New York: Basic Books.

Schmitt, M. T., & Branscombe, N. R. (2002). The internal and external causal loci of attributions to prejudice. *Personality and Social Psychology Bulletin,* 28, 620–628.

Shelton, J. N., Richeson, J. A., & Salvatore, J. (2005). Expecting to be the target of prejudice: Implications for interethnic interactions. *Personality and Social Psychology Bulletin,* 31, 1189–1202.

Spencer-Rodgers, J., Peng, K., Wang, L., & Hou, Y. (2004). Dialectical self-esteem and East-West differences in psychological well-being. *Personality and Social Psychology Bulletin,* 30, 1416–1432.

Steele, C. M. (1997). A threat in the air: How stereotypes shape intellectual identity and performance. *American Psychologist,* 52, 613–629.

Strage, A. A. (1999). Social and academic integration and college success: Similarities and differences as a function of ethnicity and family educational background. *College Student Journal, 33,* 198.

Sue, D. W., Bucceri, J., Lin, A. I., Nadal, K. L., & Torino, G. C. (2007). Racial microaggressions and the Asian American experience. *Cultural Diversity and Ethnic Minority Psychology, 13,* 72–81.

Swim, J. K., Hyers, L. L., Cohen, L. L., Fitzgerald, D. C., & Bylsma, W. H. (2003). African American college students' experiences with everyday racism: Characteristics of and responses to these incidents. *Journal of Black Psychology, 29,* 38–67.

Terrell, F., & Terrell, S. (1981). An inventory to measure cultural mistrust among Blacks. *Western Journal of Black Studies, 5,* 180–185.

Thompson, R. J., & Berenbaum, H. (2006). Shame reactions to everyday dilemmas are associated with depressive disorder. *Cognitive Therapy and Research, 30,* 415–425.

Triandis, H. C. (1989). The self and social behavior in differing cultural contexts. *Psychological Review, 96,* 506–520.

Twenge, J. M., & Crocker, J. (2002). Race and self-esteem: Meta-analyses comparing Whites, Blacks, Hispanics, Asians, and American Indians and comment on Gray, Little, and Hafdahl (2000). *Psychological Bulletin, 128,* 371–408.

U.S. Census Bureau. (2000). *Statistical abstract of the United States.* Washington, DC: U.S. Government Printing Office.

Ward, L. M., Hansbrough, E., & Walker, E. (2005). Contributions of music video exposure to Black adolescents' gender and sexual schemas. *Journal of Adolescent Research, 20,* 143–166.

Watson, D., & Friend, R. (1969). Measurement of social-evaluative anxiety. *Journal of Consulting and Clinical Psychology, 33,* 448–457.

Wright, J. C., Zakriski, A. L., & Drinkwater, M. (1999). Developmental psychopathology and the reciprocal patterning of behavior and environment: Distinctive situational and behavioral signatures of internalizing, externalizing, and mixed-syndrome children. *Journal of Clinical and Counseling Psychology, 67,* 95–107.

Zane, N. W. S., & Yeh, M. (2002). The use of culturally-based variables in assessment: Studies on loss of face. In K. S. Kurasaki, S. Okazaki, & S. Sue (Eds.), *Asian American mental health: Assessments theories and methods* (pp. 123–139). New York: Kluwer Academic.

Zhang, J., & Norvilitis, J. M. (2002). Measuring Chinese psychological well-being with Western developed instruments. *Journal of Personality Assessment, 79,* 492–511.

When Positive Stereotypes Threaten Intellectual Performance

The Psychological Hazards of "Model Minority" Status

By Sapna Cheryan and Galen V. Bodenhausen, Northwestern University

Abstract

Asian-American women's performance on a test of quantitative skill was studied as a function of whether their Asian, female, or individual identity was salient at the time of testing. In previous research, ethnicity salience was found to result in enhanced math performance among Asian women. However, the investigators relied on a subtle manipulation of ethnicity salience that likely did not invoke concerns about group reputation nor make salient the common cultural stereotypes concerning Asians' mathematical prowess. We induced a focus on ethnic identity in a manner that was likely to make other people's high performance expectations more salient. Under these conditions, ethnicity salience resulted in diminished ability to concentrate, which in turn led to significantly impaired math performance. Thus, although people commonly hold positive stereotypes about Asians' mathematical skills, making these stereotypes salient prior to performance can create the potential for "choking" under the pressure of high expectations.

A number of recent investigations have shown that negative stereotypes can undermine the academic performance of even very talented members of the stereotyped group. For example, African-American students were found to perform significantly more poorly than their European-American counterparts on a test that was characterized as diagnostic of intelligence, but when the same test was characterized in a manner that undermined the relevance of prevailing stereotypes of intellectual inferiority, differential performance was eliminated (Steele & Aronson, 1995). Similar results have emerged regarding other stereotyped groups, including Caucasian students of low socioeconomic backgrounds (Croizet & Claire, 1998) and women performing in mathematical and technical domains (e.g., Spencer, Steele, & Quinn, 1999). The picture emerging from this growing literature reveals that negative stereotypes undermine performance by creating concern on the part of members of the stereotyped group that their performance might serve to confirm the negative

Sapna Cheryan & Galen V. Bodenhausen, "When Positive Stereotypes Threaten Intellectual Performance: The Psychological Hazards of 'Model Minority' Status," *Psychological Science*, vol. 11, no. 5, pp. 399–402. Copyright © 2000 by SAGE Publications, Inc. Reprinted with permission.

expectations other people hold about their group (Steele, 1997). Steele and his colleagues (e.g., Steele, 1997; Steele & Aronson, 1995) used the term *stereotype threat* to refer to the extra cognitive burden involved in worrying about confirming the low performance expectations of others.

Recently, Shih, Pittinsky, and Ambady (1999) reported intriguing evidence that intellectual performance can be moderated by manipulations influencing the salience of stereotyped social identities. Shih et al. examined the influence of gender versus ethnicity salience on mathematics performance in a sample of Asian-American women. This manipulation is particularly interesting because one of the relevant identities ("woman") is typically negatively stereotyped in the domain of quantitative skill (e.g., Benbow, 1988), whereas the other ("Asian") is typically positively stereotyped in this domain (e.g., Kao, 1995). Confirming the logic of Steele's stereotype-threat hypothesis, Shih et al. found in two experiments that the participants in the gender-prime condition performed more poorly on a mathematics test than a control group of Asian-American women. Intriguingly, Shih et al. also found a positive effect of the ethnicity prime in one of their experiments. Specifically, participants prompted to think of themselves in terms of their Asian identity earned higher math scores than participants in the control condition. This result suggests that although negative stereotypes can threaten intellectual performance, positive stereotypes can actually provide a performance boost.

Although the data reported by Shih et al. (1999) did not provide evidence as to the processes mediating the "stereotype boost" effect seen in the ethnicity-prime condition, previous research suggests one likely candidate. Specifically, it is likely that activating an identity that is associated with positive stereotypes leads to confidence and expectations for personal success, which have been shown to facilitate actual performance (e.g., Baumeister, Hamilton, & Tice, 1985). However, the research of Baumeister et al. reveals a crucial moderator of the effects of expectations for success. When such expectations are held privately, they are likely to provide a confidence boost that contributes to successful performance. However, when a positive performance is anticipated by an external audience, an individual may experience apprehension about meeting those high expectations, and such feelings can lead to the phenomenon known as "choking under pressure." Thus, the effects of positive expectancies need not always be beneficial.

The ethnicity-salience manipulation used by Shih et al. (1999) was purposely chosen to be subtle and indirect. It involved asking respondents whether they lived in coed housing (gender salience) or spoke more than one language (ethnicity salience). The manipulation made no reference to how other people view the groups in question, so it was unlikely to create much of a sense of public, external expectations for performance. For this reason, any positive expectations for math performance among the Asian-American students were likely to be operating in the private sphere that has been found to enhance performance (Baumeister et al., 1985). However, one can readily imagine a different performance context in which high expectations for the performance of one's group are more salient. Would these more public expectations still provide a performance boost, or could they possibly lead to choking? In the present experiment, we tested the idea that positive stereotypes can also threaten performance by creating concern about failure to meet the high expectations held for one's group. We repeated the basic experiment conducted by Shih et al., giving Asian-American women a challenging mathematics test after making salient their ethnic or gender identity. However, we changed the identity manipulation in order to make public, group-related expectancies more salient. We also examined a range of potential mediating variables in order to understand the psychological reasons for any observed effects of the identity-salience manipulation on mathematical performance.

Method

Overview

Forty-nine self-identified Asian-American women were recruited for the study. All were undergraduates enrolled at a Midwestern university. We restricted the sample to students who reported that math performance was very important to them (operationalized as a rating of 5 or 6 on a 6-point scale of math importance). This restriction was imposed because previous research suggested that the effects of stereotype threat are limited to individuals who value the performance domain highly (e.g., Aronson et al., 1999). Each student participated individually and was randomly assigned to one of three identity salience conditions (ethnic identity, gender identity, or a personal identity control condition). After completing a questionnaire designed to manipulate identity salience, the respondents completed a quantitative skills test and then completed a post test questionnaire assessing several reactions to the test.

Procedure and Materials

Participants reported to a laboratory room individually to participate in a study examining "predictors of math ability." Thus, in line with most previous research in which effects of stereotype threat have been demonstrated, the test was presented as diagnostic of the stereotyped ability. The various tasks were administered in a private cubicle containing a computer. The first task was a 10-item survey designed to manipulate identity salience. In the ethnicity condition, the 10 items were taken from the Collective Self-Esteem Scale (Luthanen & Crocker, 1992) and adapted specifically to ethnic identity (e.g., "Overall, my race is considered good by others," "I am a worthy member of the racial group I belong to"). In the gender condition, the same items were reworded to focus on gender instead of ethnicity. This salience manipulation was expected to be much more likely than the procedure used by Shih et al. (1999) to make public, group-based performance expectancies salient to the participants. In the control condition, no social identity was made salient; instead, the students answered 10 questions about their personal, individual identity.

After completing the initial questionnaire, participants were given 20 min to complete a challenging quantitative skills test consisting of 20 multiple-choice items taken from previous versions of the Graduate Record Examination. After completing the math test, the students were asked to answer a final questionnaire containing items measuring several potential mediators, including, among others, (a) task motivation, (b) ability to concentrate on the task, and (c) self-handicapping (i.e., excuses for poor performance, such as getting little sleep the previous night). Finally, participants were debriefed and offered $5 compensation for their participation.

Results

Math Performance

Following Shih et al. (1999), we measured math performance by computing the ratio of the number of questions answered correctly to the number of questions attempted (see also Steele & Aronson, 1995).[1] In the control, personal-identity condition (n = 16), students correctly answered an average proportion of .83 of the items (SD = 0.09). In line with the possibility that positive expectations for performance could cause choking under pressure when the positively stereotyped Asian identity was salient, performance in the ethnicity condition (n = 16) was markedly lower, $M = .71$, $SD = 0.17$. In contrast, performance in the gender condition (n = 17) was comparable to performance in the control condition, $M = .81$, $SD = 0.14$. A one-way analysis of variance confirmed the significant effect of the identity-salience manipulation, $F(2, 46) = 4.04$, $p < .025$. Planned contrasts confirmed specifically that performance was significantly lower in the ethnicity condition than in the control condition, $t(46) = 2.63$, $p < .015$ (all reported p values are two-tailed); however, there was no reliable difference between the gender condition and the control condition, $t(46) = 0.40$, $p > .65$. Thus, we did not observe a gender threat effect in this sample (see the Discussion section).

Potential Mediators

As was the case in the studies of Shih et al. (1999), we found that task motivation was not influenced by our identity-salience manipulation. Students in all conditions reported being motivated. We also did not find any differential invocation of post hoc excuses for poor performance (such as life stress or poor sleep on the previous night). However, we did find evidence that lower performance in the ethnicity condition was attributable in large part to impaired concentration in this condition. Participants in the ethnicity-salience condition reported that they had experienced significantly poorer ability to concentrate during the math task than did participants in the control condition, Ms = 4.00 *(SD = 1.32)* versus 5.13 *(SD = 1.41)*, respectively, on a 7-point scale; $t(30) = 2.34$, $p < .025$.[2] This pattern is consistent with the possibility that concerns about living up to the high expectations held for Asians impeded performance by interfering with participants' mental focus during the math test. To test this possibility, we conducted a series of regression analyses. The resulting regression coefficients

---

[1]In as much as the great majority of respondents completed all or almost all of the test items, results were substantially similar when the absolute frequency of correct responses was analyzed.

[2]Concentration scores of the students in the gender-salient condition were at an intermediate level, $M = 4.59$, and were not reliably different from scores for the control condition, $t(31) = 1.13$, $p > .25$.

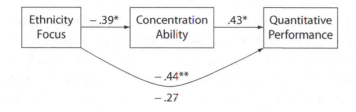

Figure. 1. Mediation of ethnicity-salience effects on math performance. The regression coefficient shown above the arrow from ethnicity focus to quantitative performance is for the direct pathway between these variables; the coefficient below this arrow is from an analysis in which the effects of the concentration variable were statistically controlled. *p < .05. **p < .01.

are depicted in Figure 1, which shows that ethnicity focus was associated with significantly reduced concentration ability; in turn, concentration ability was positively related to math performance. More crucial for our mediational argument, the significant direct pathway from ethnicity focus to math performance (shown above the arrow) is reduced to nonsignificance when the effects of the concentration variable are statistically controlled (shown below the arrow). The modified Sobel test advocated by Kenny, Kashy, and Bolger (1998) indicated that the reduction in the path coefficient was marginally significant, Z = 1.65, p < .10. These results confirm that the deleterious impact of ethnicity focus on math performance was partially mediated through the effects of identity salience on participants' ability to concentrate on the math problems.[3]

Discussion

These results extend current understanding of the role of identity issues in academic performance in several important ways. Most notably, these findings show that even a positively stereotyped social identity can constitute a threat to academic performance. Unlike Shih et al. (1999), we found that focusing our Asian-American participants' attention on their ethnicity did not improve their performance; instead,

---

[3]We of course could not ask participants about their ability to concentrate on the math problems prior to undertaking the test, and to do so during the test could itself have interfered with their mental focus. Thus, this measure (as well as all the potential mediators) was assessed immediately after the math test. This could create some interpretational ambiguity, because it is possible that the respondents who experienced difficulty on the test reported concentration problems as a way of rationalizing or explaining their performance. Two facts argue against this interpretation. First, there were many possible mediators assessed, and any one of them could have been used as a post hoc basis for explaining poor performance. None of these other measures were related to performance, however. Thus, it does not appear that our participants' responses to the mediational questions served a rationalization strategy. Rather, their reports of concentration ability seem to reflect their actual state of mind during the test. Second, mediational analyses in which the causal direction was reversed (i.e., poor performance was assumed to cause reports of concentration problems) did not yield meaningful results.

it created difficulties in concentration that translated into significantly impaired performance. Whereas Shih et al. relied on a relatively subtle means for making ethnicity salient, we used a procedure that made participants reflect on how their ethnic group is viewed publicly. This focus presumably led them to contemplate the possibility of failing to exhibit the positive quantitative skills commonly expected of Asians. Just as fear of confirming a negative stereotype can undermine performance, so can fear of failing to confirm a positive stereotype. However, the latter effect appears to be limited to conditions in which public expectations of success are salient (Baumeister et al., 1985). When expectations of success are activated in a more private fashion, membership in a positively stereotyped group may confer performance benefits (as in the experiment by Shih et al.).

Although Asian Americans are often characterized as a "model minority" (Kao, 1995), this characterization may in itself be quite limiting (Lee, 1996). Asians may well have good reason to be concerned about the consequences of failing to live up to the positive stereotypes held about their group, because previous research suggests that they can pay a heavy cost for falling short. Ho, Driscoll, and Loosbrock (1998) found that Asian-American students who performed poorly on a mathematical test were given substantially fewer points by graders than European-American students who performed identically. Failing to meet high expectations can thus be accompanied by greater punishment than would have occurred in the absence of any particular expectations. Add to this the possibility that one's poor performance may undermine the reputation of one's group, and there is ample reason why Asian students may experience unique performance pressures when positive stereotypes of their ethnic group are activated.

This research also underscores the fluidity of self-definition and its role in academic performance. Being Asian, per se, was not the issue; rather, the crucial factor concerned whether participants thought about themselves in terms of a (potentially) stereotyped identity. In this regard, it is interesting to note that the gender-salience manipulation we used failed to create any stereotype-threat effects among our participants. These results are actually similar to those obtained by Shih et al. in their experiment most analogous to ours, in which they used a sample of Asian women from the United States (Shih et al., 1999, Experiment 1). In that study, performance of students in the gender salient condition was not substantially different from performance of students in the control condition (mean proportion correct = .43 and .49, respectively; a direct statistical comparison of these means was not provided). It may be that the particular test items used were not difficult enough to generate gender-based stereotype-threat effects (cf. Spencer et al., 1999), although they were sufficiently difficult to create problems for our ethnicity-focused participants. Another potential explanation may lie in the possibility that Asian women are less susceptible to gender-related stereotype threat than other women, because they can call upon an identity dimension that is positively stereotyped in the math domain (i.e., the Asian side of their identity) to bolster their private confidence in themselves, should they begin to experience gender-related threat. In this sense, their latent, positively stereotyped identity constitutes a ready basis for private self-affirmation (Steele, 1988) when negative gender stereotypes are salient. This possibility awaits further empirical exploration. The present findings should therefore certainly not be taken as evidence against the more general existence of gender-based stereotype-threat effects in the domain of math performance.

Whatever the reason for the lack of impact of negative, gender-based stereotypes in the present study, the findings with respect to ethnic stereotypes document a striking effect. Specifically, positive stereotypes (at least when they form the basis for salient public expectations) can place a considerable burden on members of the stereotyped group, adversely affecting their performance in the stereotyped domain. Future research needs to further explore the conditions under which both positive and negative stereotypes can undermine achievement in consequential settings such as academic performance.

Acknowledgments—We are grateful to Shira Gabriel, Adam Galinsky, Wendi Gardner, Gifford Weary, and two anonymous reviewers for their helpful comments and suggestions.

References

Aronson, J., Lustina, M.J., Good, C., Keough, K., Steele, C.M., & Brown, J. (1999). When white men can't do math: Necessary and sufficient factors in stereotype threat. *Journal of Experimental Social Psychology*, 35, 29–46.

Baumeister, R.F., Hamilton, J.C., & Tice, D.M. (1985). Public versus private expectancy of success: Confidence booster or performance pressure? *Journal of Personality and Social Psychology*, 48, 1447–1457.

Benbow, C.P. (1988). Sex differences in mathematical reasoning ability in intellectually talented preadolescents: Their nature, effects, and possible causes. *Behavioral and Brain Sciences*, 11, 169–232.

Croizet, J.-C., & Claire, T. (1998). Extending the concept of stereotype threat to social class: The intellectual underperformance of students from low socioeconomic backgrounds. *Personality and Social Psychology Bulletin*, 24, 588–594.

Ho, C.P., Driscoll, D.M., & Loosbrock, D.L. (1998). Great expectations: The negative consequences of falling short. *Journal of Applied Social Psychology*, 28, 1743-1759.

Kao, G. (1995). Asian Americans as model minorities? A look at their academic performance. *American Journal of Education*, 103, 121–159.

Kenny, D.A., Kashy, D.A., & Bolger, N. (1998). Data analysis in social psychology. In D.T. Gilbert, S.T. Fiske, & G. Lindzey (Eds.), *The handbook of social psychology* (4th ed., Vol. 1, pp. 233–265). Boston: McGraw-Hill.

Lee, S.J. (1996). *Unraveling the "model minority" stereotype.* New York: Teachers College Press.

Luthanen, R., & Crocker, J. (1992). A collective self-esteem scale: Self-evaluation of one's social identity. *Personality and Social Psychology Bulletin*, 18, 302–318.

Shih, M., Pittinsky, T.L., & Ambady, N. (1999). Stereotype susceptibility: Identity salience and shifts in quantitative performance. *Psychological Science, 10, 80–83.*

Spencer, S.J., Steele, C.M., & Quinn, D.M. (1999). Stereotype threat and women's math performance. *Journal of Experimental Social Psychology, 35, 4–28.*

Steele, C.M. (1988). The psychology of self-affirmation: Sustaining the integrity of the self. In L. Berkowitz (Ed.), *Advances in experimental social psychology* (Vol. 21, pp. 261–302). San Diego: Academic Press.

Steele, C.M. (1997). A threat in the air: How stereotypes shape intellectual identity and performance. *American Psychologist, 52,* 613–629.

Steele, C.M., & Aronson, J. (1995). Stereotype threat and the intellectual test performance of African Americans. *Journal of Personality and Social Psychology,* 69, 797–811.

Field Experiments Examining the Culture of Honor

The Role of Institutions in Perpetuating Norms About Violence

By Dov Cohen, University of Illinois at Urbana-Champaign
Richard E. Nisbett, University of Michigan

Two field experiments illustrate how institutions of the US South and West can help perpetuate violence related to a culture of honor. In Study 1, employers across the United States were sent letters from job applicants who had allegedly killed someone in an honor-related conflict. Southern and western companies were more likely than their northern counterparts to respond in an understanding and cooperative way. In Study 2, newspapers were sent facts for a story concerning a stabbing in response to a family insult. Southern and western papers created stories that were more sympathetic toward the perpetrator and presented his actions as more justified than northern papers did. Control conditions in both studies showed that the greater sympathy of southern and western institutions involves honor-related violence, not all violence or crime in general. Findings highlight the importance of examining the role of institutional behavior in perpetuating culture.

The standard view of the Old South and West is that these regions accepted, and even glorified, certain types of violence. In these frontier areas where the law was weak, where one's wealth could be rustled away instantly, and where citizens had to depend on themselves for protection, violence—or at least the threat of it—became a powerful force in social interaction. Insults or any challenge indicating that a person could be pushed around had to be met with harsh retaliation so that a man would not be branded an "easy mark."

Anthropologists call societies that hold such violent norms *cultures of honor*. Such cultures have been created independendy many times and in many places the world over (Gilmore, 1990; Nisbett & Cohen, 1996; Schneider, 1971). And the conditions that can give rise to cultures of honor—weak or absent law enforcement, portable (and, therefore, stealable) wealth, economic uncertainty, and high variability of economic outcomes—are present today in pockets all over the world, from the inner cities of the United States to sparsely populated regions of Asia, Europe, and Micronesia. In such societies, in

Dov Cohen & Richard E. Nisbett, "Field Experiments Examining the Culture of Honor: The Role of Institutions in Perpetuating Norms About Violence," *Personality and Social Psychology Bulletin*, vol. 23, no. 11, pp. 1188–1199. Copyright © 1997 by SAGE Publications, Inc. Reprinted with permission.

which one is vulnerable to predation, it becomes adaptive for one to adopt a tough, don't-mess-with-me stance.

Many subcultures within the United States can be characterized as possessing some version of a culture of honor, undoubtedly contributing to the high rate of violence in this country. What is striking, however, is not that cultures of honor exist where the conditions that created them are still in place but that some of these cultures continue to persist, even after there may be no functional reason for individuals to behave that way.

The regional cultures of honor in the South and West are good examples of this persistence. For the most part, the South and West are no longer frontier, herding regions where social and economic circumstances make the culture of honor a functional adaptation. Yet, the cultures in these regions remain strong. In this article, we use two field experiments to demonstrate that the culture of honor continues to exist in the South and the West at an institutional (as well as individual) level. Institutional supports for violence may well "feed back" and help to perpetuate that culture.

Examining Culture

Psychologists are used to studying culture at the level of individual attitudes and behaviors. But as Miller and Prentice (1994) showed, collective norms exist that cannot be derived by simply aggregating individual attitudes. Understanding the collective is not just a matter of assessing the individuals in it and then summing their scores on some dimension (see also Kuran, 1995; Schelling, 1978; Sunstein, 1995). To examine culture, one needs to go beyond the level of the individual and examine public representations (Sperber, 1990). To say that one culture is more violent than another does not mean simply that there are more violent individuals in one culture; it normally means that there are more institutional, social, and collective supports for violence in that culture. Culture exists, and can be studied, at the collective, public level as well as the individual, private level.

Although behaviors are ultimately performed by individuals or groups of individuals, such behaviors can carry profound cultural consequences when they affect institutional policies or public representations. Behavior takes on the imprimatur of cultural approval as people act in their "official" roles. In this way, public representations can feed back and influence what is defined as culturally acceptable, worthy of reward or punishment. In this article, we try to demonstrate two mechanisms by which this happens: (a) the social stigma or lack of stigma for violent acts and (b) media representations of violence as heinous and unacceptable or as justified and understandable.

Persistence of a Culture of Honor in the South and West

There is evidence from a number of different methods that a culture of honor does indeed persist in the modern South and West. Such evidence comes from analyses of homicide records, attitude surveys, laboratory experiments, aggregate behavioral data, and laws and social policies.

The white homicide rates of the South and West far surpass those of the North (see discussions by Baron & Straus, 1988, 1989; Gastil, 1971; Hackney, 1969; HuffCorzine, Corzine, & Moore, 1986,

1991; Kowalski & Peete, 1991; Land, McCall, & Cohen, 1990; Lee, 1995a; Nisbett & Cohen, 1996, chap. 2; Nisbett, Polly, & Lang, 1995; Reaves & Nisbett, 1995). The differences can be quite dramatic. For example, Nisbett and his colleagues (Nisbett & Cohen, 1996, chap. 2; Nisbett et al., 1995; Reaves & Nisbett, 1995) showed that homicide rates in small towns in the South are triple those of small towns in the North. Importantly, the effect is limited to differences between southern and northern Whites. Regional differences do not exist for Black homicide rates, suggesting that it is something about White southern culture (rather than just living below the Mason-Dixon Line) that elevates southern White homicide rates.

Further, in a more detailed analysis, Nisbett and colleagues (Nisbett, 1993; Nisbett & Cohen, 1996; Nisbett et al., 1995) showed that it is only conflict-, argument-, or brawl-related homicides—not homicides committed in the context of other felonies such as robbery—that are elevated in the South and West. This pattern was also confirmed by Rice and Goldman (1994), who found not only that southerners were more likely to kill over arguments but also that they were more likely to kill people they knew. "Both of these findings," Rice and Goldman argued, "are consistent with common cultural explanations for southern violence" (p. 381).

In attitude surveys, White southern (and, to a lesser extent, western) respondents are more likely to endorse violence consistent with culture-of-honor norms (Cohen & Nisbett, 1994; Nisbett & Cohen, 1996). Although they are not more likely to endorse violence of all sorts, they are more likely to endorse it when used for self-protection, to answer an affront, or to socialize children. Ellison (1991) also found that "native southerners are disproportionately inclined to condone defensive or retaliatory forms of violence" (p. 1223). Thus, there seems to be a coherent ideology of violence for southern Whites revolving around culture-of-honor concerns (see also work by Baron & Straus, 1989, pp. 165-169; Ellison & Sherkat, 1993; Reed, 1981).

In laboratory experiments, southern White males respond differently to an insult than do their northern White male counterparts. After they are insulted, southern subjects become more (a) angry, (b) convinced that their masculine reputation has been damaged, (c) cognitively primed for aggression, (d) physiologically stressed and aroused, (e) physiologically prepared for aggression (as indicated by increases in testosterone level), (f) domineering in subsequent encounters with other people, and (g) physically aggressive in their behavior in subsequent challenge situations (Cohen, Nisbett, Bowdle, & Schwarz, 1996).

The cultures of the South and (especially) the West are also more likely to approve of violence as shown by subscriptions to violent magazines, viewership of violent television programs, production of college football players, hunting license applications, national guard enrollments, and a number of other indicators in Baron and Straus's (1989) Legitimate Violence Index. Lee (1995a, 1995b) came to a similar conclusion in his analysis of magazine subscription rates, arguing that the West (and, to a lesser extent, the South) was higher in its machismo interests. It was these regions where people were most likely to read magazines "in which physical strength, self-defense, weapons, combat, and sex are prominent themes" (Lee, 1995b, p. 91).

Finally, the laws of the South and West are more likely to endorse violence consistent with a strong ethic of self-protection and honor. Southern and western states are more likely than their northern counterparts to have (a) looser gun control laws, (b) laws allowing people to use violence in defense of self and property (including laws allowing people to stand their ground and kill instead of retreating), and (c) legislators who are more likely to vote hawkishly on national defense issues (Cohen, 1996). The present work supplements this body of research by adding another method—field experiments— to supply more converging, real-world evidence that the South and West possess a culture of honor and, moreover, that this culture has self-sustaining aspects.

Study 1: Sanctions By Employers For An Honor-Related Killing

If violence is less stigmatized in the South and West than in the North, then we should see this in institutional practices, such as the hiring of employees. People who have committed crimes of violence in defense of their honor should be seen less as undesirable criminals and more as decent citizens who deserve a break. Thus, if a letter inquiring about employment were sent to companies describing a person who had good credentials but who also had been convicted for honor-related violence, then the letter should receive a warmer, more promising response from companies in the South and West. To provide a tighter test of the hypothesis, organizations in the North, South, and West that were part of the same company chain were compared. Some employers were sent a letter describing an honor-related crime (the homicide condition), and others were sent a control letter describing a crime not involving personal honor (the theft condition).

Method

Materials

Letters inquiring about employment were sent to companies across the United States. The applicant described himself as a qualified, hard-working 27-year-old man who was relocating to the area. In the homicide condition, the third paragraph read as follows:

> There is one thing I must explain, because I feel I must be honest and I want no misunderstandings. I have been convicted of a felony, namely manslaughter. You will probably want an explanation for this before you send me an application, so I will provide it. I got into a fight with someone who was having an affair with my fiancee. I lived in a small town, and one night this person confronted me in front of my friends at the bar. He told everyone that he and my fiancee were sleeping together. He laughed at me to my face and asked me to step outside if I was man enough. I was young and didn't want to back down from a challenge in front of everyone. As we went into the alley, he started to attack me. He knocked me down, and he picked up a botde. I could have run away and the judge said I should have, but my

pride wouldn't let me. Instead I picked up a pipe that was laying in the alley and hit him with it. I didn't mean to kill him, but he died a few hours later at the hospital.

I realize that what I did was wrong.

In the theft condition, the third paragraph read as follows:

There is one thing I must explain, because I feel I must be honest and I want no misunderstandings. I have been convicted of a felony, namely motor vehicle theft. You will probably want an explanation for this before you send me an application, so I will provide it. I have no excuse for my behavior. I was young and I needed money. I had a wife and kids and by stealing a couple of expensive cars, I was able to give them what I always needed to give them and pay off the bills I owed. I never intended to cause the car owners any serious trouble. I was sentenced for grand theft auto and am very sorry for my crime. I was desperate but now I realize this is no excuse.

I realize that what I did was wrong.

All letters continued and requested an application for employment, the name and phone number of a contact person, and hours when the applicant might stop by for an interview.

Sample

Procedure for sampling. A letter (of either the honor or theft type) was mailed to 921 organizations. These organizations were businesses that were part of five national chains: a general merchandise store chain, a low-end motel chain, a high-end hotel chain, a family restaurant chain, and a motorcycle dealership chain. The chains were chosen because they represented a diverse cross section of the economy, operated nationwide, and accepted applications by mail. And importantly, we could find listings for the locations of all their outlets in the United States.

The particular businesses were selected by figuring out how many outlets would represent the state (based on its population) and then sampling every nth outlet within that state. Businesses from the South were oversampled so that this region could be broken out if necessary in the analysis stage. Thus, for each chain, approximately 100 letters were sent to southern companies in that chain, and 100 letters were sent to nonsouthern companies in that chain. (Because not all states had enough stores to fill their quota of letters, there were somewhat less than 1,000 letters sent.)

Following census categorization, we defined the South as Census Divisions 5, 6, and 7: Delaware, Maryland, Virginia, West Virginia, North Carolina, South Carolina, Georgia, Florida, Kentucky, Tennessee, Alabama, Mississippi, Arkansas, Louisiana, Oklahoma, and Texas. Washington, D.C., is also defined as the South by the census but was excluded for the studies of this article because it is probably not representative of either northern or southern culture.

The West was defined as Census Divisions 8 and 9, excluding Alaska and Hawaii. (This includes New Mexico, Arizona, Colorado, Utah, Nevada, Wyoming, Idaho, Montana, California, Oregon, and

Washington.) Alaska and Hawaii were excluded from the West because they do not share the common historical heritage of the region. All other states not in the South or West are obviously in the third category of states. In this article, these states are referred to as *northern* merely as a shorthand way of referring to nonsouthern and nonwestern states. The definitions of these regions are consistent with other work on regional differences and violence (see Baron & Straus, 1988,1989; Cohen, 1996; Cohen & Nisbett, 1994; Nisbett, 1993; Nisbett & Cohen, 1996; Nisbett et al., 1995).

After the study was completed, debriefing letters were sent to all organizations, whether they responded to the original letter or not The debriefing letter contained a brief summary of the study and its purposes. The few employers who contacted us after receiving our debriefing letter were very positive about the study and found the topic quite important.

Response rates. Of the 921 letters sent, 9 were returned as undeliverable. A total of 112 responses were received, for an overall response rate of 12%. Northern companies were more likely to respond to the letters than were southern and western companies, as indicated by logistic regression analysis, $f(908) = 2.93$, $p < .01$. The response rate for the northern-homicide condition was 16% of 149 letters; for northern-theft condition, 17.5% of 154 letters; for southern and western-homicide condition, 11% of 308 letters; and for southern and western-theft condition, 9% of 301 letters. One might have expected northern companies to respond more often to a theft letter than to an honor letter, whereas southern and western companies might respond more often to an honor letter than to a theft letter. This was indeed the pattern, but the interaction was far from significant. This lack of interaction, however, aids us in interpreting the content of the letters. Differential response rates (for which there was no interaction) cannot account for the interaction effects on the compliance and tone indexes that follow.

Measures

What is crucial for our purposes is the content of the response letters. An entirely unsympathetic letter basically shuts the door on the applicant, ends communication, and may be worse than no response at all. In contrast, a letter that is cooperative, fills the person's requests, and is generally sympathetic would clearly be positive and an invitation to further communication. This was why we analyzed the responses we received for (a) compliance with requests and (b) the tone of the letter or note (if enclosed).

Compliance, tone, and job availability items. We noted whether each organization complied with the requests of the letter by sending an application, the name of a contact person, the phone number for the contact, and hours or days to stop by. Some potential employers sent back a business card and a note or a letter, and these responses were noted as well. For each of the above items, the organizations received a score of 1 if the response included the item and a 0 if it did not. The scores were then summed over the six items to compute a compliance index.

When a letter was received from an organization, its tone was evaluated by two judges who were blind to condition. The tone items were scored for how encouraging the letter was (4-point scale), how understanding it was (4-point scale), how personal it was (3-point scale), and whether it mentioned an appreciation for the applicant's candor (dichotomous scale). All scores were turned into dichotomous variables (for example, encouraging or not, understanding or not, etc.) and then summed. (Variables were dichotomized because a 0-1 scale was the simplest meaningful metric that could be common to all four items of the tone index.)

On one question, raters also coded how available the note indicated that jobs were in that organization. The codes for this question were as follows: 0 = we cannot hire felons, 1 = there are no jobs now, 2 = there are no jobs now but we will keep your materials on file or no mention about jobs, and 3 = there are jobs available.

Coding. Codes for the items of the compliance index (the presence of a note or letter, an application form, etc.) were obvious from inspection. The various measures used to create the compliance index were moderately correlated with each other. Ruder-Richardson formula 20 was used to compute an internal consistency score (analogous to Cronbach's alpha) for the compliance index (r = .48) (Carmines & Zeller, 1979, p. 48; Rosenthal & Rosnow, 1991, p. 49).

For the tone index, we examined interrater agreement by computing Cohen's Kappas for the dichotomous ratings of how encouraging, understanding, and personal the letters were (Cohen, 1960). Cohen's Kappas were .58, .81, and .79, respectively (all significant at $p < .001$). Coder scores were averaged together before being combined into a scale. The reliability coefficient for the scale was .76, using Ruder-Richardson formula 20.

For the codings of job availability, nine categories were originally used, but then we collapsed this down to the four ordinal categories indicated above for greater reliability. Because of the objective nature of these categories, an interrater agreement score was not computed, and coder ratings were not averaged together. Rather, any discrepancies in coding (of which there were only five) were resolved by a third coder who was blind to condition.

Results

The prediction was that southern and western companies would be more accepting than northern companies of the homicide letter applicant but that the regions would not differ in their treatment of the theft applicant.[1]

Compliance scores. As may be seen in Table 1, the mean compliance scores differed significantly as a function of region and condition in the way predicted.[2] Compliance scores were approximately equal for both regions (or even slightly higher in the North) for the theft letter. But for the homicide letter, compliance scores were higher for companies in the South and West than for companies in the North. The contrast was significant at $p < .06$, $t(108) = 1.91$. The effect size (r = .18) was in the small-to-moderate-size range.[3]

Tone index. Letters or notes were enclosed for 78 responses. As may be seen in Table 1, the predicted pattern for the index of the tone items again held. Control letters were responded to with about the same degree of warmth and understanding in all regions. But honor letters were responded to more warmly in the South and West than in the North. The contrast was significant, $t(74) = 2.02$, $p < .05$. The effect size (r = .23) was in the small to moderate range.

Job availability. As predicted, there was little difference between northern versus southern and western companies for the theft letter (northern control = 2.0, southern control = 2.05). And as predicted,

TABLE 1. Compliance With Requests, Warmth of Response, and Indication of Job Availability for Honor Applicants and Control Applicants to Companies in the North, South, and West, Study 1

	Honor Letter	Control Letter
Compliance index		
North	2.83 (1.27)	3.15 (1.35)
South and West	3.52 (1.39)	2.93 (1.27)
Interaction p < .06		
Tone of response		
North	0.75 (0.83)	1.39 (1.30)
South and West	1.69 (1.59)	1.43 (1.47)
Interaction p < .05		
Job availability item		
North	1.71 (0.61)	2.00 (0.49)
South and West	1.96 (0.36)	2.05 (0.38)
Interaction p < .11		

NOTE: Standard deviations are in parentheses.

northern companies were less welcoming for the homicide letter than southern and western companies were (northern honor = 1.71, southern honor = 1.96). However, the standard contrast was not significant (p level = .11), £(74) = 1.62. The effect size (r = .19) was in the small to moderate range.

Interactions between region, letter type, and organization. The interactions of interest were obviously the Region x Type of Letter interactions. But one might also wonder whether these interactions would be strengthened or weakened, depending on the type of organization that was responding. They were not. The p levels for the three-way interaction between region, letter type, and organization type were all nonsignificant (p > .80 for the compliance index, p > .65 for the tone index, and p > .20 for the job availability item). There were, however, some effects for type of organization (not involving the region variable). Perhaps, these reflect the effects of organizational culture on the employment process and workplace environment (for research on organizational or small-group culture, see, for example, Levine & Moreland, 1991; Lewis, 1989; Martin, 1992; Pratt, 1994; Pratt & Rafaeli, 1996; Schein, 1990; Tichy & Cohen, 1996). Without greater ethnographic information on the organizations in our study, however, speculation about effects involving organization type would have little meaning.

Summary and discussion. In sum, for our measures of tone and compliance, control letters were treated about equally everywhere, whereas the honor letters were responded to more positively in the South and West than in the North. The only item for which the standard contrast did not achieve significance was the job availability item. Perhaps the job availability item was different because it was the response that was most constrained by reality. That is, managers are relatively free to write response letters with any tone that they feel is appropriate, but it would take an outright lie to say that there is no job when jobs are available. Still, it is probably worth noting that the northern-homicide condition was the only condition in which a manager wrote back that he could not hire felons and in which not a single manager wrote back that jobs were available.

Consistent with this, we might note that perhaps the greatest signs of cultural difference involved the more extreme responses to the letters. In response to the homicide letter, no northern manager sent back a complete package of items, and none received the highest scores on the tone index. In contrast, southern and western employers could be quite warm toward the applicant in the homicide condition: One quarter of all southern and western employers responded to the homicide letter in a way that earned the highest score on the tone index.

A qualitative example may help make this point more vividly. In response to the applicant who had killed the man who provoked him, one southern store owner wrote back that although she had no jobs, she was sympathetic to the man's plight:

> As for your problem of the past, anyone could probably be in the situation you were in. It was just an unfortunate incident that shouldn't be held against you. Your honesty shows that you are sincere....
>
> I wish you the best of luck for your future. You have a positive attitude and a willingness to work. Those are the qualities that businesses look for in an employee. Once you get settled, if you are near here, please stop in and see us.

No letter from a northern employer was anywhere near as sympathetic toward this man who killed in defense of his honor.

Study 2: Portrayals Of Honor-Related Violence In The Media

In a classic study, Bartlett (1950) showed that as stories are remembered and retold, they are distorted in ways that make sense according to the culture of the listener. We propose that the same phenomenon should occur for northern and southern listeners who are told about an incident involving honor-related violence. Specifically, in retelling a story, southern and western storytellers should be more likely than their northern counterparts to mention provocations and explain the violence in a fashion that is more sympathetic to the perpetrator.

One could examine this phenomenon at the individual level by giving a story to northerners, southerners, and westerners and seeing how they organize and retell it. But one can also examine this phenomenon in a context in which it has potential collective consequences. A reporter working for a newspaper is not just an individual but—acting in an institutional role—also creates a public representation for mass consumption.

The reporter's retelling of the story obviously reaches more people than any given individual's retelling, and by virtue of the paper's status, the story becomes a public representation of the way things are (or should be). News stories are not just objective statements of facts; they are statements of values about what a culture views as relevant, appropriate, and acceptable (see, for example, Binder, 1993; Faludi, 1991; Lee, Hallahan, & Herzog, 1996; Meyers, 1994; Morris & Peng, 1994). Thus, through the power of the reporter's role, private representations become public representations that can feed back on and influence the private representations of others (see Kuran, 1995).

One cannot just compare actual news stories about violence in defense of honor in these regions, because differences in the articles could be due to differences in "objective" facts or in "subjective" interpretations. The present study controlled for this problem by sending out a fact sheet describing a fictional honor-related stabbing to newspapers in the North, West, and South. The papers were asked to turn these events into a story (for pay) as it would appear in the paper. The prediction was that newspapers in the South and West would treat the honor-related violence more sympathetically, portray the violence as more justified, describe the assaulting person as being less blameworthy, and downplay any aggravating circumstances. For this story, we described events revolving around a central culture-of-honor concern— namely, insults or attacks against female family members (Fiske, Markus, Kitayama, & Nisbett, in press). WyattBrown (1982, p. 53) described how insults against female members of the family were treated with utmost seriousness in the Old South, and Cohen and Nisbett (1994) showed that this is still true today.

A control story giving facts for a violent crime that was not honor related allowed for a tighter test of the hypothesis. We expected that stories written by southerners, westerners, and northerners would not differ in the degree of sympathy expressed for such a crime.

College newspapers were used because we assumed compliance rates would be higher for them than for professional newspapers. This probably provides for a conservative test of our hypothesis, because college newspapers (relative to rural papers, for example) are written by and produced for a more liberal segment of the population. There was also another advantage to using college newspapers, as these papers were overwhelmingly staffed by reporters who grew up in the same region where they went to school.

Method

Materials

We created a set of facts to be used as the basis for two news stories and sent them to college newspapers across the country. A cover letter explained that the research concerned how newspapers turn a collection of facts into a news story. The letter said it would probably take about 1 hr to turn the facts into news stories and offered the reporter or the general fund of the paper $25 for the help. Thus, reporters knew they were participating in a study (although they were blind to its purpose and hypotheses). The stories had to include a headline and be no longer than 250 words each. A brief questionnaire also asked how much space the paper would allot each story and for demographic information about the reporter.

The fact sheets contained many miscellaneous facts, as well as some that were highly relevant for a culture-of-honor interpretation. Some of the salient facts from the stories are summarized here:[4]

Honor story. Victor Jensen stabbed Martin Shell. Jensen is a 28-year-old Caucasian who works as a janitor at Warren High School, and Shell is a 27-year-old Caucasian who works as a mechanic at the Bradley GM car dealership. Shell is currently in stable condition at Mercy Hospital after last night's incident.

Shell dated Jensen's sister, Ann, for about a month, but they broke up a few weeks before the party. Ann was present at the party, but she was not involved in the stabbing.

Witnesses told police that Shell and Jensen talked to each other throughout the evening. Around 1:30 a.m., Shell spilled a glass of beer on Jensen's pants. The two began arguing and had to be separated by others at the party. Shell shouted that Jensen's sister, Ann, was "a slut." Jensen then started to walk toward Shell but was restrained by three other people at the party. Several men at the party were heard to make comments about what they would do if someone said that about their sister.

Around 1:45 a.m., Jensen left the party. As Jensen was leaving, Shell and his friends laughed at Jensen. Shell then shouted that both Jensen's sister and mother were "sluts." When Jensen returned to the party around 1:55 a.m., he demanded that Shell take back his comments "or else." Shell laughed at Jensen and said, "Or else what, Ram bo? "Jensen then pulled a 4-in. knife out of his jacket and stabbed Shell twice. Shell was unarmed at the time of the stabbing.

Several quotes expressing opinions about the incident from both Jensen's and Shell's statements to police were also included.

Control story. Robert Hansen pistol-whipped John Seger. Seger was working at a 7-11 convenience store when Hansen robbed the store and pistol-whipped Seger. Hansen took the $75 that was in the cash register and a carton of cigarettes. Seger is a 22-year-old Caucasian and is in stable condition at Mercy Hospital. Hansen is a 19-year-old Caucasian and is in custody at the Washtenaw County Jail. Hansen was convicted on a charge of simple assault 6 months ago and served 2 days in jail.

According to the police report about the robbery, Hansen showed the pistol and demanded that Seger open the store's safe. The pistol was not loaded, according to police. Seger told Hansen that he did not know the combination to the safe, and he offered Hansen the $75 in the cash register.

Seger tried to open the safe but kept insisting he did not know the combination. Hansen then pistol-whipped Seger, striking him five times in the head with the butt of his weapon. When Seger fell to the ground, Hansen spit on him, swore at him, and kicked him in the stomach.

Several quotes from Hansen's and Seger's statements to the police were given, including a few from Hansen stating that money was stolen from him earlier in the evening and he was mad about that.

Sample

Sampling was done from a list of colleges in the *1994 World Almanac* (Famighetti, 1993). Once a college was selected, its student newspaper was found through a listing in the *1994 Editor and Publisher Yearbook* (I. Anderson, 1994). To be eligible for selection, a college had to be a 4-year school and have a student enrollment of at least 5,000.

A total of 303 letters were sent out to colleges across the country. No region of the country was oversampled; 154 letters went to colleges in the North, 53 went to colleges in the West, and 96 went to colleges in the South. Responses were received from 47 schools in the North (31%), 15 schools in the West (28%), and 32 schools in the South (33%). Of the 94 responses that were received, 83 were written by White reporters. It is only the White responses that are reported below, because previous research indicates that the relevant regional differences may exist only among Whites (Nisbett & Cohen, 1996; Nisbett et al., 1995).

Consistent with previous research focusing on White non-Jewish populations, we excluded predominantly Jewish and historically Black schools from our sample (Cohen, Nisbett, et al., 1996; Nisbett & Cohen, 1996). We also excluded schools located in Washington, D.C. (because this region is representative of neither northern nor southern culture) and University of Michigan schools (because of the remote possibility that a reporter might be familiar with our hypotheses).

Measures

Three coders rated the honor and control stories for tone and content. The coders were not blind to the experimental hypotheses or, obviously, to the type of story—honor versus control—but they were blind to what region the story came from.

We computed a justification index, examining whether writers reported or ignored nine key facts relevant to determining how justified the attack was. We constructed the index by giving papers a point for mentioning each act Shell took to provoke Jensen and a point for ignoring each act that aggravated the nature of Jensen's crime. The six actions that Shell took to provoke Jensen were spilling beer on him, insulting his sister once, insulting her again, laughing at him, insulting his mother, and laughing at him or insulting him when he asked for a retraction. The three aggravating circumstances to Jensen's crime were that Jensen returned to the party 10 min, or some time later, with a knife (suggesting premeditation); that Jensen stabbed Shell twice (or multiple times); and that Shell was unarmed at the time he was attacked. The items in the justification index were dichotomously scored, and the index had an internal consistency score of $r = .49$, using Ruder-Richardson formula 20. (Because of the objective nature of the items—a fact was either mentioned or it was not—an interjudge reliability score was not computed.)

We also computed a blameworthiness index. Coders rated the tone of the article on several dimensions: whether the most important factor leading to the stabbing seemed to be an insult from Shell to Jensen (vs. an argument between the two), whether the incident that started the whole conflict seemed to be a provocation from Shell to Jensen (vs. an argument between the two), whether Shell or Jensen seemed to be more at fault, whether the focus of the story was on the person doing the provoking or the person who did the stabbing (thus emphasizing either the situational or the dispositional causes of the attack), whether Shell could be characterized as an innocent victim or someone who got what he deserved, whether Jensen could be characterized as a hothead or a man defending his honor, and whether the story in general could be characterized as being about a psycho or a hothead or a man defending his honor. The intraclass correlation for judges' ratings was .77, as given by Shrout and Fleiss's (1979)

TABLE 2. Justification and Blameworthiness Indexes for the Honor Story for Papers in the North, South, and West, Study 2

	North	South and West	P<
Justification index	3.37 (1.87)	4.21 (1.43)	.02
Blameworthiness index	0.17 (0.75)	-0.10 (0.68)	.09

NOTE: Standard deviations are in parentheses.

formula (3,1). Judges' ratings were averaged together to form the final index. The alpha coefficient for this index, reflecting how well the individual items held together, was .89. Higher numbers on the index indicated more blameworthiness.

Also, there was one question for both the honor and the control story that asked judges to rate (on a 4-point scale) how sympathetically each story portrayed the offender. We analyzed these data using a 2 x 2 ANOVA with region as one factor and type of crime as the other. (Justification and blameworthiness indexes were not analyzed using an interaction strategy because there were no justification or blameworthiness items in the control story that were directly analogous to those in the honor story. The control story was, after all, a classic felony assault.) Based on the difference scores of sympathy for the honor offender minus sympathy for the control offender, we also categorized newspapers into those that treated the honor-related offender more sympathetically than the control offender and those that did not. For the categorizations, the associated pairwise Kappas for the three judges were .56, .26, and .21, all significant at $p < .05$.

Finally, in addition to rating the actual story, judges also rated just the lead and headline of the story. Thus, they scored whether insult, argument, or honor were mentioned in the headline or first sentence. And they rated whether the headline or first sentence seemed to indicate that the story was about a psycho or a hothead or a man defending his honor. Judges also examined the use of quotes by Shell and Jensen (some of which related to an honor theme and some of which did not).

For the control story, judges rated the content and tone of the story on a number of dimensions— for example, whether the robbery or the beating seemed to be the focus of the story, whether different circumstances of the crime were mentioned, whether different aspects of Hansen's background were mentioned, and whether different quotes from Hansen and Seger were used. The regions were not predicted to differ in their treatment of the control story.

Results and Discussion

Justification. As may be seen in the first line of Table 2, southern and western papers were likely to see the crime as more provoked and less aggravated than their northern counterparts did, $t(81) = 2.33$, $p < .02$. This effect was of moderate size, $d = .51$.[5]

Blameworthiness. As may be seen in the second line of Table 2, in the tone of their articles, southern and western papers were less likely to blame Jensen for stabbing Shell than northern papers were, $t(81)$ = 1.74, $p < .09$. The effect size ($d = .38$) was in the small to moderate range.

Sympathy. Examining the raw sympathy scores for each story, there was a trend for southern and western papers to treat the honor-related offender more sympathetically and for northern papers to treat the non-honor-related offender more sympathetically, interaction , $F(1, 79) = 2.17$, $p < .15$ (effect size, $r = .16$, was in the small to moderate range). If papers are simply categorized according to which offender they treated most sympathetically, we found that only 19% of southern and western papers treated the nonhonor crime at least as sympathetically as the honor crime, whereas twice as many northern papers (39%) did so, $\chi^2(1, N= 83) = 4.03$, $p < .04$. The effect size measure for the χ^2 statistic, w, was .22, or in the small to moderate range (Cohen, 1977, chap. 7).

Leads, headlines, and quotes. There were no significant differences in the content of the lead sentence and headline or in the use of quotes by Shell and Jensen.

Control story. Although there were several differences in how papers across the country treated the honor-related story, there were virtually no differences in how they treated the control story. Only three items showed even marginally significant differences, and these three indicated that northern papers showed more sympathy than southern and western papers for the man who beat the clerk during the robbery. Thus, the differences found on the story concerning honor-related violence do not reflect an approval of all sorts of violence; rather, they reflect a sympathy among southern and western papers that is specifically focused on honor-related violence.

Demographic items. Demographic information requested at the end of the questionnaire revealed few differences among reporters from the different regions. Their newspapers did not differ in the size of their circulation, nor did the reporters differ in their age, sex, or year in school. Thus, controlling for circulation, gender, age, and year in school using multiple regression equations changed the results very little.

Controlling for demographics also made little difference because the demographic variables were themselves relatively uncorrelated with our dependent variables of justification, blameworthiness, and sympathy. Using multiple regressions, we found only a weak tendency for men to assign less blame than women to the honor-related offender. Effects of age, year in school, and the paper's circulation on our dependent variables were very slight. Race was also not a confound in these data because we analyzed only the 83 White respondents. Results were similar, however, if the 11 non-White respondents were added to the analysis.

Demographic questions also revealed that most reporters had grown up in the region in which they were currently attending school. Indeed, there were only two cases in which southern and western reporters wrote for northern papers and only three cases in which northern reporters wrote for southern and western papers.

In summary, the papers of the South and West treated honor-related violence more sympathetically in both tone and content than did the papers of the North. The articles from the South and West portrayed the honor-related violence as more justified, less aggravated, and more the fault of the provoker. The control stories indicated that papers of the South and West were not more sympathetic toward violence in general but that sympathy was limited to honor-related violence.

Discussion

The results of these two field experiments indicate that violence related to honor is less stigmatized by institutions of the South and West than by those of the North. In Study 1, southern and western employers responded in a warmer, more sympathetic, and more cooperative way to a person convicted of an honor-related killing than they did to a person convicted of a non-honor-related crime. The reverse was true of northern employers. In Study 2, southern and western newspapers treated a violent crime in defense of honor in a more sympathetic and understanding way than did northern newspapers. As predicted, no differences were found for a story concerning violence not related to honor.

A few issues and concerns should be noted here. One ethical concern is the deception used in Study 1. Although it would have been nice if organizations had known up front that they were involved in a study, one might wonder whether the results of Study 1 would be very convincing if they had been so informed. Deception was used in this field experiment because there is no reason to assume that people are aware of—or would truthfully report—the values guiding their behavior toward job applicants with various histories. Starting with LaPiere's (1934) research, it has been shown that the real behavior of workers within an organization is often poorly reflected by its professed values and that "as if" questions may provide poor guides to actual practices. In more recent times, Salancik (1979) argued that it is often necessary to use experimentation to "stimulate" an organization and discover its true orientation. Deception in this case was mild and required little effort from experimental participants—sending application forms and, in some cases, a brief note. The costs and benefits must be weighed in deciding whether to use deception, and obviously, reasonable people can and will disagree on whether a study merits its use. In this case, we felt it did.

A more theoretical concern involves the interpretation of the present two studies. Some readers might wonder about the distinction between a culture of honor and a macho culture. Such concerns should be put in context by noting that macho culture is a version of a more general culture of honor (Gilmore, 1990). That is, all cultures of honor emphasize masculinity, toughness, and the ability to protect one's own. Cultures of honor differ from each other, however, in the amount of swagger and attitude they require versus the amount of politeness and gentility they require (E. Anderson, 1994; Cohen, Vandello, Puente, & Rantilla, 1996; Pitt-Rivers, 1965, 1968). Differences between such cultures are interesting and need exploration, but they are all still rightfully considered variations of a general culture of honor.

On a more concrete level, there are some concerns having to do with specific aspects of the studies in this article. One concern involves whether the results can be generalized to real behavior. This certainly is not an issue for Study 1, in which people thought they were responding to real job applicants. It is of some concern for Study 2, in which it is possible that different results would be obtained if reporters were not aware they were participating in a study. (This is obviously the flip side of the ethical issue involving deception discussed above.)

There are plausible hypotheses for why reporters writing a real story might produce stories that muted their own personal bias. However, it is also quite possible that if reporters were writing a real story, the salience of the audience might cause them to be even more sensitive to prevailing cultural norms, and thus regional differences would become even more magnified (see Kuran, 1995). A nice follow-up study might involve examining how actual news stories (of some notoriety) are treated by correspondents from newspapers around the nation. In addition, if one were concerned with editing and presentation issues, then one could examine how wire stories— from the Associated Press, for example—were cut, restructured, and played up or played down by various papers across the country. Such studies might provide details about the process by which news is "distorted."

Another concern has to do with the actual effects in this article. They are not large. In fact, they are almost uniformly in the small to moderate range, using Cohen's (1977) criteria. But it is their consistency—within this package of two studies and together with the results of our lab experiments, archival studies, and attitude surveys— that give us confidence in the results (Nisbett & Cohen, 1996).

Finally, there is the issue of the representativeness of the organizations that responded in both studies. A problem with field experiments is that the response rate can be relatively low. And perhaps this was to be expected given the nature of our requests here. In Study 1, for example, it is possible that the low response rate from this study was due to the applicant in both cases having a criminal record. Although low response rates are problematic, there are two major reasons for why our concerns with this are tempered. First, concerns are allayed to some extent by the comparability of responses in the control conditions of both experiments. The non-honor-related crime was treated equivalently by employers and by newspapers in the North, West, and South, suggesting that any response bias probably affected all regions equally. And also, our concerns are tempered to a larger extent by placing the studies in their broader context. Again, the field experiments presented here give results very consistent with a line of research by Nisbett, Cohen, Reaves, and others, pointing to systematic cultural differences between the South and West versus the North. Through attitude surveys, analyses of laws and social policies, homicide records, and lab experiments, this research has established the existence of regional differences in matters having to do with violence and gender roles. The two field experiments fit well with this line of work, adding to the evidence and suggesting some institutional mechanisms through which the cultures of the South and West are perpetuated.

Study 1 tells us something about the sort of feedback given to men who have committed crimes of violence related to honor. Feedback from northern employers is more likely to convey to such men that they are undesirable, unsympathetic, and unforgiven for their crimes, whereas feedback from southern employers is more likely to convey to these men that they are normal people who got caught in unfortunate situations—situations that "anyone" could have been in—and that their behavior in those situations "shouldn't be held against" them (as one southern letter writer indicated). Thus, Study 1 shows that institutions—as well as individuals—participate in the stigmatization, or lack of stigmatization, of violence.

Our speculation is that Study 1 underestimates regional differences regarding how men who perpetuate culture-of-honor violence are treated. At an early stage of the application process ("please send me an application and information"), most national chains probably have either (a) a policy of treating all applicants equally or (b) a policy of treating convicted felons more harshly than other applicants, regardless of what crime they committed. If so, then the opportunity for differential treatment would have been constrained in this study. Thus, one might expect to see even more differential treatment in institutional and especially in interpersonal situations in which there were not such constraints. Consider, for example, everyday social interactions, personal relationships, less formal organizational settings, or other situations in which association is more voluntary. As one Texas hotel manager called to tell us after receiving the debriefing letter, he had a lot of "empathy" as a person with the man who fought after the "dishonoring of his girlfriend." And he would "not have a problem with this guy being my neighbor, having my kids go over and play in his yard ... getting to know him. But as an employer, I can't hire him" because of the legal issues involved. We suspect, then, that the feedback and stigmatization (or lack of it) evidenced in Study 1 would be greatly amplified in many less constrained interpersonal and institutional settings in the real world.

Study 2 indicates another way in which institutions can contribute to collective representations that support violence. By treating violence as sympathetic, justified, or legitimately provoked, the media can help feed cultural notions about when such behavior is appropriate. And Study 2 demonstrates that there are clear cultural differences in how papers of the North, West, and South present honor-related violence and explain it to their readers.

Newspapers are just one source of collective storytelling, however. It seems remarkable that such differences were found between the stories of the South and West and stories of the North when both sets of newspapers were given the exact same facts. Newspapers are institutions that are supposed to report such stories objectively and according to journalistic formula. One can only imagine what would happen on the next iterations—as readers not bound by a journalist's sense of objectivity and closeness to the facts retell the story to others, who then retell the story to still others, who then retell the story, and so on. As this game of "telephone" continues and stories spread throughout a community, stories would probably stray further and further from the facts and become molded into culturally prescribed myths. These communal myths could both reflect the biases of the culture and serve to perpetuate it—defining some violent actions as sympathetic or even heroic (for discussions of public narratives and communal experiences, see also Bartlett, 1950, p. 173; Faludi, 1991, chap.1; Gates, 1995).

Researchers in cultural psychology need to examine all sorts of mechanisms by which a culture gets perpetuated—interpersonal interactions, familial socialization, and real or imagined peer enforcement of norms. We also cannot forget that we live our lives constrained by institutions—our media, our workplaces, our legal system, and our economic system. In this light, the mutually reinforcing effects of culture and social structure are extremely important to examine. Just as culture and the individual mind reinforce and strengthen each other (Fiske et al., 1997), so, too, do culture and our social structures.

Presently, we are a long way from understanding the mechanisms through which institutions (or even individuals) perpetuate a culture of honor. However, these field experiments—seen in the context of the laboratory experiments, attitude surveys, policy analyses, and homicide data—suggest that institutions, such as corporations and the media, at least reflect the norms of their culture. As a consequence, they may produce public representations that perpetuate the culture and keep it strong even after the culture has outlived its original purpose.

Notes

1. The appropriate contrast to test this prediction is +1, -1, 0, 0 (Rosenthal & Rosnow, 1985). Effect size measures for the interaction contrast follow formulas given by Rosenthal and Rosnow (1991, p. 470), and interpretations of their magnitude follow Cohen's (1977) conventions.

2. All p levels are two-tailed.

3. The contrast reported in the text puts together companies from the South with those of the West. This was done because the small number of responses from the West (n = 14) could make estimates unreliable. Nevertheless, analyses that examine the North, West, and South separately—using a contrast of -2, 1, 1, 0, 0, 0—give similar results. This contrast gives significance levels of $p < .02$ for the compliance index and $p < .06$ for the analysis of the tone of the letters.

4. The complete set of facts for the stories—as well as information about means and standard deviations for individual items from Studies 1 and 2—can be obtained by corresponding with the first author.

5. Data in Study 2 were analyzed with t tests between papers of the North versus papers of the South and West Again, this was done because the small number of western responses (n = 12) could make estimates unreliable. However, results look very similar if the papers are separated into three regions—North, West, and South—and a contrast of -2, +1, +1 is used. The //levels for the main variables using this contrast were as follows: justification index, p< .005; blameworthiness index, $p < .05$; greater sympathy for the offender in the honor story versus the control story, $p < .03$. In general, responses from the West tended to be even stronger than those from the South.

References

Anderson, E. (1994). The code of the streets. *Atlantic Monthly,* 5, 81–94.

Anderson, I. E. (Ed.). (1994). *Editor and publisher international yearbook.* New York: Editor and Publisher.

Baron, L., & Straus, M. A. (1988). Cultural and economic sources of homicide in the United States. *Sociological Quarterly,* 29, 371–392.

Baron, L., & Straus, M. A. (1989). *Four theories of rape in American society: A state-level analysis.* New Haven, CT: Yale University Press.

Bartlett, F. C. (1950). *Remembering: A study in experimental and social psychology.* Cambridge, UK: Cambridge University Press.

Binder, A. (1993). Constructing racial rhetoric: Media depictions of harm in heavy metal and rap music. *American Sociological Review,* 58, 753–767.

Carmines, E. G., & Zeller, R. A. (1979). *Reliability and validity assessment.* Newbury Park, CA: Sage.

Cohen, D. (1996). Law, social policy, and violence: The impact of regional cultures. *Journal of Personality and Social Psychology,* 70, 961–978.

Cohen, D., & Nisbett, R. E. (1994). Self-protection and the culture of honor: Explaining southern violence. *Personality and Social Psychology Bulletin,* 20, 551–567.

Cohen, D., Nisbett, R. E., Bowdle, B. F., & Schwarz, N. (1996). Insult, aggression, and the southern culture of honor: An "experimental ethnography." *Journal of Personality and Social Psychology,* 70, 945–960.

Cohen, D., Vandello, J., Puente, S., & Rantilla, A. (1996). *"When you call me that, smile!": How norms for politeness and aggression interact in the southern culture of honor.* Unpublished manuscript, University of Illinois.

Cohen, J. (1960). A coefficient of agreement for nominal scales. *Educational and Psychological Measurement,* 20, 37–46.

Cohen, J. (1977). *Statistical power analysis for the behavioral sciences.* New York: Academic Press.

Ellison, C. G. (1991). An eye for an eye? A note on the southern subculture of violence thesis. *Social Forces,* 69, 1223–1239.

Ellison, C. G., & Sherkat, D. E. (1993). Conservative Protestantism and support for corporal punishment. *American Sociological Review, 58,* 131–144.

Faludi, S. *(1991). Backlash: The undeclared war against American women.* New York: Crown.

Famighetti, R. (Ed.). (1993). *The world almanac and book of facts.* Mahwah, NJ: Funk & Wagnalls.

Fiske, A. P., Markus, H., Kitayama, S., & Nisbett, R E. (in press). The cultural matrix of social psychology. In D. T. Gilbert, S. T. Fiske, & G. Lindzey (Eds.), *Handbook of social psychology* (4th ed). Boston: McGraw-Hill.

Gastil, R. D. (1971). Homicide and a regional culture of violence. *American Sociological Review, 36,* 412–427.

Gates, H. L. Jr. (1995, October 23). Thirteen ways of looking at a Black man. *The New Yorker,* pp. 56–65.

Gilmore, D. D. (1990). *Manhood in the making: Cultural concepts of masculinity.* New Haven, CT: Yale University Press.

Hackney, S. (1969). Southern violence. In H. D. Graham & T. R. Gurr (Eds.), *The history of violence in America* (pp. 505–527). New York: Bantam Books.

Huff-Corzine, L., Corzine, J., & Moore, D. C. (1986). Southern exposure: Deciphering the South's influence on homicide rates. *Social Forces, 64,* 906–924.

Huff-Corzine, L., Corzine, J., & Moore, D. C. (1991). Deadly connections: Culture, poverty, and the direction of lethal violence. *Social Forces, 69,* 715–732.

Kowalski, G. S., & Peete, T. A. (1991). Sunbelt effects on homicide rates. *Sociology and Social Research, 75,* 73–79.

Kuran, T. (1995). *Private truths, public lies: The social consequences of preference falsification.* Cambridge, MA: Harvard University Press.

Land, K. C., McCall, P. L., & Cohen, L. E. (1990). Structural covariates of homicide rates: Are there any invariances across time and social space. *American Journal of Sociology, 95,* 922–963.

LaPiere, R. T. (1934). Attitudes vs. actions. *Social Forces, 13,* 230–237.

Lee, F., Hallahan, M., & Herzog, T. (1996). Explaining real-life events: How culture and domain shape attributions. *Personality and Social Psychology Bulletin, 22,* 732–741.

Lee, R. S. (1995a). Machismo values and violence in America: An empirical study. In L. L. Adler & F. L. Denmark (Eds.), *Violence and the prevention of violence* (pp. 11–31). Westport, CT: Praeger.

Lee, R .S. (1995b). Regional subcultures as revealed by magazine circulation patterns. *Cross-Cultural Research, 29,* 91–120.

Levine, J. M., & Moreland, R L. (1991). Culture and socialization in work groups. In L. B. Resnick, J. M. Levine, & S. D. Teasley (Eds.), *Perspectives on socially shared cognition* (pp. 257–279). Washington, DC: American Psychological Association.

Lewis, M. (1989). *Liar's poker.* New York: Norton.

Martin, J. (1992). *Cultures in organizations.* New York: Oxford University Press.

Meyers, M. (1994). News of battering. *Journal of Communication, 44,* 47–63.

Miller, D. T., & Prentice, D. A. (1994). Collective errors and errors about the collective. *Personality and Social Psychology Bulletin, 20,* 541–550.

Morris, M. W., & Peng, K. (1994). Culture and cause: American and Chinese attributions for social and physical events. *Journal of Personality and Social Psychology, 67,* 949–971.

Nisbett, R. E. (1993). Violence and U.S. regional culture. *American Psychologist, 48,* 441–449.

Nisbett, R E., & Cohen, D. (1996). *Culture of honor: The psychology of violence in the South.* Boulder, CO: Westview.

Nisbett, R. E., Polly, G., & Lang, S. (1995). Homicide and regional U.S. culture. In R. B. Ruback & N. A. Weiner (Eds.), *Interpersonal violent behaviors* (pp. 135–151). New York: Springer.

Pitt-Rivers, J. (1965). Honour and social status. In J. G. Peristiany (Ed.), *Honour and shame: The values of Mediterranean society* (pp. 21–77). London: Weidenfeld and Nicolson.

Pitt-Rivers, J. (1968). Honor. In D. Sills (Ed.), *International encyclopedia of the social sciences* (pp. 503–511). New York: Macmillan.

Pratt, M. G. (1994). *The happiest, most dissatisfied people on earth: Ambivalence and commitment among Amway distributors.* Unpublished doctoral dissertation, University of Michigan.

Pratt, M. G., & Rafaeli, A. (1996). *Multi-layered identities: Organizational dress as a symbol of complex social identities in organizations.* Manuscript submitted for publication.

Reaves, A. L., & Nisbett, R E. (1995). *The cultural ecology of rural White homicide in the southern United States.* Unpublished manuscript, University of Michigan.

Reed, J. S. (1981). Below the Smith and Wesson line: Reflections on southern violence. In M. Black & J. S. Reed (Eds.), *Perspectives on the American South: An annual review of society, politics, and culture* (pp. 922). New York: Cordon & Breach Science.

Rice, T. W., & Goldman, C. R. (1994). Another look at the subculture of violence thesis: Who murders whom and under what circumstances. *Sociological Spectrum, 14,* 371–384.

Rosenthal, R., & Rosnow, R. L. (1985). *Contrast analysis.* Cambridge, UK: Cambridge University Press.

Rosenthal, R., & Rosnow, R. L. (1991). *Essentials of behavioral research.* New York: McGraw-Hill.

Salancik, G. R. (1979). Field stimulations for organizational behavior research. *Administrative Science Quarterly, 24,* 638–649.

Schein, E. H. (1990). Organizational culture. *American Psychologist, 45,* 109–119.

Schelling, T. C. (1978). *Micromotives and macrobehavior.* New York: Norton.

Schneider, J. (1971). Of vigilance and virgins: Honor, shame and access to resources in Mediterranean societies. *Ethnology, 10,* 1–24.

Shrout, P. E., & Fleiss, J. L. (1979). Intraclass correlations: Uses in assessing rater reliability. *Psychological Bulletin, 86,* 420–428.

Sperber, D. (1990). The epidemiology of beliefs. In C. Fraser & G. Gaskell (Eds.), *The social psychological study of widespread beliefs* (pp. 25–44). Oxford, UK: Clarendon.

Sunstein, C. R (1995, December 25). True lies. *The New Republic,* pp. 37–41.

Tichy, N., & Cohen, E. (1996). *The leader driven organization.* Unpublished manuscript, University of Michigan.

Wyatt-Brown, B. (1982). *Southern honor: Ethics and behavior in the Old South.* New York: Oxford University Press.

The Mentor's Dilemma

Providing Critical Feedback Across the Racial Divide

By Geoffrey L. Cohen, Claude M. Steele, Lee D. Ross, Stanford University

Two studies examined the response of Black and White students to critical feedback presented either alone or buffered with additional information to ameliorate its negative effects. Black students who received unbuffered critical feedback responded less favorably than White students both in ratings of the evaluator's bias and in measures of task motivation. By contrast, when the feedback was accompanied both by an invocation of high standards and by an assurance of the student's capacity to reach those standards, Black students responded as positively as White students and both groups reported enhanced identification with relevant skills and careers. This "wise," two-faceted intervention proved more effective than buffering criticism either with performance praise (Study 1) or with an invocation of high standards alone (Study 2). The role of stigma in mediating responses to critical feedback, and the implications of our results for mentoring and other teacher-student interactions, are explored.

The mentor who wants to provide constructive performance feedback faces a dilemma. Information about shortcomings in the student's work, and pointed suggestions for improvement, can undermine the student's self-confidence and motivation to succeed. Providing critical feedback that encourages rather than discourages the recipient is a challenge for all teachers (Bruner, 1962; Daloz, 1986; Sansone, Sachau, & Weir, 1989), tutors (Lepper, Aspinwall, & Mumme, 1990), managers (Weisinger, 1990), coaches (Horn, 1985), and other educators. But the dilemma is particularly acute when potentially threatening scholastic feedback must be provided to minority students facing negative stereotypes about their group's intellectual capacities.

Minority students are aware that important people in their schooling environment may doubt their ability and belonging (Steele, 1992,1997; Steele & Aronson, 1995).

Critical feedback, accordingly, may be especially threatening to these students because instead of merely offering information about areas in need of improvement, it raises the prospect that they have been judged in light of a negative stereotype. This "attributional ambiguity" constitutes a double-edged sword (Crocker & Major, 1989; Crocker, Voelkl, Testa, & Major, 1991). Although it may protect

Geoffrey L. Cohen, Claude M. Steele & Lee D. Ross, "The Mentor's Dilemma: Providing Critical Feedback Across the Racial Divide," *Personality and Social Psychology Bulletin*, vol. 25, no. 10, pp. 1302–1318. Copyright © 1999 by SAGE Publications, Inc. Reprinted with permission.

students' self-esteem by allowing them to attribute negative feedback to racial bias rather than short-comings in their own performance, it also may lead them to dismiss rather than act on potentially useful criticism—especially when the criticism comes from a White evaluator rather than a Black one (Banks, Stitt, Curtis, & McQuarter, 1977; Crocker & Major, 1989; Crocker et al., 1991; see also Kleck, 1966).

"Stereotype threat" may create additional consequences for minority students' motivation upon receiving negative feedback (see Steele, 1992, 1997; Steele & Aronson, 1995; Spencer, Steele, & Quinn, 1997). In the context of a broadly disseminated stereotype, the decision to renew or increase one's efforts carries a threatening possibility. While further effort increases chances for success, it also may increase the cost of failure because such failure threatens to confirm the alleged limitation in ability both in the eyes of others and perhaps in one's own eyes as well. Rather than expose themselves to such peril, minority students may respond to critical feedback by withdrawing from the performance task, especially insofar as that feedback made them doubt their ability to reach the higher performance standard it demanded. To further protect self-regard, minority students also may adopt the psychological defense of disidentification, that is, diminishing the importance of the relevant domain of achievement as a basis of self-esteem (Steele, 1992, 1997). This self-protective response may further discourage the effort and risk-taking that could boost self-esteem through success in meeting higher performance standards.

The challenge facing the mentor is thus to provide feedback in a *wise* manner, that is, in a manner that discourages expectations and attributions of racial bias and that minimizes stereotype threat. We borrow the term wise from the keen-eyed sociologist Erving Goffman (1963), who in turn borrowed it from the gay subculture of the 1950s. In its original use, the term referred to nonstigmatized individuals who were recognized for their ability to see the full humanity of those bearing a stigma. Our use vis-a-vis intervention strategies has a similar connotation. Wise strategies for assisting minority students are those that assure the students that they will not be judged stereotypically—that their abilities and "belonging" are assumed rather than doubted (Steele, 1992, 1997).

Some features of wise strategies are suggested by successful interventions that, in defiance of troubling statistics on minority achievement, have raised the grades, test scores, and college prospects of at-risk and minority youth (Comer, 1980,1988; Kleinfeld, 1975; Lepper et al., 1990; Lepper, Woolverton, Mumme, & Gurtner, 1993; Mathews, 1988; Treisman, 1985; see Cose, 1997; Steele, 1997, for reviews). The educators in these programs all refute negative stereotypes by conveying a clear faith in each student's intellectual potential. But they do not impart this message by assigning easier work to ensure student success or by offering heavy doses of unstinting praise—all too common tactics of well-meaning but unwise teachers. Indeed, several authors offer detailed discussions of the dangers of "overpraising" and "underchallenging" members of stereotyped groups (Dweck, Davidson, Nelson, & Enna, 1978; Fernandez, Espinosa, & Dornbusch, 1975; Harber, 1998; Kleinfeld, 1975; Massey, Scott, & Dornbusch, 1975; Mathews, 1988; Steele, 1992, 1997; see also Barker & Graham, 1987; Dawes, 1994; Meyer et al., 1979; Mueller & Dweck, 1998). Rather, minority students in all of these otherwise diverse success stories are challenged with high performance standards—standards that *presume* their motivation and ability to succeed. The educators often go an important step further by explicitly assuring students of their capacity to meet those standards through greater effort.

Anecdotal evidence illustrates the effectiveness of setting and maintaining high standards. Jaime Escalante (whose work was portrayed in the movie *Stand and Deliver* and documented by Mathews, 1988) challenged his East Los Angeles Latino students to take and pass the advanced placement (AP) exam in calculus. Escalante's students met this standard. In fact, they accounted for 27% of all Mexican Americans receiving college credit on their AP exam, and the rate of advanced placement compared favorably with that obtained in many privileged, suburban schools. Xavier University, which, despite its small size and scant endowment, sends more Black students to medical schools than any other university, and Georgia Tech, which enjoys exceptional success in graduating minority students from its engineering curriculum, similarly set highly demanding standards (see Steele, 1992, 1997; also Cose, 1997).

The invocation of high standards is apt to be of limited value unless the student is assured, implicitly or explicitly, that he or she is capable of reaching the higher standard. Successful interventions thus continually convey the message that students can succeed through effort and persistence (Mathews, 1988; see also Cose, 1997). In a sense, the message is that academic ability, or even so called intelligence, is not fixed or immutable. Rather, it can be enhanced through effortful practice and the cultivation of specific skills (see Dweck, Chiu, & Hong, 1995; Dweck & Leggett, 1988; Ericsson, 1993). As Dweck and her colleagues have shown (see also Nicholls, 1978), students who believe in the immutability of intelligence focus on "performance goals;" they seek to demonstrate rather than enhance their competence and are apt to withdraw from tasks where they risk failure. In the face of the inevitable setbacks and frustrations that accompany the pursuit of high standards, stereotype-threatened students may thus need to be assured that, with greater effort, they can increase their capacities.

Not coincidentally, the most successful academic programs aimed at minority youth often are presented as honorific rather than remedial, with correspondingly higher standards for student performance (Steele, 1992, 1997). The assurance that students can reach the higher standards is implicit in their recruitment. Students in Urie Treisman's (1985) rigorous calculus workshops at Berkeley, for example, are told that their invitation to join the "special honors program" is based on their prior records and demonstrated academic potential. Other features of the program reinforce high standards and refute alleged limitations in ability. For example, interracial group study sessions allow students to observe one another wrestle with the assigned work. They come to see their own frustration with the course material not as unique to themselves (and thus an indication of limited ability) but as a response to demanding work that is common to all students, Black and White alike (see also Prentice & Miller, 1993). Treisman's program raised the percentage of Black undergraduates who passed 1st-year calculus from 60% to 97%. In spite of the program's small size—students meet 6 to 8 hours each week during their freshman year—it also increased the percentage of Black students who ultimately completed college by 40%.

Our review suggests the wisdom of combining the invocation of high standards with the assurance of students' capacity to reach those standards. Such a two-faceted intervention, we argue, is especially germane to the concerns of the mentor who must provide feedback across racial lines. The invocation of high standards alone may encourage minority students to attribute critical feedback to rigorous performance standards rather than to racial bias (see Banks et al., 1977). But the assurance that the student can meet the higher standard may be necessary to diminish the threatening possibility that the student has reached a group-based limitation in ability. In a sense, it is the explicitness of these messages that may be disproportionately important for students who face negative stereotypes. Nonminority students receiving unbuffered rigorous criticism, we argue, will be more inclined than minority students to automatically infer high standards and to further assume that the critic felt that they could meet these standards.

The two experiments reported here examined the response of Black and White students to critical feedback. Our first study pitted the effectiveness of the wise combination of explicit invocation of high standards, and assurance that the student could meet those standards, against the more commonplace tactic of accompanying criticism with a buffer of performance praise. Providing such a buffer of praise is a strategy advocated both by some organizational theorists and some educators of minority students and one frequently practiced by White evaluators giving feedback to Black students (Harber, 1998). Our second study compared the effects of the same wise, two-faceted intervention, with those of invoking high standards in the absence of the relevant personal assurance.

The paradigm we developed was one in which students wrote and then received critical feedback on a letter of commendation for their most memorable and effective teacher, coach, or mentor—with the prospect of ultimately having their letter published. This paradigm was noteworthy in several respects. First, in contrast to the performance task used in many feedback studies, our students' task was highly motivating, personally relevant, and one for which they were uniquely qualified. Second, the relevant feedback consisted not of an arbitrary numerical ranking or rating of performance but of detailed criticisms and suggestions for improvement. Students could see a clear (indeed, authentic) connection between the feedback and the specifics of their work. Third, our dependent variable measures included particularly natural and appropriate measures of task motivation, that is, students' expressed belief in their capacity to improve their letter and their interest in undertaking further revision.

Study 1

In the first of two experimental sessions, Black and White college students were asked to write a letter of commendation for their favorite teacher, ostensibly for potential publication in an education journal. In the second session, a week later, students in three conditions received critical feedback pointing out weaknesses and suggesting strategies for improvement from a reviewer that they presumed to be White. In an "unbuffered criticism" condition, the students received this critical feedback with no further comment. In a "wise criticism" condition, students received the same critical feedback buffered with an explicit invocation of high standards and an assurance of the particular student's capacity to reach those standards. In a "positive buffer" condition, students received the critical feedback buffered only by general praise of their performance.[1]

Three types of dependent variable measures were used. One measure assessed students' perceptions of the bias showed toward them on the part of the reviewer. A second set of measures assessed motivation at the task, specifically, participants' belief in their ability to improve their work with greater effort and their interest in revising and resubmitting their letter. (Such measures were specifically attuned to the concerns of the mentor, that is, whether the student, upon receiving critical feedback, believes that he or she can now do better and wishes to try again.) A third set of dependent measures assessed general feelings of identification with the more global academic skills relevant to the letter-writing task. (In addition to their intuitive appeal, the validity of our motivation and identification dependent measures is supported by a principal component analysis reported in each of the Results sections.)

Our working hypothesis (following Crocker et al., 1991, and Banks et al., 1977) was that Black students would respond to unbuffered criticism more negatively than would White students. That is, Black students would rate the criticism as more biased, and feel less motivated, than their White peers. Our main concern, however, was the extent to which the tactic of accompanying the criticism with an explicit invocation of high standards and an assurance of the student's capacity to reach those standards would attenuate those negative effects and thus reduce or eliminate the relevant race differences in response to criticism. We further predicted that our two-faceted intervention would reduce the differences between Black and White students' responses to criticism more than would the inclusion of general praise to buffer the criticism.

Method

Participants

All but 4 participants were recruited by telephone from a registrar's list of Stanford undergraduates and paid $10 for their participation. Only self-classified Black and White students who had not taken any courses in introductory or social psychology (and thus were unlikely to be suspicious about the purpose of the study) qualified for participation in the study from this list. The other 4 participants (2 Blacks and 2 Whites) were recruited by telephone from an introductory psychology course within the 1st week of the course before any discussion of relevant issues and subject matter; these students received course credit for their participation.

A total of 45 Black and 48 White students were assigned at random to the three criticism conditions. However, data from 2 of these participants were discarded prior to analysis; 1 Black student who voiced suspicion about our interest in race and 1 White student who received feedback that erroneously referred to his male teacher as "she."

Procedure

Students participated in the study individually, although in some instances, 2 students heard the initial introduction to the study together before being escorted into separate rooms to complete the experimental task.[2] Each student took part in two sessions, writing an account of a favorite teacher during the first session and receiving feedback on that account during the second session.

Session 1. Each student was greeted by an experimenter (a White male or White female) who escorted him or her to a laboratory room and then proceeded to elaborate on the ostensible purpose of the study. Students were told that the study concerned the psychology of effective teaching and that its objective was to uncover those qualities that define excellence in teaching. Their task, it was explained, would be to write a "letter of commendation" for their favorite teacher, who could be an elementary or secondary schoolteacher, a university professor, a tutor, or a coach—anyone who they felt had "made an important contribution to their personal growth." Students were led to believe that the researchers would seek to publish the best letters in an education journal.

To strengthen the link between the letter-writing task and more general academic skills relevant to negative minority-group stereotypes, students were told that their task would "require the same skills necessary for writing an effective paper. ... You'll have to communicate your ideas clearly, make intelligent points and back them up with supporting arguments, and maintain a coherent organization and structure." The experimenter went on to explain that in the first session, students would write the letter and that in the second session a week hence, their letters would be returned to them with comments provided by a reviewer from a research panel—comments that might help them improve their letter if they decided to revise it.

Students next were asked to read and sign a participation consent form. As they were reading the form, the experimenter reminded participants of a request (made at the time of their recruitment) that they bring to the study a photograph of themselves, ideally with their favorite teacher, that would accompany their letter should it be published. When (in all but two cases) students indicated that they had forgotten or been unable to find such a photograph, the experimenter said, "No problem, but if it's okay with you, we'd like to take your picture at the end of today's session because we like to get snapshots of our recommenders for the journal in case we decide to publish what you write." All students agreed to this request. (In the two cases in which the student had brought a photograph, the experimenter said, "Good. We'll attach that to your letter at the end of today's session because we like to get snapshots of our recommenders for the journal in case we decide to publish what you write.") This use of the photographs would later serve to alert students that their racial identity would be known to their evaluator.

Letter-writing task. Printed across the top of the letterhead that students were told to use for their task was the heading "Letter of Recommendation for————for Recognition in Teaching Excellence." Students were instructed to write the name of their teacher on the blank line of this header, to begin writing their letter on the same page, and to use additional blank sheets as necessary. They also were told that they could write a rough draft or outline first if they liked. After 40 minutes, the experimenter checked on the student's progress. Students were given as much time as they needed to finish their letters, and most finished within 45 minutes (with a range from 20 to 75 minutes).

Session 1 (pre-manipulation) measures. After completing the letter-writing task, all students were given an initial questionnaire that included three critical items designed to assess motivation regarding the letterwriting task. These items asked, "How much do you think you could improve your letter given the opportunity to revise it?" "How much interest do you have in revising your letter before submitting it to the journal for the final time?" and "How important is it to you to do a good job on your letter of recommendation?"[3] Three other items measured identification with the more global skills underlying both the specific letter-writing task and written communication more generally. These items asked, "How important is being a good writer to your view of yourself?" "How open are you to career options that would require writing skills?" and "How would you rate your overall competence as a writer?" Students responded using appropriately labeled 7-point scales.[4]

After completing the questionnaire, students were photographed using a Polaroid Instant Camera. The experimenter explained again that a copy of the photo would be used in the journal should their entry be accepted for publication. Participants were then asked to staple their photograph to their letter, thereby ensuring that they were aware that their race would be known by the reviewer who would read and evaluate their letter. They also were asked to put their entry in a large mailing envelope to be deposited in a box in the hallway upon their departure. Before leaving, students were scheduled for the next session, given a reminder slip listing its date and time, and either paid $5 or assured that they would receive the relevant course credit.

Session 2. Approximately 1 week later, students returned for the second session, whereupon the experimenter greeted them and handed students a sealed envelope containing both their letter and a handwritten review by an alleged reviewer. Students were told that they would be allowed to revise their letter and resubmit it to the journal. The experimenter told each student to take his or her time reading their letter and the review, then left the room. The first page of this review was a summary sheet that indicated the student's name and entry number, their teacher's name, and the name of the purported reviewer who had evaluated their letter (i.e., "Dr. Gardiner Lindsay," which is a name that pilot testing had established as recognizably Caucasian).

Critical feedback. Each letter was marked with handwritten corrections of errors in spelling and grammar; in addition, there were comments (approximately eight in number) regarding particular shortcomings in style, structure, and wording (i.e., "awkward," "confusing," or "unclear") as well as specific suggestions for improvement. Each letter also received two check marks, placed in the margins, acknowledging good points. This feedback had been provided by assistants trained in providing useful critical reactions but blind to the letter writer's race and experimental condition.

At the end of each letter, there was a general critique of the student's performance, which was again handwritten and signed by Gardiner Lindsay; the critique, which follows, appeared to be individualized but was actually identical (except in the use of appropriate masculine versus feminine pronouns) for all students receiving critical feedback (and that addressed limitations that were, in fact, characteristic of virtually all the students' letters):

Student's name:

Your letter needs work in several areas before it can be considered for publication. In addition to some routine editorial suggestions that I've offered, most of my comments center on how you could breathe more life into your letter and make the description of your favorite teacher and her [his] merits more vivid, personal, and persuasive. As it stands, your letter is vague and rambling—long on adjectives and short on specific illustrations. You describe your teacher's dedication and commitment, but you haven't explained why your teacher is more exemplary in her [his] contribution, more deserving of recognition, than most of the other nominees cited by other writers. In particular, it would be helpful to be more specific when you describe your teacher, to pay closer attention to the details that inspired your high opinion of her [him]. What were some of the specific things your teacher did that set her [him] apart from all other teachers you've encountered in your life? You cover this at certain points in your letter, and it is there that your letter begins to come to life—you need to sustain this.

One last comment: If you choose to revise your letter, you should spend significantly more time explaining your teacher's impact on your own personal growth. What made her [his] influence so much more important than other teachers in your life? Perhaps hadn't seen before, perhaps she [he] helped you to see your potential. Sometimes you touch on this but you fail to build on it. You need to discuss the long-term imprint [teacher's name] has left on you in greater detail—this enduring impact is perhaps the strongest testimony of a teacher's success.

Experimental conditions. Students returning for the second session were randomly assigned to one of three criticism conditions. Students in the unbuffered criticism condition received the criticism described above without further comment. Students in the wise criticism condition received that criticism prefaced with the following comments designed to ward off potentially destructive attributions by explicitly invoking high standards while assuring the particular student that he or she could meet such standards:

It's obvious to me that you've taken your task seriously and I'm going to do likewise by giving you some straightforward, honest feedback. The letter itself is okay as far as it goes—you've followed the instructions, listed your teacher's merits, given evidence in support of them, and importantly, produced an articulate letter. On the other hand, judged by a higher standard, the one that really counts, that is, whether your letter will be publishable in our journal, I have serious reservations. The comments I provide in the following pages are quite critical but I hope helpful. Remember, I wouldn't go to the trouble of giving you this feedback if I didn't think, based on what I've read in your letter, that you are capable of meeting the higher standard I mentioned.

By contrast, students in the positive buffer condition received the same general criticism described above but prefaced with the following comments:

Overall, nice job. Your enthusiasm for your teacher really shows through, and it's clear that you must have valued her [him] a great deal. You have some interesting ideas in your letter and make some good points. In the pages that follow, I've provided some more specific feedback and suggested several areas that could be improved.

Session 2 (post-manipulation) measures. After reading their letter and review, students filled out a questionnaire containing the same task motivation and identification items that had been included in the Session 1 questionnaire. An additional item, embedded among three other incidental items on a page titled "Impressions of the Reviewer," asked students to rate the reviewer's bias on a scale from 1 *(not at all biased)* to 7 *(extremely biased).*

Debriefing. At the conclusion of the second session, in a postexperimental interview, students were first probed for possible suspicion and then informed about the general purpose of the study. The experimenter not only revealed the deceptive elements in the feedback and purported rationale for the study but also offered an account of the study's real concerns and the psychological processes under investigation (using a "process debriefing" procedure espoused by Ross, Lepper, & Hubbard, 1975). Students were informed of the study's focus on strategies for attenuating adverse responses to criticism, but most were not informed of our interest in race because such a disclosure would rule them out as prospective participants for future research on stereotype threat at Stanford and was unnecessary in making their participation in the study an interesting and satisfying experience. Finally, students were thanked for their participation and either paid $5 or again assured that they would receive the relevant course credit.

Results

Analyses revealed no main effects or interactions involving gender of participant or experimenter; these variables, accordingly, receive no further consideration in our report.

Creation of "Task Motivation" and "Identification With Writing Skills" Composites

To lend empirical support to the validity of the motivation and identification constructs, a principal component analysis using varimax rotation was performed on the six premanipulation measures of task motivation and identification. As expected, the component analysis produced two discrete components, accounting for 64.7% of the variance in the response measures. The first component, accounting for 38.5% of the variance, encompassed the three items pertaining to identification with writing skills (eigenvalue = 2.31). The second component, accounting for 26.5% of the variance, encompassed the three items pertaining to task motivation (eigenvalue = 1.56). All items loaded highly on their respective components (loadings ranged from .68 to .84) and none had a substantial loading (i.e., greater than .25) on a component other than its own. Premanipulation and postmanipulation composites were created for both components. That is, the three premanipulation items for each component and the three postmanipulation items for each component (standardized to equate their variance) were averaged to provide premanipulation and postmanipulation scores of task motivation and identification.

Ratings of Bias

Preliminary overall analysis. A 2 x 3 (i.e., Race x Criticism Condition) ANOVA was performed for ratings of bias. The omnibus ANOVA tests revealed a marginal main effect of race, with Black

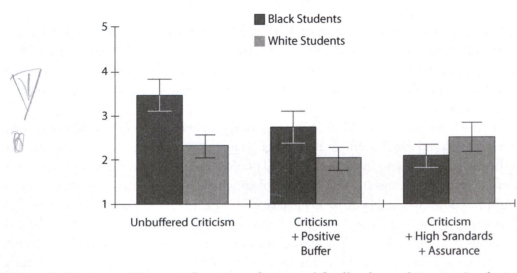

Figure 1. Ratings of bias as a function of race and feedback condition in Study 1.

students rating the reviewer as somewhat more biased (M= 2.75) than White students (M= 2.26), $F_{(1,85)}$ = 3.29, p= .07, and a borderline Race x Condition interaction, F(2,85) = 3.08,p= .05, indicating that this race effect varied as a function of criticism condition. Figure 1 displays the six relevant cell means.

Unbuffered criticism versus wise criticism. More important than these overall analyses are the specific comparisons involving Black and White students in the two conditions most relevant to our hypotheses. Our first concern was whether, as predicted, Black students receiving unbuffered criticism would rate the reviewer as more biased than would White students. Our second and more critical question was the extent to which our wise intervention, that is, the invocation of high standards accompanied by the assurance that the particular student could meet those standards, would attenuate the adverse effects of such criticism and reduce the relevant race difference.

As Figure 1 attests, Black students receiving unbuffered criticism rated the reviewer as more biased *(M* = 3.47) than did White students receiving the same criticism (M= 2.31), <85) = 2.53, *p* < .02. However, as predicted, this between-race difference was eliminated when the criticism was accompanied by the combination of high standards and assurance. Indeed, in the face of such wise feedback, Black students rated the reviewer somewhat lower in bias (M= 2.04) than did White students (M= 2.47). Evidence for the relevant interaction effect is provided by a weighted contrast comparing the size of the race effect in the unbuffered criticism condition with that in the wise criticism condition (with weights of 0 assigned both to White and Black participants in the criticism plus positive buffer condition). This analysis yielded a significant contrast, t(85) = 2.41, p< .02. (In the case of ratings of bias, however, between-race comparisons may be inappropriate because White students may have interpreted the term *bias* to mean hostility toward them personally rather than animus toward members of their race. Thus, it is perhaps more relevant simply to note that, as predicted, Black students in the unbuffered criticism condition rated the reviewer as significantly more biased than did Black students in the wise criticism condition, t[85] = 3.02, p< .005.)

Criticism plus positive buffer condition. In the criticism plus positive buffer condition, the relevant race difference was smaller but still apparent, t(85) = 1.60, *p* < .12, with the mean bias rating provided by Black students (M= 2.73) falling squarely between those provided by Black students in the other two criticism conditions (see Figure 1). (A simple within-race contrast, in which Black students in the positive buffer condition are compared with Black students in the wise criticism condition, yields a similar *t* value, t[85] = 1.47, *p* < .15.) A reasonable description of the data—and one that is consistent with our predictions and conceptual analyses—is that the Black-White difference is greatest in face of unbuffered criticism, smaller when the same criticism is buffered by positive feedback, and nonexistent (indeed, slightly reversed) when this criticism is buffered by high standards and a personal assurance. A contrast testing the relevant linear decrease in this racial difference (i.e., assigning weights of +1 to White students in each of the three conditions and weights of -3, -1, and +1 to Black students in the unbuffered criticism, criticism plus positive buffer, and wise criticism conditions, respectively) yields a highly significant tvalue, t(85) = -3.551, p< .001, and most important, such a contrast accounts for the vast majority (90%) of between-cell variance. Simply comparing the size of the race effect in the wise criticism condition with that in the other two criticism conditions similarly yielded a significant result, /(85) = 2.40, *p* < .02, as did simply comparing the bias rating of Black students in the unbuffered criticism condition with that of Black students in the two other criticism conditions, t(85) = 2.67, p< .01.

Task Motivation

Preliminary overall analyses. A 2 x 3 ANCOVA was performed on self-reported, postmanipulation task motivation using premanipulation task motivation as a covariate. This analysis revealed a marginal main effect of condition, such that motivation was lower in the unbuffered criticism condition (M= -0.20) than either in the criticism plus positive buffer condition (M= 0.07) or in the wise criticism condition (M= 0.12), F(2,84) = 2.74, *p* = .07. This overall analysis also revealed a Race x Condition interaction, F(2,84) = 3.11,p< .05. Once again, however, it is more specific comparisons that are of greatest interest (see Figure 2 for the adjusted cell means).

Unbuffered criticism versus wise criticism. As in the case of our bias measure, we expected to find a race difference in motivation in the unbuffered criticism condition but to find such a difference attenuated or eliminated in the two-faceted wise criticism condition. This expectation, bolstered by the finding of a significant association between perceived bias and lack of motivation (r= -.27, *p* < .01), proved accurate. In the face of unbuffered criticism, Black students reported lower motivation (M= -.48) than did White students (M= .09), t(84) = -2.75, *p* < .01. By contrast, when the same criticism was accompanied by the invocation of high standards and appropriate assurance, the task motivation of Black students was notably increased. Indeed, they reported slightly higher motivation (M= .20) than did White students in the same condition (M= .05). A weighted contrast comparing the size of the race effect in the unbuffered criticism condition with that in the wise criticism condition (with weights of 0 assigned both to White and Black students in the criticism plus positive-buffer condition) again yielded a significant contrast, /(84) = 2.43, *p* < .02.

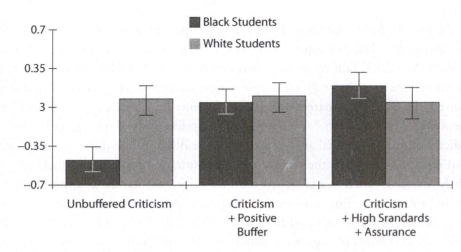

Figure 2. Task motivation as a function of race and feedback condition in Study 1.

Criticism plus positive buffer condition. Once more, the mean for Black students in the criticism plus positive buffer condition (M= .05) fell between those for Black students in the other two criticism conditions, although closer to that in the wise criticism condition than the unbuffered criticism condition. Also, as with ratings of bias, the race difference in responses on the task motivation measure was greatest in the unbuffered criticism condition, smaller in the positive buffer condition, and nonexistent (indeed, slightly reversed) in the wise criticism condition. Again, as with the bias measure, a contrast testing the relevant linear decrease in the racial difference proved highly significant, t(84) = 3.31, *p* < .002, and accounted for 84% of the between-cell variance. Simply comparing the size of the race effect in the wise criticism condition with that in the other two conditions yields a marginally significant result, t(84) = 1.80, p < .08.

Identification With Writing Skills

Preliminary overall analysis. A 2 x 3 ANCOVA was performed for postmanipulation identification, with premanipulation identification as a covariate. The omnibus tests revealed only a marginal main effect of condition, reflecting the fact that among Black and White students alike, identification with writing skills was lower in the face of unbuffered criticism (M= -.10), and also in the face of the same criticism buffered by positive feedback (M= -.06), than in the wise criticism condition offering both the high standards invocation and the appropriate assurance (M= .16), F(2, 84) = 2.63,p< .08. Figure 3 displays the relevant adjusted means.

Unbuffered criticism versus wise criticism. In contrast to the case for the perceived bias and task motivation measures, Black and White students in the unbuffered criticism condition differed little on this measure, *t* < 1, and the weighted contrast involving race and criticism condition failed to show any interaction effect, *t* < 1. This absence of an interaction effect, however, should not obscure the fact that the wise criticism condition accomplished its pedagogical goal. That is, Black students who received wise criticism showed greater identification with writing skills (M= .18) than those who received the

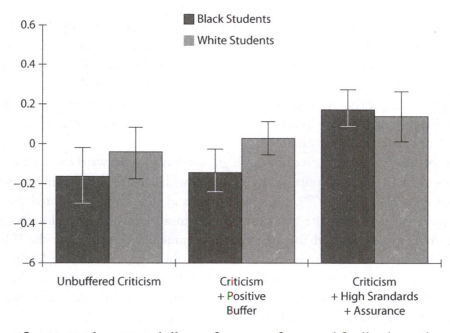

Figure 3. Identification with writing skills as a function of race and feedback condition in Study 1.

unbuffered criticism (M=-.16), t(84) = 1.96, p= .05. The failure to obtain a significant interaction effect simply reflects the fact that White students showed a similar, albeit smaller (statistically insignificant), difference in responding to the two relevant criticism conditions.

Criticism plus positive buffer condition. The mean identification score among Black students in the criticism plus positive buffer condition was as low (M= -.15) as that of students receiving unbuffered criticism (M= -.16). Simply contrasting these two conditions with the wise criticism condition yielded a statistically significant result, t(84) = 2.20, p< .05.

Discussion

As predicted, Black students generally responded less favorably to unbuffered criticism than did White students, both in ratings of bias and in measures of task motivation. The relevant race difference in response was somewhat reduced when the criticism was buffered with praise of the student's work, but it was totally eliminated (indeed, even slightly reversed) only when the criticism was buffered with the wise combination of an explicit invocation of high standards and an appropriate assurance that the student in question could meet such standards. Our wise criticism condition also best served to bolster the willingness of students, Black and White alike, to identify themselves with the more global academic skills involved in their letter-writing task.

An obvious question arising from this study is whether the effects obtained in the wise criticism condition were due solely to the attributional benefit of evoking high standards or whether the additional assurance regarding the student's capacity to reach those standards was necessary. Study 2

Study 2

began the effort to disentangle these two elements of the wise criticism manipulation by introducing a condition that invoked high standards but that made no assurance regarding the student's capacity to reach those standards. We predicted that this condition would be less effective than the two-faceted wise criticism condition offering the extra assurance of the student's ability to reach the standard. Specifically, our working hypothesis was that invoking high standards alone might suffice to deflect attributions of bias but would leave intact the stereotype threat created by the delivery of criticism and hence would not enhance task motivation.

The prediction that the simple evocation of high standards would ward off attributions of bias is consistent not only with our conceptual analysis but also with prior findings from the previously cited study by Banks and colleagues (1977). Black participants in that study discounted the objectivity of performance feedback from a White evaluator, relative to a Black one, and also chose to persever-ate on their own strategies rather than adopt those recommendations made by the White evaluator. Interestingly, this reluctance to trust and to comply with the suggestions of the White evaluator was eliminated when, prior to the exercise, students were told that the evaluator would win money if participants excelled at the task. Simply making explicit the evaluator's goals, it seems, clarified the motives behind the feedback and forestalled attributions of prejudice.

We expected the simpler tactic of making explicit high standards to similarly forestall perceptions of prejudice and racial bias by providing a compelling external attribution for the feedback. That is, in the face of an invocation of high standards alone, Black students would see the criticism as motivated by the reviewer's demands for excellence rather than by any personal or group animus (an attribution perhaps made implicitly by White students in the absence of the explicit invocation of standards). At the same time, we expected this "high standards only" condition to leave unaddressed the stereotype threat to Black students introduced by the negative feedback. To prevent depressed task motivation, according to our working hypothesis, it would be necessary to attenuate stereotype threat through the additional assurance that the student was personally capable of meeting the higher standard—that is, by providing the same wise two-faceted intervention featured in Study 1.

Study 2

The explicit invocation of high standards, accompanied by the assurance of the student's personal capacity to reach those standards, we have argued, is analogous to the strategy used by mentors, teach-ers, and academic intervention programs that provide critical feedback while successfully addressing the concerns of minority students. The results of Study 1 attested to the efficacy of such feedback. Study 2 attempts to demonstrate that personal assurance is a necessary component of wise critical feedback—that, although the invocation of high standards alone may forestall attributions of racial bias, it does not sufficiently address the negative motivational consequences of the stereotype threat evoked by pointed criticism. (The issue of whether such assurance is not only necessary but sufficient is not addressed by our research design but will be discussed later in this article.) Accordingly, Black and White students in two conditions of our second study again received either critical feedback alone or such feedback accompanied by an invocation of high standards and a personal assurance of their capacity to reach those standards. In an additional condition, however, students received criticism accompanied by an invocation of high standards without such assurance.

Design and Participants

The design of the experiment featured a 2 x 3 (i.e., Race x Criticism Condition) factorial design in which 80 Black and 73 White participants (all recruited from a registrar's list) were randomly assigned to condition and received either unbuffered criticism, criticism buffered by an invocation of high standards alone, or criticism buffered both by that invocation and by an assurance of the student's capacity to reach the relevant standards. As in Study 1, ratings of the reviewer's bias, task motivation, and identification with writing skills were used as the dependent measures. The data of 5 participants who either failed to return to their scheduled second session or expressed suspicion about the purpose of the study or the authenticity of the feedback were discarded prior to analysis.

Procedure

Two minor changes were made in the procedure of Study 2. First, students were paid $12 (rather than $10) for their participation. Second, the experimenter (again, either a White male or a White female) waited 45 minutes (instead of 40) before checking on the student's progress during Session 1 (to give students more time to produce a satisfactory letter of commendation). The dependent variable questionnaire also was altered slightly. The task motivation composite now included only two items, one asking the extent to which students felt they could improve their performance with further effort and the other assessing students' interest in revising the letter. The writing-skills identification composite now also included two sets of items, one asking the general importance of writing skills to students' view of themselves and a second set of items assessing students' openness to various career possibilities (such as author, journalist, and editor) that demand writing skills (Stoutemeyer & Steele, 1997).

The major change in procedure, however, was the addition of the new high standards only condition and the elimination of the positive buffer (and bland praise) conditions. The unbuffered criticism and wise criticism conditions were identical to those in Study 1. In the new high standards only condition, the criticism delivered to students was prefaced by comments that invoked the relevant standards but then proceeded to justify those standards not with an assurance regarding the student's capacity but with an emphasis on the reviewer's commitment to the journal considering the student's efforts. The comments for the high standards only condition were as follows:

It's obvious to me that you've taken your task seriously and I'm going to do likewise by giving you some straightforward, honest feedback. The letter itself is okay as far as it goes—you've followed the instructions, listed your teacher's merits, given evidence in support of them, and importantly, produced an articulate letter. On the other hand, judged by a higher standard, the one that really counts, that is, whether your letter will be publishable in our journal, I have serious reservations. The comments I provide in the following pages are quite critical but I hope helpful. Remember, I wouldn't go to the trouble of giving you this feedback if I weren't committed to the quality of this journal—I want to uphold the highest standards for what I consider a suitable entry, for you or any student whose work is under consideration.

As noted, all participants again received critical comments and suggestions appropriate to their particular letters along with two critical paragraphs, at the end of the letters, identical for participants in all conditions. After reading the feedback, students completed the dependent measures. Then, as in Study 1, they were thoroughly debriefed using a process debriefing procedure (Ross et al., 1975), thanked for their participation, and paid.

Results

For all but one measure, there were neither main effects nor interactions involving gender of participant (nor were there effects involving gender of experimenter). Accordingly, with the exception to be noted, this factor will receive no further attention in our report of the results of Study 2. Also, some students omitted answers to one or more questions, resulting in variable degrees of freedom for different measures.[5]

Creation of Task Motivation and Identification With Writing Skills Composites

Principal component analysis, using varimax rotation, again produced two discrete components that accounted for 71 % of the variance in the Session 1 premanipulation response measures. The first component, encompassing the two items pertaining to task motivation, accounted for 41.1 % of the variance (eigenvalue = 1.65). The second component, encompassing the two items pertaining to identification with writing skills, accounted for 29.4% of the variance (eigenvalue = 1.18). Once again, all items loaded highly on their respective components (loadings ranged from .82 to .85) and none had a substantial loading (i.e., greater than .11) on a component other than its own. As in Study 1, "premanipulation" and "postmanipulation" composites were created both for task motivation and identification, with responses on the two relevant items in each composite standardized to equate their variance and then averaged to provide single premanipulation and postmanipulation scores.

Ratings of Bias

Our basic prediction was that Black students would perceive the reviewer as more biased than would White students in the unbuffered criticism condition but that this difference would be attenuated or even disappear in the two conditions where the criticism was accompanied by an invocation of high standards. A 2 x 3 ANOVA (i.e., Race x Criticism Condition) performed on students' ratings of bias (see Figure 4) yielded the predicted Race x Condition interaction, $F(2, 140) = 3.39$, $p < .05$.

As in Study 1, Black students in the unbuffered criticism condition rated the reviewer as more biased (M = 3.04) than did White students (M= 2.00), $t(140) = 2.44$, $p < .02$. By contrast, Black students in the two high standards conditions rated the reviewer as no higher in bias (M= 2.30) than

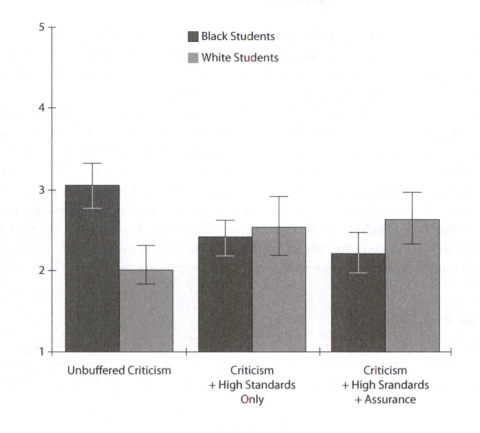

Figure 4. Ratings of bias as a function of race and feedback condition in Study 2.

did their White peers (M= 2.59). The relevant test of our hypothesis—a weighted contrast comparing the size of the race effect in the unbuffered criticism condition with that in the two conditions where the criticism was accompanied by an invocation of high standards—also proved significant, $t(140) = 2.56$, $p < .02$. (As we noted in reporting the results of Study 1, comparisons of bias ratings by Black and White students may be misleading. However, orthogonal within-race comparisons reveal, as predicted, that Black students rated the reviewer as more biased in the unbuffered criticism condition than in the two high standards conditions, $/[140] = 2.09$, $p < .05$, whereas there was no reliable difference between their bias ratings in the two high standards conditions, $t < 1$.)

Task Motivation

A simple between-participants analysis of variance was performed on postmanipulation task motivation due to a violation of the homogeneity of regression slopes assumption of covariance analysis. The invocation of high standards alone sufficed to deflect attributions of bias, but it did not prove sufficient to raise Black students' motivation to the level observed in the wise criticism condition featuring both high standards and the added assurance. The relevant analysis yielded a significant Race x Condition interaction, $F(2, 140) = 3.12$, $p < .05$. Black students reported significantly greater motivation in the wise criticism condition than they did in either the unbuffered criticism condition, t(140) = 2.01, *p* < .05, or the criticism plus high standards only condition, t(140) = 2.16, p < .05. By contrast, the motivation of White students showed no significant differences across conditions (all relevant contrasts yielded *p* values > .19). Figure 5 displays the six relevant cell means.

Black students in the unbuffered criticism and the criticism plus high standards only conditions also showed marginally lower task motivation (M= -.19) than did White students in the same conditions (M = .09), t(140) = -1.83, *p* < .07. (Introducing quality of students' letters [assessed by a coder unaware of students' condition or race] as a covariate raised the relevant *t* value to -2.35, *p* < .02.) By contrast, Black students in the wise criticism condition were somewhat more motivated at their task (M = .27) than were their White peers (M = -.06), t(140) = 1.54. (Introducing quality of students' letters as a covariate lowered the relevant *t* value, t< 1.) Evidence for the hypothesized Race x Condition interaction effect is provided by a weighted contrast that compared the race difference in the unbuffered criticism condition and criticism plus high standards only condition with that in the wise criticism condition, t(140) = 2.30, p< .05.

Identification With Writing Skills

An ANCOVA was performed on our measure of general identification with writing skills (using premanipulation identification as the covariate). On this measure, gender interacted significantly with race, such that Black males showed lower identification with writing skills than did Black females,

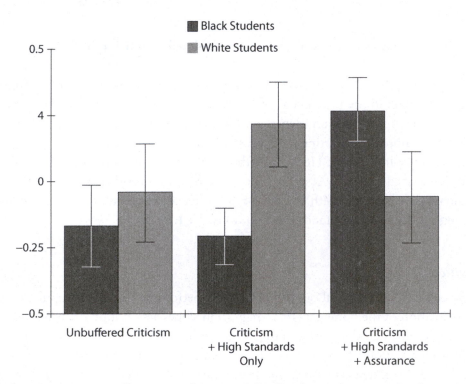

Figure 5. Task motivation as a function of race and feedback condition in Study 2.

whereas the reverse was true for White students, F(1, 128) = 11.42, $p < .001$. Otherwise, there were no significant main or interaction effects involving race or criticism condition (all ps > .20). In particular, Black and White students showed similar levels of identification with writing skills both in the wise criticism condition and in the criticism plus high standards only condition. However, a planned contrast comparing Black students' identification with writing skills in the unbuffered criticism condition (M = -0.20) with their identification in the wise criticism condition (M= 0.01) yielded a marginally significant tvalue, t(128) = -1.77, p< .08. (One could argue for a one-tailed test, which would yield a p value of .04, because we are replicating an effect obtained in Study 1.) In addition, the level of general identification with writing skills by Black students in the unbuffered criticism condition proved to be marginally lower than that of White students in the same condition (M= 0), t(128) = -1.67, p < .10.

Racial Differences in Performance: A Potential Mediator?

On average, the letters of Black students were rated less positively than those produced by White students (again, as assessed by a coder unaware of students' race or condition). Accordingly, we conducted further analyses to determine whether this difference in performance (and perhaps even a resulting difference in harshness of feedback or in anticipated difficulty of achieving a satisfactory revision) could have played a role in our main findings. When we simply control for differences in rated letter quality in an ANCOVA, the Race x Feedback interactions most relevant to our predictions remain statistically significant, both for task motivation and ratings of bias. Indeed, when the analysis controls for performance, the relevant contrast involving the identification measure for Black students in the unbuffered criticism condition versus Black students in the wise criticism condition becomes stronger. Furthermore, when we perform a regression analysis including letter quality as a continuous variable, we find no trace of a three-way interaction among race, feedback, and performance. Thus, the simple Race x Condition interactions we report remain constant across levels of letter-writing performance.

Moreover, the racial difference in performance logically could work against our hypothesis rather than for it. That is, the receipt of harsher criticism, or other evidence of weaker performance, could enhance rather than attenuate students' motivation to revise—especially insofar as students who performed less well might feel that they could more easily improve their performance. Indeed, among both Black and White students across all conditions, lower performance did in fact prove to be significantly associated with greater postmanipulation task motivation, r(145) = .21, p = .01. Black students' lower performance, therefore, should have led them to increase their motivation more than White students, not less. In sum, students' level of performance does not qualify our main findings—that is, whereas the invocation of high standards, and accompanying assurance, exerted little if any influence on White students, this intervention significantly raised motivation and reduced perceptions of bias among Black students.

Discussion

The results of Study 2 confirmed and extended those of Study 1. When negative feedback was presented without additional information, Black students again responded less favorably than did White students. When the same feedback was accompanied by an explicit invocation of high standards and an assurance that the student was capable of meeting those standards, Black students again responded as favorably, if not more favorably, than did White students. This effect was seen on ratings of bias and task motivation, and to a lesser extent, in measures assessing identification with writing skills more generally. Furthermore, whereas an invocation of high standards alone reduced attributions of bias among Black students, it was insufficient to raise their task motivation.

General Discussion

Minority students may wonder whether they are being viewed through the lens of a stereotype rather than judged on their own merits and recognized for their full potential. The challenge facing the mentor is to provide critical feedback in a manner that discourages attributions of bias and that refutes the threatening limitation alleged by the stereotype. Although our studies focus on minority students, this challenge arises in any context where students face group-based doubts about their abilities or "belonging" within a given domain of achievement. Thus, as Spencer et al. (1999) and Steele (1997) argue, stereotype threat also affects women working in math and the physical sciences.

The present studies offer two findings that speak to this challenge. First, we showed that whereas unbuffered criticism neither prompted attributions of bias nor undermined motivation on the part of White students, such criticism had precisely those effects on Black students. Second, we demonstrated that a wise, theory informed intervention—that is, one that both invoked high standards and assured students of their capacity to reach those standards—eliminated this race difference in response to criticism. In fact, the motivation of Black students provided with criticism in this wise manner improved so dramatically that it slightly surpassed that of their White peers. Study 1 further showed this wise feedback to be more effective than the common tactic of buffering criticism with nonspecific praise; Study 2 demonstrated that although the invocation of high standards in the absence of the assurance could deflect attributions of racial bias, it could not fully raise Black students' motivation.

Before discussing these results further, one specific finding from Study 2 merits further comment. Whereas the invocation of high standards alone did not sustain Black students' task-specific motivation, it did suffice to maintain their identification with the general domain of writing skills. It is possible that our highly selected students may have been more secure about their general academic abilities than about their capacity to excel at the specific novel task that our studies introduced. It also is possible that the invocation of high standards, even in the absence of personal assurance, created a context in which the negative feedback had fewer esteem-threatening consequences (see Bruner, 1996; Lepper, 1988; Lepper et al., 1990, 1993; Steele, 1992, 1997). The explicit reference to high standards allowed students to treat the criticism not as diagnostic of an underlying lack of ability on their part, or even of a failure in their particular performance, but rather as a reflection of the exacting standards of their reviewer.

Although such an external attribution would protect students' self-esteem, and thereby forestall any need for defensive disidentification from the achievement domain, we believe it left intact their apprehension concerning future performance. That is, Black students in the high standards only condition still had reason to worry about their prospects for future success at the task and, more specifically, their capacity to meet the reviewer's standards. They still faced the discouraging possibility that further effort might meet not with success but with failure and that they might thereby confirm a negative stereotype—a possibility that might even have become more salient to them when they received criticism regarding their essay. In short, Black students in the high standards only condition may have been free to maintain their identification with the general domain of achievement but discouraged from risking further investment in the specific task at hand.

Consideration of Underlying Processes

Our wise intervention was designed to assure Black students that they would not be judged stereotypically. Black students, we contend, felt that they could trust their critic's motives and that they could safely invest their effort, and even their identity, in the task before them. The invocation of high standards ruled out racial bias as a potential motivation behind the feedback, and the assurance reduced the threat of confirming a group-based limitation in ability. Support for this conceptual analysis was provided primarily by the specific Race x Treatment interactions we obtained. Our statistical analyses allowed us to test predictions about the conditions under which Black students would report greater bias than would White students and the conditions under which they would feel less motivation. Our analyses also largely confirmed our predictions about the specific measures and specific conditions that would reveal differences in the response between Black students and White students. In short, we believe that the interaction effects reported in Studies 1 and 2 present persuasive, if not compelling, evidence that wise feedback produced benefits for Black students by attenuating the threat of stigmatization.

Beyond our present conceptual and statistical analyses, there are also two social-psychological theories that can be called on to support the wisdom of assuring students of their capacity to reach a higher performance standard. Bandura's (1977, 1986) self-efficacy theory would point to the obvious benefits of enhancing students' confidence in their capacities. Similar advice would be offered by theorists who have examined the motivational consequences of learned helplessness and of other counterproductive attribution strategies (e.g., Diener & Dweck, 1978; Dweck, 1986; Dweck & Leggett, 1988; Weiner, 1972, 1974). That is, students manifesting learned helplessness could be expected to attribute critical feedback to uncontrollable external factors such as task difficulty or bias on the part of the evaluator, or even worse, to uncontrollable internal factors including their own lack of ability. Affirming students' ability to meet a higher standard, through further effort and incorporation of the changes suggested for improvement, would help to counteract such helplessness.

Although these theories support the wisdom of our wise intervention, they also raise the possibility that a condition that provided students with a boost in task-related efficacy but that made no mention of an elevation in standards might be sufficient to produce the benefits that we have demonstrated and discussed in the present research. At first consideration, an "assurance only" condition (i.e., where the evaluator assures students of their capacity without invoking high standards) might seem timely. On further consideration, however, it becomes clear that although such a condition would bear on theoretical and practical concerns, it would do little to clarify the mediating role of self-efficacy. Assuring Black students that they can do better without explicitly or implicitly conveying the message that doing better means meeting a higher standard would be rather empty and, hence, would constitute a weaker efficacy induction. Indeed, if the student interpreted the assurance as a message that hard work could raise the level of their performance from utter deficiency to mere adequacy, it might even be threatening and counterproductive. Researchers who want to focus on the role of self-efficacy, we believe, would be better served by testing the effects of a condition in which, prior to the presentation of any criticism, students simply receive positive feedback on their writing skills—or perhaps fortuitously overhear their evaluator praise their abilities. Although such an efficacy boost might help to relieve stereotype threat, we suspect that it would still leave Black students wondering about the critic's motives. Indeed, the additional boost in self-confidence might lead them to find racial bias a more plausible attribution for the feedback—especially if their high confidence is accompanied by the belief that their performance "in absolute terms" has been quite satisfactory.

Again, self-efficacy and learned helplessness are clearly relevant to our general concerns, but these theories cannot, in their simplest form, explain our overall pattern of findings. An adequate theoretical treatment must explain why our wise feedback condition offered benefits unique to Black students. In particular, a satisfactory self-efficacy account of our findings must explain why the motivation of Black students suffered a unique drop in the unbuffered criticism condition and why it was uniquely enhanced in the wise criticism condition. Only by recognizing the significance of race, and the threat of stigmatization, can any theory reasonably address our findings.

Clearly, a self-efficacy account would be reasonable if Black students began the experimental task with lower self-efficacy than White students and thus were in greater need of a boost in efficacy. Our data, however, suggest that this was not the case. Prior to the presentation of the critical feedback, Black students and White students did not differ on any motivational premeasure, including an item that specifically asked students whether they thought they could improve the letter they wrote if given the opportunity to revise it. Moreover, recent investigations (including one national, longitudinal study, and one comprehensive review of the relevant research) find no evidence of preexisting racial differences in academic-related self-efficacy, expectancies for success, or negative attributional styles (see Graham, 1994; Tashakkori, 1993; Tashakkori & Thompson, 1991). Black students, accordingly, should not have benefited uniquely from any manipulation that merely offered a general boost in self-efficacy.

In one important respect, however, conceptual analyses involving stereotype threat, attributional style, and self-efficacy converge. Each suggests that although minority students may not generally be prone to undue doubts about their academic efficacy, or to harmful attributions concerning the causes of academic failure, they may find such doubts more readily triggered when they are confronted with criticism or when they experience performance frustration. In a sense, Black students' self-efficacy may be reasonably high but nevertheless fragile—at least in domains in which the stereotype poses a relevant explanation for negative feedback or frustration (see, in particular, Study 3 of Steele & Aronson, 1995). We hope that our present analysis invites theorists to consider factors such as stereotype threat and their role in mediating the maintenance of efficacy beliefs over time and across situations. An examination of such factors is crucial to a complete account of individual and group differences in motivation and performance.

In considering other theoretical perspectives, we also believe that part of the effectiveness of wise feedback may indeed lie in the message it conveys about the malleable nature of ability—the message that greater effort will yield performance that surpasses the capacities demonstrated to date (Dweck et al., 1995; Dweck & Leggett, 1988; see also Butler, 1987; Earley, 1986; Koestner, Zuckerman, & Koestner, 1987, 1989; Sansone et al., 1989). Again, however, the fact that we obtained Race x Treatment interactions rather than main effects of treatments must be addressed. The malleability message, we argue, should be particularly important for students who are targets of ability-stigmatizing stereotypes, because these stereotypes imply that ability (or lack of ability) is a fixed group attribute rather than a malleable aspect of the self. Indeed, as we noted in introducing our studies, the guiding philosophy of many of the most successful programs aimed at minority youth is an emphasis on the malleable nature of academic ability—the message that "intelligence can be taught" (Whimbey, 1975).

Theoretical and Practical Implications

The findings documented here point out the obstacles in the classroom posed by race. The mentor trying to convey feedback to the Black student may face a situation in which there is a possibility of mistrust—a mistrust that arises not from the disposition of mentor or student but from race and the meaning imputed to it in our society. To use the terminology of J. J. Gibson's (1979) ecological approach to perception, race constitutes an "affordance" of mistrust—where an affordance is a situational or contextual factor that invites a particular perception of the object of judgment (see also Baron & Boudreau, 1987). The challenge to the wise mentor, accordingly, is to establish a learning environment that "affords" more constructive perceptions.

The need to combat the effects of racial stigmatization does not oblige the educator to withhold critical feedback, to lavish praise, or to otherwise lower performance standards in the hope of sustaining student motivation. Rather than altering the content of instruction, the educator might instead consider modifying the context in which such instruction occurs. In the case of our highly selected Black students, motivation was sustained not by diluting the one-and-a-half pages of criticism offered or by softening its tone. What proved effective was providing the relevant criticism in a context in which its critical nature could be readily attributed to the existence of high and consistent standards and a belief in the student's capacity to reach them.

We have argued that our wise intervention served to buffer students from the sting of negative feedback. But an alternative possibility exists that we think merits further investigation. We suspect that the effectiveness of the two-faceted wise intervention depends on the provision of rigorous feedback. Had the feedback been cursory rather than critical, students might have doubted the sincerity of the reviewer's self-proclaimed high standards. Indeed, the additional assurance might have seemed condescending if it had accompanied milder feedback (see Lepper et al., 1990, 1993). The critical nature of the feedback used in our studies, we contend, helped both to reinforce the message that high standards were being applied and to justify the provision of the assurance. What is more, it is likely that the rigor of the feedback also communicated the critic's interest in helping the student to reach the higher standard. Many students remarked in the debriefing session that they had been impressed by the rigor of the criticism and that seldom in their undergraduate careers had a teacher or professor taken their efforts so seriously. A valuable question for future research, accordingly, is whether our wise intervention requires the additional evidence of attention and personal concern implicit in such feedback. Effective educators and academic programs convey an unflagging faith in their minority students' potential. But at the same time they do not hesitate to call attention to the gap between students' current performance and the level that they could achieve with unstinting effort (see Vygotsky, 1978).

In sustained relationships with students, the wise mentor, of course, does not simply speak of high expectations and a faith in students' potential. He or she also buttresses this message through expenditures of time and effort, by giving detailed attention to the student's performance, and by providing an empowering pattern of feedback over time (e.g., Dweck et al., 1978; see also Aronson & Linder, 1965; Jones, 1963). Outside such a relationship (or in trying to initiate one), the teacher providing critical feedback must find other means to deflect attributions of racial bias and to sustain motivation and academic identification. It was in the absence of such a relationship that our wise (but relatively minor) intervention shielded Black students from the consequences of negative racial stereotypes.

In a real sense, the challenge for the mentor of minority students, whether in the day-to-day interactions of an enduring relationship, or in single encounters about a specific academic product, is to make explicit the message that is apt to be implicit for at least the more privileged of nonminority students. This message of belonging, and of still untapped intellectual potential, is vital. As *Los Angeles Times* columnist Frank del Olmo (cited in Mathews, 1988) observed, the less effective educators expect little from their Black and Latino students and ultimately see their expectations confirmed in poor grades and high dropout rates. By contrast, the successful teachers of minority students "share one thing in common . . . they truly believe that their students can succeed in school, and they act on that conviction" (p. 289).

Notes

1. An additional "bland praise" condition, in which students returning to the second session received a few phrases of nonspecific praise, was later added to this basic 2 x 3 factorial design. It was included mainly to demonstrate that it was criticism, and not feedback in general, to which Black students would respond differently from White students. Our results confirmed this expectation and also demonstrated that bland praise alone generally proved less effective than wise criticism in motivating students (although the nature of our dependent variables made relevant between-condition comparisons awkward and problematic). No further discussion of this condition will be offered in this necessarily brief report of our research.

2. Pairs comprised either 2 White participants or a White and a Black participant but never 2 Black participants. Because of the relatively small number of Black students on campus, we worried that the presence of 2 Black students might evoke suspicions regarding the study's concern with race. Thorough postexperimental debriefing

revealed no student (with the exception of the 1 Black student, noted earlier, whose data were discarded) who voiced any suspicion regarding the significance of race in our study.

3. With one exception, the individual items constituting the task motivation composite were highly correlated (ranging from r= .40 to r= .65), a result reflected in the principal component analyses reported in our Results sections. The item "How important is it to you to do a good job on your letter?" was only weakly correlated with the item "How much do you think you could improve your letter given an opportunity to revise it?" (r= .16). Accordingly, this item was dropped in Study 2. We should note, however, that excluding this item in Study 1 would not change the statistical significance of any effects involving the relevant composite measure.

4. Several potential covariates also were measured. These included students' self-reported perceptions of the quality of their letter, students' self-esteem (assessed by Rosenberg's, 1965, self-report instrument), and students' self-reported verbal and math Scholastic Aptitude Test (SAT) scores. None of the assessed covariates proved a consistent and significant predictor or possible mediator of the effects to be reported, and accordingly, none receives further consideration in this article.

5. One outlier (a White student in the unbuffered criticism condition) provided a bias rating more than 3 standard deviations away from his group mean. We opted to omit his data for analysis of the bias item. Doing otherwise—for example, "Windsorizing" his response (by reducing it to equal the next most extreme score in his cell) or even including his response without alteration—would have lowered the significance of our omnibus analysis, but left intact the interaction effect most relevant to our hypothesis. Resorting entirely to nonparametric analyses similarly would have lowered significance levels but still confirmed the relevant interaction effect involving race and feedback condition.

References

Aronson, E., & Linder, D. (1965). Gain and loss of esteem as determinants of interpersonal attractiveness. *Journal of Experimental Social Psychology*, 1, 156–171.

Bandura, A. (1977). Self-efficacy: Toward a unifying theory of behavior change. *Psychological Review, 84*, 191–215.

Bandura, A. (1986). *Social foundations of action: A social-cognitive theory.* Englewood Cliffs, NJ: Prentice Hall.

Banks, W. C., Stitt, K. R., Curtis, H. A., & McQuarter, G. (1977). Perceived objectivity and the effects of evaluative reinforcement upon compliance and self-evaluation in Blacks. *Journal of Experimental Social Psychology, 13*, 452–463.

Barker, G. P., & Graham, S. (1987). Developmental study of praise and blame as attributional cues. *Journal of Educational Psychology*, 79, 62–66.

Baron, R. M., & Boudreau, L. A. (1987). An ecological perspective on integrating personality and social psychology. *Journal of Personality and Social Psychology, 53*, 1222–1228.

Bruner, J. S. (1962). *On knowing: Essays for the left hand.* Cambridge, MA: Harvard University Press.

Bruner, J. (1996). *The culture of education.* London: Harvard University Press.

Butler, R. (1987). Task-involving and ego-involving properties of evaluation: Effects of different feedback conditions on motivation perceptions, interest, and performance. *Journal of Educatonal Psychology*, 79, 474–482.

Comer, J. P. (1980). *School power: Implications of an intervention project.* New York: Free Press.

Comer, J. P. (1988). Educating poor minority children. *Scientific America,* 259(5), 42–48.

Cose, E. (1997). *Color-blind: Seeing beyond race in a race-obsessed world.* New York: Harper Collins.

Crocker, J., & Major, B. (1989). Social stigma and self-esteem: The self-protective properties of stigma. *Psychological Review*, 96, 608–630.

Crocker, J., Voelkl, K., Testa, M., & Major, B. (1991). Social stigma: The affective consequences of attributional ambiguity. *Journal of Personality and Social Psychology, 60,* 218–228.

Daloz, L. A. (1986). *Effective teaching and mentoring.* San Francisco: Jossey-Bass.

Dawes, R. M. (1994). *House of cards: Psychology and psychotherapy built on myth.* New York: Free Press.

Diener, C. I., & Dweck, C. S. (1978). An analysis of learned helplessness: Continuous changes in performance, strategy and achievement cognitions following failure. *Journal of Personality and Social Psychology, 36,* 451–462.

Dweck, C. (1986). Motivational processes affecting learning. *American Psychologist,* 41, 1040–1048.

Dweck, C., Chiu, C., & Hong, Y. (1995). Implicit theories and their role in judgments and reactions: A world from two perspectives. *Psychological Inquiry, 6,* 267–85.

Dweck, C., Davidson, W., Nelson, S., & Enna, B. (1978). Sex differences in learned helplessness: II. The contingencies of evaluative feedback in the classroom. *Developmental Psychology, 14,* 268–276.

Dweck, C., & Leggett, E. L. (1988). Asocial-cognitive approach to motivation and personality. *Psychological Review,* 95, 256–273.

Earley, P. C. (1986). An examination of the mechanisms underlying the relation of feedback to performance. *Academy of Management Journal, 33,* 87–105.

Ericsson, K. A. (1993). The role of deliberate practice in the acquisition of expert performance. *Psychological Review,* 100, 363–06.

Fernandez, C., Espinosa, R., & Dornbusch, S. (1975). *Factors perpetuating the low academic status of Chicano high school students (Memorandum No. 138).* Stanford, CA: Stanford University, Center for Research and Development in Teaching.

Gibson, J. J. (1979). *The ecological approach to visual perception.* Boston: Houghton Mifflin.

Goffman, E. (1963). *Stigma: Notes on the management of a spoiled identity.* Englewood Cliffs, NJ: Prentice Hall.

Graham, S. (1994). Motivation in African Americans. *Review of Educational Research, 64,* 55–117.

Harber, K. (1998). Feedback to minorities: Evidence of a positive bias. *Journal of Personality and Social Psychology, 74,* 622–628.

Horn, T. S. (1985). Coaches' feedback and changes in children's perceptions of their physical competence. *Journal of Educational Psychology,* 77, 174–186.

Jones, E. E. (1963). *Ingratiation: A social psychological analysis.* New York: Appleton Century Crofts.

Kleck, R. (1966). Physical stigma and nonverbal cues emitted in face-to-face interaction. *Human Relations,* 21, 19–28.

Kleinfeld, J. (1975). Effective teachers of Eskimo and Indian students. *School Review,* 83, 301–344.

Koestner, R., Zuckerman, M., & Koestner, J. (1987). Praise, involvement and intrinsic motivation. *Journal of Personality and Social Psychology, 53,* 383–390.

Koestner, R., Zuckerman, M., & Koestner, J. (1989). Attributional focus of praise and children's intrinsic motivation: The moderating role of gender. *Personality and Social Psychology Bulletin, 15,* 61–72.

Lepper, M. R. (1988). Motivational considerations in the study of instruction. *Cognition and Instruction,* 5, 289–309.

Lepper, M. R., Aspinwall, L. G., & Mumme, D. L. (1990). Self-perception and social-perception processes in tutoring: Subtle social control strategies of expert tutors. In J. M. Olson & M. P. Zanna (Eds.), *Self-inference processes: The Ontario symposium* (Vol. 6, pp. 217–237). Hillsdale, NJ: Lawrence Erlbaum.

Lepper, M. R., Woolverton, M., Mumme, D. L., & Gurtner, J. (1993). Motivational techniques of expert human tutors: Lessons for the design of computer-based tutors. In S. P. Lajoie & S. J. Derry (Eds.), *Computers as cognitive tools* (pp. 75–105). Hillsdale, NJ: Lawrence Erlbaum.

Massey, G. C., Scott, M. V., & Dornbusch, S. M. (1975, November). Racism without racists: Institutional racism in urban school. *Black Scholar,* pp. 10–19.

Mathews, J. (1988). *Escalante: The best teacher in America.* New York: Henry Holt and Company.

Meyer, W. U., Bachmann, M., Biermann, U., Hempelmann, M., Ploger, F. O., & Spiller, H. (1979). The informational value of evaluative behavior: Influences of praise and blame on perceptions of ability. *Journal ofEducational Psychology,* 71, 259–268.

Mueller, C. M., & Dweck, C. S. (1998). Praise for intelligence can undermine children's motivation and performance. *Journal of Personality and Social Psychology,* 75, 33–52.

Nicholls, J. G. (1978). The development of the concepts of effort and ability, perception of own attainment, and the understanding that difficult tasks require more ability. *Child Development,* 49, 800–814.

Prentice, D. A., Miller, D. T. (1993). Pluralistic ignorance and alcohol use on campus. *Journal of Personality and Social Psychology,* 64, 243–256.

Rosenberg, M. (1965). *Society and the adolescent self-image.* Princeton, NJ: Princeton University Press.

Ross, L., Lepper, M. R., & Hubbard, M. (1975). Perseverance in self-perception and social perception: Biased attributional processes in the debriefing paradigm. *Journal of Personality and Social Psychology,* 32, 880–892.

Sansone, C., Sachau, D. A., & Weir, C. (1989). Effects of instruction on intrinsic interest: The importance of context. *Journal of Personality and Social Psychology,* 57, 819–829.

Spencer, S., Steele, C. M., & Quinn, D. (1999). Under suspicion of inability: Stereotype threat and women's math performance. *Journal of Experimental Social Psychology,* 35, 4–28.

Steele, C. M. (1992, April). Race and the schooling of black Americans. *Atlantic Monthly,* 68–78.

Steele, C. M. (1997). A threat in the air: How stereotypes shape the intellectual identities and performance of women and African Americans. *American Psychologist,* 52, 613–629.

Steele, C. M., & Aronson, J. (1995). Stereotype threat and the intellectual test performance of African Americans. *Journal of Personality and Social Psychology,* 69, 797–811.

Stoutemeyer, K., & Steele, C. M. (1997). *The effects of stereotype threat on women's self-esteem, identification with math, and math performance.* Unpublished manuscript.

Tashakkori, A. (1993). Race, gender and pre-adolescent self-structure: A test of construct-specificity hypothesis. *Personality and Individual Differences,* 14, 591–598.

Tashakkori, A., & Thompson, V. D. (1991). Race differences in self-perception and locus of control during adolescence and early adulthood: Methodological implications. *Genetic, Social, & General Psychology Monographs,* 117, 113–152.

Treisman, P. U. (1985). *A study of the mathematics performance of Black students at the University of California, Berkeley.* Unpublished manuscript.

Vygotsky, L. V. (1978). *Mindin society.* Cambridge, MA: Harvard University Press.

Weiner, B. (1972). *Theories of motivation: From mechanism to cognition.* Chicago: Markham.

Weiner, B. (1974). *Achievement motivation and attribution theory.* Morristown, NJ: General Learning Press.

Weisinger, H. (1990). *The critical edge: How to criticize up and down your organization and make it pay off.* New York: Perennial Library.

Whimbey, A. (1975). *Intelligence can be taught.* New York: E. P. Dutton.

How Terrorism News Reports Increase Prejudice Against Outgroups

A Terror Management Account

By Enny Das, Brad J. Bushman, Marieke D. Bezemer, Peter Kerkhof, and Ivar E. Vermeulen

Abstract

Three studies tested predictions derived from terror management theory (TMT) about the effects of terrorism news on prejudice. Exposure to terrorism news should confront receivers with thoughts about their own death, which, in turn, should increase prejudice toward outgroup members. Non-Muslim (Studies 1-3) and Muslim (Study 3) participants were exposed to news about either Islamic terrorist acts or to control news. When Dutch filmmaker Theo van Gogh was murdered in Amsterdam by an Islamic extremist during data collection of Study 1, this event was included as a naturally occurring factor in the design. Consistent with TMT, terrorism news and Van Gogh's murder increased death-related thoughts. Death-related thoughts, in turn, increased prejudiced attitudes toward outgroup members, especially when participants had low self-esteem, and when terrorism was psychologically close. Terrorism news may inadvertently increase prejudiced attitudes towards outgroups when it reminds viewers of their own mortality.

Introduction

In recent years, terrorist attacks have become a salient threat to Western countries. News broadcasts frequently report about the threat of Muslim extremist terrorist acts, using vivid pictures of terrorist bombings, buildings crashing down, and people being killed in the name of the Islam and Allah. At the same time, different socio-cultural and religious groups appear to be drifting apart. For example, European adolescents set ablaze Muslim schools after news reports on Muslim extremist terrorism, and individuals with an Arab background have been reported to foster more extreme anti-European

Enny Das, Brad J. Bushman, Marieke D. Bezemer, Peter Kerkhof & Ivar E. Vermeulen, "How Terrorism News Reports Increase Prejudice Against Outgroups: A Terror Management Account," *Journal of Experimental Social Psychology*, vol. 45, no. 3, pp. 453–459. Copyright © 2009 by Elsevier Science & Technology Journals. Reprinted with permission.

sentiments (BBC, 2004). This rift between groups with different backgrounds may not be a coincidence; the immense fear elicited by terrorism news reports may inadvertently increase prejudice against outgroups.

The present research tests the effects of terrorism news on prejudice against Arabs and Europeans. Terror management theory provides the theoretical foundation for the research. Terrorism news was manipulated across studies, and also induced by real-world events in Study 1. On November 2nd, 2004, the well-known Dutch filmmaker Theo van Gogh was murdered by an Islamic extremist, two months after the release of his highly controversial film about the abuse of Muslim women, titled *Submission*. Because the murder occurred in the middle of data collection, it allowed us to test whether real-life terrorism news produces the same effects as our experimental manipulation of terrorism news.

A terror management account of prejudice

According to terror management theory (TMT; Greenberg, Pyszczynski, & Solomon, 1986), human beings are biologically predisposed toward survival, just like all animals. The uniquely human capacity for self-reflection, however, makes people aware that someday they will die. TMT proposes that thoughts of one's inevitable death create a potential for terror. To avoid becoming paralyzed by this terror, people immerse themselves in cultural systems and worldviews that offer them literal immortality (e.g., the promise of an afterlife after one's death) or symbolic immortality (e.g., being remembered by others after one's death). Faith in one's cultural worldview thus functions as a buffer against death-related anxiety.

TMT provides a powerful theoretical framework for explaining the origins and consequences of terrorism and political violence (Pyszczynski, Greenberg, & Solomon, 2003). Recent studies support a TMT account of the origins of political ideology and violence by showing that mortality salience increased violent resistance against political interventions (Hirschberger & Ein-Dor, 2006), support for violent military interventions (Pyszczynski et al., 2006) and willingness to sacrifice ones life for political or religious ideology (Pyszczynski et al., 2006; Routledge & Arndt, 2007). Because the main goal of terrorist acts is the "intentional generation of massive fear" (Cooper, 2001, p. 883), terrorism news may also increase worldview defense such as prejudice against outgroups, or increased support for one's country and government. This may be especially likely for terrorist attacks that are perceived as psychologically or physically close.

Unfortunately, empirical evidence about the consequences of terrorism is mainly indirect, by focusing on the role of mortality salience rather than directly testing the effects of terrorism news. One study showed that experimentally induced thoughts of death enhanced support for US president George W. Bush. Also, priming participants subliminally with 9/11 stimuli increased death-related thoughts (Landau et al., 2004). Another study showed that after a mortality salience manipulation, securely attached participants increased their support for a liberal presidential candidate, whereas less securely attached participants increased their support for a conservative presidential candidate (Weise et al., 2008). One study conducted more direct tests of the effects of terrorism news reports, but could not establish effects on death thought accessibility (Ullrich & Cohrs, 2007).

The present studies add to the literature by providing an extensive test of a TMT account of terror-induced prejudice. A TMT account of prejudice differs from other perspectives in three important ways. First, several theorists have argued that prejudice is an inevitable consequence of categorization processes (e.g., Allport, 1954; Tajfel, 1981). For instance, when news reports link Arabs to terrorist acts, this automatically reinforces the "Arab equals bad" stereotype, thus increasing prejudice against Arabs. In contrast, TMT proposes that prejudice can be regarded as a specific type of worldview defense that results from the suppression of death-related thoughts. Contrary to a stereotype generalization account of prejudice, TMT attributes a pivotal role to thoughts about death in predicting prejudice. However, empirical support for a link between death-related thoughts and prejudiced attitudes is lacking. Although there is evidence that mortality reminders can increase worldview defenses against people of a different race or religion (Greenberg, Schimel, Martens, Solomon, & Pyszczynski, 2001; Greenberg et al., 1990), death-related thoughts have remained the missing link.

This research tests the full causal chain from terrorism news to death-related thoughts to prejudice against outgroup members. The classical TMT account is that death-related thoughts mediate between terrorism news and prejudice. We compare these findings to a model in which death-related thoughts moderate the relationship between terrorism news and prejudice. This is reminiscent of well-known priming theories of news effects (e.g., Iyengar & Kinder, 1987). According to these theories, news determines not so much what people think, but what they think about (the agenda setting effect, McCombs & Shaw, 1972). What people think about, in turn, becomes an important evaluation standard for judging "reality" (the media priming effect, Iyengar & Kinder, 1987). For example, news about economic crisis may increase the accessibility of thoughts and fears about such a crisis in the public, which, in turn, may "prime" public perceptions of employment policy, or political actors, and cause a shift in voting behavior. Likewise, terrorism news reports may increase the accessibility of thoughts of one's own mortality, which, in turn, may become an important evaluation standard for judging outgroup members, public policies, and politicians. Studies 1 and 2 test both mediation and moderation models of terrorism news effects.

A second difference between a TMT account of prejudice and other accounts concerns the role of self-esteem. TMT proposes that self-esteem protects individuals from the anxiety that arises as they become aware of their own demise, and thus functions as a buffer against mortality reminders (Greenberg et al., 1992, 1993; Harmon-Jones et al., 1997). The anxiety buffering function of self-esteem is unique to a TMT account of prejudice and sets it apart from an intergroup threat account of terrorism news effects on prejudice.

According to intergroup threat accounts, terrorism news poses a threat to one's group and therefore threatens collective and personal self-esteem, which in turn affects reactions to outgroup members (see Riek, Mania, & Gaertner, 2006, for a meta-analysis). Importantly, in conditions of threat, high self-esteem promotes rather than reduces prejudice (e.g., Aberson, Healy, & Romero, 2000; Crocker, Thompson, McGraw, & Ingerman, 1987). In contrast, TMT proposes that in conditions of a specific threat of death, high self-esteem reduces rather than promotes prejudice. However, empirical support for this proposition is lacking. Study 2 is the first to test the effects of self-esteem on terror-induced prejudice.

A third difference between a TMT account of prejudice and other accounts concerns the role of specific outgroups. According to a stereotype generalization account of terror-induced prejudice, news about Muslim extremist terrorist threats is most likely to increase prejudice against Arabs among Westerners, because the stereotype "Arab = bad" generalizes to all individuals who are thought to belong to this socio-cultural group (Tajfel & Turner, 1979). In contrast, TMT proposes that terror-induced prejudice is not contingent upon the socio-cultural group portrayed in the news, or upon a viewer's background. Rather, terrorism news may increase prejudice against *any* outgroup, regardless of a viewer's socio-cultural background, when it confronts viewers with their own mortality. Thus, terrorism news may increase prejudice against Arabs for Europeans, and prejudice against Europeans for Arabs. This assertion is tested in Study 3.

Overview

Three studies tested the effects of news on terrorism on prejudice against outgroups. According to TMT, terrorism news may increase prejudice against outgroups when it confronts viewers with their own mortality. In Study 1 we manipulated news on terrorism and included the murder of filmmaker Van Gogh as a real-world factor in the design, and tested whether death-related thoughts mediated or moderated the effects of terrorism news on prejudice. Study 2 extended these findings by testing whether the effects on death-related thoughts and prejudice are mitigated by self-esteem. Finally, Study 3 tested the effects of terrorism news on prejudice against outgroups among Muslim and non-Muslim respondents.

Study 1

In Study 1, participants viewed news content about Islamic terrorist attacks or about the Olympic Games (control). Theo van Gogh was murdered by an Islamic extremist in the middle of data collection. Thus, half of the participants in Study 1 were also exposed to Van Gogh's murder. We test the classical TMT model in which death-related thoughts mediate the relationship between terrorism news and prejudice, and compare it to a model in which death-related thoughts moderate the relationship between terrorism news and prejudice.

Method

Participants and design

To ensure a diverse sample, 100 white European volunteers (40 men, 60 women) recruited via advertisements across different regions of the Netherlands. To avoid a selection bias, participants were told that the researchers were studying a variety of issues (e.g., news content, multicultural societies). The mean age of participants was 35 (*SD* = 10 years). About 48% of the participants were Protestant, 10% Catholic, and 42% were atheist. None were Muslim.

Participants were randomly assigned to one of two groups in a 2 (terrorism news vs. Olympic game news) between-subjects factorial design. The second factor was not manipulated, but occurred naturally during the data collection process. About half the participants *(N = 44)* were tested before the highly publicized murder of Dutch filmmaker Theo van Gogh, whereas the others *(N = 56)* were tested after his murder.

Procedure

After informed consent was obtained, participants first reported their age, gender, religious background, and political preference. By the flip of a coin, participants then watched 12 min of programming from the Dutch news (NOS) about terrorism committed by Islamic extremists or about the Olympic Games. The terrorism news showed the September 11th, 2001 terrorist attack on the World Trade Center in New York City, the January 18th, 2002 terrorist attack during a Bar Mitzvah in Hadera, Israel, and the September 3rd, 2004 terrorist attack on a school in Beslan, Russia. The other participants watched segments from the 2004 Olympic Games in Athens, Greece (e.g., the arrival of the Olympic flame in Amsterdam).

Next, participants completed a word fragment task that contained 17 death-related items (e.g., in Dutch the fragment *doo_* can be completed as *dood* [dead], *doos* [box], or *doof* [deaf]). Participants then completed a measure of prejudicial attitudes toward Arabs (Bushman & Bonacci, 2004). Sample items include "Even for Arabs who live in the Netherlands, their first loyalty is to their home country rather than to the Netherlands" and "If there are too many Arabs in the Netherlands, our country will be less safe." (1 = *totally disagree,* 10 = *totally agree;* Cronbach's α = 0.92). Finally, participants were thanked, debriefed, and dismissed.

Results

Preliminary analyses

Because the Van Gogh murder was a naturally occurring factor in our design, it is important to show that there are no systematic differences between participants who were tested before versus after his murder. That is, it is important to rule out differential subject selection as a threat to the validity of our design (Cook & Campbell, 1979). There are three reasons why we can rule out this threat. First, commitment to participate was obtained *before* Van Gogh was murdered. Thus, knowledge about the murder could not have influenced participation rates before versus after the murder. Second, there were no differences in participation rates before versus after the murder. All those who agreed to participate, did in fact participate. Third, political preferences were similar for individuals who participated before and after the murder, $v^2(9) = 0.22, p > 0.99$.[1]

---

[1]Degrees of freedom are nine because participants listed a total of 10 political parties.

Main analyses

Death-related thoughts

A 2 (terrorism vs. control news) x 2 (before vs. after Van Gogh murder) ANOVA showed a significant interaction between news content and Van Gogh's murder, $F(1, 96) = 4.18$, $p < 0.05$. Before Van Gogh's murder, death-related words were higher for participants who saw terrorism news than for participants who saw Olympic Games news, $Ms = 3.17$ and 2.59, respectively, $F(1, 96) = 3.14$, $p < 0.08$, $d = 0.36$. After Van Gogh's murder, death-related words were equally high regardless of whether participants saw terrorism news or Olympic Games news, $Ms = 2.80$ and 3.22, respectively, $F(1, 96) = 1.21$, $p < 0.273$, $d = 0.22$. There were no other significant effects.

Predicting prejudice against Arabs

Regression analysis was used to test the effects of terrorism news, the murder of Van Gogh, and death-related thoughts on prejudiced attitudes toward Arabs. We first tested the possibility of mediation following Baron and Kenny (1986). However, because death-related thoughts did not significantly predict prejudice ($t(93) = 0.94$, $p = 0.35$) the conditions for mediation were not met. Thus, the findings do not support a model where death-related thoughts mediate the effects of terrorism news on prejudice against Arabs.

Next, we tested a moderation model. The regression model contained death-related word completions (mean centered), news content (control = -1, terrorism = +1), time of participation (before Van Gogh's murder = -1, after Van Gogh's murder = +1), and their interactions (see West, Aiken, & Krull, 1996). The results showed a marginally significant interaction between time of participation and death-related completions, $t(93) = 1.70$, $p = 0.094$. Before Van Gogh was murdered, death-related thoughts were not significantly related to prejudiced attitudes toward Arabs, $t(42) = -0.43$, $p = 0.67$, $b = -0.10$ and b = -0.08. After Van Gogh was murdered, the more death-related thoughts people had, the more prejudiced their attitudes were toward Arabs, $t(52) = 0.187$, $p = 0.07$, $b = 0.49$ and b = 0.26. No other significant effects were found.

Discussion

Study 1 showed that terrorism news and Van Gogh's murder increased death-related thoughts. Death-related thoughts, in turn, led to more prejudiced attitudes towards Arabs, but only after Van Gogh's murder. These findings suggest that death-related thoughts moderate the relationship between terrorism news and prejudice, supporting a media priming account of the relationship between death-related thoughts and prejudice (Iyengar & Kinder, 1987). In a classical TMT account of prejudice, death-related thoughts should mediate the effect of Van Gogh's murder on prejudice against Arabs. Our findings suggest an alternative interpretation, in which the Van Gogh murder primed unconscious death anxiety, which, in turn, became "attached" to attitudes toward Arabs. Van Gogh's murder triggered a fear-based judgment of the Arab population, with high levels of unconscious fear predicting higher prejudice against Arabs. Overall, these findings resemble well-known priming accounts of news effects frequently observed in media studies (e.g., Iyengar & Kinder, 1987), in which the news determines not so much what people think, but what they think about (cf. the accessibility construct). What people think about, in turn, becomes an important evaluation standard for judging "reality."

The present study also shows some unexpected patterns. First, although terrorism news and Van Gogh's murder appeared to have similar effects on death-related thoughts, closer inspection of the means show that terrorism news increased death-related thoughts before the murder of Van Gogh, but not after. These findings suggest a ceiling effect, in which already activated death-related thoughts remain at the same level when a second terrorism news report comes in. Also contrary to expectations, terrorism news did not affect prejudice against Arabs. Although Van Gogh's murder was highly publicized and occurred close by, whereas the terrorism acts shown in the news clips occurred in other countries (i.e., USA, Israel, Russia). These findings suggest that terrorism news is most likely to increase prejudiced attitudes when the news is (psychologically or physically) close.

Study 2

In Study 2, we used a terrorism news story about a bomb threat on Amsterdam central train station, in order to ascertain that the news was perceived as psychologically close. The main goal of Study 2 was to provide further evidence for a unique TMT account of prejudice by testing the effects of self-esteem. According to TMT, terror-induced prejudice will be most pronounced for people with low self-esteem, and the accessibility of death thoughts should be positively linked to prejudice, especially for people with low selfesteem. Study 2 used an implicit measure of prejudice against Arabs to provide convergent evidence for a TMT account of prejudice.

Method

Participants

Participants were 101 white European volunteers (39 men, 62 women) who were recruited via a university website. Their mean age was 29 (SD = 11 years). About 32% were Protestant, 14% Catholic, 51% atheist, and 3% other. None were Muslim.

Procedure

Participants were told that the researchers were studying the relationship between news messages and cognitive abilities. After informed consent was obtained, participants reported their age, gender, religious background, and political preference. Next, they completed the 10-item Self-Esteem Scale (Rosenberg, 1965). Sample items include "I feel that I have a number of good qualities" and "I take a positive attitude toward myself." Each item was rated on a four-point scale (1 = *strongly disagree*, 4 = *strongly agree* and Cronbach α = 0.79).

Next, participants were randomly assigned to read a negative news article, either about terrorism or about animal abuse. The terrorism article described a bomb threat at the Amsterdam central train station. It said the suspected terrorist, a member of Al-Qaeda (Osama bin Laden's terrorist network), had been arrested, and that he had the bomb materials and plans in his possession. The animal abuse article described the stabbing of a pony with a sharp object. It said that the animal had survived the attack, but was permanently crippled. As in Study 1, participants completed word fragments as a measure of death-related thoughts. Participants then completed the implicit association test (IAT, e.g., Greenwald, McGhee, & Schwartz, 1998). The IAT has been shown to reliably measure prejudice at the implicit, unconscious level on the basis of reaction times to target words. Implicit tests of prejudice have the advantage of avoiding several demand characteristics associated with explicit measures of prejudice. Participants were told to classify words into categories as quickly as possible, while making as few mistakes as possible. We used European names (e.g., Maarten, Marcel) versus Arab names (e.g., Akbar, Mohammed), and good words (e.g., joy, love) versus bad words (e.g., evil, terrible). On the first test, participants pressed one button if the word was "European Name or Good," and they pressed another button if the word was "Arab Name or Bad." On the second test, the process was reversed (i.e., "European Name or Bad" versus "Arab name or Good"). Each test consisted of 25 trials. The difference in reaction times between the two tests was used to measure prejudiced attitudes.[2] Specifically, positive scores denote prejudiced attitudes toward Arabs, whereas negative scores denote prejudiced attitudes toward Europeans. Finally, participants were debriefed.

Results

Death-related thoughts

As hypothesized, a one-way ANOVA on death word completions showed that participants in the terrorism news condition had more death-related word completions (M = 2.00, SD = 1.25) than did participants in the control news condition (M = 1.40, SD = 1.15), F(1, 99) = 6.32, p < 0.02, d = 0.51.

Predicting prejudiced attitudes toward arabs

Regression analysis was used to predict prejudiced attitudes toward Arabs, and to test the mediating or moderating role of death related thoughts. First, we tested whether news content (animal abuse = -1, terrorism = +1), self-esteem (mean centered), and the interaction between news content and self-esteem (see West et al., 1996) were related to prejudice against Arabs, and whether this relationship was mediated by

---

[2]Actually, a D measure was calculated by dividing the difference in reaction time between the two tests by the standard deviation of the reaction time scores of the test block (cf. Greenwald, Nosek, & Banaji, 2003). This measure is similar to the wellknown effect-size measure d, but not identical. Specifically, whereas the standard deviation in D is calculated using scores from both tests, the standard deviation in d is calculated using a pooled within-treatment standard deviation (Greenberg et al., 2003). Research has shown that the D score compensates for differences caused by cognitive skills of the participant (Cai, Sriram, Greenwald, & McFarland, 2004).

death-related thoughts (mean centered). The analysis revealed a significant main effect for news content, $t(95) = 2.69$, $p < 0.01$, $b = 0.15$ and $b = 0.26$, with higher levels of prejudice in the terrorism news condition. However, similar to Study 1, death-related thoughts did not significantly predict prejudice ($t(95) = 1.76$, $p = 0.19$). Hence, the conditions for mediation were not met (cf. Baron & Kenny, 1986).

Next, we tested the possibility of moderation. Death-related word completions (mean centered), and the interactions between death-related thoughts, self-esteem, and news content were added to the regression model. The results showed a nearly significant main effect for news content, $t(91) = 1.77$, $p < 0.09$. This main effect, however, was qualified by interaction effects. There was a significant interaction between news content and self-esteem, $t(91) = -2.22$, $p < 0.03$. Self-esteem decreased prejudice against Arabs in the terrorism news condition, $t(20) = -2.06$, $p < 0.06$, $b = -0.26$, $b = -0.42$. Self-esteem had no significant relationship with prejudice in the control condition, $t(17) = 0.84$, $p = 0.414$, $b = 0.17$ and $b = 0.20$. Finally, a significant three-way interaction between news content, self-esteem, and death-related thoughts was also observed, $t(91) = -2.09$, $p < 0.04$. Prejudice against Arabs increased with higher death-related thought accessibility, but only for low self-esteem participants exposed to terrorism news. In all other conditions, the relationship between death-related thought accessibility and prejudice was non-significant (see Fig. 1).

Discussion

In Study 2, terrorism news increased death-related thoughts. Death-related thoughts, in turn, increased prejudiced attitudes towards Arabs, especially in individuals with low self-esteem. These findings replicate the moderating role of death-related thoughts observed in Study 1, and suggest that death-related thoughts become linked to prejudice against outgroups after watching terrorism news. Importantly, the findings also support a unique TMT account of prejudice by showing that self-esteem functions as a buffer against the effects of terrorism news. Thus, terrorism news is most likely to increase prejudice for viewers who suffer from low self-esteem.

Study 3

Studies 1 and 2 used participants with a European background, and showed that terrorism news may increase prejudice against Arabs. Another unique proposition in TMT is that terrorism news may increase prejudice against *any* outgroup member, regardless of the outgroup's role in the news, and regardless of a viewer's background. This hypothesis was tested in Study 3. Terrorism news was expected to increase prejudice against Europeans for Muslim participants, and to increase prejudice against Arabs for non-Muslim participants.

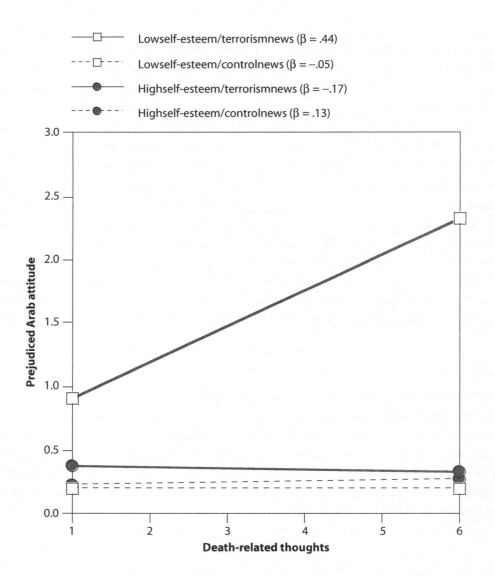

Figure 1. Relationship between death-related thoughts and prejudiced attitudes towards Arabs for participants high and low in self-esteem who were exposed to either terrorism news or control news (Study 2).

Method

Participants and materials

Participants were recruited via flyers at a University campus, and online banners placed at different Arab-Dutch websites. Participation was on a voluntary basis, and was encouraged by awarding gift vouchers of Euro 25 (about $37) in a lottery. The mean age of participants (98 women, 81 men) was 28 *(SD* = 11.53). Of the total population, 47.5% were Muslim, 29.6% were Christian, 9.5% were Catholic, 10.6% were atheist, and 8.2% had a different religious background. As expected, there was a significant correlation between country of origin defined as (parents) being born in a country and religious background. Specifically, the vast majority of participants with a Dutch, British, German, or Belgian background were atheist, Christian, or Catholic, whereas virtually all participants from Morocco, Egypt, Pakistan, Iran, and Iraq were Muslim. In order to assess the effects of religious background, participants were categorized into "Muslim" (n = 85, 47.5%) or "non-Muslim" (n = 94, 52.5%).

The procedure was similar to that used in Study 2: participants first completed demographic measures and were then randomly assigned to read a negative news article about terrorism or about animal abuse. Participants then completed the Implicit Association Test (IAT, e.g., Greenwald et al., 1998) with European names (e.g., Maarten, Marcel) versus Arab names (e.g., Akbar, Mohammed), and good words (e.g., joy, love) versus bad words (e.g., evil, terrible). Finally, participants were debriefed.

Results

Implicit prejudiced attitudes

A 2 (news article: terrorism vs. control) x 2 (religious background: Muslim vs. non-Muslim) ANCOVA, with attitudes toward a Dutch multicultural society as the covariate, revealed a main effect for background, $F(1,135) = 22.53$, $p < 0.001$, g = 0.14. As expected, Muslim participants generally scored below zero on the IAT, denoting prejudice against Europeans (M = -0.29, SD = 0.75), whereas non-Muslim participants generally scored above zero, denoting prejudice against Arabs (M = 0.29, SD = 0.65). More important, there was a significant interaction between news article and religious background, $F(1,135) = 3.93$, $p = 0.05$, $\eta^2_p = 0.03$. As can be seen from Fig. 2, news on terrorism increased polarization between groups with different backgrounds. Specifically, prejudiced attitudes toward outgroup members were most pronounced after reading terrorism news, $F(1,135) = 24.23$, $p < 0.001$, $\eta^2_p = 0.15$. This differentiation between groups was much less pronounced after reading control news, $F(1,135) = 3.55$, $p < 0.07$, $\eta^2_p = 0.03$.

Discussion

In Study 3, terrorism news increased prejudice against Arabs for non-Muslims, and increased prejudice against Europeans for Muslim audiences. These findings further support a TMT account of terror-induced prejudice, and make other accounts of prejudice less likely. Specifically, if prejudice against Arabs was caused by the negative image of Arabs created by terrorism news, then terrorism news should have increased prejudice against Arabs, but not against Europeans. However, terrorism news also increased prejudice against Europeans, a group not linked to stereotypical images of Islamic terrorists. These findings support a TMT account of terror-induced prejudice, in which terrorism news may increase prejudice against any outgroup when it confronts viewers with their own mortality.

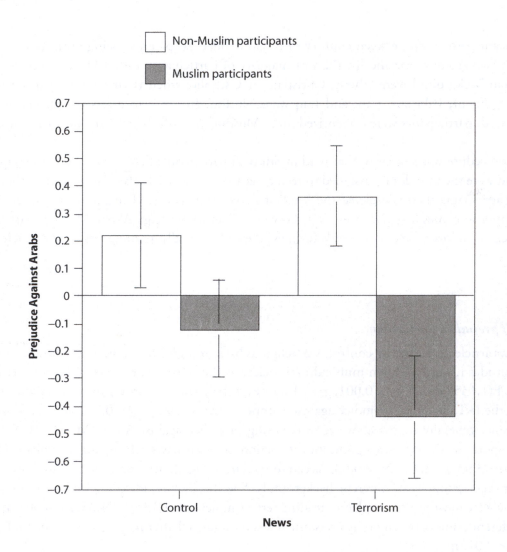

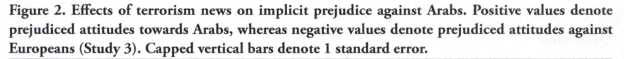

Figure 2. Effects of terrorism news on implicit prejudice against Arabs. Positive values denote prejudiced attitudes towards Arabs, whereas negative values denote prejudiced attitudes against Europeans (Study 3). Capped vertical bars denote 1 standard error.

General discussion

Three studies tested the effects of terrorism news on prejudiced attitudes toward outgroups. Based on terror management theory (TMT; Greenberg et al., 1986), we hypothesized that news reports about terrorism would remind people of their own mortality, which, in turn, would increase prejudiced attitudes. In Study 1, the murder of Dutch filmmaker Van Gogh and news reports of terrorist attacks in the US, Israel, and Russia, increased death-related thoughts. Death-related thoughts, in turn, predicted prejudiced attitudes towards Arabs, but only after Van Gogh's murder. In Study 2, news on a terrorist threat close by increased death-related thoughts, which, in turn, predicted implicit prejudice against Arabs for individuals with low self-esteem. Finally, Study 3 replicated the effect of news on terrorism on prejudice against Arabs for nonMuslim participants, and further showed that terrorism news increased prejudice against Europeans for Muslim participants.

TMT provides a unique account of prejudice by proposing that prejudice against outgroups can result from an attempt to suppress the terror evoked by thoughts of death. The present research is the first to document the full causal chain from a terrorist act to death-related thoughts to prejudice, and suggest a media priming account of the relationship between death-related thoughts and prejudice (Iyengar & Kinder, 1987). Specifically, terrorism news triggers an unconsciously activated fear of death, which then becomes the basis for judging outgroups. As a result, individuals will exhibit higher levels of prejudice against outgroups to the extent that they are more terrified after watching terrorism news. Similar patterns of findings have often been reported in the research area of media effects, where news issues often become an important evaluation standard for judging "reality," an effect termed media priming. Likewise, (news reports about) terrorist acts may bring about thought of one's own mortality, which subsequently affect how the public views involved groups, policies, and politicians (also see Landau et al., 2004). In the case of terrorism news, unconsciously activated fears thus become linked to social judgment processes.

TMT predicts that death-related thoughts will always trigger some type of worldview defense (Greenberg et al., 1986). Nevertheless, little is known about the relationship between the accessibility of specific situational cues and the subsequent "selection" of certain types of worldview defenses. Research suggests that situational cues can affect the activation of constructs following death-related thoughts, and thus affect the specific types of worldview defenses that are triggered across contexts. For instance, mortality salience increased the accessibility of nationalistic thoughts for men and romantic thoughts for women in one study (Arndt et al., 2004). However, when America was made salient prior to other manipulations, reminders of death also increased the accessibility of nationalistic thoughts for women. Another way of looking at the present findings, then, is that news reports increase the salience of specific types of worldview defense, and have some sort of "steering effect" on how people respond to their death-related thoughts. If this reasoning is correct, terrorism news may steer death-related thoughts in the direction of prejudice against salient outgroup members, whereas news about a famine in a third world country may steer death-related thoughts in the direction of, for instance, increased consumption (Arndt et al., 2004).

Importantly, our findings also show that terrorism news may increase prejudice against different outgroups (i.e., Arabs, Europeans), regardless of whether they are linked to news content. These findings reduce the plausibility of a stereotype generalization account of terror-induced prejudice. Specifically, if terror-induced prejudice was caused by the negative image of Arabs created by terrorism news, then prejudice should have increased against Arabs, but not Europeans. However, Study 3 showed that terrorism news also increased prejudice against Europeans for Muslim participants, thus suggesting a more general account of terrorism news effects in which terrorism news can increase prejudice against any outgroup in viewers who are confronted with their own mortality.

One limitation of the present research is that it did not explicitly document the relationship between death-related thoughts and prejudice against Europeans for individuals with a Muslim background for practical reasons (Study 3), thus making the findings liable to alternative interpretation. For instance, it may be that Muslim participants who were exposed to terrorism news scored higher on prejudice against Europeans because they reasoned that Europeans were probably going to blame Arabs for the terrorist act committed by a few Islamic extremists, and that this shows how shallow and prejudiced Europeans are. In this case, prejudice against Europeans may be prompted by anger, or disappointment, rather than by an unconscious fear of death. Future studies should focus on further documenting the relationship between death-related thought and prejudice against different outgroups. Also, although the present research suggests that the psychological and physical proximity of news on terrorism may play an important role in triggering death salience and worldview defenses, we did not explicitly test this reasoning. Future research should include explicit manipulations of the psychological or physical distance of terrorism news to verify our reasoning.

Finally, the present research also point to a possible antidote against the negative side effects of terrorism news. Specifically, Study 2 showed that news on terrorism is most likely to increase prejudice for individuals suffering from low self-esteem. Other perspectives have proposed that high self-esteem promotes rather than reduces prejudice under conditions of threat (e.g., Aberson et al., 2000). TMT is unique in proposing that self-esteem serves as a psychological buffer against death concerns, and thus attenuates the effect of death thought suppression on worldview defense (Greenberg et al., 1992, 1993; Harmon-Jones et al., 1997). This means that factors that temporarily or permanently boost self-esteem are likely to mitigate negative effects of terrorism news. This seems of particular importance in view of the negative social and political consequences of terrorism news.

Acknowledgments

We thank Jamie Arndt, Rowell Huesmann, and Sander Koole for their useful suggestions on an earlier draft of this manuscript. We also thank Sander Kooistra for his help with the IAT programming for Study 2.

This research was supported by a Faculty Fellowship grant awarded to the first author by the Centre for Comparative Social Studies at the Faculty of Social Sciences of VU University, Amsterdam.

References

Aberson, C. L., Healy, M. R., & Romero, V. L. (2000). Ingroup bias and self-esteem: A meta-analysis. *Personality and Social Psychology Review, 4,*157–173.

Allport, G. W. (1954). *The nature of prejudice.* Reading, MA: Addison-Wesley

Arndt, J., Cook, A., & Routledge, C. (2004). The blueprint of terror management: Understanding the cognitive architecture of psychological defense against the awareness of death. In: J. Greenberg, S. L. Koole, & T. Pyszczynski (Eds.), *Handbook of experimental existential psychology* (pp. 35–53). New York: Guilford Press.

Baron, R. M., & Kenny, D. A. (1986). The moderator-mediator variable distinction in social psychological research: Conceptual, strategic, and statistical considerations. *Journal of Personality and Social Psychology, 51,*1173–1182.

BBC (2004, November 9). Dutch Islamic school set ablaze. http://news.bbc.co.uk/1/ hi/world/europe/3997943.stm Downloaded 26.01.05.

Bushman, B. J., & Bonacci, A. M. (2004). You've got mail: Using e-mail to examine the effect of prejudiced attitudes on discrimination against Arabs. *Journal of Experimental Social Psychology, 40,* 753–759.

Cai, H., Sriram, N., Greenwald, A. G., & McFarland, S. G. (2004). The implicit association test's D measure can minimize a cognitive skill confound: Comment on McFarland and Crouch. *Social Cognition, 22,* 673–684.

Cook, T. D., & Campbell, D. T. (1979). Quasi-experimentation: Design and analysis issues for field settings. Boston: Houghton Mifflin Co.

Cooper, H. H. A. (2001). Terrorism: The problem of definition revisited. *American Behavioral Scientist, 44,* 881–893.

Crocker, J., Thompson, L. L., McGraw, K. M., & Ingerman, C. (1987). Downward comparison, prejudice, and evaluations of others: Effects of self-esteem and threat. *Journal of Personality and Social Psychology, 52,* 907–916.

Greenberg, J., Pyszczynski, T., & Solomon, S. (1986). The causes and consequences of a need for self-esteem: A terror management theory. In: R. F. Baumeister (Ed.), *Public and private self.* (pp. 189–212). New York: Springer-Verlag.

Greenberg, J., Pyszczynski, T., Solomon, S., Pinel, E., Simon, L., & Jordan, K. (1993). Effects of self-esteem on vulnerability-denying defensive distortions: Further evidence of an anxiety-buffering function of self-esteem. *Journal of Experimental Social Psychology, 29,* 229–251.

Greenberg, J., Pyszczynski, T., Solomon, S., Rosenblatt, A., Veeder, M., Kirkland, S., et al. (1990). Evidence for terror management II: The effects of mortality salience on reactions to those who threaten or bolster the cultural worldview. *Journal of Personality and Social Psychology, 58,* 308–318.

Greenberg, J., Schimel, J., Martens, A., Solomon, S., & Pyszczynski, T. (2001). Sympathy for the devil: Evidence that reminding whites of their mortality promotes more favorable reactions to white racists. *Motivation and Emotion, 25,* 113–133.

Greenberg, J., Solomon, S., Pyszczynski, T., Rosenblatt, A., Burling, J., Lyon, D., et al. (1992). Assessing the terror management analysis of self-esteem: Converging evidence of an anxiety-buffering function. *Journal of Personality and Social Psychology, 63,* 913–922.

Greenwald, A. G., McGhee, D. E., & Schwartz, J. L. K. (1998). Measuring individual differences in implicit cognition: The implicit association test. *Journal of Personality and Social Psychology, 74,* 1464–1480.

Greenwald, A. G., Nosek, B. A., & Banaji, M. R. (2003). Understanding and using the implicit association test: An improved scoring algorithm. *Journal of Personality and Social Psychology, 85,* 197–216.

Harmon-Jones, E., Simon, L., Greenberg, J., Pyszczynski, T., Solomon, S., & McGregor, H. (1997). Terror management theory and self-esteem: Evidence that increased self-esteem reduces mortality salience effects. *Journal of Personality and Social Psychology, 72,* 24–36.

Hirschberger, G., & Ein-Dor, T. (2006). Defenders of a lost cause: Terror management and violent resistance to the disengagement plan. *Personality and Social Psychology Bulletin, 32,* 761–769.

Iyengar, S., & Kinder, D. R. (1987). *News that matters.* Chicago: The University of Chicago Press.

Landau, M. J., Solomon, S., Greenberg, J., Cohen, F., Pyszczynski, T., Arndt, J., et al. (2004). Deliver us from evil: The effects of mortality salience and reminders of 9/11 on support for President George W. Bush. *Personality and Social Psychology Bulletin, 30,* 136–1150.

McCombs, M. E., & Shaw, D. L. (1972). The agenda-setting function of mass media. *Public Opinion Quarterly,* 36, 176–187.

Pyszczynski, T. A., Abdollahi, A., Solomon, S., Greenberg, J., Cohen, F., & Weise, D. (2006). Mortality salience, martyrdom, and military might: The great satan versus the axis of evil. *Personality and Social Psychology Bulletin,* 32, 525–537.

Pyszczynski, T. A., Greenberg, J., & Solomon, S. (2003). *In the wake of 9/11: The psychology of terror.* Washington, DC: APA Press.

Riek, B. M., Mania, E. W., & Gaertner, S. L. (2006). Intergroup threat and outgroup attitudes: A meta-analytic review. *Personality and Social Psychology Review,* 10, 336–353.

Rosenberg, M. (1965). *Society and the self-image.* Princeton, NJ: Princeton University Press.

Routledge, C., & Arndt, J. (2007). Self-sacrifice as self-defense: Mortality salience increases efforts to affirm a symbolic immortal self at the expense of the physical self. *European Journal of Social Psychology,* 38, 531–541.

Tajfel, H. (1981). *Human groups and social categories: Studies in social psychology.* Cambridge, England: Cambridge University Press.

Tajfel, H., & Turner, J. C. (1979). An integrative theory of intergroup conflict. In: W. G. Austin & S. Worchel (Eds.), *The social psychology of intergroup relations* (pp. 33–47). Chicago: Nelson-Hall.

Ullrich, J., & Cohrs, J. C. (2007). Terrorism salience increases system justification: Experimental evidence. *Social Justice Research,* 20, 117–139.

Weise, D. R., Pyszczynski, T., Cox, C. R., Arndt, J., Greenberg, J., Solomon, S., et al. (2008). Interpersonal politics: The role of terror management and attachment processes in shaping political preferences. *Psychological Science,* 19, 448–455.

West, S. G., Aiken, L. S., & Krull, J. L. (1996). Experimental personality designs: Analyzing categorical by continuous variable interactions. *Journal of Personality,* 64, 1–48.

On the Nature of Prejudice

Automatic and Controlled Processe

By John F. Dovidio, Colgate University; Kerry Kawakami, University of Nijmegen, The Netherlands; Craig Johnson, Hofstra University; Brenda Johnson, Colgate University, and Adaiah Howard, Colgate University

The present research, involving three experiments, examined the existence of implicit attitudes of Whites toward Blacks, investigated the relationship between explicit measures of racial prejudice and implicit measures of racial attitudes, and explored the relationship of explicit and implicit attitudes to race-related responses and behavior. Experiment 1, which used a priming technique, demonstrated implicit negative racial attitudes (i.e., evaluative associations) among Whites that were largely disassociated from explicit, self-reported racial prejudice. Experiment 2 replicated the priming results of Experiment 1 and demonstrated, as hypothesized, that explicit measures predicted deliberative race-related responses (juridic decisions), whereas the implicit measure predicted spontaneous responses (racially primed word completions). Experiment 3 extended these findings to interracial interactions. Self-reported (explicit) racial attitudes primarily predicted the relative evaluations of Black and White interaction partners, whereas the response latency measure of implicit attitude primarily predicted differences in nonverbal behaviors (blinking and visual contact). The relation between these findings and general frameworks of contemporary racial attitudes is considered. © 1997 Academic Press

The distinction between explicit and implicit memory processes has recently received substantial empirical attention (e.g., Loftus & Klinger, 1992; Schacter, 1990; Wegner & Bargh, 1997). Similarly, Greenwald and Banaji (1995; Banaji & Greenwald, 1994) have emphasized the importance of distinguishing between explicit and implicit indices of attitudes. Explicit measures of attitudes operate in a conscious mode and are exemplified by traditional self-report measures. Implicit attitudes, in contrast, operate in an unconscious fashion and represent "introspectively unidentified (or inaccurately identified) traces of past experience that mediate favorable or unfavorable feeling, thought, or action toward social objects" (Greenwald & Banaji, 1995, p. 8). The present research, involving three experiments, examined the existence of implicit racial attitudes of Whites toward Blacks, investigated

John F. Dovidio, Kerry Kawakami, Craig Johnson, Brenda Johnson & Adaiah Howard, "On the Nature of Prejudice: Automatic and Controlled Processes," *Journal of Experimental Social Psychology*, vol. 33, no. 5, pp. 510–540. Copyright © 1997 by Elsevier Science & Technology Journals. Reprinted with permission.

the relationship between explicit measures of racial prejudice and implicit measures of attitudes, and explored the relationship of explicit and implicit attitudes to race-related responses and behaviors.

Although intuitively one might expect that unconscious activation of general associations or attitudes, as assessed in response latency paradigms, and self-reported prejudice may be rooted in the same experiences and socialization history and thus be directly related, research typically does not support this expectation (Banaji & Greenwald, 1995; Devine, 1989; Fazio, Jackson, Dunton, & Williams, 1995; Gaertner & McLaughlin, 1983). Theoretically, response latency measures and self-report measures may reflect the distinction between activation and application identified by Gilbert and Hixon (1991). The presentation of an attitude object may automatically activate an associated evaluation from memory (Fazio et al., 1995) which *may* influence subsequent judgments. However, as Gilbert and Hixon (1991) argue, automatic activation "does not mandate such use, nor does it determine the precise nature of its use. It is possible for activated information to exert no effect on subsequent judgments or to have a variety of different effects" (p. 512). Thus, it is quite possible that response latency measures of activation and self-report prejudice measures could be empirically unrelated.

A dissociation between response latency measures of implicit attitudes and self-reported attitudes may be likely to be observed for socially sensitive issues (Dovidio & Fazio, 1992) and particularly for racial attitudes. Devine (1989), for example, proposed that high- and low-prejudiced people are equally knowledgeable about cultural stereotypes about minority groups and similarly activate these stereotypes automatically with the real or symbolic presence of a member of that group. Low and high-prejudiced individuals differ, however, in their personal beliefs and their motivations to control the potential effects of the automatically activated cultural stereotypes. Lower prejudiced people are more motivated to control, suppress, and counteract their initial, automatic, biased reactions. Thus unconscious associations, which are culturally shared and automatically activated, may be disassociated from expressions of personal beliefs that are expressed on self-report measures of prejudice and systematically vary.

A dissociation between automatic responses and self-reported prejudice is also consistent with other conceptions of the current nature of racial prejudice among Whites, such as the aversive racism and the symbolic (or modern) racism framework. These frameworks suggest that, whereas traditional forms of prejudice are direct and overt, contemporary forms are indirect and subtle. Aversive racism (see Dovidio & Gaertner, 1991, 1997; Dovidio, Mann, & Gaertner, 1989; Gaertner & Dovidio, 1986; Kovel, 1970) has been identified as a modern form of prejudice that characterizes the racial attitudes of many Whites who endorse egalitarian values, who regard themselves as nonprejudiced, but who discriminate in subtle, rationalizable ways. According to the aversive racism perspective, many Whites who consciously and sincerely support egalitarian principles and believe themselves to be nonprejudiced also unconsciously harbor negative feelings and beliefs about Blacks, which may be based in part on almost unavoidable cognitive, motivational, and sociocultural processes (see Gaertner & Dovidio, 1986). These unconscious negative feelings and beliefs may be implicit attitudes, whereas the conscious, self-reported egalitarian attitudes of aversive racists may represent explicit attitudes.

According to symbolic racism theory (Sears, 1988) and its related variant modern racism theory (McConahay, 1986), negative feelings toward Blacks that Whites acquire early in life persist into adulthood but are expressed indirectly and symbolically, in terms of opposition to busing or resistance to preferential treatment, rather than directly or overtly, as in support for segregation. McConahay (1986) further proposes that because modern racism involves the rejection of traditional racist beliefs and the displacement of anti-Black feelings onto more abstract social and political issues, modern racists, like aversive racists, are relatively unaware of their racist feelings. This conception of prejudice, like the aversive racism framework, would also suggest a potential dissociation between explicit and implicit racial attitudes.

The first experiment in the present set of studies used a priming procedure to assess the implicit racial attitudes of Whites. The relationship between this implicit measure of attitudes and explicit, self-report measures of racial bias was also explored. The second experiment also assessed implicit and explicit racial attitudes but, in addition, investigated how well these measures predicted deliberative judgments (of the guilt of a Black defendant) and spontaneous reactions (in a word-completion task). The third experiment tested the relative predictive validity of implicit and explicit measures of racial attitudes on relatively deliberative ratings of Blacks and Whites and relatively spontaneous nonverbal behaviors during actual interracial interaction.

SUMMARY OF THE 3 EXPERIMENTS

Experiment 1

This experiment was designed to assess the implicit attitudes of Whites about Blacks and Whites. Previous research has demonstrated relationships between racial category primes and evaluations in response latency paradigms (e.g., Dovidio, Evans, & Tyler, 1986), but the research did not necessarily demonstrate automatic processes (Bargh, 1994; Greenwald & Banaji, 1995). Participants were made aware that the study focused on judgments about racial categories, and participants were aware of the potential relationships between the stimuli. In addition, the parameters used in the Dovidio et al. (1986) study (stimulus onset asynchronies of 2500 ms) may have permitted conscious processing, which could allow intentional suppression of negative attitudes within this paradigm (cf. Judd, Park, Ryan, Brauer, & Kraus, 1995). Thus, these findings may represent "controlled" rather than "automatic" processing (Posner & Snyder, 1975).

To examine automatic processes, the present study used a modified version of the subliminal priming procedure introduced by Perdue, Dovidio, Gurtman, and Tyler (1990, Experiment 3). In that experiment, ingroup and outgroup pronoun primes ("we" and "they") were presented very rapidly on a computer screen and then visually masked to prevent participants' awareness of the presence of the prime. The mask was a string of letters designed to cue the category "persons" or, in the control condition, "houses." Similarly to the priming task used by Dovidio et al. (1986), the participant's task was to decide whether the target word that followed could ever describe the cued category, persons or houses. Perdue et al. found that the masked ingroup prime that was presented outside of awareness facilitated responses, relative to the outgroup prime, to positive target words.

In the present experiment, the primes were schematic faces of Black and White men and women and a control prime (X), which were masked by figures representing the cued categories of persons and houses (see also Bargh & Chen, 1996). The target word stimuli were the evaluatively positive and negative non-stereotypical words used by Dovidio and Gaertner (1993) in their studies of racial associations and evaluations. The present study, using procedures that potentially offer evidence of automatic activation, was intended to complement the findings of Dovidio and Gaertner (1993) and Fazio et al. (1995), who used supraliminal priming techniques, demonstrating implicit bias in the racial attitudes of Whites. It was hypothesized that racial primes would automatically activate biased evaluations among White participants. Specifically, a Racial Prime X Target Word Favorability interaction was predicted such that participants would respond faster to positive words following a White prime than a Black prime and faster to negative words following a Black prime than a White prime. The relationship between explicit and implicit attitudes was also investigated. To examine whether the activation of implicit attitudes would be moderated by the participants' prejudice, participants also completed explicit (i.e., self-report) racial attitudes measures: Brigham's (1993) Attitudes Toward Blacks Scale and McConahay's (1986) Modern Racism scale.

Method

Participants. Participants were 12 White male and 12 White female undergraduates from a northeastern liberal arts college who participated to fulfill one option of a course requirement. These participants were recruited from a pool of 124 students who completed Brigham's (1993) 20-item Attitudes Toward Blacks Scale and a 5-item version of McConahay's (1986) Modern Racism Scale at the beginning of the semester. Item responses were assessed on 5-point Likert scales. For this sample of 124 students, the Cronbach a for the Attitudes Toward Blacks Scale was .87 and for the Modern Racism Scale was .78. The correlation between these two scales was .74.

Procedure. Participants were informed by a White female experimenter that the study examined how people categorize people and objects. Test stimuli for the categorization task that represented positive and negative nonstereotypic characteristics were based on previous research. Three positive and three negative traits that had been pretested for nonstereotypicality and for favorability (−3 to + 3) were used. These were the same stimuli employed by Dovidio and Gaertner (1993) and by Perdue et al. (1990, Experiment 3). The three positive traits were good (mean evaluation = +2.15), kind (mean evaluation = +2.25), and trustworthy (mean evaluation = +2.65); the three negative characteristics were bad (mean evaluation = −2.30), cruel (mean evaluation = −2.65), and untrustworthy (mean evaluation = −2.20).

The main experiment used a procedure that was a variation of a subliminal priming procedure employed by Perdue et al. (1990, Experiment 3), which combined the method of Dovidio et al. (1986), who studied stereotypic and evaluative associations of racial categories, with the method of Bargh and Pietromonaco (1982), who investigated subliminal influences on impression formation. Specifically, participants in the Perdue et al. (1990) study were informed that the study examined "how quickly and accurately people categorize objects and persons." In that experiment, they were told that either the letter string PPPPP, which represented the category *person,* or the letter string HHHHH, which symbolized the category *house,* would be presented on a computer screen and followed by an adjective (the test stimuli). The responses to the person category were of primary theoretical interest.

Perdue et al. (1990) also incorporated into their method procedures for subliminal priming (see Bargh & Pietromonaco, 1982) using an ingroup designator (we), an outgroup designator (they), and a control prime (xxx) that preceded a person category (PPPPPP) or a house category (HHHHHH) cue. The distance from the participant's eyes to the center of the CRT, where the fixation point (*) was situated, was set at 56 cm so that the prime stimuli would be presented outside the participant's foveal visual field. Sequentially, participants were (a) initially presented for 75 ms with a subliminal prime (e.g., we, they, or xxx) that was located 3.6 cm to the left or right of the fixation point, (b) presented for 250 ms with a target category cue, PPPPPP for a person or HHHHHH for a house, that visually masked the initial prime, (c) presented with a test word that did or did not commonly describe a person (e.g., drafty), and (d) asked to indicate by pressing the appropriate key (yes or no) whether a test word could ever describe a member of the cued category (i.e., a person or a house).

In the present study, the priming stimuli were schematic faces of Black and White men and women. These stimuli were constructed using Mac-a-Mug software. Two Black male faces, two White male faces, two Black female faces, and two White female faces were systematically constructed to be comparable (at least based on self-reported rating involving 30 White students) in perceived attractiveness, intelligence, friendliness, and likability. Samples of these faces are presented in Fig. 1. These faces, along with a control prime of X, replaced the word primes (we, they, and xxx) used by Perdue et al. (1990). In addition, based on pretesting, the exposure time for these primes was substantially shortened. The exposure time was limited by the hardware used to administer the stimuli, a Power Macintosh 7200 (75 MHz). Specifically, the refresh rate of the monitor resulted in a minimum presentation time of 15 ms and a maximum of 30 ms. These times are similar to those used for the subliminal presentation of photographs of African American and Caucasian faces by Bargh and Chen (1996) using a Gateway 486 computer with a VGA color monitor (13–26 ms). The 2 X 1.75 in. facial primes in the present study were immediately masked by geometrical figures, a "P" within an oval signifying a *person* or an "H" within a rectangle representing a *house*, occupying the same area. Geometrical figures were used as visual masks rather than letter strings (e.g., PPPPPP) in order to fully cover the area of the screen occupied by the facial primes. The cued category, which visually masked the facial or control prime, appeared on the screen for 250 ms. Then the test word (a positive or negative word or one of the six words that do not normally describe persons) was presented until the participant pressed the decision key, or up to 750 ms. There was a 1.5 s interval between trials.

These exposure times were selected, in part, to produce short SOAs (<300 ms) between the initial facial or control prime and the test word, which have been identified as a parameter for eliciting automatic (vs controlled) responses with supraliminal presentations (Banaji & Hardin, 1996; Neely, 1977, 1991). Whereas the short SOAs were used to create conditions requiring efficient processing, subliminal priming was used to establish the automatic criterion of unawareness (Bargh, 1994).

Overall, the experiment consisted of 120 trials. Sixty trials were of theoretical interest. Each of the six person-descriptive words was paired with one White female, one Black female, one White male, and one Black male face presented once to the left of the fixation point and once to the right of the fixation point (48 trials), and each person-descriptive word was paired with the control (X) prime once to the left and once to the right of the fixation point (12 trials). Six house-descriptors (drafty, furnished, leaky,

Figure 1. Samples of schematic faces used as priming stimuli.

roomy, thatch, wooden) were used for the 60 distractor trials (48 trials pairing non-person descriptors with the face primes, plus 12 trials with the control prime). Participants were familiarized with the procedure and equipment before participating. To allow participants to become familiar with the task, the first six trials were arranged not to be trials of theoretical interest. Two orders of trials were used across subjects; one was a randomly determined order (except for the first six trials) and the other was the reverse order. In addition, the locations of the "yes" and "no" keys (Z and M on the keyboard) were counter-balanced across subjects.

The primary dependent measure was the response latency of each prime-category-test word combination. An error was scored if the participant gave no response to one of the person-descriptive test words on a trial in which the person category was cued (the P within the oval symbol) or if, following the person-category cue, the participant indicated that the person-descriptive test word could not describe a person. Response latencies for the trials of theoretical interest that were three or more standard deviations beyond each participant's mean response times were identified as outliers (less than 2.5% of the distribution of response times) and excluded from the analysis; the remaining response times were subjected to a logarithmic transformation (see Blair & Banaji, 1996; Ratcliff, 1993). The transformed values associated with each of the three positive and negative stimulus words were averaged, and deviation scores were created by subtracting the transformed response latencies for the positive and negative control prime conditions from the times for each of the four face-prime conditions (reflecting the Race X Sex of prime combinations). Analyses were conducted on the transformed data, but the untransformed means (in ms) are presented in figures and reported in the text.

To determine whether participants were, in fact, unaware of the subliminal primes (Greenwald, Klinger, & Liu, 1989), participants were probed about the masked primes during debriefing. No participant reported that he or she had seen a face prime. In addition, a pilot guessing study (see Bargh & Pietromonaco, 1982; Perdue et al., 1990) was conducted in which 12 participants were run through a 48-trial procedure similar to the main experiment but were asked to guess what the initial prime was. Comparable to the rates reported by Bargh and Pietromonaco (1982), Devine (1989), and Perdue et al. (1990) with words as primes, on only 17 of the 576 trials (3%) did these participants accurately identify the prime. These data support the results of the debriefing and indicate that the conditions for automatic priming without conscious awareness were met.

Results

Preliminary analysis revealed an overall error rate that was low (<2%) and not systematically related to the experimental conditions. A 2 (Participant Sex) X 2 (Stimulus Order) X 2 (Race of Facial Prime: White and Black) X 2 (Sex of Facial Prime) X 2 (Favorability of Target Word: Positive and Negative) analysis of variance with repeated measures on the last three independent variables was performed on the deviation scores from baseline. The predicted Race Prime X Target Word Favorability interaction was obtained, $F(1, 20) = 7.32$, $p < .014$, uncomplicated by any higher-order interactions. The untransformed means for the White, Black, and control prime conditions are illustrated in Fig. 2. Planned comparisons revealed, as predicted, that response times to negative target words were significantly faster following the Black than following the White prime, Ms = 795 vs 908 ms, Deviation Ms = −72 vs +41 ms, $t(23) = 3.91$, $p < .001$. This effect seemed to reflect a facilitation effect relative to the control condition for the Black prime. Response times to negative words were faster following the Black prime than the control (X) prime, $t(23) = 2.89$, $p < .008$; there was no significant difference in response times between the White prime and the control prime conditions, $p > .44$. Also as predicted, response times to positive words were significantly shorter following the White than following the Black prime, Ms = 701 vs 755 ms, Deviation Ms = −123 vs −69 ms, $t(23) = 2.26$, $p < .033$. This result reflected primarily a facilitating effect for the White prime. Response times to positive words were significantly faster following the White prime than following the control prime, $t(23) = 4.16$, $p < .001$. Response times were somewhat but not significantly ($p > .10$) faster following the Black prime than the control prime (see Fig. 2).

To examine the relationship between explicit measures of prejudice and response latency measures of attitudes, scores on the Attitudes Toward Blacks Scale (mean = 2.89, $SD = 0.32$) and on the Modern Racism Scale (mean = 1.57, $SD = 0.50$) were correlated with response latency measures of bias. The

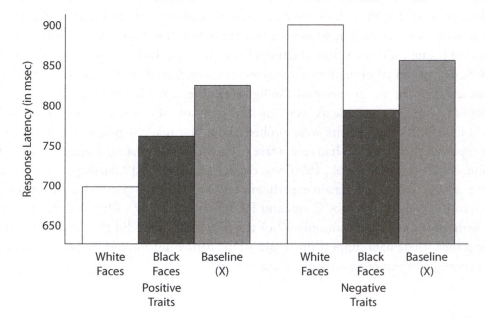

Figure 2. Experiment 1: The effects of racial prime and target word favorability on response latencies.

primary measure used in this and in the subsequent experiments represented the degree to which participants responded faster to negative words following the Black prime than following the White prime, combined with the degree to which participants responded faster to positive words following the White prime than following the Black prime. This measure is the weighted combination (i.e., +1, − 1, − 1, +1) of response latencies associated with the Race Prime X Target Word Favorability interaction for each participant. Higher scores indicate greater racial bias. This response latency measures was somewhat, but not significantly, correlated with Modern Racism scores $(r[22] = .15, p = .48)$ and Attitudes Toward Blacks scores $(r[22] = .28, p = .19)$. In addition, four supplementary measures were computed for this and the subsequent studies representing each of the four possible simple effects for the 2 X 2 interaction. As illustrated in Table 1, the correlations between these measures and Modern and Old-Fashioned Racism were of similar magnitude and also not statistically significant.

Discussion

The results of Experiment 1 complement the findings of Dovidio and Gaertner (1993) and Fazio et al. (1995), who found evidence of implicit negative racial attitudes among Whites toward Blacks using supraliminal priming techniques. As predicted, in Experiment 1 White participants responded faster to positive words following a White prime than following a Black prime and faster to negative words following a Black than following a White prime. Furthermore, the use of facial primes rather than

TABLE 1. Correlations between Response Latency Measures of Bias and Self-Report Measures of PREJUDICE

Response latency measures of bias	Experiment one		Experiment two		Experiment three	
	Modern racism scale	Attitudes toward blacks scale	Modern racism scale	Old-fashioned racism scale	Modern racism scale	Old-fashioned racisms scale
1. Combination of faster for positive words following a White prime and to negative words following a Black prime	+.15, $p < .48$	+.28, $p < .19$	+.60, $p < .01$	+.49, $p < .01$	+.01, $p < .98$	-.07, $p < .71$
2. Faster to negative relative to positive words following a Black prime	+.17, $p < .44$	+.25, $p < .23$	+.42, $p < .02$	+.33, $p < .07$	-.02, $p < .90$	-.02, $p < .92$
3. Faster to positive relative to negative words following a White prime	+.03, $p < .89$	+.13, $p < .56$	+.42, $p < .02$	+.35, $p < .06$	+.03, $p < .86$	-.05, $p < .78$
4. Faster to negative words following a Black prime than following a White prime	-.01, $p < .98$	+.09, $p < .67$	-.13, $p < .47$	-.22, $p < .24$	+.04, $p < .84$	-.08, $p < .68$
5. Faster to positive words following a White prime than following a Black prime	+.21, $p < .32$	+.30, $p < .16$	+.69, $p < .01$	+.62, $p < .01$	-.03, $p < .87$	-.01, $p < .94$

semantic primes (e.g., Blacks, Whites) provides more direct evidence that these are implicit *racial* attitudes, not simply connotations of the colors black and white (Williams, Tucker, & Dunham, 1971).

The response latency measures of evaluative activation, representing implicit racial attitudes, were only weakly correlated with explicit measures of prejudice. This finding is consistent with the results of Fazio et al. (1995) and offers further evidence of implicit evaluative biases that may not be predicted from self-report measures of prejudice. This dissociation between explicit and implicit measures of racial bias is also consistent with the contemporary perspectives on racial attitudes, such as Devine's (1989) disassociation framework, the aversive racism perspective (Gaertner & Dovidio, 1986), and symbolic (Sears, 1988) and modern racism (McConahay, 1986) theories.

If there is a dissociation between explicit and implicit attitudes, as the work of Fazio et al. (1995) and Experiment 1 suggest, then self-report and response latency measures of attitudes may differentially predict race-related behaviors. For example, as proposed by Fazio et al. (1995), response latency techniques may represent "an indirect, unobtrusive measure of attitude" (p. 1014). Alternatively, self-reported attitudes and response latency measures of attitudes may both be valid measures of attitudes (one conscious, the other unconscious) that predict different types of behaviors. Experiment 2 therefore further explored the implicit racial attitudes and the relative predictive validity of self-report and response latency measures on race-related responses.

Experiment 2

Research concerning attitudes as predictors of behavior has moved from the issue of *whether* there is a relationship to *what* the nature of that relationship is (Fazio, 1990; Zanna & Fazio, 1982). The nature of the attitude-behavior relationship may be affected by the way attitudes are measured and the type of behavior that is being examined. With respect to measuring attitudes, Dovidio and Fazio (1992) have argued that one difficulty in assessing attitudes for socially sensitive issues, such as racial prejudice, is that people may consciously alter their responses to conform to prevailing norms (Gaertner & Dovidio, 1986). With respect to behavior, Fazio (1990) proposed that there are fundamental differences between behavioral responses that are based on conscious deliberation (involving an analysis of costs and benefits) and responses that are based on spontaneous reaction to an attitude object or issue. Experiment 2 examined how conscious (explicit) and nonconscious (implicit) racial attitudes predict Whites' spontaneous and deliberative interracial responses.

Theoretically, racial attitudes may be examined at three different levels. First, there may be *public* attitudes. Individuals may publicly express socially desirable (nonprejudiced) attitudes even though they are aware that they privately hold other, more negative attitudes (Sigall & Page, 1971; Roese & Jamieson, 1993). Direct measures of traditional racist attitudes, such as McConahay's (1986) Old-Fashioned Racism Scale, are very susceptible to this type of impression management and thus may reflect this type of orientation (McConahay, Hardee, & Batts, 1981). Second, there may be *personal, conscious* aspects of racial attitudes. In contrast to public attitudes that are related to impression management, these personal attitudes are influenced by an individual's private standards and ideals (Devine

& Monteith, 1993). For example, according to the aversive racism perspective (Gaertner & Dovidio, 1986), Whites may express attitudes that are consistent with their nonprejudiced self-image but that do not reflect their *un*conscious negative feelings toward Blacks. Indirect self-report measures of prejudice, such as McConahay's (1986) Modern Racism Scale, have been designed to minimize public impression management and produce a more valid measure of personal attitudes (cf. Fazio et al., 1995). Modern racism is presumed to be a more subtle manifestation of prejudice in that bias is expressed in rationalizable ways that do not challenge a person's nonprejudiced self-image (see, however, Fazio et al., 1995). At a third level are *implicit* attitudes (Greenwald & Banaji, 1995), unconscious feelings and beliefs which are often different from personal or public attitudes (Experiment 1; see also Fazio et al., 1995). As illustrated in Experiment 1, response latency techniques may be used to assess implicit attitudes.

Which level represents a White person's "true" racial attitude? We propose that each of these levels represents a "true" aspect of an attitude and that the central question should be instead, "Which aspect of an attitude best predicts which type of behavior?" Our general position, which is guided by Fazio's MODE Model, is that implicit (unconscious) aspects of an attitude will best predict spontaneous behavior (see also Bargh & Chen, 1996), personal attitudes will best predict private but controlled responses (Crosby, Bromley, & Saxe, 1980), and public aspects of attitudes should best predict behavior in situations in which social desirability factors are salient. This framework is consistent with Fazio et al.'s (1995) recent research demonstrating the predictive validity of response-latency measures of racial attitudes. Direct ratings concerning the legitimacy of the Rodney King verdict and the illegitimacy of the anger of the Black community were correlated mainly with self-reported prejudice (Modern Racism); these responses did not correlate with the response-latency measure. However, the response-latency measure correlated more highly with the *relative* responsibility ascribed to Blacks and Whites for the tension and violence that ensued after the verdict, perhaps a more subtle and indirect manifestation of racial bias, than did the Modern Racism scores. Experiment 2 examined, in particular, the relationships among Old-Fashioned, Modern, and response-latency measures of Whites' racial attitudes and spontaneous and deliberative race-related decisions.

The study involved two ostensibly unrelated parts: (1) measures of racial attitudes and (2) race-related decisions. The measures of racial attitudes included the response-latency task of Experiment 1 and two self-report measures. The self-report measures were McConahay's (1986) Old-Fashioned Racism Scale, which assesses overt bias, and Modern Racism Scale, which was designed to be an indirect measure of subtle personal prejudice. The decision-making part of the present research included tasks that varied along a deliberative-spontaneous dimension (Fazio, 1990). Two of the tasks involved juridic judgments of the guilt or innocence of Black male defendants. These are deliberative tasks and, based on pilot research, perceived as public measures of racial attitudes. Spontaneous responses were measured in a variation of Gilbert and Hixon's (1991) word completion task. Participants performed this task under the "cognitive busy" conditions used by Gilbert and Hixon (1991, Expt. 1) while alternating decision tasks. On alternate trials, participants classified faces presented on a computer as Black (African American) or White (which served as a prime for the following trial) and completed words by pressing an appropriate key (e.g., an "a" or "u" to complete "B_D"). The measure of racial bias was the extent to which participants created more negative words following Black than White faces.

It was predicted that the response latency measure of implicit attitudes would predict answers to the word-completion task. This task requires rapid and relatively spontaneous responses under demanding circumstances that likely inhibit conscious control of responses motivated by social desirability concerns or the desire to maintain personal egalitarian standards. As Fazio et al. (1995) posited, "It is for such relatively uncontrollable classes of behavior that the effects of any automatically activated personal evaluations are likely to be most apparent" (p. 1020). Alternatively, it was hypothesized in the present experiment that self-report measures of prejudice would significantly predict juridic judgments, for which motivations to comply with both social norms and personal standards of egalitarianism would be salient, and there would be ample time to consider these factors in formulating a response. For this task, participants would have both the opportunity and motivation (see Fazio, 1990) to act in a manner consistent with their professed racial attitudes.

Method

Participants. Twenty White male and 13 White female first- and second-year undergraduates participated to complete one option of a course requirement.

Procedure. The study consisted of two, ostensibly unrelated, parts. Participants were informed that the two parts were being conducted by different groups working on different research projects. Participants were further informed that students were scheduled for both studies because each took one-half hour to complete; performing both would enable the participant to earn a full hour's research participation credit.

The first part of the study was again introduced by a White female experimenter as an experiment about how people categorize persons and objects. It closely resembled the priming procedure used in Experiment 1. The major differences were that (1) the control prime (X) was not included in order to reduce the amount of time participants performed the priming task, and (2) only male faces were used as primes, to be consistent with the juridic judgments in the second phase of the experiment that involved only male defendants. Theoretically, group stereotypes may be associated more strongly with men than with women (Eagly & Kite, 1987) and possibly intergroup attitudes, but no differences for sex of the target were obtained in Experiment 1. The test stimuli were exactly the same: three positive traits (good, kind, and trustworthy), three negative characteristics (bad, cruel, and untrustworthy), and the six nonperson descriptors. The same instructions and parameters for the presentation of the stimuli were also used. The elimination of the control prime reduced the number of trials presented from 120 in Experiment 1 to 96 in this experiment. The 48 trials of theoretical interest involved each of the six person-descriptive words paired twice with each White male and Black male face presented, once paired on the left of the fixation point and once on the right of the fixation point. Two female participants reported during debriefing that they saw some face primes during the task. Their data were excluded from subsequent analyses. Response latencies for the trials of theoretical interest that were three or more standard deviation points beyond each participant's mean response times were identified as outliers (less than 2.0% of the distribution of response times) and excluded from the analysis. The remaining response times were log transformed. The transformed values associated with each of the three positive and negative stimulus words were averaged for Black and White prime conditions.

Following the priming task, participants completed an "opinion questionnaire" that included a 7-item Old-Fashioned Racism Scale (McConahay, 1986) and a 7-item Modern Racism Scale. Participants responded to these items on 5-point Likert scales. For the participants in this study, the Cronbach a was .79 for the Old-Fashioned Racism Scale (M = 1.55, SD = .64) and .88 for the Modern Racism Scale (M = 1.85, SD = .86).

After completing this phase of the study, participants were escorted by another White female experimenter to a cubicle in another part of the research area. They were then informed that this project investigated how people make decisions about others under different circumstances. This second session involved two types of tasks presented in counterbalanced order across subjects. One set of tasks, which was intended to foster deliberative decision-making, involved simulated juridic judgments. Participants were informed that the "purpose of this part of the study is to learn more about how individuals make decisions about jurors. You will be presented with two cases and asked to indicate a verdict for each. … For each case, you have been given a summary of the crime, the prosecution's evidence, and the defense's evidence. Please read the materials carefully." The cases were adapted from materials used in studies by Bodenhausen and Lichtenstein (1987) and Faranda and Gaertner (1979). Judgments were reported on 11-point scales ranging from 0, indicating "definitely innocent," to 10, indicating "definitely guilty." One case involved "a 30-year-old Black man" who was a defendant in a robbery and murder case in which the victims were a White storekeeper and his granddaughter. The defendant was identified by a witness who "had been standing in the backroom during the robbery" and who later pursued the assailant and "reported seeing the robber run into an apartment house two blocks away." The other case involved "a 27-year-old Black male" defendant who was accused of attacking a White man in an alley behind a bar. The victim and defendant "were observed quarrelling by other bar patrons earlier in the evening," and the defendant "was seen leaving the bar about 10 minutes before the attack occurred." Responses to these two cases were positively correlated, r(29) = .39, p < .032, and were averaged together for subsequent analyses.

The other task in this phase of the research, which was designed to assess more spontaneous responses, was a word-completion task based on the method used by Gilbert and Hixon (1991). In the cognitive-busy condition of Gilbert and Hixon's (1991, Experiment 1) study, participants were asked to complete word stems (e.g., N_P) while attempting to remember an 8-digit number. Participants in the present study were informed that this segment of the session involved sequentially making decisions on two different and unrelated tasks, a "multiple decision task." It was explained that in many occupations (such as air-traffic controller) it is necessary for people to handle "simultaneous task demands." The task used in the present study was a variation of Gilbert and Hixon's (1991) cognitive-busy procedure in which participants were asked to remember an 8-digit number while performing the word-completion task. In addition, cognitive demand was created by asking participants to perform two different tasks sequentially on alternate trials under limited time constraint. These tasks were presented on the computer screen. The first task in each pair required the participant to categorize a male schematic face (including the same faces used as the primes in the response latency study) as Black or White by pressing an appropriate key. This task was used to provide a racial prime. The second task in each pair, which immediately followed the participant's response on the categorization task, was to complete a word by typing in the missing letter. Participants had 10 s to make this decision before the next trial began.

The response of interest was whether the participant provided a letter that completed a positive or negative word. Word stems were chosen based on pretesting (see Gilbert & Hixon, 1991) that indicated that they could be completed as positive, neutral, or negative words (i.e., with more than one probable answer). For example, B_D completed with an "a" would produce a negative word, but completed with an "i" would produce a neutral word. The word stem "LO_AL" could be completed with a "y" creating a positive word or a "c" creating a neutral word. There were 24 word stems of this type, 12 paired with a Black face and 12 paired with a White face. The pairings were counterbalanced across two sets of stimuli. The word stems that were used were HA_E, RU_E, PRO_ANE, _IGHT, _URE, _INISTER, LO_D, GO_D, POLI_E, BU_, MA_, _ITY, W_RM, _AGE, WI_E, S_ORT, LA_Y, _RUNK, CLEA_, B_D, S_AVE, MEA_, LO_AL, and POO_. A pool of potential word completions were generated during pretesting, and these responses were then identified by participants in the pilot study *(n = 12)* as positive, negative, or neutral words. Two raters, unaware of the primed racial category, coded the word completions of each participant in the present study as a positive (+ 1), neutral (0), or negative (−1) from this predetermined list of potential word completions. When a word completion occurred that was not on the list (approximately 2% of the time), the coders reached agreement on the score assigned. Scores for the words paired with Black and White faces were separately summed and then subtracted from one another. More positive scores represented more positive word completions following the White faces (or, alternatively, more negative scores following Black faces).

Results

The analyses examined results for the priming task, then the relationships among explicit and implicit measures of prejudice, and finally the relationship between the explicit and implicit measures of prejudice and participants' judgments of guilt of Black defendants and race-related differences in word completions.

Priming and response latencies. Preliminary analysis demonstrated that the overall error rate was low (3.0%) and not systematically related to the experimental conditions. For the latency measure, the 2 (Participant Sex) X 2 (Stimulus Order) X 2 (Race of Facial Prime: White and Black) X 2 (Favorability of Target Word: Positive and Negative) analysis of variance, with repeated measures on the last two independent variables demonstrated the predicted Race Prime X Target Word Favorability interaction, $F(1, 27) = 5.51$, $p < .026$. This effect was uncomplicated by any higher-order interactions. As anticipated, response times to negative target words were significantly faster following the Black prime than following the White prime, $Ms = 751$ vs 883 ms, $t(30) = 4.16$, $p < .001$. Response times were slightly, but not significantly, faster to positive words following the White primes than following the Black primes, $Ms = 660$ vs 663 ms, $p > .62$.

Implicit and explicit measures of prejudice. Unlike Experiment 1 and previous research (e.g., Fazio et al., 1995), there were positive correlations between the explicit measures of prejudice employed in this experiment and response-latency measures of bias (see Table 1). In particular, the primary response-latency measure of bias correlated .60 ($p < .01$) with Modern Racism and .49 ($p < .01$) with Old-Fashioned Racism. Old-Fashioned Racism and Modern Racism were highly related, r(29) = .78, $p < .001$.

Prejudice, juridic judgments, and word completions. Beyond providing a replication of Experiment 1, the primary focus of this experiment was to investigate the relationships between implicit and explicit measures of bias and subsequent race-related judgments. It was hypothesized that explicit measures of prejudice would primarily predict the deliberative juridic judgments whereas response-latency bias (represented by the sum of the two components—the extent that participants responded slower to positive words and faster to negative words after a Black prime than a White prime) would predict the results of the word-completion task, which required more spontaneous actions. The pattern of Pearson correlations was generally consistent with these hypotheses. Ratings of Black defendant guilt across the two cases was significantly related to Old-Fashioned Racism scores, r(29) = .51, $p < .003$, and Modern Racism scores, r(29) = .38, $p < .033$, but not to response-latency bias, $r = .02$. In contrast, response-latency bias was correlated with more negative word completions following Black than following White faces, r(29) = .48, $p < .007$, whereas Old-Fashioned Racism, r(29) = .10, $p < .583$, and Modern Racism, r(29) = .14, $p < .462$, did not. Ratings of guilt and word-completion bias were nonsignificantly, negatively related, r(29) = -.15, $p < .423$.

In addition, to evaluate the predictions, regression equations were computed in which the dependent variables were, separately, ratings of guilt and wordcompletion bias, and the independent variables were Old-Fashioned Racism scores, Modern Racism scores, and response-latency bias considered simultaneously. For the equation for ratings of guilt, $F(3, 27) = 4.68$, $p < .01$, Old-Fashioned Racism was the only significant predictor, $\beta = .56$, $p < .034$. Modern Racism had a nonsignificant positive relation, $\beta = .15$, $p = .582$, and response-latency bias had a nonsignificant negative effect, $\beta = -.35$, $p = .082$. For word-completion bias, F(3, 27) = 43.41, $p < .04$, response-latency bias was the only significant predictor, $\beta = .63$, $p < .005$. When the predictor variables were considered simultaneously, Old-Fashioned Racism ($\beta = -.04$, $p = .871$) and Modern Racism ($\beta = -.20$, $p = .483$) had nonsignificant negative relations.[1] These findings are consistent with predictions.

---

[1]Because of the high correlations among the three predictor variables (i.e., Modern Racism, Old-Fashioned Racism, and response latency bias), supplementary analyses were performed. These analyses do not alter the conclusions from the primary analyses. For ratings of guilt, for example, the p for response latency bias was .01 ($p = .948$) when it was the only predictor variable. This finding suggests that the marginally significant p of $-.35$ ($p = .082$) that was obtained when all three predictors were considered simultaneously may be an artifact of multicollinearity among the independent variables. Regression analyses were also performed entering only one of the explicit measures of prejudice (i.e., Modern or Old-Fashioned Racism) simultaneously with the response latency measure. The results are the same except that when Modern Racism is considered without Old-Fashioned Racism, it is a significant predictor of ratings of Black defendant guilt, p = .58, $p < .010$.

Discussion

The results were consistent with our predictions and supported a multidimensional view of racial attitudes. Explicit and implicit racial attitudes predicted race-related decisions—but different ones. As expected, ratings of the guilt of a black defendant were correlated most strongly with Old-Fashioned Racism ratings but also significantly with Modern Racism. As with Fazio et al.'s (1995) findings for ratings about the Rodney King verdict, ratings of guilt were not predicted by the response-latency measure. In contrast, bias in the wordcompletion task, a more spontaneous type of response, was significantly predicted by response-latency scores and not by either self-report measure of prejudice. The relationship between the response-latency measure of bias and the wordcompletion task, which was performed with a high level of cognitive busyness, reflects the efficiency of implicit attitude activation. Efficiency, defined as a process requiring few attentional resources, is a fundamental quality of automatic activation (Bargh, 1994).

Experiment 2, which generally replicated the pattern of bias in implicit racial attitudes of Experiment 1, extends our previous research and complements the conclusions of Fazio et al. (1995) by demonstrating that variability in response latencies may reflect systematic and meaningful individual differences in implicit attitudes. However, we note some inconsistencies and limitations in the results. First, although it is plausible that implicit and explicit measures of attitudes may correlate to some extent, particularly if they are rooted in common experiences and socialization, the magnitude of the correlation of response-latency bias with Modern and Old-Fashioned Racism scores was unexpectedly high given the results of Experiment 1, other previous research (Fazio et al., 1995), and the demonstrations of dissociations between implicit and explicit cognition more generally (Wegner & Bargh, 1997). Second, we recognize that although our results were consistent with predictions derived from Fazio's (1990) MODE Model, our findings are preliminary, and support should be interpreted with some caution. Deliberative and spontaneous behaviors, in general, are difficult to define theoretically or operationally and may involve other dimensions. In the present study, for example, the juridic judgment tasks and the word-completion task differed along the deliberative/spontaneous dimension but varied also in terms of the nature of the decision (e.g., legal and person-specific vs category-based). One possible interpretation might be that implicit attitudes are irrelevant when it comes to important social behaviors, for which self-reported attitudes are important. In addition, although judgments like those reflected in simulated juridic decisions have been used as behavioral intentions in previous research (e.g., Brigham, 1971), they may not fully represent the responses that might occur during actual trials (Costanzo & Costanzo, 1994) or in more common face-to-face interaction. However, indicating some degree of external validity, the results of analog studies of racial biases in juridic decisions generally parallel the findings of archival research on the outcomes of actual court cases (Johnson, 1985). Furthermore, although a measure of spontaneous response, it could be reasonably argued the Gilbert and Hixon (1991) word-fragment completion task reflects another measure of racial prejudice more than it does discriminatory behavior. Even so, the significant correlation between the response-latency measure and word-completion responses and the weak relationship between the self-report measures of racial attitudes and word-completion responses offer some support for the implicit-explicit attitude dichotomy outlined by Greenwald and Banaji (1995). Nevertheless, given the plausible alternative interpretations of Experiment 2 and the disparity in correlations between implicit and explicit measures of attitudes in the first two experiments, a third study was performed that again used response latency and self-report measures of prejudice but involved responses to specific black and white persons in face-to-face interaction.

Experiment 3

This third experiment investigated how implicit and explicit measures of racial attitudes may differentially predict the responses of White participants to Black and White partners during face-to-face interaction. As a measure of explicit attitudes, participants were asked to evaluate both other interactants on a series of rating scales. Such direct measures have been identified as being reactive measures that are sensitive to racial concerns and can produce deliberative attempts to appear nonprejudiced among people motivated to appear so (Crosby et al., 1980; Dovidio & Fazio, 1992; Gaertner & Dovidio, 1986; Sigall & Page, 1971). Nonverbal behaviors were used to represent more spontaneous forms of behavior. As Fazio et al. (1995) propose, "Nonverbal behavior, in particular, may be subject to 'leakage' of negativity that an individual is experiencing, despite the individual's effort to behave in a nonprejudiced manner" (p. 1026).

Crosby et al. (1980) identified nonverbal behavior as a viable, unobtrusive measure of racial attitudes. They note, "Because nonverbal behavior generally lies outside of conscious awareness and control, nonverbal behavior may be considered less subject to social desirability effects than are verbal attitude reports" (p. 555). Consistent with this assumption, their review of the literature revealed, first, that there was stronger evidence of racial bias among studies using nonverbal measures than those using self-report measures, and second, that for studies employing both types of measures there was a dissociation between verbal and nonverbal measures. Crosby et al. concluded that the "nonverbal behavior studies of racism imply that whites still discriminate against blacks in terms of behaviors that lie largely out of awareness. This is true even for whites who do not discriminate in terms of behaviors that fall under more conscious control, such as verbal reports" (p. 556). We acknowledge that nonverbal behaviors can be deliberately regulated with some success, and this control can be improved by practice, experience, and knowledge (DePaulo, 1992; DePaulo & Friedman, 1997). Nevertheless, people generally monitor and control their nonverbal behaviors less frequently and effectively than they do their verbal behaviors (Harper, 1985). Thus, nonverbal behaviors represent *relatively* spontaneous social behaviors.

Participants in Experiment 3 took part in two ostensibly unrelated sessions. The first session, as in Experiment 2, was designed to assess implicit and explicit racial attitudes. The second session was described as part of an interview requirement for a psychology course. During this session, participants were asked to discuss a series of questions presented by a Black female and a White female interviewer who behaved in a preprogrammed, well-rehearsed manner. At the end of the session, the participants were asked to evaluate both interviewers—a deliberative response to these particular people. In addition, the session was videotaped and participants' nonverbal behaviors were later coded. These behaviors represented relatively spontaneous reactions to the interviewers.

In particular, two measures of nonverbal behavior were studied in Experiment 3. One was visual contact or gaze. Higher levels of visual contact (i.e., percent of time spent looking at another) reflect greater attraction (Exline, 1972; Kleinke, 1986; Kleinke, Meeker, & LaFong, 1974; Harper, 1985), intimacy (Rubin, 1970), and respect (Dovidio, Brown, Heltman, Ellyson, & Keating, 1988; Efran, 1968; Efran & Broughton, 1966; Fugita, 1974). The other measure was blinking. Higher rates of blinking have been demonstrated to be related to higher levels of negative arousal and tension (Doering, 1957; Exline, 1985; Kanfer, 1960). Both of these nonverbal behaviors are particularly difficult to monitor and control (see Ellyson & Dovidio, 1985).

Following the rationale developed for Experiment 2, it was predicted that the explicit measures of prejudice, Modern and Old-Fashioned Racism, would primarily predict bias in the evaluations of Black relative to White interviewers. In contrast, the response-latency measure of negative racial attitude was expected to be the best predictor of nonverbal reactions—specifically higher rates of blinking and lower percentages of visual contact with the Black relative to the White interviewer.

Method

Participants. Participants were 14 White male and 19 White female second-, third-, and fourth-year undergraduates who were paid five dollars for their participation.

Procedure. This study also consisted of two supposedly unrelated parts. Participants were informed that the two parts were being conducted by different experimenters who were pooling their funds to recruit participants.

The first session was again introduced by a White female experimenter as an experiment about how people categorize persons and objects. Its procedures and materials were identical to those used in Experiment 2. Participants performed the priming task first and then completed the "opinion questionnaire" that included a 7-item Old-Fashioned Racism Scale (McConahay, 1986) and a 7-item Modern Racism Scale. Participants responded to these items on 5-point Likert scales. The Cronbach a for participants in this study was .69 for the Modern Racism Scale. The Cronbach a for the Old-Fashioned Racism Scale for this sample was unexpectedly low, .32, perhaps due to the restricted range of responses. The mean score on the 1–5 scale was 1.28 with a standard deviation of 0.34. Two-thirds of the respondents had scores of 1.00, 1.14, or 1.28—the three lowest possible scores. The mean score for the Modern Racism Scale was 1.67, with a standard deviation of 0.51. Old-Fashioned and Modern Racism scores were highly correlated, r(31) = .74, p < .001.

After completing the first phase of the research, participants were met by a second White female experimenter and escorted to another room to begin an ostensibly unrelated study. They were informed that this session was part of an "interview practicum" for a psychology class and that they would be interviewed by one or more advanced psychology students. The experimenter presented an overview of the procedure and explained that the session would be videotaped for later evaluation. The room contained two chairs separated by a 3-ft-square table. One camera was situated behind the participant's chair and directed toward the interviewer's chair; another camera was located behind the interviewer's chair and directed toward the participant's chair. These images and the conversation were recorded using equipment in an adjacent cubicle.

After answering any questions the participant posed, the experimenter announced that she would now get the interviewer. Each participant interacted with two interviewers, one Black female and one White female college student, in counterbalanced order across participants. Two different pairs of Black and White interviewers were used in the present research. Each interviewer asked the participant to respond to one question or situation. These tasks were pretested to insure that they were involving and generated fairly lengthy responses and that men and women (as well as Blacks and Whites) would report being and be perceived as being equally knowledgeable about the topic (see Dovidio et al., 1988).

Two set of questions were used for each session. The two questions in one set were: (1) Dating in the 1990's has some advantages and disadvantages to dating in earlier eras. Please consider and discuss what you personally feel are these advantages and disadvantages; and (2) First-year college students often bring more than they need to college. Please identify three or four things that are most essential for first-year students to bring, as well as the three or four things that first-year students are most likely to bring to college and do not need.

The two questions in the other set involved hypothetical situations in which participants were asked to make decisions: (1) You are in a boat with four other people. The boat begins to sink, and the closest land is five miles away. … The lifeboat will only carry three people. … List, in order (1 to 5) the priority of people for the lifeboat: you, a 60-year-old male doctor, a pregnant woman, a 5-year-old boy, the boy's father; and (2) A husband and wife are recently married. The husband tells the wife he must go on a business trip. … After he leaves, the distraught wife asks the ferryman … to take her to the other side of the river where she visits an old boyfriend and spends the night with him. The next morning … when she reaches the ferry she realizes that she has no money; the ferryman does not let her on board. … She runs to an old bridge, stumbles apparently accidentally, and falls into the river and drowns. Rank order the following people in terms of responsibility for her death: husband, self, ferryman, boyfriend, husband's job. The particular set of questions assigned to Black and White interviewers was varied across participants, as well as the order in which the two questions in each set were asked.

After introducing herself, the interviewer presented each question once verbally, asked the participant "to think for a minute or so" about his or her answer before responding, and then repeated the question. Interviewers were trained to maintain a steady gaze while the participant responded, looking away only to avoid appearing to stare (Exline, 1972). Interviewers were also instructed to nod periodically to show responsiveness and, if the participant completed her response in less than one minute, to ask, "Can you elaborate [or expand] on that?" After the participant finished his or her response, the interviewer excused herself and left the interview room to retrieve the experimenter. The experimenter returned and briefly informed the participant of the second interview. She left and returned with the second interviewer. Participants were not informed of how many interview questions or interviewers there would ultimately be.

At the end of the second interview session, the experimenter returned with questionnaires "to assess participants' responses to the interviews." Participants were asked to evaluate both interviewers, sequentially by the order of their appearance, on 7-point semantic differential scales adapted from previous research (Dovidio et al., 1988) and designed to assess evaluation of the interviewers. Factor analyses with varimax rotation, performed separately on ratings of the Black and White interviewers, each demonstrated that the evaluative items loaded on the same factor. These items were then averaged to form an evaluative score for each interviewer. The evaluative items were unlikable-likable and insincere-sincere (Cronbach a for the White interviewer = .59; for the Black interviewer = .60). A relative evaluation score was then computed by taking the difference between evaluative ratings of the White and Black interviewers. To assess self-perceptions of their behavior, participants were also asked to rate, using the same set of semantic differential items, how they behaved toward each interviewer. The Cronbach a for the evaluative items was .79 for interaction with the White interviewer and .83 for interaction with the Black interviewer.[2] A relative score was also computed for this measure.

Nonverbal behaviors were coded from the videotapes from the angle over the interviewer's shoulder using the procedures outlined in Dovidio et al. (1988). With respect to the behavior of the participants, two coders, uninformed about the hypotheses and unaware of the race of the interviewer, independently recorded (1) the amount of time (in seconds) that participants responded to each question, the amount of time (in seconds) they made visual contact with the interviewer during that period, and the number of times the participant blinked during that period. Reliability, as determined by the intraclass correlation coefficient, was .99 for speaking time with the White interviewer and .99 for speaking time with the Black interviewer, .85 for visual contact with the White interviewer and .90 for visual contact with the Black interviewer, and .96 for blinking with the White interviewer and .97 for blinking with the Black interviewer. The average for the two coders on each measure was computed. The rate of blinking was calculated as the number of blinks divided by the time of the response period. The percent of time in visual contact was the time in visual contact divided by the response time, which was then multiplied by 100. The behaviors of the interviewer were also coded. There was no difference across the interviewers in visual contact, the number and rate of nods, and the number of times the interviewer prodded the participant for elaboration on the response. In addition, preliminary analyses revealed no differences in results between the two sets of interviewers. Consequently, this factor is not included in the analyses reported.

Results

The analyses first examined response latencies in the priming task, next the relationship between explicit and implicit measures of prejudice and the relationships of these variables to relative evaluations and nonverbal responses to Black and White interviewers, and then how participants perceived their own behavior.

---

[2]The factor analyses of the semantic differential ratings of the interviewers and of participants' own behaviors also yielded a second, potency dimension. The potency items were submissive-dominant, powerless-powerful, irresponsible-responsible, and confused-confident. For interviewer ratings, the Cronbach a was .73 for the White interviewer and .74 for the Black interviewer. For self-perceptions of one's own behavior, the Cronbach a's were .86 for interactions with the White interviewer and .85 for interactions with the Black interviewer. In contrast to the results subsequently reported for evaluative ratings, there were no consistent effects for the potency ratings. Details of these analyses are available from the first author.

Priming and response latencies. Preliminary analysis demonstrated that the overall error rate was low (2.8%) and not systematically related to the experimental conditions. The occurrence of outliers was again rare (2.6%). For the latency measure, the 2 (Participant Sex) X 2 (Stimulus Order) X 2 (Race of Facial Prime: White and Black) X 2 (Favorability of Target Word: Positive and Negative) analysis of variance, with repeated measures on the last two independent variables revealed a marginally significant Race Prime X Target Word Favorability interaction, $F(1, 29) = 3.29$, $p < .08$. This effect was independent of sex and order; no higher-order interactions were obtained. As predicted and found for the first two studies, response times to negative target words were significantly faster following the Black prime than following the White prime, Ms = 911 vs 1020 ms, $t(32) = 3.72$, $p < .001$. As in Experiment 2, however, there was no significant difference for positive words as a function of the racial prime, $p = .20$. In fact, response times were slightly slower following the White primes than following the Black primes, Ms = 814 vs 777 ms. Overall, though, the interaction pattern closely replicates the results of Experiment 2, which used the same priming procedure and stimuli.

Prejudice, evaluations and nonverbal behaviors. In this study, the primary response-latency measure of bias was uncorrelated with Modern Racism, $r(31) = .01$, $p = .98$, and with Old-Fashioned Racism, $r(31) = -.07$, $p = .71$. The four supplementary measures of response latency bias were also uncorrelated with the explicit measures of prejudice (see Table 1).

It was hypothesized that explicit measures of prejudice would primarily predict relative evaluations of Black and White interviewers, whereas response-latency bias would primarily predict nonverbal behaviors. Zero-order correlations generally supported these predictions. For ratings of the interviewers, the extent to which participants evaluated the White interviewer more favorably than the Black interviewer was positively correlated with both Modern Racism, $r(31) = .54$, $p < .001$, and Old-Fashioned Racism, $r(31) = .37$, $p < .034$. Participants who scored higher on the Modern and Old-Fashioned Racism scales evaluated the Black interviewer less favorably than the White interviewer. The response-latency measure of bias was not associated with ratings of evaluation, $r(31) = .02$, $p < .93$.

In contrast to the results for ratings of the interviewers and consistent with the predictions, significant correlations were obtained between the nonverbal behaviors and the response-latency measure of bias but not between the nonverbal behaviors and self-report measures of prejudice. For the response-latency measure, higher levels of racial bias were associated with higher rates of blinking with the Black than with the White interviewer, $r(31) = .43$, $p < .012$, and with less visual contact, $r(31) = -.40$, $p < .022$. Scores on the Modern and Old-Fashioned Racism scales were not related to relative rates of blinking, rs = .07 and -.04, ps > .70, or to visual behavior, rs = .20 and .02, ps > .25. As in Experiment 2, regression equations were also computed in which the dependent variables were, separately, ratings of the interviewers and the two nonverbal behaviors; the independent variables were Old-Fashioned Racism scores, Modern Racism scores, and response-latency bias considered simultaneously. For the equation for bias in evaluative ratings, $F(3,29) = 4.06$, $p < .017$, Modern Racism was the only significant predictor, $\beta = .58$, $p < .018$. Old-Fashioned Racism ($\beta = -.05$, $p < .83$) and response-latency bias ($\beta = .01$, $p < .95$) were nonsignificant predictors.

For the equation predicting relative rates of blinking, $F(3, 29) = 2.39$, $p < .089$, response-latency bias was the only significant predictor, $\beta = .42$, $p < .018$. Modern Racism ($\beta = .16$, $p < .51$) and

Old-Fashioned Racism (β = -.13, p < .59) had nonsignificant relations. In the equation for percent of time with visual contact, F(3, 29) = 3.21, p < .038, response-latency bias was again the only significant predictor, β = -.42, p < .014. The effect for Old-Fashioned Racism was nonsignificant (β = -.33, p < .17), but the effect for Modern Racism unexpectedly approached significance (β = -.45, p < .067). Participants higher in Modern Racism tended to have greater visual contact with White than with Black interviewers. Overall, the results are consistent with predictions.

Finally, to compare how participants scoring relatively high or low in explicit and implicit measures of prejudice responded to Black and White interviewers in terms of mean levels of responses to the Black and White interviewers, 2 (High vs Low in Modern Racism, determined by a median split) X 2 (High vs Low in Response Latency Bias, determined by a median split) X 2 (Participant Sex) X 2 (Race of Interviewer) analyses of variance (ANOVA), with repeated measures on the last factor, were performed. It was expected that effects for ratings of the interviewers would primarily be a function of scoring high or low in Modern Racism,[3] not a function of performance on the response-latency task. In contrast, it was anticipated that effects for the nonverbal behaviors would be related more to performance on the response-latency task than to self-reported prejudice.

The ANOVA on the evaluative scores demonstrated, as expected, a Modern Racism X Interviewer Race interaction, F(1, 25) = 6.99, p < .014. Low prejudice-scoring participants indicated more favorable evaluations of the Black interviewer than of the White interviewer, Ms = 5.93 vs 4.62, t(13) = 2.59, p < .022. In contrast, high prejudice-scoring participants evaluated the White interviewer more positively than the Black interviewer, Ms = 4.79 vs 5.26, t(18) = 2.11, p < .049.

The analysis for rates of blinking demonstrated, as anticipated, a Response-Latency Bias X Interviewer-Race interaction, F(1, 25) = 51.88, p < .001. Participants scoring above the median on the response-latency measure of bias exhibited a significantly higher rate of blinking with the Black interviewer than with the White interviewer, Ms = 0.44 vs 0.26, t(16) = 2.96, p < .009. Participants scoring below the median had a somewhat but not significantly lower rate of blinking with the Black relative to the White interviewer, Ms = 0.25 vs 0.37, t(15) = −1.48, p < .16. Unexpectedly, a Modern Racism X Interviewer Race interaction was also obtained, F(1, 25) = 29.47, p < .001. Low prejudice-scoring participants showed equivalent rates of blinking with Black and White interviewers, Ms = 0.35 vs 0.39, t(13) = −0.40, p < .70, whereas high prejudice-scoring participants showed a somewhat higher rate of blinking with the Black interviewer than with the White interviewer, Ms = 0.34vs0.26, t(18) = 1.65, p < .12. As hypothesized, the interaction effect was considerably more pronounced when participants were classified as high or low in prejudice on the response-latency measure than on the Modern Racism scale. The ANOVA for percent of visual contact revealed a significant Response-Latency Bias X Interviewer-Race interaction, F(1, 25) = 4.97, p < .035. Participants scoring above the median on the response-latency measure of bias looked somewhat less at the Black interviewer than at the White interviewer, Ms = 47.6% vs 62.7%, t(16) = −1.07, p < .31; in contrast, participants scoring below the median looked more at the Black than the White interviewer, Ms = 50.3% vs 40.0%, t(15)

---

[3]A parallel set of analyses was conducted using the median split on Old-Fashioned Racism scores. The results resembled those obtained for Modern Racism but were much weaker and nonsignificant.

= 2.42, $p < .029$. The Modern Racism X Interviewer-Race interaction did not approach significance, $F < 1$.

Perceptions of own behavior. Participants were also asked to rate their own behavior toward Black and White interviewers on the evaluative items. Analyses of variance demonstrated that, overall, participants reported behaving equally positively toward the Black and White interviewers, Ms = 4.89 vs 4.92, $F < 1$. Consistent with the expectation that self-reports would predict overt manifestations of bias, Modern Racism scores were positively correlated with ratings of behaving more favorably toward the White interviewer than the Black interviewer, $r(31) = .37$, $p < .037$; the correlation was also positive but somewhat weaker and nonsignificant for Old-Fashioned Racism scores, $r = .12$. The weakest correlation was, as anticipated, for response latency bias, $r = .07$.

Self-perceptions of behaving positively, however, were not related to differences in the nonverbal behaviors displayed with White and Black interviewers: relative rate of blinking, $r = —.17$; relative time in visual contact, $r = —.03$. Thus, how participants perceived their own behavior was largely independent of the differences in nonverbal behavior that they displayed with Black and White interviewers.

Discussion

[handwritten annotation: , not a big sample size though overall]

Experiment 3 provides converging evidence to the findings and conclusions of the first two studies. The priming task again revealed evidence of systematic, negative implicit attitudes of Whites toward Blacks. The pattern of results closely paralleled those of Experiment 2, which used essentially the same priming procedure. Race Prime X Target Word Favorability interactions were obtained ($p < .03$ for Experiment 2; $p < .08$ for Experiment 3), and the effect of the racial primes was more pronounced for negative words than for positive words. A Race Prime X Trait Favorability X Study (Experiment 2 vs Experiment 3) analysis of variance performed on the transformed response-latency scores revealed a significant Race Prime X Trait Favorability interaction across the two studies, $F(1, 62) = 8.14$, $p < .006$. This effect was comparable across the two experiments; the Study X Race Prime X Trait Favorability interaction did not approach significance, $F(1, 62) = 0.36$, $p < .550$. Overall, participants responded faster to negative words following a Black prime than following a White prime; the difference was not statistically significant for positive words. These findings provide additional evidence of systematically negative implicit attitudes of Whites toward Blacks.

This study also complements Experiment 2 by offering support for the hypothesis that implicit attitudes would primarily predict more spontaneous race-related behaviors, whereas self-reported racial prejudice would primarily predict more deliberative responses. Experiment 3 involved actual face-to-face interaction and the measures used to represent spontaneous responses (nonverbal behaviors vs word completions) and deliberative response (evaluations vs juridic judgments of guilt) were quite different from those used in Experiment 2. Nevertheless, like those of Experiment 2, the data from Experiment 3 support these hypotheses.

We acknowledge, however, that a definitive taxonomy of spontaneous and deliberative behavior does not exist and that a comparison across different types of responses can involve variations along multiple dimensions. The parallel results we observed for very different operationalizations of these concepts across Experiments 2 and 3 lend support to our framework, but future studies might attempt to use the same dependent measures while manipulating circumstances that would permit or promote deliberative responding to varying degrees. Previous research supporting the MODE Model (e.g., Sanbonmatsu & Fazio, 1990) has examined the effects of manipulations of motivation and opportunity for deliberation on subsequent heuristic and deliberative decision-making. Future research on race-related decisions could similarly manipulate motivation by varying the degree to which participants' responses would be public or anonymous (Crosby et al., 1980) and opportunity by varying time pressure for making the decision. Alternatively, the research on subtle forms of racism may provide paradigms for examining the differential validity of implicit and explicit attitudes. Research supporting the aversive racism framework, for example, has found that discrimination against Blacks by Whites is unlikely to occur when norms for appropriate behavior are clear but often does occur when Whites can justify or rationalize a negative response on the basis of some factor other than race (e.g., by diffusing responsibility; Gaertner & Dovidio, 1977). Whereas explicit attitudes may predict Whites' responses in the former case, implicit attitudes may predict discrimination in the latter case. In general, then, our experiment not only provides evidence that response-latency measures can systematically predict subsequent race-related responses but also suggests when these effects occur.

We also note that because some behaviors are more spontaneous, that does not mean that they are necessarily less consequential in their effects than are more deliberative behaviors. Nonverbal behaviors, for instance, can have a profound impact on people's perceptions of and reactions to others (DePaulo & Friedman, 1997). In addition to communicating attraction and attitude, nonverbal behaviors can shape the nature of interactions, subtly influencing outcomes in systematic ways. Word, Zanna, and Cooper (1974) demonstrated the potential adverse impact of nonverbally mediated expectancy effects in interracial interactions. They found that White interviewers behaved less positively nonverbally with Blacks than with Whites. Furthermore, interviewers who were trained to exhibit these less positive nonverbal displays produced inferior applicant performance among naive White interviewees than did interviewers trained with the more favorable displays associated with Whites. Outside the laboratory, nonverbal communication of warmth is a key factor communicating teachers' expectations of students (Harris & Rosenthal, 1985). These nonverbal cues can be detected from very short (e.g., 30-s) segments of behavior (Ambady & Rosenthal, 1993). Thus, although bias may be unconscious and transmitted in subtle ways, its impact can be quite significant.

The effects of this subtle transmission of bias may also be quite insidious and contribute to distrust and suspicion between Blacks and Whites. Participants in Experiment 3 reported that they acted in an equally likable and sincere manner with Black and White partners, but their nonverbal behaviors were inconsistent with their perceptions—and perhaps with their intentions. As suggested by the aversive racism framework, racial bias may be manifested outside of one's awareness. Thus, in interracial interaction Whites may intend to convey a positive and friendly attitude toward their Black partner and believe that they have succeeded. In assessing the behavior of the White person, however, Blacks may not only consider the overt, consciously controlled behavior of the partner, but also concentrate on the less conscious behaviors (such as eye contact and nonverbal expression of discomfort) that Whites may have difficulty monitoring and controlling. Thus, while the White person may feel that he or she is acting in a personable and accepting manner, in the same interaction the Black partner may be attuned to the negative or mixed-message inadvertently sent (see Devine, Evett, & Vasquez-Suson, 1996), which produces a very different, potentially conflicting, perspective that can contribute to racial tension and distrust. This line of reasoning is consistent with the finding of Fazio et al. (1995) that a Black experimenter's perceptions of White participants' friendliness was better predicted by their implicit attitudes than by their explicit attitudes.

General Discussion

A meta-analysis across the three experiments reveals clear evidence of a negative response-latency bias among participants. Overall, across the three studies, response-latency bias corresponding to the Race X Target Word Favorability interaction (i.e., the extent to which participants responded more slowly to positive words and more quickly to negative words following a Black prime than following a White prime) was statistically reliable, mean $r = .447$, $z = 4.18$, $p < .001$, fail-safe number = 18. Corresponding to the simple effects tests, the meta-analytic effect of Prime was significant for negative target words, mean $r = .593$, $z = 5.97$, $p < .001$ (one-tailed), but was only marginally significant for positive words, mean $r = .176$, $z = 1.54$, $p = .062$ (one-tailed). These findings further demonstrate the existence of implicit attitudes in general (Greenwald & Banaji, 1995), support Wegner and Bargh's (1997) conclusion that "the automatic activation of evaluations or attitudes by the mere presence of the attitude object in the environment is a ubiquitous phenomenon" (p. 25), and converge with studies showing systematic implicit racial biases among Whites (Devine, 1989; Dovidio & Gaertner, 1993; Fazio et al., 1995; Judd et al., 1995; Lepore & Brown, 1997).

Furthermore, in the present research, this effect was obtained despite the fact that these same participants scored very low on self-report measures of the traditional form of prejudice represented by Old-Fashioned Racism (Experiment 2: $M = 1.55$; Experiment 3: $M = 1.28$, on a 1–5 scale) and low on a measure intended to assess a more contemporary and subtle form of bias, Modern Racism (Experiment 1, $M = 1.57$; Experiment 2: $M = 1.85$; Experiment 3: $M = 1.67$, also on a 1–5 scale; see also Fazio et al., 1995). Whereas the aversive racism framework (Dovidio & Gaertner, 1997; Gaertner & Dovidio, 1986) has presented it as a theoretical assumption rather than an empirical demonstration, this pattern offers direct evidence that many Whites who report being nonprejudiced on traditional measures of prejudice do indeed harbor unconscious negative attitudes toward Blacks.

The present research, however, also further calls into question whether the Modern Racism Scale is a nonreactive measure of racial prejudice (McConahay, 1986, p. 577). One criticism has been that the scale confounds political conservatism with prejudice (Sniderman & Tetlock, 1986a, 1986b). What the present research also suggests is that it may now be closely aligned with traditional racism. Although scores on the Modern Racism Scale were generally higher than those on the Old-Fashioned Racism Scale, scores on the Modern Racism Scale were highly correlated with measures of more traditional forms of racism across the three studies. As a consequence of the closer alignment with traditional racism, Modern Racism may no longer represent a subtle manifestation of personal attitudes but may be a public expression that is shaped significantly by social desirability concerns (see also Fazio et al., 1995). As McConahay (1986) anticipated, "new items will have to be generated for the Modern Racism Scale as new issues emerge in American race relations and some of the current scale items become more reactive" (p. 123). This may help explain why the results for Modern Racism and measures of traditional racism were generally similar across our three experiments.

The reactivity of the Modern Racism Scale and particularly the Old-Fashioned Racism Scale might also help to account for the quite variable set of correlations between self-report measures of prejudice and the response-latency measure of bias across our three experiments. In Experiment 1, the combined measure of response-latency bias (i.e., the extent to which participants responded more slowly to positive words and more quickly to negative words following a Black prime than a White prime) correlated somewhat but not significantly positively with Modern Racism (r = .15) and Attitudes Toward Blacks Modern Racism (r = .28); in Experiment 2 significant positive relationships were found between the response-latency measure and Modern Racism (r = .60) and Old-Fashioned Racism (r = .49); in Experiment 3, the comparable correlations were again weak and nonsignificant (rs = .01 and —.07). The significant positive correlations between implicit and explicit attitudes were obtained when the level of racial bias expressed on the self-report scales was highest (Modern Racism mean for Experiment 2 = 1.85, for Experiment 3 = 1.67, for Experiment 1 = 1.57 [on a 5-item scale]). Old-Fashioned Racism scores were significantly higher (p < .04) in Experiment 2 than in Experiment 3. (The Old-Fashioned Racism Scale was not used in Experiment 1.)

It is possible that, with experience at college, students become increasingly aware of norms of being nonprejudiced and perhaps come to internalize these norms, producing lower levels of self-reported racial prejudice. Consistent with this reasoning, participants in Experiment 3 who displayed very low levels of Old-Fashioned Racism were advanced undergraduates who volunteered to participate. Participants in Experiments 1 and 2 were primarily first-year students. Jackman and Muha (1984) argue that better educated people are the most sophisticated practitioners of racial bias. This reasoning suggests that correlations between implicit and explicit racial attitudes would be stronger for subgroups whose norms are more permissive of the overt expression of bias. The relationship would be weaker for people who adhere more to nonprejudiced norms. This represents one potential avenue for future research to consider.

The fact that negative attitudes may exist and be expressed automatically does not mean that racial bias is inevitable or immutable and may, in fact, suggest ways of producing truly nonprejudiced attitudes—implicitly as well as explicitly. The work of Devine (1989; Monteith & Devine, 1993) suggests that implicit prejudice is like a "bad habit." It is an overlearned response that can be unlearned. An important first step is making people aware of discrepancies between their conscious ideals and automatic negative responses. By making these nonconscious negative responses conscious, it may be possible to take advantage of the genuinely good intentions of aversive racists to motivate them to gain the experiences they need to unlearn one set of responses and learn the new set that they desire.

Research by Devine and Monteith (1993) illustrates how awareness of inconsistency between one's interracial behavior and one's egalitarian standards produces a negative emotional reaction and a genuine motivation to behave in a more egalitarian fashion in the future. Specifically, they found that people who indicated that they were relatively nonprejudiced exhibited feelings of guilt and compunction when they became aware of discrepancies between their potential behavior toward minorities (i.e., what they would do) and their personal standards (i.e., what they should do). These emotional reactions, in turn, can motivate people to control subsequent spontaneous stereotypical responses and behave more favorably in the future (Monteith, 1993). Recently, Blair and Banaji (1996) demonstrated that conscious efforts to suppress stereotypically biased reactions can inhibit even the immediate activation of normally automatic associations. Although implicit negative racial attitudes among Whites may be generally unconscious and automatic, these responses are not inevitable.

The present study also raises important questions for future research. More work is needed on the measurement characteristics (e.g., reliability, convergent validity) of priming techniques and other measures of implicit attitudes. If response-latency techniques are to be used as individual-difference measures for predicting future behavior, their psychometric properties need to be more firmly understood and established. Understanding these properties may help to account for the highly variable correlations between implicit and explicit measures of attitudes across the present three studies and other research (e.g., Fazio et al., 1995). With respect to behavior, the spontaneous-deliberative distinction requires further conceptual refinement that identifies the factors (e.g., cognitive effort, evaluative concerns) that critically define behaviors as deliberative. Nevertheless, the present study continues to suggest the importance of recognizing the subtlety and complexity of Whites' contemporary racial attitudes and of appreciating how these attitudes combine to shape the interracial behaviors of Whites toward Blacks and the reciprocal actions of Blacks toward Whites.

References

Ambady, N., & Rosenthal, R. (1993). Half a minute: Predicting teacher evaluations from thin slices of nonverbal behavior and physical attractiveness. *Journal of Personality and Social Psychology, 64*, 431–441.

Baker, S. M., & Devine, P. G. (1988, April). Faces as primes for stereotype activation. Paper presented at the 60th annual meeting of the Midwestern Psychological Association, Chicago.

Banaji, M. R., & Greenwald, A. G. (1995). Implicit gender stereotyping in judgments of fame. *Journal of Personality and Social Psychology, 68*, 181–198.

Banaji, M. R., & Greenwald, A. G. (1994). Implicit stereotyping and prejudice. In M. P. Zanna and J. M. Olson (Eds.), *The psychology of prejudice: The Ontario symposium* (Vol. 7, pp. 55–76). Hillsdale, NJ: Erlbaum.

Banaji, M. R., & Hardin, C. D. (1996). Automatic gender stereotyping. *Psychological Science, 7*, 136–141.

Bargh, J. A. (1994). The Four Horsemen of automaticity: Awareness, intention, efficiency, and control in social cognition. In R. S. Wyer & T. K. Srull (Eds.), *Handbook of social cognition* (2nd ed., Vol. 1, pp. 1–40). Hillsdale, NJ: Erlbaum.

Bargh, J. A., & Chen, M. (1996). *The chameleon effect: Automatic social perception produces automatic social behavior.* Manuscript submitted for publication.

Bargh, J. A., & Pietromonaco, P. (1982). Automatic information processing and social perception: The influence of trait information presented outside of awareness on impression formation. *Journal of Personality and Social Psychology, 43*, 437–449.

Blair, I., & Banaji, M. R. (1996). Automatic and controlled processes in gender stereotyping. *Journal of Personality and Social Psychology, 70*, 1142–1163.

Bodenhausen, G. V., & Lichtenstein, M. (1987). Social stereotypes and information processing strategies: The impact of task complexity. *Journal of Personality and Social Psychology, 52*, 871–888.

Brigham, J. C. (1971). Racial stereotypes, attitudes, and evaluations of and behavioral intentions toward Negroes and Whites. *Sociometry, 34*, 360–380.

Brigham, J. C. (1993). College students' racial attitudes. *Journal of Applied Social Psychology, 23*, 1933–1967.

Costanzo, S., & Costanzo, M. (1994). Life and death decisions: An analysis of capital jury decision-making under the special issues sentencing framework. *Law and Human Behavior, 18*, 151–170.

Crosby, F., Bromley, S., & Saxe, L. (1980). Recent unobtrusive studies of black and white discrimination and prejudice: A literature review. *Psychological Bulletin, 87*, 546–563.

DePaulo, B. M. (1992). Nonverbal behavior and self-presentation. *Psychological Bulletin, 111*, 203–243.

DePaulo, B. M., & Friedman, H. S. (1997). Nonverbal communication. In D. T. Gilbert, S. T. Fiske, & G. Lindzey (Eds.), *The handbook of social psychology* (4th Ed.). New York: McGraw-Hill.

Devine, P. G. (1989). Stereotypes and prejudice: The automatic and controlled components. *Journal of Personality and Social Psychology, 56*, 5–18.

Devine, P. G., Evett, S. R., & Vasquez-Suson, K. A. (1996). Exploring the interpersonal dynamics of intergroup contact. In R. M. Sorrentino & E. T. Higgins (Eds.), *Handbook of motivation and cognition* (Vol. 3 pp. 423–464). New York: Guilford.

Devine, P. G., & Monteith, M. J. (1993). The role of discrepancy-associated affect in prejudice reduction. In D. M. Mackie & D. L. Hamilton (Eds.), *Affect, cognition, and stereotyping: Interactive processes in intergroup perception* (pp. 317–344). Orlando, FL: Academic Press.

Doering, D. G. (1957). *The relation between manifest anxiety and rate of eyeblink in stress situations.* (Report No. 6, Project No. NM130199). San Antonio, TX: U.S. Air Force School of Aviation Medicine, Brooks Air Force Base.

Dovidio, J. F., Brigham, J. C., Johnson, B. T., & Gaertner, S. L. (1996). Stereotyping, prejudice, and discrimination: Another look. In N. Macrae, C. Stangor, & M. Hewstone (Eds.), *Foundations of stereotypes and stereotyping* (pp. 276–319). New York: Guilford.

Dovidio, J. F., Brown, C. E., Heltman, K., Ellyson, S. L., & Keating, C. F. (1988). Power displays between women and men in discussions of gender-linked tasks: A multichannel study. *Journal of Personality and Social Psychology, 55*, 580–587.

Dovidio, J. F., & Ellyson, S. L. (1985). Patterns of visual dominance behavior in humans. In S. L. Ellyson & J. F. Dovidio (Eds.), *Power, dominance, and nonverbal behavior* (pp. 129–149). New York: Springer-Verlag.

Dovidio, J. F., Evans, N., & Tyler, R. B. (1986). Racial stereotypes: The contents of their cognitive representations. *Journal of Experimental Social Psychology, 22*, 22–37.

Dovidio, J. F., & Fazio, R. H. (1992). New technologies for the direct and indirect assessment of attitudes. In J. Tanur (Ed.), *Questions about survey questions: Meaning, memory, attitudes, and social interaction* (pp. 204–237). New York: Russell Sage Foundation.

Dovidio, J. F., & Gaertner, S. L. (1991). Changes in the nature and expression of racial prejudice. In H. Knopke, J. Norrell, & R. Rogers (Eds.), *Opening doors: An appraisal of race relations in contemporary America* (pp. 201–241). Tuscaloosa, AL: Univ. of Alabama Press.

Dovidio, J. F., & Gaertner, S. L. (1993). Stereotypes and evaluative intergroup bias. In D. M. Mackie & D. L. Hamilton (Eds.), *Affect, cognition, and stereotyping* (pp. 167–193). San Diego: Academic Press.

Dovidio, J. F., & Gaertner, S. L. (1997). On the nature of contemporary prejudice: The causes, consequences, and challenges of aversive racism. In J. Eberhardt & S. T. Fiske (Eds.), *Racism: The problem and the response.* Newbury Park, CA: Sage.

Dovidio, J. F., Mann, J. A., & Gaertner, S. L. (1989). Resistance to affirmative action: The implication of aversive racism. In F. A. Blanchard & F. J. Crosby (Eds.). *Affirmative action in perspective* (pp. 83–102). New York: Springer-Verlag.

Eagly, A. H., & Kite, M. E. (1987). Are stereotypes of nationalities applied to both women and men? *Journal of Personality and Social Psychology,* 53, 451–462.

Efran, J. S. (1968). Looking for approval: Effects of visual behavior of approbation from persons differing in importance. *Journal of Personality and Social Psychology,* 10, 21–25.

Efran, J. S., & Broughton, A. (1966). Effects of expectancies for social approval on visual behavior. *Journal of Personality and Social Psychology,* 4, 103–107.

Ellyson, S. L., & Dovidio, J. F. (Eds.) (1985). *Power, dominance, and nonverbal behavior.* New York: Springer-Verlag.

Exline, R. V. (1972). Visual interaction: The glances of power and preference. In J. K. Cole (Ed.), *The Nebraska symposium on motivation,* 1971 (pp. 163–208, Vol. 19). Lincoln, NE: Univ. of Nebraska Press.

Exline, R. V. (1985). Multichannel transmission of nonverbal behavior and the perception of powerful men: The presidential debates of 1976. In S. L. Ellyson & J. F. Dovidio (Eds.), *Power, dominance, and nonverbal behavior* (pp. 183–206). New York: Springer-Verlag.

Faranda, J., & Gaertner, S. L. (1979, March). *The effects of inadmissible evidence introduced by the prosecution and the defense, and the defendant's race on the verdicts by high and low authoritarians.* Paper presented at the annual meeting of the Eastern Psychological Association, New York.

Fazio, R. H. (1987). Self-perception theory: A current perspective. In M. P. Zanna, J. M. Olson, & C. P. Herman (Eds.), *Social influence: The Ontario symposium* (Vol. 5, pp. 129–150). Hillsdale, NJ: Erlbaum.

Fazio, R. H. (1990). Multiple processes by which attitudes guide behavior: The MODE model as an integrative framework. In M. P. Zanna (Ed.), *Advances in experimental social psychology* (Vol. 23, pp. 75–109). Orlando, FL: Academic Press.

Fazio, R. H., Jackson, J. R., Dunton, B. C., & Williams, C. J. (1995). Variability in automatic activation as an unobtrusive measure of racial attitudes: A bona fide pipeline? *Journal of Personality and Social Psychology,* 69, 1013–1027.

Fazio, R. H., & Zanna, M. P. (1981). Direct experience and attitude-behavior consistency. In L. Berkowitz (Ed.), *Advances in experimental social psychology* (Vol. 14, pp. 162–202). New York: Academic Press.

Fugita, S. S. (1974). Effects of anxiety and approval on visual interaction. *Journal of Personality and Social Psychology,* 29, 586–592.

Gaertner, S. L., & Dovidio, J. F. (1977). The subtlety of white racism, arousal, and helping behavior. *Journal of Personality and Social Psychology,* 35, 691–707.

Gaertner, S. L., & Dovidio, J. F. (1986). The aversive form of racism. In J. F. Dovidio & S. L. Gaertner (Eds.), *Prejudice, discrimination, and racism* (pp. 61–89). Orlando, FL: Academic Press.

Gaertner, S. L., & McLaughlin, J. P. (1983). Racial stereotypes: Associations and ascriptions of positive and negative characteristics. *Social Psychology Quarterly,* 46, 23–30.

Gilbert, D. T., & Hixon, J. G. (1991). The trouble of thinking: Activation and application to stereotypic beliefs. *Journal of Personality and Social Psychology, 60,* 509–517.

Greenwald, A. G., & Banaji, M. R. (1995). Implicit social cognition: Attitudes, self-esteem, and stereotypes. *Psychological Review, 102,* 4–27.

Greenwald, A. G., Klinger, M. R., & Liu, T. J. (1989). Unconscious processing of dichoptically masked words. *Memory and Cognition, 17,* 35–47.

Harris, M. J., & Rosenthal, R. (1985). Mediation of interpersonal expectancy effects: 31 meta-analyses. *Psychological Bulletin, 97,* 363–386.

Harper, R. G. (1985). Power, dominance, and nonverbal behavior: An overview. In S. L. Ellyson & J. F. Dovidio (Eds.), *Power, dominance, and nonverbal behavior* (pp. 29-48). New York: Springer-Verlag.

Jackman, M. R., & Muha, M. J. (1984). Education and intergroup attitudes: Moral enlightenment, superficial democratic commitment, or ideological refinement? *American Sociological Review, 49,* 751–769.

Johnson, S. L. (1985). Black innocence and the white jury. *Michigan Law Review, 83,* 1611–1708.

Judd, C. M., Park, B., Ryan, C. S., Brauer, M., & Kraus, S. (1995). Stereotypes and ethnocentrism: Diverging inter-ethnic perceptions of African American and White American Youth. *Journal of Personality and Social Psychology, 69,* 460–481.

Kanfer, F. H. (1960). Verbal rate, eyeblink, and content in structured psychiatric interviews. *Journal of Abnormal and Social Psychology, 61,* 341–347.

Kleinke, C. L. (1986). Gaze and eye contact: A research review. *Psychological Bulletin, 100,* 78–100.

Kleinke, C. L., Meeker, F. B., & LaFong, C. (1974). Effects of gaze, touch, and use of name on evaluation of "engaged" couples. *Journal of Research in Personality, 7,* 368–373.

Kovel, J. (1970). *White racism: A psychohistory.* New York: Pantheon.

Lepore, L., & Brown, R. (1997). Category and stereotype activation: Is prejudice inevitable? *Journal of Personality and Social Psychology, 72,* 275–287.

Loftus, E. F., & Klinger, M. R. (1992). Is the unconscious smart or dumb? *American Psychologist, 47,* 761–765.

McConahay, J. B. (1986). Modern racism, ambivalence, and the modern racism scale. In J. F. Dovidio & S. L. Gaertner (Eds.), *Prejudice, discrimination, and racism* (pp. 91–125). Orlando, FL: Academic Press.

McConahay, J. B., Hardee, B. B., & Batts, V. (1981). Has racism declined in America? It depends upon who is asking and what is asked. *Journal of Conflict Resolution, 25,* 563–579.

Monteith, M. (1993). Self-regulation of prejudiced responses: Implications for progress in prejudice reduction efforts. *Journal of Personality and Social Psychology, 65,* 469–485.

Neely, J. (1977). Semantic priming and retrieval from lexical memory: Roles of inhibitionless spreading, activation and limited-capacity attention. *Journal of Experimental Psychology: General, 106,* 226–254.

Neely, J. (1991). Semantic priming effects in visual word recognition: A selective review of current findings and theories. In D. Besner & G. Humphreys (Eds.), *Basic processes in reading: Visual word recognition* (pp. 264–336). Hillsdale, NJ: Erlbaum.

Perdue, C. W., Dovidio, J. F., Gurtman, M. B., & Tyler, R. B. (1990). "Us" and "Them": Social categorization and the process of intergroup bias. *Journal of Personality and Social Psychology, 59,* 475–486.

Posner, M. I., & Snyder, C. R. (1975). Attention and cognitive control. In R. L. Solso (Ed.), *Information processing and cognition: The Loyola symposium* (pp. 55–85). Hillsdale, NJ: Erlbaum.

Ratcliff, R. (1993). Methods for dealing with reaction time outliers. *Psychological Bulletin,* 114, 510–532.

Roese, N. J., & Jamieson, D. W. (1993). Twenty years of bogus pipeline research: A critical review and meta-analysis. *Psychological Bulletin,* 114, 363–375.

Rubin, Z. (1970). Measurement of romantic love. *Journal of Personality and Social Psychology,* 16, 265–273.

Sanbonmatsu, D. M. & Fazio, R. H. (1990). The role of attitudes in memory-based decision making. *Journal of Personality and Social Psychology,* 59, 614–622.

Schacter, D. L. (1990). Introduction to "Implicit memory: Multiple perspectives." *Bulletin of the Psychonomic Society,* 28(4), 338–340.

Sears, D. O. (1988). Symbolic racism. In P. A. Katz & D. A. Taylor (Eds.), *Eliminating racism: Profiles in controversy* (pp. 53–84). New York: Plenum.

Sigall, H., & Page, R. (1971). Current stereotypes: A little fading, a little faking. *Journal of Personality and Social Psychology,* 18, 247–255.

Sniderman, P. M., & Tetlock, P. E. (1986a). Symbolic racism: Problems of motive attribution inpolitical analysis. *Journal of Social Issues,* 42, 129–150.

Sniderman, P. M., & Tetlock, P. E. (1986b). Reflections on American racism. *Journal of Social Issues,* 42, 173–187.

Wegner, D. M., & Bargh, J. A. (1997). Control and automaticity in social life. In D. T. Gilbert, S. T. Fiske, & G. Lindzey (Eds.), *The Handbook of Social Psychology* (4th Ed.). New York: McGraw-Hill.

Williams, J. E., Tucker, R. D., & Dunham, F. Y. (1971). Changes in the connotations of color names among Negroes and Caucasians. *Journal of Personality and Social Psychology,* 19, 222–228.

Word, C. O., Zanna, M. P., & Cooper, J. (1974). The nonverbal mediation of self-fulfilling prophecies in interracial interaction. *Journal of Experimental Social Psychology,* 10, 109–120.

Zanna, M. P., & Fazio, R. H. (1982). The attitude-behavior relation: Moving toward a third generation of research. In M. P. Zanna, E. T. Higgins, & C. P. Herman (Eds.), *Consistency in social behavior: The Ontario symposium* (Vol. 2, pp. 283–301). Hillsdale, NJ: Erlbaum.

Why Clever People Believe Stupid Things

By Ben Goldacre

> The real purpose of the scientific method is to make sure nature hasn't misled you into thinking you know something you actually don't know.
>
> —Robert Pirsig, *Zen and the Art of Motorcycle Maintenance*

Why do we have statistics, why do we measure things, and why do we count? If the scientific method has any authority—or, as I prefer to think of it, value—it is because it represents a systematic approach, but this is valuable only because the alternatives can be misleading. When we reason informally—call it intuition, if you like—we use rules of thumb that simplify problems for the sake of efficiency. Many of these shortcuts have been well characterized in a field called heuristics, and they are efficient ways of knowing in many circumstances.

This convenience comes at a cost—false beliefs—because there are systematic vulnerabilities in these truth-checking strategies that can be exploited. This is not dissimilar to the way that paintings can exploit shortcuts in our perceptual system: as objects become more distant, they appear smaller, and "perspective" can trick us into seeing three dimensions where there are only two, by taking advantage of this strategy used by our depth-checking apparatus. When our cognitive system—our truth-checking apparatus—is fooled, then, much like seeing depth in a flat painting, we come to erroneous conclusions about abstract things. We might misidentify normal fluctuations as meaningful patterns, for example, or describe causality where in fact there is none.

These are cognitive illusions, a parallel to optical illusions. They can be just as mind-boggling, and they cut to the core of why we do science, rather than base our beliefs on intuition informed by a "gist" of a subject acquired through popular media: because the world does not provide you with neatly tabulated data on interventions and outcomes. Instead it gives you random, piecemeal data in dribs and drabs over time, and trying to construct a broad understanding of the world from a memory of your own experiences would be like looking at the ceiling of the Sistine Chapel through a long, thin cardboard tube: you can try to remember the individual portions you've spotted here and there, but without a system and a model, you're never going to appreciate the whole picture.

Let's begin.

Randomness

As human beings we have an innate ability to make something out of nothing. We see shapes in the clouds and a man in the moon; gamblers are convinced that they have "runs of luck;" we take a perfectly cheerful heavy metal record, play it backward, and hear hidden messages about Satan. Our ability to spot patterns is what allows us to make sense of the world, but sometimes, in our eagerness, we are oversensitive and trigger-happy and mistakenly spot patterns where none exist.

In science, if you want to study a phenomenon, it is sometimes useful to reduce it to its simplest and most controlled form. There is a prevalent belief among sporting types that sportsmen, like gamblers (except more plausibly), have runs of luck. People ascribe this to confidence, "getting your eye in," "warming up," or more, and while it might exist in some games, statisticians have looked in various places where people have claimed it to exist and found no relationship between, say, hitting a home run in one inning, then hitting a home run in the next.

Because the "winning streak" is such a prevalent belief, it is an excellent model for looking at how we perceive random sequences of events. This was used by an American social psychologist named Thomas Gilovich in a classic experiment. He took basketball fans and showed them a random sequence of Xs and Os, explaining that they represented a player's hits and misses, and then asked them if they thought the sequences demonstrated streak shooting.

Here is a random sequence of figures from that experiment. You might think of it as being generated by a series of coin tosses.

OXXXOXXXOXXOOOXOOXXOO

The subjects in the experiment were convinced that this sequence exemplified streak shooting or runs of luck, and it's easy to see why, if you look again: six of the first eight shots were hits. No, wait: eight of the first eleven shots were hits. No way is that random ...

What this ingenious experiment shows is how bad we are at correctly identifying random sequences. We are wrong about, what they should look like: we expect too much alternation, so truly random

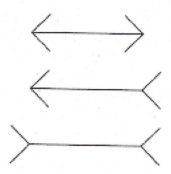

sequences seem somehow too lumpy and ordered. Our intuitions about the most basic observation of all, distinguishing a pattern from mere random background noise, are deeply flawed.

This is our first lesson in the importance of using statistics instead of intuition. It's also an excellent demonstration of how strong the parallels are between these cognitive illusions and the perceptual illusions with which we are more familiar. You can stare at a visual illusion all you like, talk or think about it, but it will still look "wrong." Similarly, you can look at that random sequence above as hard as you like: it will still look lumpy and ordered, in defiance of what you now know.

Regression To The Mean

We have already looked at regression to the mean in our section on homeopathy; it is the phenomenon, whereby, when things are at their extremes, they are likely to settle back down to the middle, or regress to the mean.

We saw this with reference to the *Sports Illustrated* jinx, but also applied it to the matter in hand, the question of people getting better; we discussed how people will do something when their back pain is at its worst—visit a homeopath, perhaps—and how although it was going to get better anyway (because when things are at their worst, they generally do), they ascribe their improvement to the treatment.

There are two discrete things happening when we fall prey to this failure of intuition. First, we have failed to spot correctly the pattern of regression to the mean. Second crucially, we have then decided that something must have *caused* this illusory pattern: specifically, a homeopathic remedy, for example. Simple regression is confused with causation, and this is perhaps quite natural for animals like humans, whose success in the world depends on our being able to spot causal relationships rapidly and intuitively: we are inherently oversensitive to them.

To an extent, when we discussed the subject earlier, I relied on your goodwill and on the likelihood that from your own experience you could agree that this explanation made sense. But it has been demonstrated in another ingeniously pared-down experiment, in which all the variables were controlled, but people still saw a pattern and causality where there was none.

The subjects in the experiment played the role of a teacher trying to make a child arrive punctually at school for 8:30 a.m. They sat at a computer on which it appeared that each day, for fifteen consecutive days, the supposed child would arrive sometime between 8:20 and 8:40, but unbeknownst to the subjects, the arrival times were entirely random and predetermined before the experiment began. Nonetheless, all the subjects were allowed to' use punishments for lateness and rewards for punctuality, in whatever permutation they wished. When they were asked at the end to rate their strategy, 70 percent concluded that reprimand was more effective than reward in producing punctuality from the child.

These subjects were convinced that their intervention had an effect on the punctuality of the child, despite the child's arrival time being entirely random and exemplifying nothing more than regression to the mean. By the same token, when homeopathy has been shown to elicit no more improvement than placebo, people are still convinced that it has a beneficial effect on their health.

To recap:

1. We see patterns where there is only random noise.
2. We see causal relationships where there are none.

These are two very good reasons to measure things formally. It's bad news for intuition already. Can it get much worse?

The Bias Toward Positive Evidence

> It is the peculiar and perpetual error of the human understanding to be more moved and excited by affirmatives than negatives.
>
> —Francis Bacon

It gets worse. It seems we have an innate tendency to seek out and overvalue evidence that confirms a given hypothesis. To try to remove this phenomenon from the controversial arena of CAM—or the MMR scare, which is where this is headed—we are lucky to have more pared-down experiments that illustrate the general point.

Imagine a table with four cards on it, marked "A," "B," "2," and "3." Each card has a letter on one side and a number on the other. Your task is to determine whether all cards with a vowel on one side have an even number on the other. Which two cards would you turn over? Everybody chooses the "A" card, obviously, but like many people—unless you really forced yourself to think hard about it—you would probably choose to turn over the "2" card as well. That's because these are the cards that would produce information *consistent* with the hypothesis you are supposed to be testing. But in fact, the cards you need to flip are the "A" and the "3," because finding a vowel on the back of the "2" would tell you nothing about "all cards," it would just confirm "some cards," whereas finding a vowel on the back of "3" would comprehensively disprove your hypothesis. This modest brainteaser demonstrates our tendency, in our unchecked intuitive reasoning style, to seek out information that confirms a hypothesis, and it demonstrates the phenomenon in a value-neutral situation.

This same bias in seeking out confirmatory information has been demonstrated in more sophisticated social psychology experiments. When trying to determine if someone is an "extrovert," for example, many subjects will ask questions for which a positive answer would confirm the hypothesis ("Do you like going to parties?") rather than refute it.

We show a similar bias when we interrogate information from our own memory. In one experiment, subjects first read a vignette about a woman who exemplified various introverted and extroverted behaviors and then were divided into two groups. One group was asked to consider the woman's suitability for a job as a librarian, while the other was asked to consider her suitability for a job as a real estate agent. Both groups were asked to come up with examples of both her extroversion and her introversion. The group considering her for the librarian job recalled more examples of introverted behavior, while the group considering her for a job selling real estate cited more examples of extroverted behavior.

This tendency is dangerous, because if you ask only questions that confirm your hypothesis, you will be more likely to elicit information that confirms it, giving a spurious Sense of confirmation. It also means—if we think more broadly—that the people who pose the questions already have a head start in popular discourse.

So we can add to our running list of cognitive illusions, biases, and failings of intuition:

1. We overvalue confirmatory information for any given hypothesis.
2. We seek out confirmatory information for any given hypothesis.

Biased By Our Prior Beliefs

> [I] followed a golden rule, whenever a new observation or thought came across me, which was opposed to my general results, to make a memorandum of it without fail and at once; for I had found by experience that such facts and thoughts were far more apt to escape from the memory than favorable ones.
>
> —Charles Darwin

This is the reasoning flaw that everybody does know about, and even if it's the least interesting cognitive illusion—because it's an obvious one—it has been demonstrated in experiments that are so close to the bone that you may find them, as I do, quite unnerving.

The classic demonstration of people's being biased by their prior beliefs comes from a study looking at beliefs about the death penalty. A large number of proponents and opponents of state executions were collected. They all were shown two pieces of evidence on the deterrent effect of capital punishment: one supporting a deterrent effect, the other providing evidence against it. The evidence they were shown was as follows:

- A comparison of murder rates in one U.S. state before the death penalty was brought in, and after.
- A comparison of murder rates in different states, some with and some without the death penalty.

But there was a very clever twist. The proponents and opponents of capital punishment were each further divided into two smaller groups. So overall, half the proponents and opponents of capital punishment had their opinions reinforced by before/after data but challenged by state/state data, and vice versa.

Asked about the evidence, the subjects confidently uncovered flaws in the methods of the research that went against their preexisting view, but downplayed the flaws in the research that supported their view. Half the proponents of capital punishment, for, example, picked holes in the idea of state/

state comparison data, on methodological grounds, because that was the data that went against their view, while they were happy with the before/after data; but the other half of the proponents of capital punishment rubbished the before/after data, because in their case they had been exposed to before/after data that challenged their view and state/state data that supported it.

Put simply, the subjects' faith in research data was not predicated on an objective appraisal of the research methodology, but on whether the results validated their preexisting views. This phenomenon reaches its pinnacle in alternative therapists—or scaremongers—who unquestioningly champion anecdotal data, while meticulously examining every large, carefully conducted study on the same subject for any small chink that would permit them to dismiss it entirely.

This, once again, is why it is so important that we have clear strategies available to us to appraise evidence, regardless of its conclusions, and this is the major strength of science. In a systematic review of the scientific literature, investigators will sometimes mark the quality of the "methods" section of a study blindly—that is, without looking at the "results" section—so that it cannot bias their appraisal. Similarly, in medical research there is a hierarchy of evidence: a well-performed trial is more significant than survey data in most contexts, and so on.

So we can add to our list of new insights about the flaws in intuition:

1. Our assessment of the quality of new evidence is biased by our previous beliefs.

Availability

We spend our lives spotting patterns and picking out the exceptional and interesting things. You don't waste cognitive effort, every time you walk into your house, noticing and analyzing all the many features in the visually dense environment of your kitchen. You do notice the broken window and the missing television.

When information is made more "available," as psychologists call it, it becomes disproportionately prominent. There are a number of ways this can happen, and you can pick up a picture of them from a few famous psychology experiments into the phenomenon.

In one, subjects were read a list of male and female names, in equal number, and then asked at the end whether there were more men or women in the list. When the men in the list had names like Ronald Reagan, but the women were unheard of, people tended to answer that there were more men than women, and vice versa.

Our attention is always drawn to the exceptional and the interesting, and if you have something to sell, it makes sense to guide people's attention to the features you most want them to notice. When slot machines pay up, they make a theatrical "kerchunkkerchunk" sound with every coin they spit out, so that everybody in the casino can hear it, but when you lose, they don't draw attention to themselves. Lottery companies, similarly, do their absolute best to get their winners prominently into the media, but it goes without saying that you, as a lottery loser, have never had your outcome paraded for the TV cameras.

As we shall see, the tragic anecdotes about the MMR vaccine are disproportionately misleading, not just because the statistical context is missing, but because of their "high availability:" they are dramatic, associated with strong emotion, and amenable to strong visual imagery. They are concrete and memorable, rather than abstract. No matter what you do with statistics about risk or recovery, your numbers will always have inherently low psychological availability, unlike miracle cures, scare stories, and distressed, parents.

It's because of availability, and our vulnerability to drama, that people are more afraid of sharks at the beach, or of fairground rides on the pier, than they are of flying to Florida or driving to the coast. This phenomenon is even demonstrated in patterns of smoking cessation among doctors. You'd imagine, since they are rational actors, that all doctors would simultaneously have seen sense and stopped smoking once they'd read the studies showing the phenomenally compelling relationship between cigarettes and lung cancer. These are men of applied science, after all, who are able, every day, to translate cold statistics into meaningful information and beating human hearts.

But in fact, from the start, doctors working in specialties like chest medicine and oncology, where they witnessed patients dying of lung cancer with their own eyes, were proportionately more likely to give up cigarettes than their colleagues in other specialties. Being shielded from the emotional immediacy and drama of consequences matters.

Social Influences

Last in our whistle-stop tour of irrationality comes our most self-evident flaw. It feels almost too obvious to mention, but our values are socially reinforced by conformity and by the company we keep. We are selectively exposed to information that revalidates our beliefs, partly because we expose ourselves to *situations* in which those beliefs are apparently confirmed; partly because we ask questions that will—by their very nature, for the reasons described above—give validating answers; and partly because we selectively expose ourselves to *people* who validate our beliefs.

It's easy to forget the phenomenal impact of conformity. You doubtless think of yourself as a fairly independent-minded person, and you know what you think. I would suggest that the same beliefs were held by the subjects of Solomon Asch's experiments into social conformity. These subjects were placed near one end of a line of actors who presented themselves as fellow experimental subjects but were actually in cahoots with the experimenters. Cards were held up with one line marked on each of them, and then another card was held up with three lines of different lengths: six inches, eight inches, ten inches.

Everyone called out in turn which line on the second card was the same length as the line on the first. For six of the eighteen pairs of cards the accomplices gave the correct answer, but for the other twelve they called out the wrong answer. In all but a quarter of the cases, the experimental subjects[1] went along with the incorrect answer from the crowd of accomplices on one or more occasions, defying the clear evidence of their own senses.

That's an extreme example of conformity, but the phenomenon is all around us. Communal reinforcement is the process by which a claim becomes a strong belief, through repeated assertion by members of a community. The process is independent of whether the claim has been properly researched or is supported by empirical data significant enough to warrant belief by reasonable people.

Communal reinforcement goes a long way toward explaining how religious beliefs can be passed on in communities from generation to generation. It also explains how testimonials within communities of therapists, psychologists, celebrities, theologians, politicians, talk show hosts, and so on can supplant and become more powerful than scientific evidence.

> When people learn no tools of judgment and merely follow their hopes, the seeds of political manipulation are sown.
>
> —Stephen Jay Gould

There are many other well-researched areas of bias. We have a disproportionately high opinion of ourselves, which is nice. A large majority of the public think they are more fair-minded, less prejudiced, more intelligent, and more skilled at driving than the average person, when of course, only half of as can be better than the median.[1] Most of us exhibit something called attributional bias: we believe our successes are due to our own internal faculties, and our failures are due to external factors; whereas for others, we believe their successes are due to luck, and their failures to their own flaws. We can't all be right.

Last, we use context and expectation to bias our appreciation of a situation, because in fact, that's the only way we can think. Artificial intelligence research has drawn a blank so far largely because of something called the frame problem: you can tell a computer how to process information, and give it all the information in the world, but as soon as you give it a real-world problem—a sentence to understand and respond to, for example—computers perform much worse than we might expect, because they don't know what information is relevant to the problem. This is something humans are very good at—filtering irrelevant information— but that skill comes at a cost of ascribing disproportionate bias to some contextual data.

We tend to assume, for example, that positive characteristics cluster: people who are attractive must also be good; people who seem kind might also be intelligent and well informed. Even this has been demonstrated experimentally: identical essays in neat handwriting score higher than messy ones, and the behavior of sporting teams that wear black is rated as more aggressive and unfair than teams that wear white.

---

[1] I'd be genuinely intrigued to know how long it takes to find someone who can tell you the difference between "median," "mean," and "mode," from where you are sitting right now.

And no matter how hard you try, sometimes things just are very counter-intuitive, especially in science. Imagine there are twenty-three people in a room. What, is the chance that two of them celebrate their birthday on the same date? One in two.[2]

When it comes to thinking about the world around you, you have a range of tools available. Intuitions are valuable for all kinds of things, especially in the social domain: deciding if your girlfriend is cheating on you, perhaps, or whether a business partner is trustworthy. But for mathematical issues, or assessing causal relationships, intuitions are often completely wrong, because they rely on shortcuts that have arisen as handy ways to solve complex cognitive problems rapidly, but at a cost of inaccuracies, misfires, and oversensitivity.

It's not safe to let our intuitions and prejudices run unchecked and unexamined: it's in our interest to challenge these flaws in intuitive reasoning wherever we can, and the methods of science and statistics grew up specifically in opposition to these flaws. Their thoughtful application is our best weapon against these pitfalls, and the challenge, perhaps, is to work out which tools to use where. Because trying to be "scientific" about your relationship with your partner is as stupid as following your intuitions about causality.

Now let's see how journalists deal with stats.

---

[2]If it helps to make this feel a bit more plausible, bear in mind that you only need *any* two dates to coincide. With forty-seven people, the probability increases to 0.95; that's nineteen times out of twenty! (Fifty-seven people and it's 0.99; seventy people and it's 0.999.) This is beyond your intuition; at first glance, it (hakes no sense at all.

It's Not My Fault

When and Why Attributions to Prejudice Protect Self-Esteem

By Brenda Major, Cheryl R. Kaiser, and Shannon K. McCoy, University of California, Santa Barbara

This study tested the hypothesis that awareness of the possibility of being a target of discrimination can provide individuals with a means of self-esteem protection when they are faced with negative outcomes. Men and women contemplated being rejected from a course due to sexism, personal deservingness, or an exclusively external cause. Regardless of gender, participants in the sexism condition blamed themselves less, attributed the rejection less to internal causes, and anticipated feeling less depressed than those in the personal deservingness condition. Furthermore, the more participants discounted the rejection—blamed it more on discrimination than themselves—the less depressed emotions they anticipated feeling. Discounting did not buffer participants from feeling hostility or anxiety. These findings advance our understanding of when and why attributions to prejudice protect emotional well-being.

What are the psychological consequences of perceiving that one has been a target of prejudice—of believing that one has been discriminated against because of one's gender, ethnicity, sexual orientation, or appearance? Certainly there is ample evidence that being the target of prejudice is associated with reduced well-being (see Major, Quinton, & McCoy, 2002, for a review). Furthermore, correlational studies reveal that those who generally perceive themselves as victims of pervasive discrimination have poorer well-being than those who do not. For example, perceiving oneself as a target of discrimination is positively associated with depression among women (Kobrynowicz & Branscombe, 1997) and gay men (Diaz, Ayala, Bein, Henne, & Marin, 2001) and with lower self-esteem among women (Schmitt, Branscombe, Kobrynowicz, & Owen, 2002) and African Americans (Branscombe, Schmitt, & Harvey, 1999). (See Kaiser, Major, & McCoy, in press; Major et al., 2002; McCoy & Major, in press, for a discussion of sources of emotional variability to perceived prejudice.)

Crocker and Major (1989; Major & Crocker, 1993) ventured the provocative hypothesis that awareness of the possibility of being a target of discrimination also may provide the stigmatized with

Brenda Major, Cheryl R. Kaiser & Shannon K. McCoy, "It's Not My Fault: When and Why Attributions to Prejudice Protect Self-Esteem," *Personality and Social Psychology Bulletin*, vol. 29, no. 6, pp. 772–781. Copyright © 2003 by SAGE Publications, Inc. Reprinted with permission.

a means of self-esteem protection when they are faced with negative outcomes (see also Dion, 1975; Dion & Earn, 1975). Drawing on Kelley's (1973) discounting principle, they hypothesized that the availability of prejudice as a plausible external cause of negative outcomes might allow the stigmatized to discount their own role in producing those outcomes. Furthermore, Crocker and Major (1989) hypothesized that because prejudice is external to the self, attributing negative outcomes to prejudice should protect affect and self-esteem relative to making attributions to "internal, stable, and global causes such as lack of ability" (p. 613). They based their hypothesis on theoretical models of emotion positing that attributing negative events to causes external to the self protects affect and self-esteem, whereas attributing negative outcomes to causes internal to the self for which one is responsible, such as one's lack of deservingness, leads to negative affect and low self-esteem (e.g., Abramson, Seligman, & Teasdale, 1978; Weiner, 1985).

Recently, Schmitt and Branscombe (2002a, 2002b) challenged Crocker and Major's description of an attribution to prejudice as an external attribution. They contend that because one's group membership is an aspect of the self, attributions to prejudice have a strong internal component. Furthermore, Schmitt and Branscombe (2002a, 2002b) dispute the hypothesis that attributions to discrimination protect self-esteem. They argue that because attributions to discrimination threaten an important aspect of the self—one's social identity—making such attributions will heighten rather than decrease negative affect for members of stigmatized groups. Finally, Schmitt and Branscombe claim that attributions to discrimination are less damaging for members of high-status groups than for members of low-status groups because discrimination has a different, and more benign, meaning for the former than the latter.

In a test of their hypotheses, Schmitt and Branscombe (2002a) conducted two experiments in which participants were asked to imagine that a professor refused their request to add a closed class. In one condition (the everyone rejected condition), participants learned that the professor was a "jerk" and did not honor anyone's request to add the class. In a second condition, participants learned that the professor was "sexist" and let in no members of their own gender but let in 10 members of the other gender (the prejudice condition). The extent to which participants saw the rejection as due to discrimination, due to something about themselves (internal causes), and due to something about the professor (external causes) was assessed. In addition, participants in the second study indicated the extent to which they would experience 12 emotions, such as discouraged, blue, angry, and cruel.

Consistent with Schmitt and Branscombe's claim that attributions to prejudice have an internal component, participants in both studies rated internal causes higher when the ingroup was rejected than when everyone was rejected. However, consistent with Crocker and Major's (1989) claim that attributions to prejudice have an external component, participants in the first study also rated external causes just as high in the prejudice condition as in the everyone rejected condition. In the second study, participants rated external causes even higher when the ingroup was rejected than when everyone was rejected. Schmitt and Branscombe (2002a, Study 2) also found that women who read the "prejudice" vignette reported significantly more general negative affect than women who read the "everyone rejected" vignette. Thus, women reported more negative affect if they were rejected because of discrimination than because of purely external factors. Schmitt and Branscombe did not observe this pattern for men.

Schmitt and Branscombe's (2002a) studies make the important theoretical point that attributions to prejudice contain both an internal and an external component. Furthermore, they illustrate that for women, attributing rejection to prejudice feels worse than attributing it to purely external factors (e.g., a professor who is a "jerk"). However, Schmitt and Branscombe's studies failed to provide an adequate test of Crocker and Major's primary theoretical assumptions. An appropriate test would require (a) comparing the emotional effects of rejection due to discrimination to the emotional effects of rejection due to a lack of deservingness (e.g., a lack of ability) and (b) examining the impact of rejection due to discrimination on self-esteem-related emotions (e.g., depressed, blue) separately from its effects on other-directed emotions (e.g., angry, cruel).

Crocker and Major's discounting hypothesis does not require that attributions to discrimination are exclusively external. Rather, it assumes that an attribution to discrimination is more external than an attribution to personal deservingness. Consequently, attributing rejection to discrimination should be less painful than attributing it to internal, stable, global factors such as a lack of ability. This is the rationale guiding self-handicapping (e.g., Jones & Berglas, 1978) and excuse-making behaviors (Schlenker, Pontari, & Christopher, 2001), both of which protect self-esteem under some circumstances (Snyder & Higgins, 1988). Schmitt and Branscombe's comparison between discrimination attributions and external attributions is interesting but does not test the discounting hypotheses. An appropriate test requires comparing the emotional consequences of a discrimination attribution to the emotional consequences of an attribution to a lack of personal deservingness.

Crocker and Major's (1989; Major & Crocker, 1993) theoretical analysis also was not concerned with emotions such as anger or hostility. Rather, it addressed the implications of attributions to discrimination for self-esteem-related emotions (e.g., worthlessness, depression, sadness, shame) among the stigmatized. They predicted that attributions to discrimination can protect self-esteem from rejection or failure. They did not predict that attributions to discrimination protect the stigmatized from anger or anxiety. Indeed, in their initial test of their discounting hypothesis, they differentiated among different types of affect. Crocker, Voelkl, Testa, and Major (1991, Study 1) administered 12 mood items to women who had been evaluated by a sexist or nonsexist evaluator. These 12 items were selected from the depression, anxiety, and hostility subscales of the Multiple Affect Affective Check List (MAACL) (Zuckerman, Lubin, Vogel, & Valerius, 1964). Women who were negatively evaluated by a sexist evaluator experienced significantly less depressed emotions than women negatively evaluated by a nonsexist evaluator, but they did not experience significantly less hostile emotions or less anxious emotions. Schmitt and Branscombe (2002a, Study 2) used the same 12 mood items as Crocker et al. (1991, Study 1) but reported results based on a composite of all 12 items. In the current study, we distinguish between emotions related to depression (depressed, worthless), hostility (angry, mad), and anxiety (fearful, worried) in testing the emotional implications of rejection based on discrimination compared to a lack of deservingness.

The distinction between self-directed emotions such as depression and other-directed emotions such as hostility is a particularly important one. There is substantial evidence that the perception of injustice is associated with the emotional response of anger (see Miller, 2001, for a review). Anger is also a frequent affective response to perceiving that one is a target of discrimination (Swim, Hyers, Cohen,

& Ferguson, 2001). Consequently, one might expect people who blame rejection on discrimination to be just as angry, and perhaps angrier, than people who blame rejection on a lack of ability or on a 'jerk." Several studies on prejudice illustrate the importance of differentiating between self-directed and other-directed affect (e.g., Devine, Monteith, Zuwerink, & Elliot, 1991; Vorauer & Kumhyr, 2001). Vorauer and Kumhyr (2001), for example, found that Aboriginal participants who interacted with a White partner who was highly prejudiced experienced more negative self-esteem-related feelings but not more negative other-directed feelings, compared to those who interacted with a low-prejudiced White partner. Of importance, Aboriginal participants paired with a highly prejudiced White partner failed to recognize that they were targets of prejudice. This study suggests that when targets experience behavioral manifestations of prejudice and fail to attribute those behaviors to prejudice, they may personalize the implications of the negative behavior. In summary, one goal of this study was to test adequately the Crocker and Major (1989; Major & Crocker, 1993) discounting hypothesis using the same paradigm used by Schmitt and Branscombe (2002a).

Distinguishing Between Internal Causation and Self-Blame

The second goal of this research was to extend the self-esteem protection hypothesis proposed by Crocker and Major (1989) beyond a simple internal versus external attribution dichotomy to consider the emotional implications of attributions of responsibility and blame. Major et al. (2002) recently proposed that the dilemma that must be resolved by the stigmatized target to protect his or her self-esteem in the face of poor treatment is not "Did something internal or external to me cause this outcome?" but rather "Who is to blame for this outcome, you or me?"

A necessary component of making an attribution to discrimination is acknowledging that some part of the self (one's stigma or group membership) played a causal role in an outcome. Indeed, recognition of this fact led Crocker and Major (1994) to refine their discounting hypothesis to distinguish between attributing outcomes to one's social identity and attributing outcomes to prejudice based on one's social identity. Crocker and Major (1994) noted that although attributing treatment to one's social identity is an internal attribution, it does not necessarily carry with it the assumption of injustice, or moral wrongdoing, that attributing treatment to prejudice does. Indeed, some members of stigmatized groups may perceive that their treatment is due to others' reactions to their social identity but may perceive this treatment as legitimate. Consequently, they may not blame their negative treatment on prejudice, but rather blame it on themselves. This may occur, for example, if the target perceives a stigma to be under their personal control. A study of overweight women demonstrated this pattern (Crocker, Cornwell, & Major, 1993). Overweight women who were rejected as a partner by a man who knew their weight, attributed their rejection to their weight, but did not blame it on the man's prejudice.

Although Crocker and Major (1994) recognized that an attribution to discrimination involves the perception of moral wrongdoing on the part of another, they did not distinguish among the concepts of attributions to causality, responsibility, and blame. Some scholars argue that most respondents use these terms interchangeably (Tennen & Affleck, 1990). Others argue that these concepts should be differentiated theoretically (Fincham & Shultz, 1981; Shaver, 1985; Weiner, 1995). According to Weiner (1995), for example, holding a person responsible for an outcome is not the same as attributing the outcome to the person. He argues that even if the cause of an adverse event is located within the person and that cause is controllable by the individual, it is still possible that a judgment of responsibility will not be rendered if there are mitigating circumstances that negate moral responsibility. Furthermore, Weiner theorizes that it is judgments of responsibility (and/or blame, in the case of negative outcomes) rather than judgments about the locus of causality (internal vs. external) that are the critical determinants of emotion. A substantial amount of empirical research supports Weiner's hypotheses (see Weiner, 1995, for a review).

We believe that judgments of responsibility also play a critical role in determining when attributions to prejudice will protect self-esteem. Attributions to prejudice should be self-protective to the extent that they shift responsibility for negative events away from the self and toward discrimination (see Major et al., 2002; Major, Quinton, & Schmader, 2003; McCoy & Major, in press). In other words, attributions to discriminations should protect self-esteem when they lead individuals to discount their own responsibility for producing negative events. The discounting principle (Kelley, 1973) is based on Heider's (1958) idea that explanations of actions commonly involve a trade-off between causes internal and external to a person. A recent theoretical review indicates that internal and external causes for events are not necessarily inversely related (McClure, 1998). Often, increased ratings of internal causes have no effect on ratings of external causes, and vice versa. One implication of this analysis is that attributions to discrimination and self-blame are not necessarily inversely related. Perceiving that another person is prejudiced against one's group does not preclude blaming a negative outcome on aspects of oneself, such as one's lack of effort. Similarly, perceiving that one is poorly qualified for a position does not preclude blaming one's rejection on another's prejudice. Consequently, neither attributions to discrimination nor self-blame alone may be sufficient to mediate the relationship between negative events and emotion. The critical determinant of emotional responses is apt to be the relative degree to which individuals blame a negative event on themselves or on discrimination, that is, their degree of discounting.

A recent study by Major et al. (2003) demonstrates this point. Women in this study received negative feedback that was clearly due to sexism, possibly due to sexism, or clearly not due to sexism. Their self-esteem subsequently was assessed. The relationship between attributions to discrimination and self-esteem varied by condition; for example, it was positive in the clear sexism condition and negative in the no sexism condition. Across all conditions, however, discounting was positively related to self-esteem. That is, women who attributed negative feedback more to discrimination than to their lack of ability had higher self-esteem. Thus, in the current study, we hypothesized that the more individuals discounted a negative event (i.e., blamed it on prejudice more than on themselves) the higher their self-esteem would be.

Overview

The current study tested the key theoretical assumptions of Crocker and Major's discounting hypothesis and our self-blame discounting hypothesis, using Schmitt and Branscombe's (2002a, Study 2) paradigm. Male and female participants read a vignette in which a professor rejected their request to enroll in a course. One third read that the professor was "sexist" and excluded only members of the participant's gender. This condition was identical to the "prejudice" condition of Schmitt and Branscombe (2002a, Study 2). Another third read that the professor was "a jerk" and excluded everyone who tried to admit the class. This condition was identical to the "everyone excluded" condition of Schmitt and Branscombe (2002a, Study 2). The remaining third read that the professor "thought they were stupid" and excluded only the participant from the course in the personal rejection condition. Participants subsequently were asked to indicate the extent to which the rejection was due to discrimination, internal causes, external causes, and how much they were to blame for the rejection. We also assessed depressed, hostile, and anxious emotions and examined the impact of rejection condition on these types of emotions separately.

We predicted that ratings of self-blame would be lower in the prejudice condition compared to the personal rejection condition (Hypothesis 1). We also tested Crockerand Major's (1989) hypothesis that attributions to internal causes would be lower and attributions to external causes would be higher in the prejudice condition compared to the personal rejection condition (Hypotheses 2 and 3). We predicted that participants would report fewer depressed emotions (but not fewer hostile or anxious emotions) in the prejudice condition compared to the personal rejection condition (Hypothesis 4). Finally, we tested the hypothesis that discounting would mediate the depressed emotion effect (Hypothesis 5).

Method

Participants

Participants were 43 female and 42 male university student volunteers (M age = 20.84 years). Most participants (75%) were European American, with the remainder reporting Asian American (7.5%), Latino American (8.8%), African American (2.5%), or Other (6.3%) racial backgrounds. Male and female participants were randomly assigned to read one of three vignettes, resulting in a 2 (participant sex) X 3 (rejection condition) between-subjects design.

Procedure

Participants read a vignette, identical to that used by Schmitt and Branscombe (2002a, Study 2), in which a professor of the other sex denied them admission to a needed course. The attribution for the professor's refusal was manipulated by what a friend (who was always the same sex as the participant) said about the professor. All participants were asked to imagine the following situation:

Suppose that it's the beginning of the semester and you need an "add code" for a course required by your major. You stop by the professor's office and politely ask to be let into the class. To your disappointment, the professor turns you down and says, "Sorry, but I just can't give you an add code. Later that day, you talk to a good friend about not being able to get into the class. Your friend, a reliable source, says that he/she is not surprised the professor didn't let you into the class. He/she tells you that . . ."

For one third of the participants (prejudice condition), the friend said the professor was "sexist" and had let several members of the other gender into the class even after turning the participant down. For another one third, the friend said the professor was "a real jerk" and did not give anyone add codes (everyone rejected condition). These manipulations were identical to the prejudice and everyone rejected conditions of Schmitt and Branscombe (2002a, Study 2).[1] For the remaining third of the participants (personal rejection condition), the friend said that the professor "thought they were stupid" and had let everyone else who asked for an add code except the participant into the class.

Dependent Measures

Participants indicated the extent to which they anticipated blaming themselves for being rejected from the course ("I am to blame for not receiving an add code," "It is my fault that I did not receive an add code," $\alpha = .70$). In addition, participants indicated the extent to which they anticipated the rejection was due to internal causes ("The professor refused to give me an add code because of something about me," "The professor refused to give me an add code because of who I am," $\alpha = .82$) and external causes ("The professor refused to give me an add code because of something about her/him," "The professor's decisions were due to her/his attitudes or personality," $\alpha = .86$). The internal and external items were identical to those used by Schmitt and Branscombe (2002a). Participants also completed a two-item manipulation check on perceived discrimination ("The professor's actions were due to gender discrimination," "The professor is sexist," $\alpha = .97$). All items were rated on 7-point scales with endpoints of 1 *(not at all)* and 7 (*extremely).*

Participants then completed a 28-item mood scale. The depressed emotions measure was composed of four items from the MAACL depression subscale: discouraged, fine (reverse-coded), active (reverse-coded), and blue (these same items were assessed by Crocker et al., 1991, and Schmitt and Branscombe, 2002a, Study 2), as well as 12 additional affect items common on self-esteem scales: worthless, proud (reverse-coded), embarrassed, like a failure, disappointed in myself, pleased with myself (reverse-coded), humiliated, ashamed, inferior to others, sad, depressed, and mortified. These 18 items formed a highly reliable scale of depressed emotions ($\alpha = .94$). The hostile emotions measure was composed of four items from the MAACL hostility subscale: angry, cooperative (reverse-coded), cruel, and agreeable (reverse-coded) (these same items were used by Crocker et al. and Schmitt and Branscombe), as well as four additional items: mad, scornful, irritable, and hostile. These items formed a reliable scale ($\alpha = .83$). The anxious emotions measure was composed of the four items from the MAACL anxiety subscale used by Crocker et al. and Schmitt and Branscombe: fearful, worried, calm (reverse-coded), and secure (reverse-coded) ($\alpha = .65$).

All items were rated on 7-point scales with endpoints of 1 *(not at* all) and 7 *(extremely).* Finally, participants provided demographic information including age, gender, and race and were then thanked for their participation.

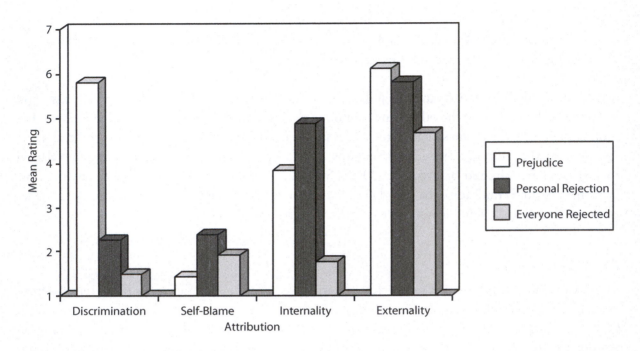

Figure 1. Mean attribution ratings as a function of experimental condition.

Results

All variables were analyzed with 2 (participant sex) X 3 (rejection condition: prejudice, personal rejection, everyone rejected) analyses of variance (ANOVAs) unless otherwise indicated. All significant effects were followed up with Bonferroni post hoc tests. Mean attributions for rejection by condition are shown in Figure 1.

Attributions to Discrimination

The manipulation check on attributions to discrimination was successful, $F(2, 79) = 92.02$, $p < .001$. Participants in the prejudice condition rated the rejection as significantly more due to discrimination ($M = 5.80$, $SD = 1.26$) than did participants in the personal rejection condition ($M = 2.27$, $SD = 1.66$). These participants, in turn, rated the rejection as significantly more due to discrimination than did those in the everyone rejected condition ($M = 1.48$, $SD = 0.87$). Women were more likely to blame the rejection on discrimination ($M = 3.42$, $SD = 2.12$) than were men ($M = 2.90$, $SD = 2.44$), $F(1, 79) = 3.97$, $p = .05$. The interaction was not significant.

Attributions for the Rejection

Self-blame. Analyses of self-blame revealed a significant main effect for rejection condition, $F(2, 79) = 5.72$, $p = .01$. Consistent with Hypothesis 1, participants in the prejudice condition were significantly less likely to imagine blaming themselves for the professor's refusal to let them in the course (M = 1.32, *SD* = 0.70) than were participants in the personal rejection condition (M = 2.39, *SD* = 1.53). Ratings of self-blame in the everyone rejected condition (M = 1.91, *SD* = 1.14) fell in between these two conditions and were not significantly different from either. Participant sex was not involved in any significant effects, Fs < 0.55, ps > .58.

Internality. Analyses of ratings of internality revealed a significant main effect for rejection condition, F(2, 79) = 31.17, *p* < .001. Consistent with Hypothesis 2, participants in the prejudice condition (M = 3.82, *SD* = 2.06) anticipated attributing the rejection less to internal causes than did those in the personal rejection condition (M = 4.89, *SD* = 1.40). Both groups rated internality significantly higher than did participants in the condition in which everyone was rejected (M = 1.76, *SD* = 0.98). There were no main effects or interactions involving participant sex, Fs < 2.25, ps > .11.

Externality. Analyses of ratings of externality revealed a significant main effect for rejection condition, F(2, 79) = 31.17, *p* < .001. Participants in the prejudice (M = 6.11, *SD* = 0.88) and personal rejection (M = 5.80, *SD* = 1.13) conditions attributed the professor's rejection of their request significantly more to external causes than did participants in the everyone rejected condition (M = 4.66, *SD* = 1.69). Although ratings of externality in the prejudice condition were higher than in the personal rejection condition, contrary to Hypothesis 3, they did not differ significantly from each other. Women (M = 5.86, *SD* = 1.14) also rated the rejection as more due to external causes than did men (M = 5.15, *SD* = 1.59), F(1, 79) = 7.22, *p* < .01. The interaction was not significant.

Emotions

Depressed emotions. As can be seen if Figure 2, rejection condition had a significant impact on participants' anticipated depressed emotions, F(2, 79) = 19.96, *p* < .001. Consistent with Hypothesis 4, participants in the prejudice condition (M = 3.10, *SD* = 0.72) anticipated feeling significantly less depressed than those in the personal rejection condition (M = 4.40, *SD* = 1.35). Participants in the personal rejection condition also anticipated feeling significantly more depressed than those in the everyone rejected condition (M = 2.80, *SD* = 0.87). The prejudice and everyone rejected conditions did not significantly differ from each other. Neither the main effect for participant sex, F(1, 79) = 2.07, *p* = .15, nor the interaction, *F* < 1, was significant.

Hostile emotions. As is illustrated in Figure 2, the analysis of hostile emotions revealed a significant main effect for rejection condition, F(2, 79) = 11.87, *p* < .001. Participants in the prejudice (M = 4.86, *SD* = 0.85) and personal rejection conditions (M = 5.07, *SD* = 1.00) imagined feeling more hostile affect compared to those in the everyone rejected condition (M = 3.97, *SD* = 0.96). The prejudice and personal rejection conditions did not significantly differ from each other. Participant sex did not produce any significant effects, Fs < 2.22, ps > .13.

Anxious emotions. Rejection condition had a significant effect on anxious emotions, F(2, 79) = 3.10, *p* = .05 (see Figure 2). Participants expected to feel more anxiety in the personal rejection condition (M = 4.17, *SD* = 1.27) than in the everyone rejected condition (M = 3.47, *SD* = 1.02). Anxiety ratings in the prejudice conditions fell in between these two conditions and did not significantly differ from

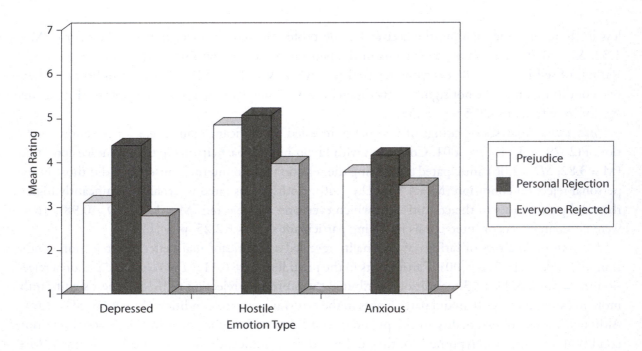

Figure 2. Mean emotional responses as a function of experimental condition.

either (M = 3.78, *SD* = 0.85). Participant sex did not produce any significant effects, Fs < 1.64, ps > .20.

Mediational Analyses

Bivariate correlations among the attributions and anticipated emotional responses to rejection among participants in the prejudice and personal rejection conditions are shown in Table 1. Overall, attributions to discrimination were negatively and significantly related to self-blame (r = -.26, *p* = .05) and negatively (but not significantly) related to internal attributions (r = -.19). Attributions to discrimination were unrelated to external attributions (r = .01). There was a negative but nonsignificant correlation between internal and external attributions (r = -.21). Furthermore, the less participants attributed their rejection to discrimination (*r* = -.49, *p* < .01) and the more they blamed it on themselves (r = .43, *p*< .01), the more they reported depressed feelings. Internal attributions also were positively related to depressed feelings (r = .26, *p* = .06). Attributions to discrimination, self blame, and internal attributions were unrelated to hostile affect or anxious affect.

According to our discounting hypothesis, awareness of the possibility that one is a target of prejudice protects self-esteem to the extent that it shifts blame for negative events toward discrimination and away from the self. Thus, we argued that the critical mediator of emotional response is the relative extent to which individuals blame negative outcomes on discrimination versus on themselves. We did not expect either attributions to discrimination or self-blame alone to mediate the relationship between experimental condition and self-esteem related negative affect.

TABLE 1. Correlations Among Attributions for Rejection and Affect

	1	2	3	4	5	6	7
1. Discrimination							
2. External	.01	_					
3. Internal	-.19	-.21	_				
4. Self-blame	-.26*	-.34*	.41**	_			
5. Depressed emotions	-49**	-.18	.26+	.43**	_		
6. Hostility	.01	.28т	.12	.00	.36**	_	
7. Anxiety	-.17	.12	.01	.14	.77**	.46**	_

NOTE: Correlations are based on only the prejudice and personal rejection conditions. N = 56. 1p = .06. *p < .05. **p < .01.

To test the discounting hypothesis, we created a discounting variable by subtracting participants' self-blame ratings from their attributions to discrimination (see also Major et al., 2003, for this technique). We then examined whether discounting mediated the effect of rejection condition on depressed emotions, following procedures specified by Baron and Kenny (1986). We examined mediation for the effects of prejudice versus personal rejection on depressed emotions because these are the conditions directly relevant to the discounting hypothesis.

Our first regression analysis (see Figure 3) examined whether experimental condition, dummy coded as 0 (personal rejection condition) and 1 (prejudice condition), was a significant predictor of depressed emotions. Results replicated those of the ANOVA reported previously (β = -.52, p < .001; R^2 = .28), F(1, 54) = 20.46, p < .001. Our second regression analyses examined whether experimental condition was a significant predictor of the discounting variable. Consistent with predictions, experimental condition was positively associated with discounting (β = .80, p< .001; R^2 = .63), F(1, 54) = 92.46, p < .001. It should be noted that discounting was negatively related to depressed emotions (r = -.57, p < .001), indicating that the more participants shifted responsibility for the rejection toward discrimination and away from the self, the less depressed emotions they imagined feeling. The third step in testing for mediation involved simultaneously entering experimental condition and discounting into a regression analysis predicting depressed emotions. The overall simultaneous regression was significant, R^2 = .30, F(2, 53) = 11.41, p < .001. This analysis revealed that discounting was a significant and negative predictor of depressed emotions (β = -.43, p < .03). Furthermore, when discounting was entered into the model, the direct relationship between experimental condition and depressed emotions was no longer significant (β = -.19, p = .32). A Sobel test examining the statistical significance of the drop in the beta for the direct path between experimental condition and depressed emotions was significant (z = 2.25, p < .03). Thus, consistent with Hypothesis 5, discounting mediated the relationship between experimental condition and depressed emotions.

Because internality ratings also were significantly lower in the prejudice condition relative to the personal rejection condition, we examined whether the discounting of internal causes relative to

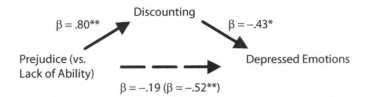

Figure 3. Discounting mediational model. *p < .05. **p < .001.

discrimination mediated the effect of experimental condition on depressed emotions. We created an internal discounting variable (internality ratings subtracted from discrimination ratings) and conducted the same series of analyses described above substituting this variable for discounting. Experimental condition was positively associated with internal discounting (β = .73, $p <$ .001, R^2 = .53), F(1, 54) = 60.01, $p <$ .001. However, in the simultaneous regression, internal discounting was unrelated to depressed emotions (β = -.25, p = .15) and the relationship between experimental condition and depressed emotions remained significant (β = -.35, $p <$ .05). Thus, the discounting of internal causes relative to discrimination did not mediate the effect of condition on depressed emotions.[2]

In separate mediational analyses, we also examined whether attributions to discrimination alone or self-blame alone mediated the relationship between experimental condition and depressed affect. Neither was a significant mediator.

Discussion

This experiment tested the hypothesis that awareness of the possibility of being a target of discrimination can provide members of stigmatized groups with a means of self-esteem protection when they are faced with negative outcomes (Crocker & Major, 1989; Dion, 1975; Dion & Earn, 1975; Major & Crocker, 1993). Crocker and Major (1989) hypothesized that because prejudice is external to the self, attributing negative outcomes to prejudice should protect affect and self-esteem relative to making attributions to "internal, stable, and global causes such as lack of ability" (p. 613). Schmitt and Branscombe (2002a) challenged this hypothesis, claiming that attributions to discrimination are not exclusively external attributions but also have a significant internal component because they implicate one's social identity. Furthermore, they claimed that attributing negative outcomes to prejudice leads to lower self-esteem among members of low-status groups relative to high-status groups. We believe that Schmitt and Branscombe's (2002a) study did not provide a fair test of Crocker and Major's discounting hypothesis. The current study was designed to do so. We also tested the hypotheses that awareness that prejudice is a potential cause of rejection leads to less self-blame than does awareness that personal deservingness may have led to rejection. In addition, we tested the hypothesis that attributions to discrimination protect self-esteem from negative events when they reduce self-blame for those events. Findings were supportive of these hypotheses.

As predicted, participants who imagined being rejected from a course by a sexist professor blamed themselves significantly less than did participants who imagined being rejected by a professor who believed that they were unintelligent. Participants in the prejudice condition also rated rejection as due significantly less to internal causes ("something about me") than did participants in the personal rejection condition. However, to our surprise, rejection due to prejudice was not rated as more external than rejection due to personal deservingness. We suspect that this may have been due to the specific wording of our personal deservingness manipulation. To make this condition as strong as the other two, the professor was described as calling the student "stupid." We suspect that students thought it was strange for professors to describe a student so callously. Consequently, they may have thought the rejection said something about the professor's character as well as their own ability level. Our results might have been even stronger had we used a more typical personal deservingness condition.

Consistent with findings of Schmitt and Branscombe (2002a, Study 2), in our study, rejection by a sexist professor was seen as due significantly more to external causes and as due significantly more to internal causes than was rejection by a professor who was a "jerk." Collectively, this pattern of findings illustrates the complex nature of attributions to discrimination. Although being rejected because of prejudice against one's group clearly implicates the self, it does not lead to as much self-blame and is not regarded as being due as much to internal causes as is being rejected because of lack of ability.

More important, participants asked to imagine that a prejudiced professor rejected them anticipated feeling significantly less depressed than participants who imagined being personally rejected because of assumed unintelligence. These findings are consistent with the hypothesis that believing that one has been rejected because of prejudice protects self-esteem relative to believing that one has been rejected because of a lack of ability. The self-protective effect of prejudice relative to personal deserving was observed among women as well as men, in contrast to Schmitt and Branscombe's (2002a) claim that prejudice is more detrimental to the self-esteem of members of low-status than high-status groups.

Results of this study emphasize the importance of distinguishing different types of emotional responses to prejudice. Crocker and Major's (1989) theoretical perspective concerned the consequences of attributions to discrimination for self-esteem-related emotions, not hostile or anxious emotions. Although participants in the prejudice condition anticipated feeling less depressed emotions than those in the personal rejection condition, they did not anticipate feeling less hostile or anxious emotions. Furthermore, although participants who were rejected because of prejudice expected to feel significantly more hostile than people in the "everyone rejected" condition, they did not expect to feel more depressed or anxious. Our results suggest that people who believe they were rejected because of prejudice will feel at least as angry as people who think they were rejected because a professor thinks they are stupid and even angrier than people who believe they (and everyone else) were rejected because someone is a jerk. These findings support Weiner's (1995) claim that different types of attributions are associated with distinct emotional responses. Ignoring these distinctions can produce misleading results.

Our conceptualization of the discounting hypothesis in terms of blame rather than attributions to internal versus external causes also received support. The more people blamed rejection on discrimination relative to blaming it on themselves, the less depression they experienced. Furthermore, discounting of self-blame mediated the effects of experimental condition on depressed emotions. Discounting of internal causes, in contrast, did not. These findings indicate that people are unlikely to derive emotional benefits from blaming negative outcomes on prejudice and discrimination if they also hold themselves (or their group) responsible for those outcomes (Major & Schmader, 2001). Indeed, judgments of justifiable negative treatment may be particularly harmful to members of stigmatized groups (Crocker at al., 1993).

A limitation of this study was its use of a vignette paradigm rather than a paradigm in which participants were actually exposed to prejudice. We used this paradigm to provide an exact replication of Schmitt and Branscombe's (2000a) study. Our results are valid only to the extent that participants were able to accurately predict their attributions and emotional responses to rejection and were willing to truthfully report them. Some emotional reactions may be less acceptable to report than others (e.g., hostility for women). Nonetheless, we feel that the theoretical benefits gained from exactly replicating the Schmitt and Branscombe (2002a) paradigm outweighed the drawbacks. Exact replication with the addition of the critical personal rejection condition allows for clear comparison across studies and permits firmer conclusions about differences observed between studies as well as provides important theoretical insights in the emotional consequences of attributions to discrimination. Furthermore, studies using more ecologically valid designs (e.g., Crocker etal., 1991; Major et al., 2003) have yielded results consistent with those of the current study.

The present research advances our understanding of when and why attributions to prejudice are self-protective. Clearly, it is overly simplistic to claim that attributing negative outcomes to prejudice protects self-esteem. Self-esteem is protected by blaming rejection on prejudice compared to blaming it on a lack of personal ability (or other indicator of a lack of deservingness). Self-esteem is not protected by blaming rejection on prejudice compared to blaming it on an indiscriminate jerk who excludes everyone. Indeed, it makes us even angrier to feel like a target of prejudice than to feel like the target of someone who excludes everyone (although it does not make us feel worse about ourselves). Thus, attributing outcomes to prejudice against one's social group may protect self-esteem only when it serves to protect an even more core component of the self. It may not feel good to blame poor outcomes on prejudice but it may feel better than blaming them on a lack of intelligence.

This statement should not be taken to imply that we see perceiving oneself as a target of discrimination as beneficial. There is substantial evidence that being exposed to prejudice threatens well-being in a variety of ways. Furthermore, individuals who chronically perceive themselves or their group as victims of prejudice have poorer psychological well-being than those who do not (see Major et al., 2002, for a review). Perceiving oneself as a target of discrimination involves recognizing that you and your group are devalued by society at large, that negative events are outside of your control, and that you are likely to face similar events in the future. Nonetheless, when one encounters a threat to the self, recognizing that discrimination may have played a role in producing that threat does have some benefits. As this study illustrates, members of stigmatized and nonstigmatized groups can feel better about themselves if they attribute a negative outcome to discrimination rather than to a lack of personal deservingness.

Notes

1. Many thanks to Michael T. Schmitt for providing us with his study stimuli.
2. We suspect that the discrepancy between our findings and those of Schmitt and Branscombe (2002a) resulted in part from their use of an affect measure that combined depressed affect with hostile affect. To investigate this possibility, we conducted a 3 (rejection condition) X 2 (participant gender) ANOVA on the same 12-item composite affect measure they used. We observed a significant main effect for rejection condition, $F(2, 79) = 9.42$, $p < .001$. Post hoc tests revealed that participants reported more general negative affect in the discrimination condition compared to the everyone rejected condition, replicating Schmitt and Branscombe's (2002a) finding. Participants also reported more general negative affect in the personal rejection condition compared to the everyone rejected condition. The discrimination and personal rejection conditions did not significantly differ from each other. The confounded nature of the composite affect measure, however, makes the meaning of this finding unclear.

References

Abramson, L. Y., Seligman, M. E., & Teasdale, J. D. (1978). Learned helplessness in humans: Critique and reformulation. *Journal of Abnormal Psychology*, 87, 49–74.

Baron, R. M., & Kenny, D. A. (1986). The moderator/mediator variable distinction in social psychological research: Conceptual, strategic, and statistical considerations. *Journal of Personality and Social Psychology*, 51, 1173–1182.

Branscombe, N. R., Schmitt, M. T., & Harvey, R. D. (1999). Perceiving pervasive discrimination among African Americans: Implications for group identification and well-being. *Journal of Personality and Social Psychology*, 77, 135–149.

Crocker, J., Cornwell, B., & Major, B. (1993). The stigma of overweight: Affective consequences of attributional ambiguity. *Journal of Personality and Social Psychology*, 64, 60–70.

Crocker, J., & Major, B. (1989). Social stigma and self-esteem: The self-protective properties of stigma. *Psychological Review*, 96, 608–630.

Crocker, J., & Major, B. (1994). Reactions to stigma: The moderating role of justifications. In M. P. Zanna & J. M. Olson (Eds.), *The psychology of prejudice: The Ontario symposium, Vol. 7* (pp. 289–314). Hillsdale, NJ: Lawrence Erlbaum.

Crocker, J., Voelkl, K., Testa, M., & Major, B. (1991). Social stigma: The affective consequences of attributional ambiguity. *Journal of Personality and Social Psychology*, 60, 218–228.

Devine, P. G., Monteith, M. J., Zuwerink, J. R., & Elliot, A. J. (1991). Prejudice with and without compunction. *Journal of Personality and Social Psychology*, 60, 817–830.

Diaz, R. M., Ayala, G., Bein, E., Henne, J., & Marin, B. V. (2001). The impact of homophobia, poverty, and racism on the mental health of gay and bisexual Latino men: Findings from 3 U.S. cities. *American Journal of Public Health*, 91, 927–932.

Dion, K. L. (1975). Women's reactions to discrimination from members of the same or opposite sex. *Journal of Research in Personality*, 9, 294–306.

Dion, K. L., & Earn, B. M. (1975). The phenomenology of being a target of prejudice. *Journal of Personality and Social Psychology, 32,* 944–950.

Fincham, F. D., & Shultz, T. R. (1981). Intervening causation and the mitigation of responsibility for harm. *British Journal of Social Psychology, 20,* 113–120.

Heider, F. (1958). The psychology of interpersonal relations. New York: John Wiley.

Jones, E. E., & Berglas, S. (1978). Control of attributions about the self through self-handicapping strategies: The appeal of alcohol and the role of underachievement. *Personality & Social Psychology Bulletin, 4,* 200–06.

Kaiser, C. R., Major, B., & McCoy, S. K. (in press). Expectations about the future and the emotional consequences of perceiving prejudice. *Personality and Social Psychology Bulletin.*

Kelley, H. H. (1973). The processes of causal attribution. *American Psychologist, 28*(2), 107–128.

Kobrynowicz, D., & Branscombe, N. R. (1997). Who considers themselves victims of discrimination? Individual difference predictors of perceived gender discrimination in women and men. *Psychology of Women Quarterly, 21,* 347–363.

Major, B., & Crocker, J. (1993). Social stigma: The consequences of attributional ambiguity. In D. M. Mackie &D. L. Hamilton (Eds.), *Affect, cognition, and stereotyping: Interactive processes in group perception* (pp. 345–370). San Diego, CA: Academic Press.

Major, B., Quinton, W., & McCoy, S. K. (2002). Antecedents and consequences of attributions to discrimination: Theoretical and empirical advances. In M. Zanna (Ed.), *Advances in experimental social psychology* (Vol. 34, pp. 251–330). San Diego, CA: Academic Press.

Major, B., Quinton, W. J., & Schmader, T. (2003). Attributions to discrimination and self-esteem: Impact of group identification and situational ambiguity. *Journal of Experimental Social Psychology, 39,* 220—31.

Major, B., & Schmader, T. (2001). Legitimacy and the construal of social disadvantage. In B. Major & J. T. Jost (Eds.), *The psychology of legitimacy* (pp. 176–204). New York: Cambridge University Press.

McClure, J. (1998). Discounting causes of behavior: Are two reasons better than one? *Journal ofPersonaliy and Social Psychology, 74,* 7–20.

McCoy, S. K. & Major, B. (in press). Group identification moderates emotional responses to perceived prejudice. *Personality and Social Psychology Bulletin.*

Miller, D. T. (2001). Disrespect and the experience of injustice. *Annual Review of Psychology, 52,* 527–553.

Schlenker, B. R., Pontari, B. A., & Christopher, A. N. (2001). Excuses and character: Personal and social implications of excuses. *Personality and Social Psychology Review, 5,* 15–32.

Schmitt, M. T., & Branscombe, N. R. (2002a). The internal and external causal loci of attributions to prejudice. *Personality and Social Psychology Bulletin, 28,* 620–628.

Schmitt, M. T., & Branscombe, N. R. (2002b). The meaning and consequences of perceived discrimination in disadvantaged and privileged social groups. In W. Stroebe & M. Hewstone (Eds.), *European review of social psychology* (Vol. 12, pp. 167–199). Chichester, UK: Wiley.

Schmitt, M. T., Branscombe, N. R., Kobrynowicz, D., & Owen, S. (2002). Perceiving discrimination against one's gender group has different implications for well-being in women and men. *Personality and Social Psychology Bulletin, 28,* 197–210.

Shaver, K. G. (1985). The attribution of blame: Causality, responsibility, and blameworthiness. New York: Springer-Verlag.

Snyder, C. R., & Higgins, R. L. (1988). Excuses: Their effective role in the negotiation of reality. *Psychological Bulletin,* 104, 23–35.

Swim, J. K., Hyers, L. L., Cohen, L. L., & Ferguson, M.J. (2001). Everyday sexism: Evidence for its incidence, nature, and psychological impact from three daily diary studies. *Journal of Social Issues,* 57, 31–53.

Tennen, H., & Affleck, G. (1990). Blaming others for threatening events. *Psychological Bulletin,* 108, 209-232.

Vorauer, J., & Kumhyr, S. M. (2001). Is this about you or me? Self versus other-directed judgments and feelings in response to intergroup interaction. *Personality & Social Psychology Bulletin,* 27, 706–719.

Weiner, B. (1985). An attributional theory of achievement motivation and emotion. *Journal of Personaliy and Social Psychology,* 92, 548–573.

Weiner, B. (1995). Judgments of responsibility: A foundation for a theory of social conduct. New York: Guilford.

Zuckerman, M., Lubin, B., Vogel, L., & Valerius, E. (1964). Measurement of experimentally induced affects. *Journal of Consulting Psychology* 28, 418–425.

Personality and Racial/Ethnic Relations

A Perspective From Cognitive-Affective Personality System (CAPS) Theory

By Rodolfo Mendoza-Denton and Michelle Goldman-Flythe, University of California, Berkeley

Abstract

The five articles in this special section examine personality and racial/ethnic relations from the perspective of Mischel and Shoda's Cognitive-Affective Personality System (CAPS) Theory. In this introductory piece, we first provide a primer on CAPS theory. In particular, we try to highlight the role that context plays in the construction and manifestation of personality as well as the dynamic ways that people interpret and react to input from their environment. We then review research on race-based rejection sensitivity as a programmatic illustration of the role expectancies play in racial/ethnic relations. Finally, we summarize and tie together the articles that comprise this section via a set of emergent themes that are common to the present contributions.

In the latter part of the 1990s, Walter Mischel and Yuichi Shoda (1995, 1998, 1999) published their Cognitive-Affective Personality System, or CAPS, theory, which attempts to account both for the stability of personality dispositions as well as the behavioral variability that characterizes people's behavior across situations or contexts. Approximately a decade later (October 2008), a Web-based Google Scholar search revealed over 800 citations for these works, underscoring the profound impact that CAPS theory has had in the field since it was first shared with the scientific community. The insights of CAPS theory have been applied to areas as varied as health psychology (Miller, Shoda, & Hurley, 1996), clinical psychology (Ayduk & Gyurak, 2008; Morf & Rhodewalt, 2001), person perception (Mendoza-Denton, Park, & O'Connor, 2007, 2008), and cultural psychology (Mendoza-Denton & Mischel, 2007). In this special section of the *Journal of Personality*, we examine CAPS theory in relation to racial and ethnic relations. More specifically, we draw on CAPS theory to help us address the following question: How do we conceptualize the relation between such a quintessentially social and contextualized phenomenon as prejudice on the one hand and personality dispositions on the other?

CAPS theory is explicitly framed as a meta-theoretical framework that sets forth a set of general principles that govern individuals' cognitive-affective dynamics vis-a-vis situations. These principles are thus applicable across a wide range of domains; however, their specific utility in a given domain is contingent on the specification of these principles. For example, a central tenet of CAPS theory (discussed in greater detail below) is that people's behavior is mediated by a network of *cognitive-affective units* that include goals, expectations, and beliefs. But *what* are the relevant such goals, expectations, and beliefs that are specific to understanding prejudice and improving racial and ethnic relations?

In answering this question, we have brought together a group of scholars whose work embodies specific instantiations of CAPS principles, allowing simultaneously for both specificity of prediction as well as an understanding of general principles at work. Sinclair, Pappas, and Lun (this issue) review research related to shared reality theory and self-stereotyping, noting that "shared reality theory contrasts with the generality of CAPS theory by making predictions regarding the nature of pertinent goals and expectations and how these constructs inter-relate to produce self-understanding in a given context." Hong, Chao, and No (this issue) discuss how people's beliefs in race as an essential versus socially constructed quality affect our perceptions of outgroup members and our intergroup interactions, focusing "on how common people's understanding about the nature of race sets up meaning systems within which they interpret and understand social information as racially keyed and, in turn, invokes a specific course of action." Butz and Plant (this issue) focus on people's motivation to control prejudice, explicitly recognizing that such motivation "is closely connected to other cognitive-affective units of personality, and together these motivational, affective, and cognitive responses influence people's responses in interracial interactions," Finally, within this introductory piece, we review research on anxious expectations of race-based rejection, highlighting how the predictions and findings regarding the psychological sequelae of such expectations provide consistent support for the principles outlined by the CAPS model. Together, these contributions provide balance by addressing personality, process, and prejudice both from the perspective of those imparting prejudice (Butz & Plant; Hong et al.,) and those who are targets of prejudice (Hong et al.,; Mendoza-Denton & Goldman-Flythe; Sinclair et al.).

Overview of this Article and of the Special Section

In this introductory article, we first provide a brief overview of CAPS theory (we refer readers to Mischel & Shoda, 2008, for a more in-depth treatment of CAPS and to Mendoza-Denton & Mischel, 2007, specifically for a discussion of social/cultural context and CAPS). Following this overview, we discuss research on *race-based rejection sensitivity* (Mendoza-Denton, Downey, Purdie, Davis, & Pietrzak, 2002; Mendoza-Denton, Pietrzak, & Downey, 2008) as a specific instantiation of CAPS that highlights the interplay of expectations and affect in determining minority individual's responding in potentially discriminatory situations and social contexts. We conclude this article by explicitly pointing out consistent themes that emerge and are illustrated in each of the research programs reviewed here. As such, this last section can be thought to provide a kind of road map to the special section, which concludes with a commentary by Mischel, Mendoza-Denton, and Hong.

Cognitive-Affective Personality System (CAPS) Theory: a Primer

Over the past two decades, a body of research has emerged recognizing that personality processes are intertwined with, and revealed through, behavioral variability across contexts (Fleeson, 2001; Fournier, Moskowitz, & Zuroff, 2008; Mendoza-Denton & Mischel, 2007; Mischel & Shoda, 1995). Imagine, for example, a midlevel executive who is kind and agreeable to her supervisors but does not address or interact with the lower level office staff. Another executive of the company, by contrast, is friendly toward the lower level staff but does not address or interact with her superiors and supervisors. Can such patterns be informative about personality process?

For this to be the case, it is necessary to establish the stability of the patterns. Person 1, for example, may not always be cold to staff and, instead, may have stayed up all night caring for a colicky baby. Person 2 may have recently heard rumors about company layoffs and may be expressly trying to remain "beneath the radar." These are examples of ways in which the relative contributions of situational factors may be understandably "discounted" in the assessment of personality dispositions (see Gilbert & Malone, 1995). However, if these patterns are indeed stable—that is, if Person 1 is *reliably* friendly to superiors and cold to staff, and Person 2 *reliably* displays the opposite pattern—they invite dynamic explanations about each person's underlying "inner lives" (e.g., Person 1 is a kiss-up that wants to get ahead; Person 2 disdains hierarchy and abhors the "fat cats" see Kammrath, Mendoza-Denton, & Mischel, 2005) and call for a theoretical framework that can somehow incorporate these dynamic explanations and account for people's stable patterns of behavioral variability across situations—their *if … then … signatures* (if Situation A, then she or he does X, but if Situation B, then she or he does Y). CAPS theory was proposed with such a goal in mind.

Do Stable Situation-Behavior Patterns Exist?

A fundamental question to address is whether *if … then …* profiles characterize, at least in part, the actual behavior of people. To explore this question, Shoda, Mischel, and Wright (1994) tracked the behavior of a group of children in relation to five psychologically meaningful situations for the campers—peers teasing, peers approaching sociably, adults warning, adults punishing, and adults praising. The data revealed predictable and nonrandom patterns of behavioral variability across situations over and above the expected situational pull on behavior (e.g., greater levels of overall aggression if provoked than if praised). To examine the *stability* of the profiles, Shoda et al. first standardized aggression scores within each situation, thus revealing a given individual's level of aggression above and beyond what would be normally expected in that situation. Each child's profile was then compared across two separate, nonoverlapping subsamples of situations, allowing the researchers to assess the stability of the situation-behavior patterns. Figure 1 shows illustrative examples of the stability of *if … then …* profiles from two of the children in the camp setting, where the solid and dotted lines represent the nonoverlapping samples of situations. As the figure shows, whereas the child represented in the top panel was reliably more aggressive than other peers when warned by an adult but not when approached sociably, the child represented in the bottom panel was less reactive when warned but became hostile when approached sociably.

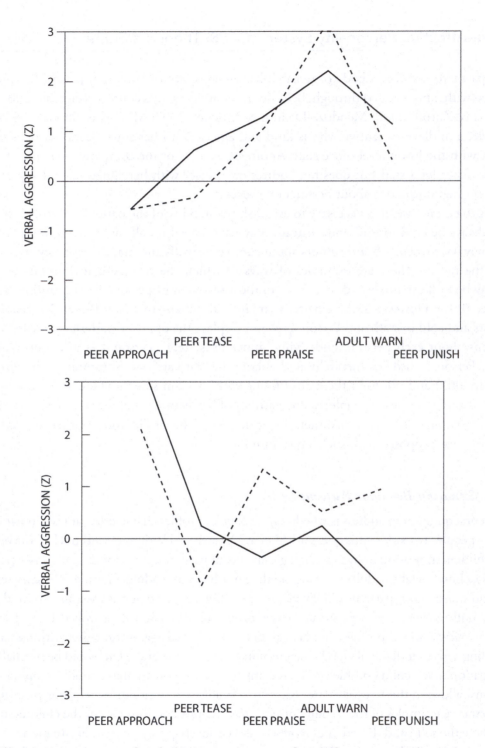

Figure 1. Illustrative patterns of verbal aggression across five different psychological situations for two children at a summer camp; solid and dotted lines represent two nonoverlapping samples of observations (from Shoda et al., 1994).

The stability coefficients ranged from .19 to .47 across the camp situations, suggesting an important and stable facet of individual differences (Shoda et al., 1994). More recently, Fournier et al. (2008) found impressive stability in people's *if … then …* profiles in social interactions with different kinds of people (e.g., agreeable-dominant people vs. quarrelsome-dominant people). English and Chen (2007) have shown, in contrast to the notion that the Asian self-concept is not stable across situations (e.g., Cousins, 1989), that Asian Americans' self-concept is quite stable *within* situation types and forms an *if … then …* pattern.

Explaining If … Then … Patterns in Personality: The Cognitive Affective Personality System

CAPS theory brings together and reflects the influence of three distinct theoretical and empirical traditions. The first influence is Mischel's (1973) cognitive-social theory and in particular the kinds of person variables that are likely to be the "nuts and bolts" of the personality system. The second influence is research and theory on connectionism (see, e.g., Read & Miller, 1998) that emphasizes interconnections between these variables (the cables that connect the bolts). The third influence is research on knowledge activation (e.g., Higgins, 1996) that specifies the principles through which such knowledge becomes activated (the switches for the bolts and cables). We discuss each of these below alongside Figure 2, which represents a schematized illustration of CAPS within its cultural context and is adapted from Mendoza-Denton and Mischel (2007).

"Units" for the System

Mischel and Shoda (1995, 1999) identified five distinct types of nuts and bolts referred to as *cognitive-affective units* or CAUs: encodings, expectancies and beliefs, affects, goals and values, and competencies and self-regulatory abilites. These CAUs summarize and organize the important social information-processing variables that have been identified in social cognition research and in cultural psychology as playing a role in behavior generation. In Figure 2, CAUs are schematized as the small circles that are within the larger circle (the person) in the center of the figure. As the articles in this special section make clear, research has identified a variety of important CAU type variables that are central to our understanding of prejudice and racial/ethnic relations: people's *motivation* to control prejudice (Butz & Plant, this issue), their *goals* to affiliate both within and across group boundaries (Sinclair et al., this issue), their *beliefs* in essentialism (Hong et al., this issue), and their anxious *expectations* of experiencing prejudice (Mendoza-Denton et al., 2002). The common focus across these is on the psychological mediating processes that underlie individual differences in behavior (the research represented here is, of course, not exhaustive; among other examples are personal *need* for structure; Neuberg & Newsom, 1993, and individual differences in promotion and prevention *goals;* Shah, Brazy, & Higgins, 2004).

We underscore that cognitive-affective units already begin to blur the line between person and context by recognizing that these aspects of the self are not biological, inborn, or otherwise "context free" but rather quite explicitly depend in their content on the input from one's environment and cultural milieu (Mendoza-Denton & Mischel, 2007; Mischel & Shoda, 1995). Further, the influence

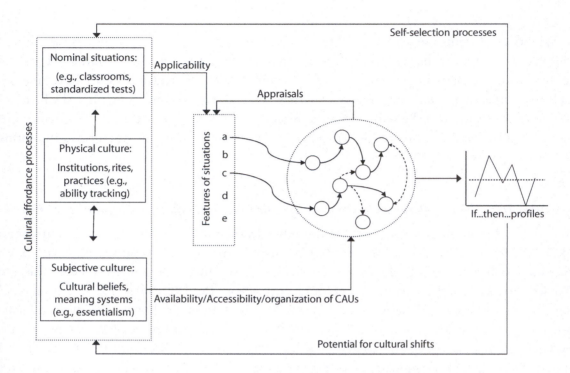

Figure 2. CAPS within its cultural context: Dynamic cultural processes (left box) both shape and are shaped by dynamic personality processes (middle circle). Adapted from Mendoza-Denton & Mischel (2007).

of culture to persons is co-constitutional, or reciprocal. People are influenced by their surrounding culture, but they also reify and reinforce cultural beliefs, goals, and values through their actions, rites, and institution (Mendoza-Denton & Mischel, 2007). This influence is schematized in the large box on the left hand side of Figure 2 labeled "cultural affordance processes." As illustrated in the figure, context can be influenced by cultural shifts that begin at the level of individual behavior (the bottom arrow in the figure) but also affects people through principles of knowledge activation (availability, accessibility, applicability, and organization, described below). As one example, valuing heritage and tradition can give rise to organizations that lobby for conservative leadership that lead to conservative legislation, which makes value-consistent behaviors more likely while increasing the accessibility of the cultural value. As another example, an essentialist belief (see Hong et al., this issue) that people are born with fixed levels of ability and intelligence has led to the creation of diagnostic "tests" for such ability and the institutionalization of practices that reinforce this fixed view such as tracking students according to ability levels in schooling. The suspicion of immutable intelligence is threatening for negatively stereotyped groups and dampens test performance (Good, Aronson, & Inzlicht, 2003). However, the same suspicion of immutable ability *protects* positively stereotyped groups and boosts their performance (Mendoza-Denton, Kahn, & Chan, 2008), further entrenching group-level differences and reinforcing notions of immutability. The implication for this special section is that the CAPS approach allows us to also consider the effects of context and culture as important influences on stable personality dynamics.

From Cognitive-Affective Units to Networks of Activation

Drawing on insights from connectionism (see Read & Miller, 1998) as well as principles of knowledge activation (e.g., Higgins, 1996), CAPS theory proposes that an individual's CAUs do not exist in isolation but rather interact with other CAUs in a dynamic network of activation (represented by the solid and dotted arrows connecting the CAUs in Figure 2). Certain representations have a positive or excitatory link to other representations in the network (the solid arrows), whereas other interconnections are inhibitory or negative (the dotted arrows). For example, for some individuals, expectations of rejection have an excitatory link to behavioral scripts of partner aggression, whereas for others the link to self-silencing and depression is stronger (Ayduk, May, Downey, & Higgins, 2003). Because some individuals share similar experiences and historical inheritances by way of shared group membership, it makes sense that CAU network differences can also occur at the group level. The richness and complexity of individual differences not only stems from the content of one's CAU's per se but also from the organization of the network, which is frequently shared by individuals with similar experiences.

Accounting for If ... Then ... Profiles

How do we go from networks of cognitive-affective mechanisms to *if ... then ...* patterns of behavior? This is the juncture at which principles of knowledge activation come into play. CAPS theory proposes that for a given CAU, its level of activation (a) is not constant and (b) depends on features of the context. Higgins (1996) distinguished specifically between *availability, accessibility,* and *applicability* with respect to knowledge structures. *Availability* refers to whether a particular cognitive-affective unit (or network of CAUs) can be found within the personality system in the first place. For example, in the case of helping behavior, research shows that even with the best intentions, sometimes people are prevented from acting because they do not know how to provide help (Latane & Darley, 1970).

Of importance here is that even though a particular CAU or subset of CAUs may be available to a person, not all of these units are activated at any one time. Thus, even though a person may potentially have a wide number of cognitive affective processes available (e.g., processes that can lead to helping or aggression or prosocial behavior), only those that are *accessible* (i.e., above a given threshold of activation) are likely to have an influence on subsequent behavior generation. Reading an article on anti-immigration protests on the train home, for example, may make nationality cognitions and scripts more accessible to the individual and thus more likely to influence a dinnertime decision to address a bilingual colleague in one language or another. Alternatively, nationality concerns may be *chronically accessible* to a person as part of his or her identity and thus more likely to be used as a framework for understanding stimuli across a wider range of contexts.

Finally, of all the beliefs, goals, values, encodings, and feelings that one can potentially experience at any given time, only those that are *relevant* in a given situation are likely to become accessible and influence subsequent behavior. This is the concept of *applicability.* For example, Banaji, Hardin, and Rothman (1993) found that participants for whom the construct "aggressive" had been primed used this construct in subsequent judgments of male targets but not of female targets. This finding illustrates accessibility effects because, in general, the term "aggressive" is applicable to male targets but not to female targets. Applicability is important because in order for particular constructs to be used, it is not enough for them to be accessible—they must also be applicable to a relevant stimulus or situation.

Nominal Versus Psychological Situations

In terms of understanding ethnic/racial relations, CAPS theory underscores how the differential availability and accessibility of constructs can yield divergent interpretations and behavioral reactions to the "same" situation (see also Mendoza-Denton & Hansen, 2007). Thus, the same *nominal* situation may yield different *psychological* situations for different groups. This was dramatically demonstrated in the United States by striking racial group differences in reactions to the O.J. Simpson 1995 criminal trial verdict (Mendoza-Denton, Ayduk, Shoda, & Mischel, 1997). This trial, which featured an African American defendant (Simpson) charged with the murder of his spouse, also featured a White police officer who may have purposefully planted a bloody glove at the crime scene—a glove that did not, in fact, fit Simpson's hand. The falsification of evidence that this implied made the issue of police bias applicable for many African Americans and contributed to elated reactions following the not-guilty verdict. Such systematic police bias was not as accessible to many White Americans, who instead decried the mountain of evidence against the defendant and thus reacted to the not-guilty verdict with dismay. Importantly, this research also identified a subset of people for whom the trial was applicable both to racial injustice as well as domestic violence and thus reacted with a complex combination of emotions. Importantly, Mendoza-Denton et al. (1997) showed that the effect of "race" as a categorical variable disappeared when these cognitive affective processes were taken into account.

A second example comes from people's reactions to the federal emergency response following the devastation of New Orleans in the wake of Hurricane Katrina. Again, whereas systematic discrimination was an applicable explanation to the federal response for African Americans (given the poorly executed response for Katrina's poorest victims, who were overwhelmingly African American), White Americans tended to favor a response that did not invoke racism per se but rather one that emphasized the magnitude of the disaster and the sheer difficulty of coordinating an effective response for anyone (Levy, Freitas, Mendoza-Denton, & Kugelmass, 2006). Levy and colleagues demonstrated that following this hurricane, African Americans' endorsement of the belief that hard work pays off (the Protestant Work Ethic, or PWE) was reduced during the months following the disaster, whereas White Americans' endorsement of this particular cultural value was not affected, presumably due to a recognition among African Americans of broader structural/institutional forces negatively impacting one's outcomes independently of one's hard work. This finding is a good illustration not only of differences in accessibility and applicability of different constructs but also of differences in the network of associated constructs (in this case, the PWE) that particular events and situations differentially activate among members of cultural groups.

Both of the above examples support the argument that ethnic/racial relations cannot be explained by sociocultural factors, group membership, or individual differences in isolation. Rather, explanations of behavior must take into account the connectedness of these variables: CAPS theory provides an explicit framework that researchers can use to manage such complexity.

Personality Processes in Context: Race-based Rejection Sensitivity

In this second section, we review research on *race-based rejection sensitivity* as one programmatic attempt to illustrate how a CAPS framework can inform our understanding of the dynamic interplay between personality and racial/ethnic relations. The CAPS framework allows us to conceptualize the ways in which prior experiences of discrimination can affect people's *expectancies* about the ways in which they might be treated in the future. Such expectancies, which can become a stable feature of a person's CAPS network (CAUs), influence subsequent cognitions and intergroup behavior. To further illustrate the complex ways in which personality and cultural context are mutually constitutive of one another (cf. Kitayama & Cohen, 2007), we contrast status-based rejection sensitivity among African Americans and Asian Americans in the U.S. context.

Theoretical Background—The Rejection Sensitivity Model

Growing out of a larger literature on attachment (see, e.g., Bowlby, 1969, 1973, 1980) emphasizing that our early experiences shape the way we function in future relationships, Geraldine Downey and her colleagues (Downey & Feldman, 1996; Feldman & Downey, 1994) have proposed a model of Rejection Sensitivity (RS), whereby prior experiences of rejection (in the form of physical or emotional abuse or neglect) lead people to develop anxious expectations of rejection; these anxious expectations are activated specifically in future situations where such rejection is applicable and possible. Once these expectations are activated, people are more likely to be vigilant for the threatening outcome (i.e., rejection), increasing the likelihood of perceiving such rejection in the behavior of their significant others. Once the rejection is perceived, the person is more likely to respond with hot, emotion-laden reactions to the event. Importantly, this dynamic, while being a stable aspect of a person's CAPS, is specifically activated only in situations that afford the possibility of rejection and has been distinguished both theoretically and empirically from generalized neuroticism (for a review of this literature, see Ayduk & Gyurak, 2008).

From Rejection Sensitivity to Race-Based Rejection Sensitivity

People can be rejected not only on the basis of their unique characteristics but also on the basis of attributes that they share with members of other groups, such as their sexual orientation (Pachankis, Goldried, & Ramrattan, 2008), their gender (London, Downey, Rattan, & Velilla, 2004; Mendoza-Denton, Shaw-Taylor, Chen, & Chang, 2009), or—the case we will focus on here—their race. Mendoza-Denton et al. (2002) postulated that direct or vicarious experiences of discrimination, mistreatment, or prejudice on the basis of one's race or ethnicity may lead to *race-based rejection sensitivity*

(RS-race), the core of which is anxious expectations of race-based rejection (research consistently points to the idea that prejudice and discrimination are experienced as rejection; Branscombe, Schmitt, & Harvey, 1999; Essed, 1991; Root, 1992). Unlike the case of personal rejection, however, with race-based rejection people can become concerned that they will be rejected on the basis of their race through either personal or *vicarious* experiences—that is, one does not need to experience the rejection oneself to understand that one can be the target of similar race-based rejection.

Different Triggers and Outcomes for Different Groups

Situations such as asking one's significant other to meet one's family have been shown to readily activate expectations of personal rejection. By contrast, race-based rejection expectations are triggered in different types of situations, and these situations differ depending on the group in question.

Mendoza-Denton et al. (2002) conducted focus groups to find out the situations that activate race-based rejection concerns among African Americans and constructed a questionnaire based on those situations. The kinds of situations included scenarios such as being stopped during a random traffic stop or being passed over for an opportunity to answer a difficult question in class. The researchers administered this questionnaire to a sample of African American, European American, and Asian American undergraduates. As expected, African Americans scored highest on the measure, whereas European American and Asian American participants scored low on the measure and did not differ. As expected, for African Americans, individual differences in RS-race predicted, over a 3-week period, reports of rejection as well as more intense feelings of alienation and rejection following the rejection. Over the course of five semesters, individual differences in RS-race as measured by the RS-race questionnaire predicted students' academic adjustment. This included students' attendance at review sessions, their comfort interacting with professors and teaching assistants, and their grade point average (GPA). However, consistent with prior research (Crocker & Major, 1989), RS-race is unrelated to self-esteem. We highlight these relationships of RS-race to the above outcomes because, as we discuss next, both triggers and outcomes are different when we consider race-based rejection sensitivity among Asian Americans.

RS-Race Among Asian Americans

As described above, the original RS-race questionnaire that was designed specifically for African Americans yielded low scores as well as low variability in anxious expectations among Asian Americans. This result can be easily misconstrued as meaning that Asian Americans do not experience as much discrimination as African Americans and is consistent with stereotypes of Asian Americans as a "model minority." However, as several researchers note, Asian Americans report experiences that contradict this notion and report that they experience just as much discrimination as other groups (Okazaki, 1997).

Chan and Mendoza-Denton (2008) recently investigated how the dynamic of race-based rejection sensitivity unfolds among Asian Americans. Focus groups revealed that the situations likely to trigger Asian Americans' concerns are much different than those triggering the concerns of African

Americans—being concerned over whether one will be invited to join an athletic game, for example, or being left out of a social evening on the assumption that nerds do not go out, seem to be the situations that resonate with Asian Americans as triggers of their race-based rejection concerns. In contrast to the findings for African Americans, Chan and Mendoza-Denton have shown that, controlling for rejection sensitivity in the interpersonal domain, the race-based rejection sensitivity scale for Asian Americans (RS-A) that resulted from these focus groups is uncorrelated with academic performance and GPA. Even more intriguingly, RS-race among Asian Americans was consistently *negatively* correlated with self-esteem and positively with depressive symptoms and social anxiety. How can we understand the different patterning of RS-race among African Americans and Asian Americans?

These group-level differences in the relationship of RS-race to particular outcomes (i.e., GPA vs. self-esteem) are reflective of the principle that stable personality dynamics are shaped and triggered by sociocultural forces. The academically related triggers and outcomes that are linked to RS-race among African Americans reflect a long and painful history related to the suspicion that African Americans are intellectually inferior to Whites (see also Hong et al., this issue). At the same time, as Chan and Mendoza-Denton (2008) argue, a powerful and meaningful civil rights movement was a catalyst that successfully increased for this group the chronic accessibility of prejudice as an explanation for negative outcomes among African Americans, thereby allowing for the protection of self-esteem (see also Twenge & Crocker, 2002, for historical data supporting this view). By contrast, Asian Americans have not had the benefit of a large-scale civil rights movement to raise collective consciousness and make discounting of negative outcomes a culturally accepted coping strategy for discrimination. As such, individual and group-level *if … then …* profiles reflect sociohistorical forces: African Americans, *if* experiencing rejection from an outgroup member, may *then* not attribute the outcome to themselves (and thus suffer no drop in self-esteem) as a result of a culturally shared set of cognitions recognizing prejudice as a source of negative outcomes. Asian Americans, *if* discriminated against, may *then* in fact feel responsible for the negative outcome (and suffer decreases in self-esteem), reflecting a lack of culturally shared protective cognitions. In other words, the same cognitive-affective dynamic—in this case anxious expectations, ready perceptions, and intense reactions to race-based rejection—can be at one level shared by members of different groups but at a second level be completely different in its triggers and consequences.

Caps "in Action:" The Contributions to this Special Section

We have reviewed research on RS-race as a specific example of how CAPS theory has informed a specific research program that focuses specifically on stigmatized group members' reactions to and coping mechanisms for the discrimination that they face. The work, though explicitly guided by CAPS theory from its inception (see Mendoza-Denton et al., 2002), nevertheless required specifying the CAUs of interest (affects and expectations), the expected *if … then …* profiles that would reflect these CAUs, as well as the particular sociohistorical realities that have shaped the specific lenses through which particular cultural groups navigate their world.

The rest of this special section highlights three more exciting research programs—on beliefs in essentialism (Hong et al.), on motivation to control prejudice (Butz & Plant), and on shared-reality theory (Sinclair et al.)—as yet other examples of CAPS theory, as it were, "in action." In each case, the authors have attempted, as we have in our treatment of RS-race, to explicitly draw links from their work to CAPS theory.

Emergent Themes

An emergent quality arises from the totality of the contributions—a set of themes that seem to run across all of the research programs that are covered here and that parallel the general principles put forward by CAPS theory (readers will also recognize them in the review above of RS-race). These themes are (a) historical and social context matters, (b) interrelations among CAUs matter, and (c) situations matter. The rest of this introduction is devoted to highlighting these themes, explicitly providing examples of how the present contributions reflect a particular theme.

Historical and Social Context Matters

Mendoza-Denton and Mischel (2007) note that "life experiences shared by members of a group—the teachings of elders, the experiences shared with others, the values imposed by society—generate a CAPS network that is immersed in and reflects the surrounding culture" (p. 182). In terms of historical context, we have reviewed above how people's anxious expectations with respect to race are borne of the fact that race has carried specific symbolic import within this country, with different groups having been subjected historically to different stereotypes (e.g., African Americans as athletic but intellectually inferior, Asian Americans as intelligent but unathletic). This historical backdrop sets the stage for the different triggers and outcomes of RS-race associated with different groups. Similarly, Butz and Plant (this issue) observe, "it is difficult to consider prejudice in contemporary society without taking into account the significant implications of social context and the norms regarding the expression of prejudice." They make the subtle but critical point that motivation to control racial prejudice develops only the presence of historically developed social sanctions against such prejudice—a condition that is much less descriptive, for example, of prejudice toward those suffering from mental illness (Hinshaw, 2007).

In terms of social context, Hong et al. (this issue) note that "lay theories of race do not exist in a social vacuum … [and] may reflect the shared consensus in the society," citing research (No et al., 2008) showing that priming people with a given lay theory from what is perceived to be a legitimate news outlet can shift people's own belief systems. Hong et al. make the important point here that an essentialist cultural zeitgeist that prizes genetically-based discoveries and explanations for human attributes can affect the chronic accessibility of an essentialist race theory at the level of the individual. Consider also the work of Sinclair et al. (this issue), who review work relevant to self-stereotyping and significant others. They discuss how, whereas women's degree of self-stereotyping is related to how they assume significant others see them and expect them to be, African Americans' self-stereotyping is unrelated to how they expect significant others to see them, because they tend to think that their significant others do not endorse these stereotypes. This is an important point because it reflects the greater overall cultural acceptance and lack of cultural inhibitions against using and applying gender stereotypes versus applying stereotypes against African Americans (see also Mendoza-Denton, Park, & O'Connor, 2008).

Interrelations Among CAUs Matter

A second theme that emerges from the four research programs included here is that beliefs, goals, expectations, and other aspects of people's "inner lives" interface and interact with each other. This, of course, underscores the principle from CAPS theory that CAUs operate within an interconnected network. Hong et al. provide an indepth review of how lay *beliefs* about race, in either essentialist or social constructionist terms, shape an entire host of downstream processes, from encoding, to inferences, to group differentiation, to stereotyping, to how then people interpret intergroup interactions. As another example, Mendoza-Denton and colleagues have shown that anxious expectations of race-based rejection affect how people subsequently *encode* future situations in which such rejection is applicable and possible, how they react behaviorally to such rejection, and how they subsequently cope in a potentially toxic environment. Sinclair et al. discuss how the strength of people's affiliative *motivation* leads them to shift their *beliefs* in tune with other people so as to increase shared reality, which can subsequently lead to self-stereotyping. Butz and Plant similarly make clear the interplay of various CAUs—people are motivated to respond without prejudice, but their specific personal *endorsement* of egalitarianism as a personal *value* affects their internal motivation and how much they value others' views affects their external motivation. Although CAPS theory brought insights from connectionism to bear on personality, in these examples we see such connections at work, no longer in the abstract form of Figure 2, but now specifically instantiated as they relate to personality and intergroup processes.

Situations Matter

One of the fundamental insights from CAPS is that situations play a fundamental role in the development and expression of personality systems. This insight may be particularly relevant in the domain of stigma, where many of today's instantiations of stigma are no longer of an overt, explicit nature. Indeed, targets of prejudice and discrimination are often confronted with "attributional ambiguity" (Crocker, Voelkl, Testa, & Major, 1991), whereby a particular negative outcome (e.g., being turned down for a job, not being voted for, getting a bad grade) can be attributed either to one's personal shortcomings or to another person's prejudice. And, as has long been noted, individual differences are most likely to emerge in ambiguous situations because people are most likely to use their pre-existing schemas to disambiguate the situation. In a demonstration of this idea, Mendoza-Denton et al. (2009) had women complete an SAT-like analogies task after having been exposed to a room in which their male evaluator's attitudes toward women were made clear through the decor, or in which his attitudes were not explicitly communicated. As expected, individual differences in gender-based rejection sensitivity predicted performance following exposure to the ambiguous room, but did not predict performance following exposure to either a chauvinist, or a progressive room. This example illustrates how expectations of discrimination can indeed affect the perception of subsequent stimuli, but situations matter in that they are differentially open to multiple interpretations. Another way in which situations matter is illustrated well by Butz and Plant through their discussion of how the context interacts with people's internal and external motivations to control prejudice to predict the success of their regulatory efforts (see Figure 1 of their article). As such, Butz and Plant show not only that internal and external motivation to control prejudice are part of the person's CAPS network, but also that the network is then related to regulatory success as a function of the situation.

Conclusions

Efforts to understand the relationship between personality and prejudice have a long and distinguished history (e.g., Adorno, FrenkelBrunswick, Levinson, & Sanford, 1950; Allport, 1954; see Brown, 1995; Zimbardo, 1970; see also Hong et al., this issue). Our aim in this special section is to take a fresh look at prejudice and racial/ ethnic relations from the perspective of CAPS theory. By reviewing four specific research programs that resonate with and specify the general principles set forth by CAPS theory, this special section attempts to shed light on the role that context plays in the expression of personality, the role that race and ethnicity play in the interpretation of context, and the implications of CAPS theory for how we understand both personality and intergroup dynamics. As the articles in this special section make clear, historical and social context matter, CAUs and their interrelationships matter, and situations matter for understanding personality and racial/ethnic relations. We hope these articles encourage interested readers to consider these broad themes vis-a-vis their own research programs as they relate to personality, process, and prejudice.

References

Adorno, T. W., Frenkel-Brunswick, E., Levinson, D. J., & Sanford, R. N. (1950). *The authoritarian personality.* New York: Harper.

Allport, G. W. (1954). *The nature of prejudice.* Reading, MA: Addison-Wesley.

Ayduk, O., & Gyurak, A. (2008). Conceptualizing rejection sensitivity as a cognitive-affective processing disposition. *Social and Personality Psychology Compass, 2,* 2016–2033.

Ayduk, O., May, D., Downey, G., & Higgins, T. (2003). Tactical differences in coping with rejection sensitivity: The role of prevention pride. *Personality and Social Psychology Bulletin, 29,* 435–448.

Banaji, M. R., Hardin, C., & Rothman, A. J. (1993). Implicit stereotyping in person judgment. *Journal of Personality and Social Psychology, 65,* 272–281.

Bowlby, J. (1969). *Attachment and loss: Vol. 1. Attachment.* New York: Basic Books.

Bowlby, J. (1973). *Attachment and loss: Vol. 2. Separation.* New York: Basic Books.

Bowlby, J. (1980). *Attachment and loss: Vol. 3. Loss, sadness, and depression*. New York: Basic Books.

Branscombe, N. R., Schmitt, M. T., & Harvey, R. D. (1999). Perceiving pervasive discrimination among African Americans: Implications for group identification and well-being. *Journal of Personality and Social Psychology, 77*, 135–149.

Brown, R. (1995). *Prejudice: Its social psychology*. Oxford, UK: Blackwell.

Chan, W. Y., & Mendoza-Denton, R. (2008). Status-based rejection sensitivity among Asian Americans: Implications for psychological distress. *Journal of Personality, 76*, 1317–1346.

Cousins, S. D. (1989). Culture and self-perception in Japan and the United States. *Journal of Personality and Social Psychology, 56*, 124–131.

Crocker, J., & Major, B. (1989). Social stigma and self-esteem: The self-protective properties of stigma. *Psychological Review, 96*, 608–630.

Crocker, J., Voelkl, K., Testa, M., & Major, B. (1991). Social stigma: The affective consequences of attributional ambiguity. *Journal of Personality and Social Psychology, 60*, 218–228.

Downey, G., & Feldman, S. (1996). Implications of rejection sensitivity for intimate relationships. *Journal of Personality and Social Psychology, 70*, 1327–343.

English, T., & Chen, S. (2007). Culture and self-concept stability: Consistency across and within contexts among Asianand European-Americans. *Journal of Personality and Social Psychology, 93*, 478–490.

Essed, P. (1991). *Understanding everyday racism*. Newbury Park, CA: Sage.

Feldman, S., & Downey, G. (1994). Rejection sensitivity as a mediator of the impact of childhood exposure to family violence on adult attachment behavior. *Development and Psychopathology, 6*, 231–247.

Fleeson, W. (2001). Toward a structureand process-integrated view personality: Traits as density-distributions of states. *Journal of Personality and Social Psychology, 80*, 1011–1027.

Fournier, M. A., Moskowitz, D. S., & Zuroff, D. C. (2008). Integrating dispositions, signatures, and the interpersonal domain. *Journal of Personality and Social Psychology, 94*, 531–545.

Gilbert, D. T., & Malone, P. S. (1995). The correspondence bias. *Psychological Bulletin, 117*, 21–38.

Good, C., Aronson, J., & Inzlicht, M. (2003). Improving adolescents' standardized test performance: An intervention to reduce the effects of stereotype threat. *Applied Developmental Psychology, 24*, 645–662.

Higgins, E. T. (1996). Knowledge activation: Accessibility, applicability, and saliance. In E. T. Higgins & A. W. Kruglanski (Eds.), *Social psychology: Handbook of basic principles* (pp. 133–168). New York: Guilford.

Hinshaw, S. P. (2007). The mark of shame: Stigma of mental illness and an agenda for change. New York: Oxford.

Kammrath, L., Mendoza-Denton, R., & Mischel, W. (2005). Incorporating *if … then …* signatures in person perception: Beyond the person-situation dichotomy. *Journal of Personality and Social Psychology, 88*, 605-613.

Kitayama, S., & Cohen, D. (2007). *Handbook of cultural psychology*. New York: Guilford.

Latane, B., & Darley, J. M. (1970). *The unresponsive bystander: Why doesn't he help?* New York: Appleton-Century-Crofts.

Levy, S. R., Freitas, A. L., Mendoza-Denton, R., & Kugelmass, H. (2006). Hurricane Katrina's impact on African Americans' and European Americans' endorsement of the Protestant work ethic. *Analyses of Social Issues and Public Policy, 6*, 75–85.

London, B., Downey, G., Rattan, A., & Velilla, E. (2004, February). *Sensitivity to gender-based rejection: Theory, validation, and implications for psychosocial well-being*. Poster presented at the annual meeting of the Society of Personality and Social Psychology, Austin, TX.

Mendoza-Denton, R., Ayduk, O. N., Shoda, Y., & Mischel, W. (1997). Cognitive-affective processing system analysis of reactions to the O.J. Simpson criminal trial verdict. *Journal of Social Issues, 53*, 563–581.

Mendoza-Denton, R., Downey, G., Purdie, V. J., Davis, A., & Pietrzak, J. (2002). Sensitivity to status-based rejection: Implications for African American students' college experience. *Journal of Personality and Social Psychology, 83*, 896–918.

Mendoza-Denton, R., & Hansen, N. (2007). Networks of meaning: Intergroup relations, cultural worldviews, and knowledge activation principles. *Social and Personality Psychology Compass, 1*, 68–83.

Mendoza-Denton, R., Kahn, K., & Chan, W. Y. (2008). Can fixed views of ability boost performance in the context of favorable stereotypes? *Journal of Experimental Social Psychology, 44*, 1187–1193.

Mendoza-Denton, R., & Mischel, W. (2007). Integrating system approaches to culture and personality: The Cultural Cognitive-Affective Processing System (C-CAPS). In S. Kitayama & D. Cohen (Eds.), *Handbook of cultural psychology*. New York: Guilford.

Mendoza-Denton, R., Park, S., & O'Connor, A. (2007). Toward a science of the social perceiver. In G. Downey, Y. Shoda, & D. Cervone (Eds.), *Persons in context: Building a science of the individual* (pp. 211–25). New York: Guilford.

Mendoza-Denton, R., Park, S. H., & O'Connor, A. (2008). Gender stereotypes as situation-behavior profiles. *Journal of Experimental Social Psychology, 44*, 971–982.

Mendoza-Denton, R., Pietrzak, J., & Downey, G. (2008). Distinguishing institutional identification from academic goal pursuit: Interactive effects of ethnic identification and race-based rejection sensitivity. *Journal of Personality and Social Psychology, 95*, 338–351.

Mendoza-Denton, R., Shaw-Taylor, L., Chen, S., & Chang, E. (2009). Ironic effects of explicit gender prejudice on women's test performance. *Journal of Experimental Social Psychology, 45*, 275–278.

Miller, S. M., Shoda, Y., & Hurley, K. (1996). Applying cognitive social theory to health protective behavior: Breast self-examination in cancer screening. *Psychological Bulletin, 119*, 70–94.

Mischel, W. (1973). Toward a cognitive social learning reconceptualization of personality. *Pyschological Review, 80*, 252–283.

Mischel, W., & Shoda, Y. (1995). A cognitive-affective system theory of personality: Reconceptualizing situations, dispositions, dynamics, and invariance in personality structure. *Psychological Review, 102*, 246–268.

Mischel, W., & Shoda, Y. (1998). Reconciling processing dynamics and personality dispositions. *Annual Review of Psychology, 49*, 229–58.

Mischel, W., & Shoda, Y. (1999). Integrating dispositions and processing dynamics within a unified theory of personality: The cognitive-affective personality system. In L. A. Pervin & O. P. John (Eds.), *Handbook of personality: Theory and research* (pp. 197–218). New York: Guilford.

Mischel, W., & Shoda, Y. (2008). Toward a unifying theory of personality: Integrating dispositions and processing dynamics within the cognitiveaffective processing system. In O. P. John, R. W. Robins, & L. A. Pervin (Eds.), *Handbook of personality psychology* (3rd ed., pp. 208–241). New York: Guilford.

Morf, C. C., & Rhodewalt, F. (2001). Unraveling the paradoxes of narcissism: A dynamic self-regulatory processing model. *Psychological Inquiry, 12*, 177–196.

Neuberg, S. L., & Newsom, J. T. (1993). Personal need for structure: Individual differences in the desire for simpler structure. *Journal of Personality and Social Psychology, 65*, 113–131.

No, S., Hong, Y., Liao, H., Lee, K., Wood, D., & Chao, M. M. (2008). Race and psychological essentialism: Lay theory of race moderates Asian Americans' responses toward American culture. *Journal of Personality and Social Psychology,* 95, 991–1004.

Okazaki, S. (1997). Sources of ethnic differences between Asian American and White American college students on measures of depression and social anxiety. *Journal of Abnormal Psychology,* 106, 52–60.

Pachankis, J. E., Goldfried, M. R., & Ramrattan, M. E. (2008). Extension of the rejection sensitivity construct to the interpersonal functioning of gay men. *Journal of Consulting and Clinical Psychology,* 76, 306–317.

Read, S. J., & Miller, L. C. (1998). Connectionist models of social reasoning and social behavior. Mahwah, NJ: Erlbaum.

Root, M. P. (1992). Reconstructing the impact of trauma on personality. In L. S. Brown & M. Ballou (Eds.), *Personality and psychopathology: Feminist reappraisals* (pp. 229–266). New York: Guilford.

Shah, J. Y., Brazy, P. C., & Higgins, E. T. (2004). Promoting us or preventing them: Regulatory focus and manifestations of intergroup bias. *Personality and Social Psychology Bulletin,* 30, 433–446.

Shoda, Y., Mischel, W., & Wright, J. C. (1994). Intraindividual stability in the organization and patterning of behavior: Incorporating psychological situations into the idiographic analysis of personality. *Journal of Personality and Social Psychology,* 67, 674–687.

Twenge, J. M., & Crocker, J. (2002). Race and self-esteem: Meta-analyses comparing Whites, Blacks, Hispanics, Asians, and American Indians and comment on Gray, Little, and Hafdahl (2000). *Psychological Bulletin,* 128, 371–408.

Zimbardo, P. G. (1970). The human choice: Individuation, reason, and order versus deindividuation, impulse, and chaos. In W. J. Arnold & D. Levine (Eds.), *Nebraska Symposium on Motivation,* 1969. Lincoln: University of Nebraska Press.

Networks of Meaning

Intergroup Relations, Cultural Worldviews, and Knowledge Activation Principles

By Rodolfo Mendoza-Denton* and Nina Hansen, University of California, Berkeley

Abstract

In this article, we bring advances in the fields of social cognition, personality, and culture to bear on the topic of intergroup relations. Specifically, principles of knowledge activation (Higgins, 1996), and of the architecture of knowledge networks (Cervone, 2005; Mischel & Shoda, 1995) are applied to understanding how cultural groups develop divergent worldviews. We discuss these principles within a recently proposed model of culture and person dynamics, the Cultural Cognitive-Affective Processing System (Mendoza-Denton & Mischel, 2007). It is argued that the underlying psychological principles that govern knowledge acquisition and activation may be universal, but that the manifestations of these processes are culture specific. More precisely, culture impacts the availability, applicability, and accessibility of knowledge, as well as the organizational relationships among constructs. Together, these processes give rise to complex *networks of meaning* that, despite diverging across cultures, can nevertheless be communicated and understood by non-natives of that culture.

CCAPS

Networks of Meaning: Understanding Cultural Worldview Differences Through Principles of Knowledge Activation

A recent poll in which 14,000 people across 13 nations worldwide were interviewed (Pew Global Attitudes Project, 2006) found striking differences in how non-Muslim Westerners and Muslims around the world see each other. When non-Muslim Westerners were asked whether Muslims are fanatical or not, the majority of participants agreed to the question. More precisely, 83% of the Spanish, 78% of the German, 50% of the French, 48% of the British, and 43% of the American participants affirmed this question. When asked the *same* question with reference to Westerners, 68% of the Jordanian, 67% of the Turkish, 61% of the Egyptian, 41% of the Indonesian, and 24% of the Pakistani participants

Rodolfo Mendoza-Denton & Nina Hansen, "Networks of Meaning: Intergroup Relations, Cultural Worldviews, and Knowledge Activation Principles," *Social and Personality Psychology Compass*, vol. 1, no. 1, pp. 68–83. Copyright © 2007 by John Wiley & Sons, Inc. Reprinted with permission.

agreed to this question. A second question asked participants whether the other group is respectful toward women. The results revealed that 83% of the Spanish, 80% of the German, 77% of the French, 59% of the British, and 69% of the American participants viewed Muslims as disrespectful to women. Similarly, 53% of the Jordanian, 39% of the Turkish, 52% of the Egyptian, 50% of the Indonesian, and 52% of the Pakistani participants viewed Westerners as lacking respect toward women.

What makes people from different groups unable to see eye-to-eye on certain issues? Why are the perspectives of these groups so different, and how can we account for broad group differences while simultaneously allowing for within-group variability as above? Historically, a principal goal of intergroup relations research has been to try to shed light on the psychological mechanisms that can help account for such discrepancies in worldviews. According to *Realistic Intergroup Conflict Theory* (Campbell, 1965), for example, conflict or competition between social groups leads to a devaluation of the other group because of the threat to the realization of the goals of one's in-group (Alexander, Brewer, & Hermann, 1999; Hogg, 2000; Sassenberg, Moskowitz, Jacoby, & Hansen, 2007; Shah, Kruglanski, & Thompson, 1998). Whereas in this case conflict between groups is based on material resources, it can also be based on symbolic or identity characteristics. In the latter vein, *Social Identity Theory* (Tajfel, 1978; Tajfel & Turner, 1979) posits that people strive for positive self-esteem as members of the social groups they belong to. As such, groups are motivated to compare each other and strive to evaluate the in-group more positively and out-groups more negatively. According to the *Ingroup Projection Model* (Mummendey & Wenzel, 1999), people who belong to a particular group tend to generalize (project) their own group's typical attitudes and characteristics to the broader, superordinate category (e.g., "humans"), thereby making their own group's perspective normative. As a consequence of this process, the more group members perceive their own in-group as prototypical, the more the attitudes toward an out-group become negative (Waldzus, Mummendey, Wenzel, & Weber, 2002).

As the examples above make clear, theoretical and empirical advances have yielded important answers to understanding the puzzle of intergroup divergences in worldview. In this article, we contribute to this literature by attempting to explain difference through common ground that is, by attempting to understand cultural differences in worldviews through the articulation of potentially universal psychological principles that govern how knowledge is acquired, activated, and used to interpret the world (cf. Higgins, 1996; Hong & Mallorie, 2004; Kashima, 2001). In so doing, we review a recently proposed model in which cultural differences in social behavior are seen as meaningful manifestations of a dynamic, culturally constituted information processing system. This system, which we call the "Cultural Cognitive-Affective Processing System" (C-CAPS; Mendoza-Denton & Mischel, 2007), allows us to understand how culture influences information processing dynamics to yield culture-specific worldviews.

Culture, Person, and Intergroup Relations

What is culture? What is person? And what can their interrelationship reveal about the rise of intergroup tension? Psychologists have long been interested in the ways in which culture influences people as a way of understanding cultural differences in social behavior. Early attempts to characterize the relationship between culture and person sought to describe general personality types that were prevalent in one culture or another. Benedict (1934), for example, described two broad personality types of the Southwest Pueblos, the Dionysian and the Appolonian, with the former having a generalized love for excess and the latter as sober and mistrustful of excessive behavior. Later, research on the "national character" and the "dominant personality" of cultural groups (e.g., Linton, 1945; Kardiner, 1945) attempted to explain intergroup discord and conflict in terms of the different personalities that were prevalent (and prone to conflict) in a given culture. Today, the tradition of searching for cultural differences in personality is principally carried on by research that characterizes cultures in terms of the Big Five: openness to experience, agreeableness, conscientiousness, neuroticism, and extraversion (e.g., Allik & McCrae, 2004; McCrae & Allik, 2002).

Nevertheless, explaining *how* members of different cultural groups can come to see the world so differently requires moving toward a model that is able to capture the process through which a culture influences the stable, characteristic ways that people think, and the way that they use acquired knowledge to navigate their world. It involves a view of "personality" not just as a description of broad behavioral tendencies (e.g., "Mehmet is gentle;" or "Johann is close minded"), but also as the way that people construe their world, the goals that they strive to achieve, the fundamental beliefs that they hold, and the values that they hold dear.

Toward an Information-Processing Account of Cultural Worldviews

Over the past 25 years, advances in the science of social cognition (see Cervone, 2005; Mischel & Shoda, 1998) have provided new clues toward understanding how cultural forces shape individual behavior (Kashima, 2001; Mendoza-Denton, Shoda, Ayduk, & Mischel, 1999). This general approach focuses on the social and cognitive-mediating processes that motivate people to behave in their characteristic ways (Bandura, 1982, 1986; Cantor, 1990, 1994; Cantor & Kihlstrom, 1987; Dodge, 1993; Dweck, 2006; Higgins, 1996; Mischel, 1973, 1990). A crucial aspect of the social cognitive orientation for researchers interested in culture lies in its emphasis on the mediating *psychological processes* underlying behavior the ways in which a person's stable encodings, beliefs, expectations, goals, emotions, and self-regulatory strategies influence behavior in relation to relevant features of situations (Mischel, 1973; Mischel, Shoda, & Mendoza-Denton, 2002). The approach harnesses behavioral variability across situations to understand such psychological processes (Mischel et al., 2002). How can such behavioral variability yield clues about psychological processes?

An example from the US context is useful here. As Cohen, Nisbett, Bowdle, and Schwarz (1996) note, data consistently suggest greater rates of violence in the American South than in the North. For example, homicide rates in the South and West have been shown to be higher than they are in the North for argument-related homicides (Nisbett & Cohen, 1996). At the same time, however, the South is also widely regarded for its politeness and charm. Charleston, South Carolina, for example, has been ranked for 10 straight years as the USA's most polite city in national polls (CNN, 2005).

Cohen et al. (1996) demonstrated this seemingly contradictory pattern in a laboratory setting. The researchers recruited participants who were either from the North or from the South, and created an experimental situation in which the participants needed to go back and forth across a narrow hallway. A research assistant (who, unbeknownst to the participant, was part of the experimental setup) was standing in front of a file cabinet in the middle of the hallway, purportedly looking for documents. In one condition, the research assistant acted annoyed by the inconvenience of having to let the participant pass, slamming the drawer, insulting the participant, and bumping the participant intentionally. In the other condition, the participant was not bumped or insulted. A few minutes later, as the participant walked back from the hallway, a new research assistant appeared and walked in the opposite direction on a direct collision course with the participant unless someone moved.

Among Northern participants, the bumping manipulation did not have a significant effect on the distance at which the participant gave way to the oncoming confederate, moving out of the way approximately 70 inches before a potential collision across both conditions. Among Southern participants, however, there was a clear effect of experimental condition. When Southern participants had been previously insulted, they subsequently moved out of the way of the other confederate at an average distance of 37 inches. Tellingly, however, when Southern participants had *not* been bumped, they actually gave way much *earlier* than Northern participants, moving out of the way 108 inches before a potential bump. Independent observers' ratings of the dominance of the participants showed that while bumped Southern subjects seemed more aggressive and threatening than Northern participants, Southern participants who had not been bumped actually seemed less so than Northern participants.

Given the above data, a description of the people of the American South in terms of broad behavioral tendencies (e.g., not agreeable, or agreeable) would yield contradictory descriptions, each of which would miss important and stable aspects of the culture. The reconciliation of these surface-level inconsistencies in behavior requires a different type of explanatory model and provides a key to understanding cultural dynamics of personality on a dynamic level.

Cohen and Nisbett (1994, 1997) have provided a historically informed, compelling reconciliation of such apparent inconsistencies. According to these researchers, the South's economy was historically herding based, yet law enforcement was difficult in part due to low population densities. This combination led to a cultural adaptation over time in which honor and reputation became critical elements in the protection of one's property and name. The culture became characterized by strong vigilance to disrespect and ready use of violence in response to it. At the same time, in a context where violence is a consequence of disrespect, unambiguous displays of respect when not looking for trouble became highly adaptive, and readily adopted (Cohen, Vandello, Puente, & Rantilla, 1999). As such, a view of Southern cultural dynamics that focuses on the historically transmitted importance of valuing *honor* helps us understand otherwise contradictory behavior. Over time, a concern over honor has not only shaped people's values and the way in which situations may be psychologically characterized, but also in the behavioral possibilities that are afforded within the cultural system (Cohen, 1998; Norenzayan & Heine, 2005).

Culture and the "active ingredients" of personality

When variability in behavior across situations is stable, it readily invites questions about a person's construals of different situations, and the relevant motivations, goals, expectations that are associated with these construals (Kammrath, Mendoza-Denton, & Mischel, 2005; Mendoza-Denton, Park, & O'Connor, forthcoming; Plaks, Shafer, & Shoda, 2003). Consider the following definitions of culture, both classical and modern:

> ... that complex whole which includes knowledge, belief, art, law, morals, custom, and any other capabilities and habits acquired by man as a member of society. (Tylor, 1871, 1)
> ... a set of meanings that human beings impose on the world. (Obeyeskere, 1981, 110)
> ... a historically transmitted pattern of meanings embodied in symbols, a system of inherited conceptions expressed in symbolic form by means of which men [and women] communicate, perpetuate and develop their knowledge about and attitudes towards life. (Geertz, 1973, 89)
> The judgmental or normative dimension, which reflects social standards and values ... the cognitive dimension, which relates to social perceptions, conceptions, attributions ... the affective dimension, the emotional structure of a social unit, including its common feelings, sources of motivations, joy and sorrow, and sense of value ... the skills dimension, signifying those special capabilities people develop to meet the demands of their social and technoeconomic environment ... the technological dimension, the notion of culture as accumulated artifacts, instrumentation, and techniques. (Gordon, 1982, 187–188)
> It includes what "has worked" in the past and can be identified by examining the extent to which psychological processes, such as beliefs, attitudes, and values, are shared and transmitted from one generation to the next. (Triandis, 1997, 442–443, on cultural syndromes)

As the definitions above illustrate, conceptions of culture have historically included some of the same "active ingredients" that help us explain surface-level inconsistencies in behavior namely, a person's goals, values, beliefs, encodings (ways of interpreting stimuli), self-regulatory mechanisms, and expectations. These units, which in the C-CAPS framework are called *cognitive-affective units* or *CAUs,* are widely agreed to be central not only to one's cultural heritage (Mendoza-Denton et al., 1999; Mendoza-Denton & Mischel, 2007), but to a dynamic conceptualization of personality (Mischel & Shoda, 1995). As Mendoza-Denton et al. (1999; Mendoza-Denton & Mischel, 2007) have posited, CAUs provide a natural bridge between cultural context on the one hand and persons on the other. Given that people navigate various worlds and roles, each person's goals, values, and other CAUs will include some CAUs that are shared broadly with other members of the superordinate culture (such as one's national group), some that are shared with smaller cultural groups (e.g., one's gender or ethnic group) as well as some idiosyncratic CAUs that are learned from specific family experiences or even private experience (Linton, 1936; Mendoza-Denton et al., 1999).

Principles of knowledge acquisition and activation

With CAUs providing a bridge for culture to influence the person (and vice versa, as discussed below), the C-CAPS framework draws on basic principles of knowledge activation (Higgins, 1996; Mischel & Shoda, 1995) to understand how cultural knowledge is acquired, activated, and used in everyday transactions. The basic architecture of the system and its governing principles organization, availability, accessibility, and applicability may broadly describe human information processing and together, give rise to different *networks of meaning* across cultural groups. We review these principles in the next section.

Organization

The C-CAPS conceptualizes the CAUs described above not as a mere collection of attributes, but rather as interacting within a stable network of activation that is, by a distinctive set of *interrelationships*. This type of model, in which representations interact within a network of relationships and constraints (e.g., Hinton, McClelland, & Rumelhart, 1986), provides a framework for conceptualizing an organized personality processing system that is sensitive to different features of situations and can respond discriminatively to them in characteristic and stable ways. As such, cultural (and individual) differences can arise not only from differences in CAUs, but also from the distinctive organization among these CAUs. For example, although concerns about discrimination and self-esteem are unrelated among African Americans (Crocker, Major, & Steele, 1998; Mendoza-Denton, Downey, Purdie, Davis, & Pietrzak, 2002), these same concerns seem to have a negative impact on self-esteem among Asian Americans (Chan & Mendoza-Denton, forthcoming).

Availability, accessibility, and *applicability* can be explained via a metaphor to coloring with crayons (Mendoza-Denton & Mischel, 2007). One can think of the world "out there" as a blank coloring book that contains a set of guidelines, yet leaves much of the final picture open to the coloring choices of cultures and individuals. Cultures are assumed to differ in the crayons that it makes *available* to its members. For example, the concept of bargaining to arrive at a price for vegetables in open markets is prevalent throughout much of West Africa, but is generally not part of the behavioral repertoire for grocery shopping in US markets. As such, a "bargaining" crayon is available to members of some cultures, but not others.

Beyond differences in the availability of constructs, cultures can also differ in the *accessibility* of available constructs. Accessibility refers to how easily a concept comes to mind; it can be thought of in terms of how easy or difficult it is to reach crayons that are in the front of one's box versus the ones in the back rows. Ease of retrieval of concepts can occur both over the short term (e.g., if one hears a lecture about the dangers of heart disease, one may be less likely to order steak for dinner that night) or have more chronic sources (e.g., when the arachnophobe is quick to interpret any speck on the wall as a spider). Going back to "the Culture of Honor" example above, the concept of "honor" is likely to be more accessible to members of this culture than to members of the Northern USA (even if the concept is available to all). As another example, by virtue of shared experiences, stigmatized group members in a culture may have concerns about discrimination more chronically accessible than non-stigmatized group members (Mendoza-Denton, Ayduk, Shoda, & Mischel, 1997).

Finally, of all the beliefs, goals, values, encodings, and feelings that one can potentially experience at any given time, only those that are *relevant* in a given situation can become activated and influence subsequent behavior. This is the concept of *applicability*. For example, Banaji, Hardin, and Rothman (1993) found that participants for whom the construct "aggressive" had been made situationally accessible used this construct in subsequent judgments of male targets, but not of female targets. This finding illustrates accessibility effects because in general, the term "aggressive" is applicable to male targets, but not to female targets. Applicability is important because in order for particular constructs to be used, it is not enough for them to be accessible they must also be applicable to a relevant stimulus or situation. In terms of the metaphor, applicability suggests that culture can influence that crayons (or constructs) one can use to color in particular aspects of one's world. For example, although the concept of *holiness* may be chronically accessible to religiously oriented individuals across cultures, the concept is differentially applicable to worldly entities (e.g., some animals are revered in one culture, but not in another). Norenzayan and Heine (2005) also propose availability, applicability, and accessibility as tools that may allow researchers to specify with greater precision the universality of a particular construct (the crayons in the metaphor above). We extend these authors' analysis by proposing that these principles *themselves* may describe universal information processing processes that give rise to cultural diversity. These principles are consistent with a growing tradition "conceptualizing human nature in terms of naturally selected psychological adaptations that are incomplete without culture-specific instantiation and coordination, which are mutually complementary and mutually necessary for psychological functioning" (Norenzayan & Heine, 2005, 778).

Back to bargaining for vegetables: given differences in the availability of different skills related to bargaining, marketplaces may prime (i.e., make accessible) not only behavioral scripts related to bargaining, but additional associated meanings that together give rise to *what it means* to engage in particular cultural practices. In West Africa, for example, haggling for prices with one's vegetable vendor is associated with relationship building, and provides a principal pathway to the development of *trust* between vendor and customer even in the presence of self-interest (to get the best price). By contrast, the network of meaning surrounding marketplaces is much different within the US context, with the concept of relationship building not accessible during monetary transactions between vendor and customer (indeed, engaging in bargaining at a US farmer's market may lead to mistrust and a distinct downturn in the vendor-customer relationship). To understand culture and cultural practices deeply, it is necessary yet not sufficient for the student of that culture to learn the behavioral scripts associated with different contexts (e.g., how to bargain appropriately or how closely to walk past someone). One must also acquire through reading, learning, observation, and experience the associated network of meanings associated with these particular practices.

Reciprocal influences of culture and person

In line with cultural psychology (see Kitayama & Cohen, 2007), the C-CAPS approach recognizes that the influence of culture to persons is co-constitutional or reciprocal. People are influenced by their surrounding culture, but they also reify and reinforce cultural beliefs, goals, and values through their actions, rites, and institution (Mendoza-Denton & Mischel, 2007). They can be relatively subtle practices that provide pathways to culturally valued practice, such as *not* having prices displayed on vegetable stands in West African marketplaces. They can also be relatively overt value displays, such as mosques or cathedrals that signify the importance of a given value system. Together, these practices and institutions make up what Triandis et al. (1980) have referred to as "physical culture," and are important because they remind us that "culture" does not manifest exclusively at the individual level. Rather, individuals create the environments and practices that reflect their important values and beliefs; these environments and practices themselves reify and perpetuate cultural values and practices. Valuing health and well-being, for example, can give rise to gymnasiums, health food stores, and advertisements featuring fit individuals, which themselves make value-consistent behaviors more likely while increasing the accessibility of the cultural value. Thus, while the current analysis focuses at the level of the individual, it is also important to recognize that culture operates at multiple, interacting levels (see Mendoza-Denton & Mischel, 2007, for a more in-depth discussion of this issue).

Information Processing and Cultural Differences

The C-CAPS approach proposes that cultural differences are in fact culturally specific manifestations of potentially universal dynamic information processing system albeit manifestations that do not end up seeing eye to eye, and can lead to conflicting worldviews. As such, the C-CAPS approach may be brought to bear on our understanding of psychological processes associated with intergroup relations.

Nominal versus psychological situations

People perceive and experience situations differently. The same *nominal* situation may yield different *psychological situations* for different people. The same cafeteria lunch with classmates, for example, may be interpreted as an opportunity to make friends for one child and as an opportunity to be rejected by another (Downey & Feldman, 1996). At the level of groups, the differential availability and accessibility of constructs can similarly yield divergent interpretations and behavioral reactions to the same nominal situation (e.g., Hansen & Sassenberg, 2006; Sechrist, Swim, & Stangor, 2004). For example, systematic group-level differences in exposure to rejection based on skin color that is, discrimination lead to similarly systematic differences in the application of racism as an explanatory construct for various sociopolitical events.

The implications of such differences for intergroup relations are dramatically demonstrated, in the US context, by striking racial group differences in reactions to the O. J. Simpson 1995 criminal trial verdict (Mendoza-Denton et al., 1997). In this case, an African American athlete and celebrity

(Simpson) was on trial for murder, but his trial was complicated by the actions of a white police officer who may have purposefully planted a bloody glove at the crime scene (a glove that did not in fact fit Simpson's hand). The suspicion of police bias made decades of judiciary injustice on the basis of race applicable to this trial for African Americans. At the same time, the applicability of such injustices to this trial was not recognized by many white Americans, who tended to discount the tainted evidence as stemming from one bad apple that did not change the "mountain of evidence" against the accused. As a result of differences in the availability, accessibility, and applicability of racism as an explanatory construct, a black-white schism occurred, leading to great racial tension surrounding the verdict at the time. The defendant's lawyer, Johnny Cochran, understood these differences and crystallized them in his closing arguments with the phrase, "If it doesn't fit, you must acquit." The phrase cleverly made reference to the bloody glove while simultaneously making an understated call for unity among members of the African diaspora with a subtle allusion to an African tradition of emphasis through rhyme (see Mendoza-Denton et al., 1997, for an in-depth discussion of this trial and issue).

Another example comes from the interpretation of the US emergency corps' response following Hurricane Katrina, which slammed into the coast of New Orleans in August 2005. A poorly executed emergency response for the hurricane's poorest victims, who were overwhelmingly African Americans, seemed to lead to systematic differences in the activation of networks of meaning among African Americans and Whites in the aftermath of the disaster. Again, whereas systematic discrimination was an applicable explanation for the federal response for African Americans, White Americans tended to favor a response that did not invoke racism per se, but rather one that emphasized the magnitude of the disaster and the sheer difficulty of coordinating an effective response for anyone (Levy, Freitas, Mendoza-Denton, & Kugelmass, 2006). Importantly, these different interpretations had downstream implications for the two groups. Levy et al. (2006) demonstrated that following this hurricane, African Americans' endorsement of the belief that hard work pays off (the Protestant work ethic) was reduced during the months following the disaster whereas white Americans' endorsement of this particular cultural value was not affected, presumably due to a recognition among African Americans of broader structural/institutional forces negatively impacting one's outcomes no matter how hard one works. This finding is a good illustration, not only of differences in accessibility and applicability of different constructs, but differences in the network of associated constructs (in this case, the Protestant work ethic) that particular events and situations differentially activate among members of cultural groups.

Toward Intergroup Tolerance

The C-CAPS framework and its proposed properties provide a useful framework through which to understand how knowledge activation processes that are shared can readily lead to differences in worldview and discord in cultural perspectives. The framework provides a first step toward making the world of the "other" more understandable less foreign and alien perhaps by understanding how common principles in information processing can lead to such differences. As such, the C-CAPS framework may be one way through which different reactions to similar nominal events can be understood not as the irrational, baseless, thoughtless reactions of another culture, but rather as differences from individuals who are similarly subject to the same principles of knowledge activation. The differences remain, but it is our hope that the framework provides one positive step toward understanding alternative worldviews from our own.

Although only a first step in a direction toward understanding, the C-CAPS framework also provides a potential route toward rapprochement of different cultures and potential reconciliation of worldviews. The C-CAPS framing suggests that cultural novices can become cultural experts through exposure, experience, and the sharing of information. Indeed, anthropological work that describes groups in their own terms, or descriptions of culture that rely on "thick description" (Geertz, 1973), are important routes toward the achievement of such rapprochement. We suggest here that such knowledge acquisition primarily operates by increasing the availability of otherwise foreign constructs. Immersion and continued exposure, however, are likely necessary to increase the accessibility of constructs that have been made newly available, and to approximate the organizational network of meaning that particular constructs are associated with.

This is not to say that the route to rapprochement does not need to overcome barriers. Members of different cultures hold stereotypes; shared beliefs about the characteristics of a different culture about each other. Fiske and Neuberg (1990) have investigated the factors that determine whether people form a first impression of an out-group member on stereotypical versus individual information. The latter is a more elaborated impression formation process on the basis of individual information, whereas choosing stereotypical/categorical information about an out-group member is the "easier" way because it requires less effort, less motivation, and less thoughtfulness. Traumatic experiences, such as those that occur in war, can also lead people to quickly generalize negative emotion broadly. "You want to scream out loud, you want to go home, …" a US solider in Iraq told CNN recently after losing one of his best friends. "You just hate seeing these people every day after one of your buddies dies" (CNN, 2007).

Increasing cultural understanding can be a daunting, difficult enterprise. We conclude with mention of one promising route toward increasing cultural competence: contact and friendship with members of a given culture. According to the *contact hypothesis* (Allport, 1954; Pettigrew, 1986), contact between different groups in society can reduce prejudice and, thus, improve intergroup relations. A long tradition of research supports the importance of contact as a principal route to positive intergroup relations (see Pettigrew & Tropp, 2006). As one example, research on the contact hypothesis has been conducted in different neighborhoods that differ in the composition of immigrants and Germans (Wagner, Christ, Pettigrew, Stellmacher, & Wolf, 2006; Wagner, van Dick, Pettigrew, & Christ, 2003). With an increased number of immigrants in a neighborhood, the chance for contact between immigrants and Germans increased as well, which in turn led to a reduction in prejudice on the German side. The more immigrants lived in the neighborhood, went into the same grade of school (Wagner et al., 2003), or were colleagues at work (Wagner et al., 2006), the more Germans had friends with an immigration background.

This last finding suggests that intergroup contact may be an important route to intergroup *friendship*, which has been identified as a particularly effective means of achieving positive intergroup attitudes (McLaughlinVolpe, Mendoza-Denton, & Shelton 2005; Paolini, Hewstone, Cairns, & Voci, 2004).

Research on the causal impact of cross-group friendship of Latino/a and white intergroup relations suggests that reductions in intergroup anxiety occur early in the development of intergroup friendship, and that such friendship can even benefit other intergroup interactions down the line (Page-Gould, Mendoza-Denton, & Tropp, forthcoming).

As Zayas, Shoda, and Ayduk (2002) have pointed out, during interpersonal (or intergroup) interaction, people can establish common ground by communicating their various goals, values, beliefs, and desires. Pettigrew (2006) has noted that the removal of threat is a first barrier in intergroup interaction that must be crossed before the development of positive affect can occur. We also view the removal of threat as also setting the groundwork for intercommunication of C-CAPS systems to occur, and potentially set the stage for cultural rapprochement and understanding coupled with positive affect.

Acknowledgment

The authors thank two anonymous reviewers for their valuable suggestions to improve this article. Both authors contributed equally to this article.

Short Biography

Rodolfo Mendoza-Denton was born in Mexico City. He lived with his family in Ivory Coast, Thailand, and the USA as a youngster, fostering an interest in culture and the different ways with which people understand the world. He enrolled at Yale University for his undergraduate studies, working with Letitia Naigles on language acquisition of Spanish and English speakers. He pursued graduate and postdoctoral study in social/personality psychology at Columbia University, where he worked with Walter Mischel and Geraldine Downey. Mendoza-Denton is currently Assistant Professor of Psychology at the University of California, Berkeley. His research focuses on stigma and intergroup relations.

Nina Hansen is currently a visiting researcher supported by a German Academic Exchange Service (DAAD) grant at the University of California, Berkeley, from where she will soon move to the University of Groningen, The Netherlands. Before coming to Berkeley, she has worked as a Postdoctor at the University of Jena (Germany). She received her Master's degree in Social Sciences from the University of Gottingen (Germany). After graduation she spent 1 year as a graduate student at the University of California, Berkeley. She holds a Ph. D. from the University of Jena (Germany). Her research focusses on responses to social discrimination and intergroup relations.

This manuscript was written when the second author was a visiting researcher at the University of California, Berkeley, under the support of a grant from DAAD. Authorship order for this article was determined by a coin toss.

Endnote

* Correspondence address: Psychology Department, University of California, 3210 Tolman Hall, Berkeley, CA 94720-1650, USA. Email: rmd@berkeley.edu.

References

Alexander, M. G., Brewer, M. B., & Hermann, R. K. (1999). Images and affect: A functional analysis of out-group stereotypes. *Journal of Personality and Social Psychology, 77*, 78–93.

Allik, J., & McCrae, R. R. (2004). Toward a geography of personality traits: Patterns of profiles across 36 cultures. *Journal of Cross-Cultural Psychology, 35*, 13–28.

Alport, G. W. (1954). *The Nature of Prejudice.* Cambridge, MA: Addison-Wesley. Banaji, M. R., Hardin, C., & Rothman, A. J. (1993). Implicit stereotyping and person judgment. *Journal of Personality and Social Psychology, 65*, 272–281.

Bandura, A. (1982). Self-efficacy mechanisms in human agency. *American Psychologist, 37*, 122–147.

Bandura, A. (1986). Social Foundations of Thought and Action: A Social Cognitive Theory. Englewood Cliffs, NJ: Prentice Hall.

Benedict, R. (1934). *Patterns of Culture.* Boston, MA: Houghton Miller. Campbell, D. T. (1965). Ethnocentric and other altruistic motives. In D. Le Vine (Ed.), *Nebraska Symposium on Motivation* (pp. 283–312). Lincoln, NE: University of Nebraska Press.

Cantor, N. (1990). From thought to behavior: "Having" and "doing" in the study of personality and cognition. *American Psychologist, 45*, 735–750.

Cantor, N. (1994). Life task problem-solving: Situational affordances and personal needs. *Personality and Social Psychology Bulletin, 20*, 235–243.

Cantor, N., & Kihlstrom, J. F. (1987). *Personality and Social Intelligence.* Englewood Cliffs, NJ: Erlbaum.

Cervone, D. (2005). Personality architecture: Within-person structures and processes. *Annual Review of Psychology, 56*, 423–452.

Chan, W., & Mendoza-Denton, R. (forthcoming). *Status-Based Rejection Sensivity among Asian Americans: Implications for Psychological Distress.*

CNN (2005, January). Charleston again ranked best-mannered city (www.CNN.com; January 14).

CNN (2007, June). Carrying friend in body bag haunts soldier (www.CNN.com; June 15).

Cohen, D. (1998). Culture, social organization, and patterns of violence. *Journal of Personality and Social Psychology, 75*, 408–419.

Cohen, D., & Nisbett, R. E. (1994). Self-protection and the culture of honor: Explaining southern violence. *Personality and Social Psychology Bulletin, 20*, 551–567.

Cohen, D., & Nisbett, R. E. (1997). Field experiments examining the culture of honor: The role of institutions in perpetuating norms about violence. *Personality and Social Psychology Bulletin, 23*, 1188–1199.

Cohen, D., Nisbett, R. E., Bowdle, B. F., & Schwarz, N. (1996). Insult, aggression, and the southern culture of honor: An "experimental ethnography." *Journal of Personality and Social Psychology, 70*, 945–960.

Cohen, D., Vandello, J., Puente, S., & Rantilla, A. (1999). "When you call me that, smile!" How norms for politeness, interaction styles, and aggression work together in southern culture. *Social Psychology Quarterly, 62,* 257–275.

Crocker, J., Major, B., & Steele, C. (1998). Social stigma. In D. T. Gilbert & S. T. Fiske (Eds.), *The Handbook of Social Psychology* (4th ed., pp. 504–553). New York: McGraw-Hill.

Dodge, K. A. (1993). New wrinkles in the person-versus-situation debate. *Psychological Inquiry, 4,* 284–286.

Downey, G., & Feldman, S. I. (1996). Implications of rejection sensitivity for intimate relationships. *Journal of Personality and Social Psychology, 70,* 1327–1343.

Dweck, C. S. (2006). *Mindset: The New Psychology of Success.* New York: Random House.

Fiske, S. T., & Neuberg, S. L. (1990). A continuum of impression formation: From category-based to individuating processes. In M. P. Zanna (Ed.), *Advances in Experimental Social Psychology* (Vol. 23, pp. 1–74). San Diego, CA,: Academic Press.

Geertz, C. (1973). The Interpretation of Cultures: Selected Essays. New York: Basic Books.

Gordon, E. (1982). Culture and ethnicity. In M. D. Levine, W. B. Cavey, A. C. Crocker & R. Gross (Eds.), *Textbook of Behavioral and Developmental Pediatrics.* Philadelphia: W. B. Sanders.

Hansen, N., & Sassenberg, K. (2006). Does social identification buffer or harm? The impact of social identification on anger after social discrimination. *Personality and Social Psychology Bulletin, 32,* 983–996.

Higgins, E. T. (1996). Knowledge activation: Accessibility, applicability, and salience. In E. T. Higgins & A. W. Kruglanski (Eds.), *Social Psychology: Handbook of Basic Principles* (pp. 133–168). New York: Guilford Press.

Hinton, G. E., McClelland, J. L., & Rumelhart, D. E. (1986). Distributed representations. In D. E. Rumelhart & J. L. McClelland (Eds.), *Parallel Distributed Processing: Explorations in the Microstructures of Cognition. Vol I, Foundations* (pp. 77–109). Cambridge, MA: MIT Press/ Bradford Books.

Hogg, M. A. (2000). Subjective uncertainty reduction through self-categorization: A motivational theory of social identity processes. In W. Stroebe & M. Hewstone (Eds.), *European Review of Social Psychology* (Vol. 11, pp. 223–255). Chichester, UK: Wiley.

Hong, Y., & Mallorie, L. A. M. (2004). A dynamic constructivist approach to culture: Lessons learned from personality psychology. *Journal of Research in Personality, 38,* 59–67.

Kammrath, L., Mendoza-Denton, R., & Mischel, W. (2005). Incorporating *if... then ...* signatures in person perception: Beyond the person-situation dichotomy. *Journal of Personality and Social Psychology, 88,* 605–613.

Kardiner, A. (1945). *Psychological Frontiers of Society.* New York: Columbia University Press.

Kashima, Y. (2001). Culture and social cognition: Toward a Social Psychology of Cultural Dynamics. In D. Matsumoto (Ed.), *The Handbook of Culture and Psychology* (pp. 325–360). New York: Oxford University Press.

Kitayama, S., & Cohen, S. (2007). *Handbook of Cultural Psychology.* New York: Guilford Press.

Levy, S. R., Freitas, A.L., Mendoza-Denton, R., & Kugelmass, H. (2006). Hurricane Katrina's impact on African Americans' and European Americans' endorsement of the protestant work ethic. *Analyses of Social Issues and Public Policy, 6,* 75–85.

Linton, R. (1936). *The Study of Man: An Introduction.* New York: Appleton-Century.

Linton, R. (1945). *The Cultural Background of Personality.* New York: Appleton-Century.

McCrae, R. R., & Allik, J. (2002). *The Five-Factor Model of Personality Across Cultures.* New York: Kluwer Academic/ Plenum Publishers.

McLaughlin-Volpe, T., Mendoza-Denton, R., & Shelton, N. (2005). Including out-group others in the self: Implications for coping with race-based rejection and alienation among minority students. In G. Downey, J. Eccles & C. Chatman (Eds.), *Navigating the Future: Social Identity, Coping and Life Tasks* (pp. 191–209). New York: Russell Sage.

Mendoza-Denton, R., & Mischel, W. (2007). Integrating system approaches to culture and personality: The cultural cognitive-affective processing system. In S. Kitayama & D. Cohen (Eds.), *Handbook of Cultural Psychology* (pp. 175–195). New York: Guilford Press.

Mendoza-Denton, R., Ayduk, O. N., Shoda, Y., & Mischel, W. (1997). Cognitive-affective processing system analyses of reactions to the O. J. Simpson Criminal Trial Verdict. *Journal of Social Issues, 53,* 563–581.

Mendoza-Denton, R., Downey, G., Purdie, V., & Davis, A. (2002). Sensitivity to status-based rejection: Implications for African-American students' college experience. *Journal of Personality and Social Psychology, 83,* 896–918.

Mendoza-Denton, R., Park, S., & O'Connor, A. (forthcoming). Toward a science of the social perceiver. In G. Downey, Y. Shoda & D. Cervone (Eds.), *Toward a Science of the Person: A Festschrift for Walter Mischel.* New York: Guilford Press.

Mendoza-Denton, R., Shoda, Y., Ayduk, O., & Mischel, W. (1999). Applying cognitiveaffective processing system (CAPS) theory to cultural differences in social behavior. In W. J. Lonner & D. L. Dinnel (Eds.), *Merging Past, Present, and Future in Cross-Cultural Psychology: Selected Papers from the Fourteenth International Congress of the International Association for CrossCultural Psychology* (pp. 205–217). Lisse, The Netherlands: Swets & Zeitlinger Publishers.

Mischel, W. (1973) Toward a cognitive social learning reconceptualization of personality. *Psychological Review, 80,* 252–283.

Mischel, W. (1990). Personality dispositions revisited and revised: A view after three decades. In L. A. Pervin (Ed.), *Handbook of Personality: Theory and Research* (pp. 111–134). New York: Guilford Press.

Mischel, W., & Shoda, Y. (1995). A cognitive-affective system theory of personality: Reconceptualizing situations, dispositions, dynamics and invariance in personality structure. *Psychological Review, 102,* 246–268.

Mischel, W., & Shoda, Y. (1998). Reconciling processing dynamics and personality dispositions. *Annual Review of Psychology, 49,* 229–258.

Mischel, W., Shoda, Y., & Mendoza-Denton, R. (2002). Situation-behavior profiles as a locus of consistency in personality. *Current Directions in Psychological Science, 11,* 50–54.

Mummendey, A., & Wenzel, M. (1999). Social discrimination and tolerance in intergroup relations: Reactions to intergroup difference. *Personality and Social Psychology Review, 3,* 158–174.

Nisbett, R. E., & Cohen, D. (1996). *Culture of Honor: The Psychology of Violence in the South.* Boulder, CO: Westview Press.

Norenzayan, A., & Heine, S. J. (2005). Psychological universals: What are they and how can we know? *Psychological Bulletin, 131,* 763–784.

Obeyeskere, G. (1981). Medusa's Hair: An Essay on Personal Symbols and Religious Experience. Chicago, IL: University of Chicago Press.

Page-Gould, E., Mendoza-Denton, R., & Tropp, L. R. *(forthcoming).* From Intergroup Anxiety to Intergroup Closeness: Stress-Reducing Effects of Cross-Ethnic Friendship.

Paolini, S., Hewstone, M., Cairns, E., & Voci, A. (2004). Effects of directions and indirect cross-group friendships on judgments of Catholics and Protestants in Northern Ireland: The mediation role of an anxiety-reduction mechanism. *Personality and Social Psychology Bulletin,* 30, 770–786.

Pew Global Attitudes Project (2006). The great divide: How Westeners and Muslims view each other. Europe's Muslims more moderate. *13-Nation Pew Global Attitudes Survey.* http://pewglobal.org/reports/display.php?ReportID=253 (last accessed September 17, 2007).

Pettigrew, T. F. (1986). The contact hypothesis revisited. In M. Hewstone & R. Brown (Eds.), *Contact and Conflict in Intergroup Encounters* (pp. 169–195). Oxford, UK: Blackwell.

Pettigrew, T. F. (2006, June). How does contact reduce prejudice? Meta-analytic tests of three mediators. In L. R. Tropp (Chair) (Ed.), *Anxiety and Trust in Intergroup Relations.* Symposium presented at the 6th biennial meeting of the Society for the Psychological Study of Social Issues, Long Beach, CA.

Pettigrew, T. F., & Tropp, L. R. (2006). A meta-analytic test of intergroup contact theory. *Journal of Personality and Social Psychology,* 90, 751–783.

Plaks, J. E., Shafer, J. L., & Shoda, Y. (2003). Perceiving individuals and groups as coherent: How do perceivers make sense of variable behavior? *Social Cognition,* 21, 26–60.

Sassenberg, K., Moskowitz, G.B., Jacoby, J., & Hansen, N. (2007). The carry-over effect of competition: The impact of competition on prejudice towards uninvolved outgroups. *Journal of Experimental Social Psychology,* 43, 529–538.

Sechrist, G. B., Swim, J. K., & Stangor, C. (2004). When do the stigmatized make attributions to discrimination occuring to the self and others? The roles of self-presentation and need for control. *Journal of Personality and Social Psychology,* 87, 111–122.

Shah, J., Kruglanski, A. W., & Thompson, E. P. (1998). Membership has its (epistemic) rewards: Need for closure effects on in-group bias. *Journal of Personality and Social Psychology,* 75, 383–393.

Tajfel, H. (1978). Social categorization, social identity and social comparison. In H. Tajfel (Ed.), *Differentiation Between Social Groups* (pp. 61–76). London: Academic Press.

Tajfel, H., & Turner, J. C. (1979). An integrative theory of intergroup conflict. In W. G. Austin & S. Worchel (Eds.), *The Social Psychology of Intergroup Relations* (pp. 33–47). Monterey, CA: Brooks/Cole.

Triandis, H. C., Lambert, W. W., Berry, J. W., Lonner, W., Heron, A., Brislin, R. W., et al. (1980). *Handbook of Cross-Cultural Psychology.* Boston, MA: Allyn and Bacon.

Triandis, H. C. (1997). Cross-cultural perspectives on personality. In R. Hogan, J. Johnson & S. Briggs (Eds.), *Handbook of Personality* (pp. 440–459). San Diego, CA: Academic Press.

Tylor, E. B. (1871). *The Origins of Culture.* Glouchester, MA: Peter Smith.

Wagner, U., Christ, O., Pettigrew, T. F., Stellmacher, J., & Wolf, C. (2006). Prejudice and minority proportion: Contact instead of threat effects. *Social Psychology Quarterly,* 69, 380–390.

Wagner, U., van Dick, R., Pettigrew, T. F., & Christ, O. (2003). Ethnic prejudice in East and West-Germany: The explanatory power of intergroup contact. *Group Processes and Intergroup Relations,* 6, 22–36.

Waldzus, S., Mummendey, A., Wenzel, M., & Weber, U. (2003). Towards tolerance: Representations of superordinate categories and perceived ingroup prototypicality. *Journal of Experimental Social Psychology,* 39, 31–47.

Zayas, V., Shoda, Y., & Ayduk, O. (2002). Personality in context: An interpersonal systems perspective. *Journal of Personality,* 70, 851–900.

Can Fixed Views of Ability Boost Performance in the Context of Favorable Stereotypes?

By Rodolfo Mendoza-Denton, Kimberly Kahn, and Wayne Chan

Abstract

Prior research has demonstrated that stereotypes affect negatively stereotyped groups in part through the implied immutability of group members' abilities. Accordingly, a belief that ability is malleable through effort and hard work has been shown to boost the performance of negatively stereotyped groups. We predicted, however, that among favorably stereotyped groups, a belief that ability is fixed would reinforce the immutability of the group differences upon which stereotype-induced social comparisons are made [Walton, G. M., & Cohen, G. L. (2003). Stereotype lift. *Journal of Experimental Social Psychology, 39,* 456–467] and result in enhanced performance. We found experimental support for these predictions in two favorably stereotyped groups in math: Asians (Study 1) and men (Study 2). Perceived difficulty of the math test helped explain the performance effects in Study 2. Implications of schooling emphasizing innate ability for exacerbating achievement gaps are discussed.

Introduction

Recent research has shown that the framing of intergroup achievement differences, particularly with reference to societally held stereotypes, has measurable effects on performance (Steele, Spencer, & Aronson, 2002). Framing a test as diagnostic of one's ability, for example, lowers the performance of group members for whom a stereotype of low ability is applicable (Steele & Aronson, 1995). Among the factors that contribute to such performance decrements is the implied immutability of stereotypic

Rodolfo Mendoza-Denton, Kimberly Kahn & Wayne Chan, "Can Fixed Views of Ability Boost Performance in the Context of Favorable Stereotypes?" *Journal of Experimental Social Psychology,* vol. 44, no. 4, pp. 1187–1193. Copyright © 2008 by Elsevier Science & Technology Journals. Reprinted with permission.

attributes: a suspicion that there is a ceiling to a given group's capabilities and potential that no amount of learning can overcome. Indeed, promoting the value of effort in academic domains (Aronson, Fried, & Good, 2002; Good, Aronson, & Inzlicht, 2003) and framing intergroup achievement differences as societal rather than biological in origin (Dar-Nimrod & Heine, 2006) has been shown to boost the performance of stigmatized group members.

In this article, we address the implications of viewing abilities as immutable versus malleable among individuals on whom stereotypes shine a favorable light. When encountering information that men are better than women at math, for example, does the same implication of fixed ability that can hinder women's performance facilitate the performance of men by entrenching the immutability of their advantage, potentially easing their concerns about performance?

While prior research has demonstrated that stereotypes can boost the performance of group members favored by such stereotypes (Walton & Cohen, 2003), the potential role that the fixedness of stereotypic attributes plays in yielding such boosts has yet to be systematically explored. We test this question in two experiments by manipulating both whether a favorable stereotype about one's group is confirmed or disconfirmed and whether ability is viewed as either fixed or malleable. In so doing, we hope to contribute to a growing body of knowledge examining the implications of fixed views of intelligence in the educational arena for perpetuating— and potentially accentuating—group differences in performance (Sternberg, 1996; Weinstein, 2005).

Lay theories of intelligence and stereotypes

Dweck and colleagues (see Dweck, 1999) have proposed that people vary in the degree to which they believe that the characteristics of a person are malleable and amenable to change. An *entity theory* refers to the belief that qualities such as intelligence are inborn, fixed, and unchangeable. By contrast, an *incremental theory* refers to the belief that abilities are malleable, with an opportunity for change through effort. The manipulation of entity versus incremental theories has short-term (Mueller & Dweck, 1998) and long-term (Henderson & Dweck, 1990; Stipek & Gralinski, 1996) implications for academic achievement, such that incremental theorists perform better over time. In the face of failure, incremental theorists view this outcome as an indication that more effort is required to succeed at the task at hand, and work harder to succeed. In contrast, entity theorists view failure as an indication that they do not have the natural talent required to succeed, and are thus more likely to disengage from tasks and domains following failure (Dweck & Sorich, 1999).

An independent line of research on stereotype threat (see Steele et al., 2002) has robustly demonstrated that people's achievement may be compromised when there is the possibility that their performance will confirm a negative stereotype. A variety of interrelated mechanisms have been proposed to account for the effects of stereotype threat (see Schmader, Johns, & Forbes, in press), including physiological stress (Blascovich, Spencer, Quinn, & Steele, 2001), arousal (O'Brien & Crandall, 2003), performance monitoring (Beilock, Jellison, Rydell, McConnell, & Carr, 2006) and cognitive demands (Croizet et al., 2004; Schmader &Johns, 2003). On a complementary level of analysis, several researchers (Aronson et al., 2002; Cokley, 2002; Good et al., 2003) have noted that negative stereotypes can be especially threatening because they carry the implication of unmodifiability—that is, that one's abilities and competence in a given domain are inherently limited by one's group membership. As such, under the suspicion of a stereotype, poor performance on a test would signify not just a low score on one test, but rather a diagnostic assessment of low capacity. Stereotype threat has been linked to disengagement and disidentification from domains in which one's identity is threatened (Major, Spencer, Schmader, Wolfe, & Crocker, 1998; Steele, 1997), which, tellingly, are the same kinds of self-protective coping strategies entity theorists have been found to use under the threat of failure (Dweck & Sorich, 1999).

Bringing together insights from the stereotype threat and entity/incremental theories literatures, Aronson and colleagues (2002) found that changing African American students' attitudes about the malleability of intelligence successfully raised their academic performance, although the intervention benefited White students as well. In addition, giving training on incremental theory to middle school students successfully eliminated the gender gap in math performance over the course of one school year (Good et al., 2003). It appears, then, that incremental training may be beneficial for members of negatively stereotyped groups, and may help reduce group differences in performance by counteracting the tendency to view stereotypes as fixed characteristics of devalued group membership.

Entity/incremental theories in the context of favorable stereotypes

Although the effects of entity versus incremental views of ability seem clear among individuals threatened by a stereotype of low ability, there is reason to believe these effects may reverse specifically when one's ingroup is perceived to have an advantage over another. *Stereotype lift* describes the phenomenon where high status group members, when primed with a negative stereotype of the devalued group, experience a performance boost presumably as a result of downward social comparison (Walton & Cohen, 2003; see also Hess & Hinson, 2006). Nevertheless, stereotype lift effects seem less robust than stereotype threat effects, opening the possibility that the relatively subtle main effect of stereotype lift may be masking interactive processes with other important variables (Marx & Stapel, 2006; Walton & Cohen, 2003).

We explore one such interaction here, arguing that an entity view of ability should specifically boost the performance of favorably stereotyped group members by assuring them that their group's advantage, relative to other groups, is immutable. As Walton and Cohen (2003) note, "stereotype-inspired social comparison may alleviate the self-doubt, anxiety, and fear of rejection that could otherwise hamper performance on important intellectual tests (p. 457)." We reasoned here that an entity theory of ability, by reinforcing the fixedness of the group differences on which such social comparisons rely, would accentuate the alleviation of such disruptive processes. Thus, while perceptions of immutable group differences should prove disruptive to performance among members of unfavorably stereotyped groups, the same immutable differences should prove beneficial to performance among members of favorably stereotyped groups. Confirmation of this hypothesis would contribute to a fuller understanding of how educational systems structured around performance and the tracking of students into ability groups (Sternberg, 1996; Weinstein, 2005) may differentially affect members of positively and negatively stereotyped groups.

Preliminary support for these hypotheses comes from Grant and Dweck (2003), who showed that an entity view of intelligence was related to enhanced achievement in a college level course relative to an incremental view, but only among already high-achieving students. Despite being consistent with our hypotheses, this study did not examine the effects of an entity theory specifically when such information is combined with favorable stereotypes. We examine this issue more directly by experimentally manipulating both stereotype information as well as entity/incremental beliefs.

The present studies

In two studies, we used established procedures and materials to experimentally manipulate participants' beliefs, and then assessed participants' test performance in GRE-like math tests. In Study 1, we examined the performance of Asian-background participants who were exposed to information that either confirmed or disconfirmed the notion that Asians outperform Whites in the domain of math, and who were exposed to either an entity or an incremental theory. In Study 2, our goal was to replicate and extend these findings to a different stereotype relevant to the math domain—that men outperform women (Spencer, Steele, & Quinn, 1999). We examined the performance of both men and women in this study, as well as their perceptions of test difficulty.

Study 1

Despite being stigmatized in the social and athletic domain (Crocker & Lawrence, 1999), individuals of Asian descent are stereotyped in the U.S. as being high achievers in academics, especially in the domain of mathematics (Lee, 1994). Aronson et al. (1999) demonstrated that a manipulation confirming the stereotype that Asians are better at math relative to Whites induced stereotype threat, and subsequent performance decrements among White students. Adopting this procedure, we exposed Asian-background students to information either confirming or disconfirming the superiority of Asians in math relative to Whites. In addition, we exposed participants to information that math achievement either stems from innate ability or from effort. We expected that in the stereotype confirmed condition, those given an entity prime would perform better than participants given an incremental prime. By contrast, with the stereotype disconfirmed and no clear advantage for one's group, we expected to replicate traditional research showing an advantage of effort over ability views on performance (e.g., Dweck, 2006).

Method

Participants

Sixty-nine English-fluent individuals (28 women; M_{age} = 19.7, SD = 1.51) of Asian descent participated in the study. Participants were enrolled in a large university in the western United States and received course credit for partaking in the study. Two participants of mixed Asian/European heritage were excluded from the final sample, as were two other participants who indicated they did not believe the manipulations. The analyses reported below are thus based on the remaining 65 participants in the sample. All participants identified "Asian" as the ethnic category that best described them. Forty-six of the participants were U.S. born. Gender, age, and birth country did not exert main or interactive effects in the analyses reported below and are not discussed further.

Procedure

Participants took part in a study, ostensibly sponsored by the University's "Center for Quantitative Reasoning and Performance," examining the factors that affect math achievement. Participants were seated at a desk and received a purported press release, enclosed in an official-looking leather folder, containing one of four manipulations. The first paragraph either confirmed an Asian-White gap in math performance (Aronson et al., 1999), or disconfirmed it by asserting equal performance between the groups. Within each of these two conditions, a second paragraph described research and testimonials asserting either that innate ability or effort was the most potent predictor of mathematical ability (Chiu, Hong, & Dweck, 1997). This resulted in four groups: stereotype confirmed/entity prime (n = 15), stereotype confirmed/incremental prime (n = 17), stereotype disconfirmed/entity prime (n = 20), and stereotype disconfirmed/incremental prime (n = 13).

Following this manipulation, participants completed a math test consisting of ten questions from Graduate Record Examination (GRE) practice tests (Robinson & Katzman, 1992). Items that 55–75%

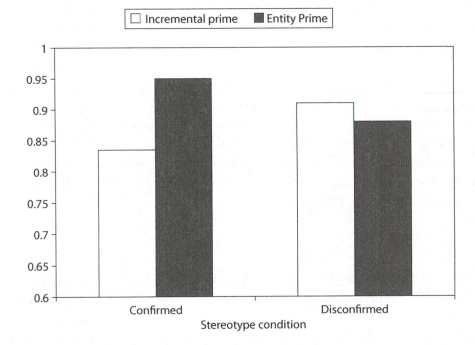

Figure 1. Quantitative test performance by condition for Asian-background students, Study 1.

of participants in national samples answered correctly were chosen to ensure our undergraduate sample could solve the GRE questions. Participants' performance, computed as a percentage of correct responses, showed that participants did well overall ($M = .89$, $SD = .14$). Following this test, participants were probed for suspicion, debriefed, and awarded course credit.

Results

A 2 (stereotype: confirmed/disconfirmed) x 2 (theory prime: entity/incremental) analysis of variance revealed no main effects of either stereotype, $F(1,61) = 0.01$, ns, or theory prime, $F(1,61) = 1.49$, ns. However, the analysis revealed the predicted stereotype x entity/incremental prime interaction, $F(1,61) = 4.11$, $p < .05$, $d = .51$. Fig. 1 shows this interaction graphically.

Planned comparisons revealed, as expected, that when the stereotype was confirmed, entity prime participants ($M = .95$, $SE = .035$) scored higher than incremental prime participants ($M = .835$, $SE = .033$; $t(30) = 2.30$, $p < .05$). When the stereotype was disconfirmed, entity prime ($M = .88$, $SE = .03$) and incremental prime ($M = .91$, $SE = .038$) participants did not differ ($t(31) = .57$, ns). The comparisons across entity prime conditions ($t(33) = 1.42$, $p = .16$) and incremental prime conditions ($t(28) = 1.44$, $p = .16$) were not statistically significant.

Discussion

Study 1 provided initial support for the predicted stereotype x entity/incremental prime interaction on test performance. In Study 2, we examined four additional issues to bolster these findings. First, we aimed to test the generalizability of the Study 1 findings by focusing on a different stereotype; namely, the stereotype that men are better than women at math. Second, Study 1 failed to find the traditionally observed advantage of incremental over entity theory on performance (see Dweck, 2006) in the absence of stereotype confirmation. Therefore we examined this specific comparison with particular interest in Study 2. Third, to establish the specificity of the predicted pattern of results, we examined the performance of both men and women. Finally, we asked participants to report on how difficult they found the test to be. We examined whether perceived test difficulty might help account for the link between the experimental manipulations and test performance, given our rationale that immutable group differences should engender threat for negatively stereotyped groups but alleviate self-doubt and anxiety for positively stereotyped groups.

Study 2

The procedure for Study 2 was similar to that of Study 1, but with four important modifications. First, the entire experiment was presented on a computer. Second, the stereotype manipulations employed in Study 2, though worded equivalently to those of Study 1, either confirmed or disconfirmed a male/female gap rather than an Asian/White gap. Third, given that participants did quite well on the math test in Study 1, and that unchallenging tests can sometimes cause a reversal of stereotype threat effects

(O'Brien & Crandall, 2003), we created a longer and more difficult math test. Finally, given that caring about how one performs in the tested domain is an important prerequisite to being affected by stereotype threat (Major et al., 1998; Steele, 1997), we also assessed this variable in Study 2.

Method

Participants

A total of 199 English-fluent students (111 women; M_{age} = 20.97, SD = 3.61) at a large University in the Western United States participated in this study for either course credit or $10 payment. Ninety-seven participants identified their background as "Asian, Asian-American, or Pacific Islander," 58 as "European-American or White," 13 as ""Hispanic or Latino," 11 as "African American or Black," 6 as "Middle Eastern," 2 as "American Indian or Alaskan Native," and 12 as "other." Forty-seven participants reported not being U.S. born. Country of birth and age did not exert main or interactive effects in the analyses reported below and are not discussed further.

One male participant who was above 3 standard deviations from the sample mean in the time taken to complete the math test was excluded from the analysis. An additional 12 participants (6 women) who did not believe the manipulation were also excluded, leaving a final sample of 186 participants (105 women) on whom the principal analyses reported below are based.

Procedure

Participants were randomly assigned to the stereotype confirmed/entity (n = 53; 30 women), stereotype confirmed/incremental (n = 54; 30 women), stereotype disconfirmed/entity (*n* = 41; 23 women), or stereotype disconfirmed/incremental (*n* = 38; 22 women) manipulations. Participants were again presented with a press release ostensibly from the University's "Center for Quantitative Reasoning and Performance" containing the manipulations. The entity/incremental manipulation remained the same as in Study 1. The stereotype confirmed/disconfirmed manipulations were altered from Study 1 to provide information about gender differences in math performance. Following the experimental manipulations, participants completed the math test. They then answered questions about the test and their performance. Participants were not given feedback on how well they did on the test. Finally, participants were debriefed, assigned course credit and dismissed.

Materials

Math test. After reading the press releases, participants completed a 20-item math test compiled from GRE practice tests (Robinson & Katzman, 1992). The test included the 10 test questions used in Study 1 as well as ten new questions answered correctly by 45–55% of original test takers. The increased difficulty of the test was reflected in lower overall performance compared to Study 1 (M = .64, SD = .24).

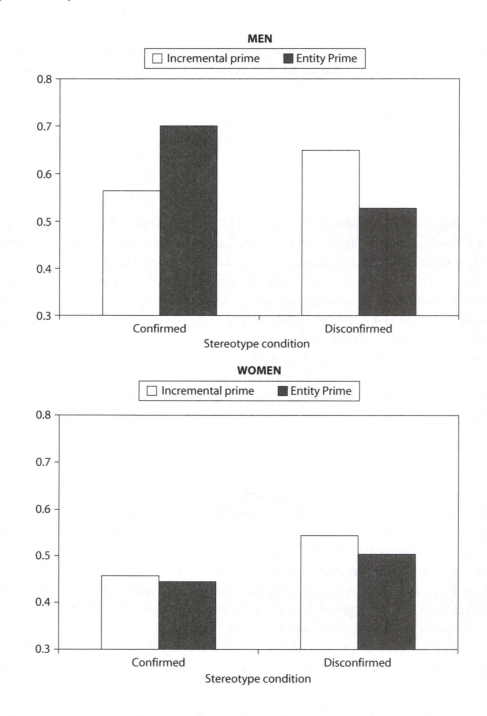

Figure 2. Quantitative test performance by condition for men & women, Study 2.

Personal investment in performance. Following research showing that the influence of stereotypes may be most pronounced among those who are invested in how they perform in the tested domain (Aronson et al., 1999; Major et al., 1998), we assessed such personal investment following the test. Using a

7point Likert-type scale, participants indicated their agreement with the following statements: "My performance on math tests influences my self-esteem/self-worth," "I don't really care what tests say about my math ability (reverse-scored)," and "Performing well on math tests is important to me" (a = 0.75, $M = 4.0$, $SD = 1.30$).

Perceived difficulty of the test. Participants answered the item "How difficult did you find the math task to be?" on a 1 ("not at all") to 7 ("very much") scale ($M = 3.51$, $SD = 1.55$).

Results and discussion

Preliminary analyses. Preliminary analyses revealed a main effect of personal investment in performance, $F(1,171) = 17.79$, $p < .001$, $d = .62$, with greater investment positively related to tested math performance. There was also a main effect of ethnicity, $F(6,171) = 9.24$, $p < .001$, $d = .45$, such that participants of Asian descent scored higher than other groups. There were no significant higher-order interactions with these variables. Subsequent analyses therefore retained these two variables as covariates. All analyses reported below are adjusted for the effects of these covariates.

Math performance

The data were analyzed using a 2 (stereotype: confirmed/disconfirmed) x 2 (theory prime: entity/incremental) x 2 (participant gender: female/male) GLM procedure with investment and ethnicity as covariates. The analysis revealed the predicted gender x stereotype x theory prime interaction, $F(1,171) = 4.17$, $p < .05$, $d = .31$. Fig. 2 shows this interaction graphically. Among men, controlling for personal investment and ethnicity, there was a significant stereotype x theory prime interaction, $F(1,171) = 9.29$, $p < .003$, $d = .46$. As the left panel of Fig. 2 shows, in the stereotype confirmed condition, entity prime participants ($M = .70$, $SE = .046$) scored significantly higher than incremental prime participants ($M = .56$, $SE = .045$; $t(45) = 2.48$, $p = .01$). By contrast, in the stereotype disconfirmed condition, entity prime participants ($M = .53$, $SE = .05$) scored marginally lower than incremental prime participants ($M = .65$, $SE = .055$; $t(32) = 1.85$, $p = .07$). Comparing men's scores across the two entity prime conditions revealed that those who had the stereotype confirmed scored significantly higher than those who had the stereotype disconfirmed ($t(39) = 2.92$, $p < .004$). The means did not differ significantly across the two incremental prime conditions, $t(38) = 1.40$, $p = .16$. This suggests that the effects of the stereotype manipulation were strongest among those with a fixed view of ability.

Among women, we observed only a main effect of stereotype manipulation, ($F(1,171) = 3.83$, $p = .05$, $d = .30$), such that women who had the stereotype confirmed ($M = .45$, $SE = .032$) performed worse than women who had the stereotype disconfirmed ($M = .52$, $SE = .037$). This is consistent with the literature on gender-based stereotype threat (e.g. Spencer et al., 1999).

Perceived difficulty of the test

Controlling for ethnicity and personal investment, we observed a significant gender x stereotype x theory prime interaction on perceived difficulty of the test, $F(1,171) = 6.35$, $p = .01$, $d = .38$. This interaction, shown in Fig. 3, mirrors the effects for test performance. More specifically, among men, the stereotype x theory prime interaction was significant, $F(1,171) = 9.48$, $p < .003$, $d = .47$. As expected, men who had the stereotype confirmed and received an entity prime found the test less difficult ($M = 2.30$, $SE = .317$) than those who had the stereotype confirmed but received an incremental manipulation ($M = 3.43$, $SE = .311$, $t(45) = 2.96$, $p < .004$). By contrast, men who had the stereotype disconfirmed and received an entity prime found the test more difficult ($M = 3.71$, $SE = .346$) than those who received an incremental prime ($M = 3.04$, $SE = .381$, $t(32) = 1.49$, $p = .14$), although this difference was not significant. Again, among men who received an entity manipulation, those who had the stereotyped confirmed felt the test was less difficult than those who had the stereotype disconfirmed, $t(39) = 3.46$, $p <.001$. Among men who received an incremental manipulation, the differences were not significant, $t(38) = .91$, $p = .36$.

Among women, we only observed a main effect of stereotype, $F(1,171) = 4.84$, $p < .03$, $d = .34$, such that women who had the stereotype confirmed ($M = 4.43$, $SE = .225$) felt the test was more difficult than women who had the stereotype disconfirmed $(M = 3.86$, $SE = .255)$.

Mediational analyses

We tested whether perceived difficulty of the test could help explain the effect of our experimental manipulations on performance. To do so, we first established that the proposed mediator, perceived test difficulty, was positively associated with test performance when controlling for ethnicity and personal investment, $F(1,177) = 78.83$, $p < .0001$, $d = 1.33$. We then regressed test performance scores onto gender, stereotype prime, theory prime, and their interactions simultaneously with perceived test difficulty. Controlling for ethnicity and personal investment, perceived test difficulty remained a significant predictor of performance, $F(1,170) = 43.01$, $p < .0001$, $d = 1.0$, whereas the previously observed gender x stereotype x theory prime interaction was no longer significant, $F(1,170) = 1.0$, $p = .32$, $d = .15$, *Sobel's* $z = 2.35$, $p < .02$. This suggests that perceived difficulty of the test is a potential mediator of the effects of the independent variables on performance.[1]

---

[1]Given that perceived difficulty was measured after the test, there remains the possibility of the reverse causal order, such that performance influenced the perceived difficulty of the test. When controlling for performance, the direct gender x stereotype x theory prime effect on perceived difficulty, albeit significantly reduced ($z = 1.95$, $p = .05$) nevertheless remained marginally significant, $F(1,170) = 3.12$, $p = .079$, $d = .27$. We retain emphasis on the alternative model (where perceived difficulty is the mediator) because participants were not given feedback on their test performance, and did not know how well they did on the test. Thus the measure of perceived difficulty more likely captured the ease with which participants felt they could complete the test questions, as we theoretically maintain.

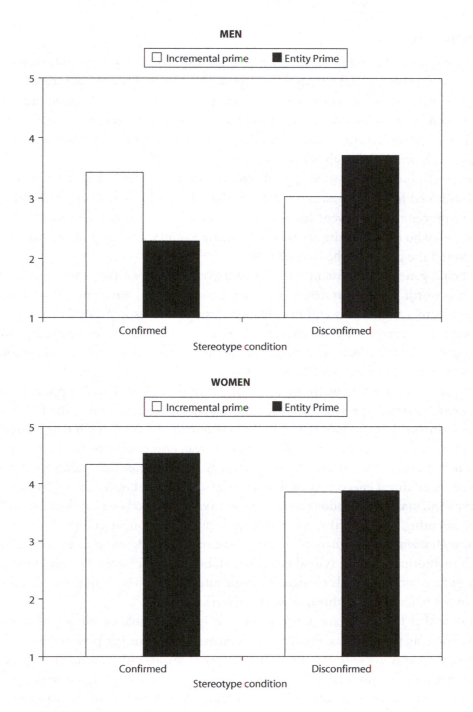

Figure 3. Perceived difficulty of the test, Study 2.

General discussion

While previous research has revealed the negative impact of entity theory on unfavorably stereotyped group members, the current study illustrates an opposite yet parallel process affecting favorably stereotyped group members in which entity views *enhance* performance. Asian-background participants in Study 1, and men in Study 2—two groups that enjoy a favorable stereotype of high math aptitude—exhibited the greatest lift in performance when they received confirmation of their in group's advantage and were given information that ability is fixed.

Consistent with research on stereotype threat, in Study 2 we found that women who had the stereotype confirmed found the test more difficult than those who did not, presumably as a result of the disruptive processes that prevent test takers from focusing on the task (Schmader et al., in press). By contrast, men who had a positive stereotyped confirmed and who were additionally primed with an entity view found the test to be the least difficult.

Despite being generally consistent with our expectations, several patterns in the data are worth discussing. It is worth noting that despite replicating the expected stereotype x theory interaction for favored groups across two studies and two different groups (Asians in Study 1; men in Study 2), we did not observe a stereotype lift main effect in either study. This pattern is consistent with the extant literature showing that lift effects are generally more subtle than threat effects, and are sometimes not significant within individual studies (Walton & Cohen, 2003).

A second pattern in our data worth noting is that even though we found support for the expected interaction between stereotype and entity/incremental manipulations among the favored groups, we did not find an interaction for the unfavored group (women) in Study 2 such that incremental beliefs buffered against stereotype threat. Here, the relatively weak effects of stereotype lift compared to stereotype threat may also prove relevant. More specifically, to the degree that stereotype threat effects are more robust, lift and threat effects may be differentially subject to influence through relatively brief and transitory experimental manipulations such as the entity/incremental one employed here. Indeed, past research documenting the protective effect of incremental beliefs on stereotype threat effect has done so either through cognitive dissonance and public commitment (Aronson et al., 2002), or through a three-month mentoring program (Good et al., 2003), both of which are relatively lengthy procedures designed to induce lasting attitude change. We hope future research will continue to address potential differences in the malleability of threat versus lift effects.

We also note that from the data presented here, it is not possible to tell the relative effects of an entity prime boosting performance versus an incremental prime hurting performance in the presence of a favorable stereotype. There is a rationale for both processes: an entity prime, as we have argued, can solidify confidence in the immutability of one's advantage. On the other hand, given an incremental prime, the inevitability of one's advantage is no longer guaranteed, potentially undermining the benefits of social comparisons. This latter possibility might shed light on the conditions under which favorable stereotypes might lead to "choking" (see Cheryan & Bodenhausen, 2000). We look forward to future research that addresses these issues.

Stereotype lift or stereotype susceptibility?

It is important to note that different mechanisms have been posited in the literature to account for performance boosts in the presence of positive stereotypes. As we have outlined, Walton and Cohen (2003) posit that downward social comparisons can alleviate performance concerns. An alternative account (see Shih, Ambady, Richeson, Fujita, & Gray, 2002; Shih, Pittinsky, & Ambady, 1999) proposes that positive stereotypes can boost performance through a more implicit priming process. According to this account, if a positive stereotype is both accessible and applicable (c.f., Higgins, 1996) to a given target, targets can become susceptible to the stereotype through a process where activated trait concepts produce corresponding behavioral tendencies (see also Dijksterhuis & Bargh, 2001).

Based on the relatively blatant nature of the stereotype manipulations used here, we believe that the effects observed in the present studies are more aligned with stereotype lift than with stereotype susceptibility accounts. The fact that we observed performance boosts with our manipulations is consistent with Walton and Cohen's (2003) finding that stereotype lift effects are equivalent across blatant (e.g., explicit mention of gender differences in the test) versus more subtle (e.g., mention of test diagnosticity) manipulations in stereotype treatment conditions. By contrast, research shows that while stereotype susceptibility effects are evident following subtle stereotype activation, blatant activation wipes out these effects, presumably because explicit activation introduces additional self-presentational concerns (Shih et al., 2002). Thus, the findings here are more consistent with the social comparison processes posited by a stereotype lift account than the priming processes posited by a stereotype susceptibility account.

Boundary conditions

Although the current findings provide initial evidence that performance may benefit from an entity theory when one already expects to do well, it is of theoretical as well as practical importance to note that people do not always perform to expectations. Despite enjoying a performance boost, members of favorably stereotyped groups can also encounter difficulties on the road to achievement—difficulties that may prove particularly damaging in the face of achievement expectations. A wealth of literature suggests that an incremental lay theory protects people when they receive failure feedback by helping them frame failure as an opportunity to grow and learn (Dweck, 2006). Conversely, as previously observed, an entity theory predisposes people to view failure information as diagnostic of their abilities, and to subsequently avoid or disidentify from the domain. Failing in a domain that one's ingroup is supposed to excel in may magnify the emotional and behavioral manifestations of entity theories (e.g., avoidance of the domain, anxiety and threat) due to a belief that if one underperforms even when one is supposed to have a sure advantage, then one must have especially low ability. Future research should address the implications of failure feedback for high status group members, both for performance as well as identity management.

Conclusions

The current studies' examination of high status groups in a short-term laboratory setting is useful in elucidating the differential implications of entity theories for our understanding of achievement gaps in the United States. The current findings, when combined with the prior literature, begin to suggest that it is not merely that low status groups are harmed by the fixed nature of stereotypes, but also that high status groups are bolstered. Americans are likely to believe in the fixed nature of intelligence and that school success is determined by natural ability (Steinberg, 1996). To the degree that the educational system reaffirms an entity view of intellectual abilities through ability tracking and intelligence testing (Weinstein, 2005), the current findings suggest an exacerbation and maintenance of performance gaps between groups about whom stereotypes exist. Further implications of the current study may be felt in areas such as career choice, such that entity-minded individuals may overselect favorably stereotyped domains in which performance is boosted. A cycle in which a favorably stereotyped groups' success then confirms societal expectations, and perpetuates inequities, understandably follows.

References

Aronson, J., Fried, C. B., & Good, C. (2002). Reducing the effects of stereotype threat on African American college students by shaping theories of intelligence. *Journal of Experimental Social Psychology, 38*, 113–125.

Aronson, J., Lustina, M. J., Good, C., Keough, K., Steele, C. M., & Brown, J. (1999). When White men can't do math: Necessary and sufficient factors in stereotype threat. *Journal of Experimental Social Psychology, 35*, 29–46.

Beilock, S. I., Jellison, W. A., Rydell, R. J., McConnell, A. R., & Carr, T. H. (2006). On the causal mechanisms of stereotype threat: Can skills that don't rely heavily on working memory still be threatened? *Personality and Social Psychology Bulletin, 32*, 1059–1071.

Blascovich, J., Spencer, S. J., Quinn, D., & Steele, C. (2001). African Americans and high blood pressure: The role of stereotype threat. *Psychological Science, 12*, 225–229.

Cheryan, S., & Bodenhausen, G. V. (2000). When positive stereotypes threaten intellectual performance: The psychological hazards of "model minority" status. *Psychological Science, 11*, 399–402.

Chiu, C., Hong, Y., & Dweck, C. S. (1997). Lay dispositionism and implicit theories of personality. *Journal of Personality and Social Psychology, 73*, 19–30.

Cokley, K. O. (2002). Testing cross's racial identity model: An examination of the relationship between racial identity and internalized racism. *Journal of Counseling Psychology, 52*, 517–526.

Crocker, J., & Lawrence, J. S. (1999). Social stigma and self-esteem: The role of contingencies of worth. In D. T. Miller & D. A. Prentice (Eds.), *Cultural divides: Understanding and overcoming group conflict* (pp. 364–392). Thousand Oaks, CA: Sage Publications.

Croizet, J., Despres, G., Gauzins, M., Huguet, P., Leyens, J., & Meot, A. (2004). Stereotype threat undermines intellectual performance by triggering a disruptive mental load. *Personality and Social Psychology Bulletin, 30*, 721–731.

Dar-Nimrod, I., & Heine, S. J. (2006). Exposure to scientific theories affect women's math performance. *Science,* 314, 435. Dijksterhuis, A., & Bargh, J. A. (2001). The perception-behavior expressway: Automatic effects of social perception on social behavior. *Advances in Experimental Social Psychology,* 33, 1–40.

Dweck, C. S. (1999). *Self-Theories: Their role in motivation, personality, and development.* Philadelphia: Taylor & Francis. Dweck, C. S. (2006). *Mindset: The new psychology of success.* New York: Random House.

Dweck, C. S., & Sorich, L. (1999). Mastery-oriented thinking. In C. R. Snyder (Ed.), *Coping: The psychology of what works* (pp. 232–251). New York: Oxford University Press.

Good, C., Aronson, J., & Inzlicht, M. (2003). Improving adolescents' standardized test performance: An intervention to reduce the effects of stereotype threat. *Applied Developmental Psychology,* 24, 645–662.

Grant, H., & Dweck, C. S. (2003). Clarifying achievement goals and their impact. *Journal of Personality and Social Psychology,* 85, 541–553.

Henderson, V. L., & Dweck, C. S. (1990). Motivation and achievement. In S. Feldman & G. Elliot (Eds.), *At the threshold: The developing adolescent* (pp. 308–329). Cambridge, MA: Harvard University Press.

Hess, T. M., & Hinson, J. T. (2006). Age-related variation in the inferences of aging stereotypes on memory in adulthood. *Psychology and Aging,* 21, 621–625.

Higgins, E. T. (1996). Knowledge activation: Accessibility, applicability, and salience. In E. T. Higgins & A. W. Kruglanski (Eds.), *Social Psychology: Handbook of basic principles* (pp. 133–168). New York: Guilford Press.

Lee, S. J. (1994). Behind the model minority stereotype: Voice of high and low achieving Asian-American students. *Anthropology and Education Quarterly,* 25, 413–429.

Major, B., Spencer, S., Schmader, T., Wolfe, C., & Crocker, J. (1998). Coping with negative stereotypes about intellectual performance: The role of psychological disengagement. *Personality and Social Psychology Bulletin,* 24, 34–50.

Marx, D. M., & Stapel, D. A. (2006). Understanding stereotype lift: On the role of the social self. *Social Cognition,* 24, 776–791.

Mueller, C. M., & Dweck, C. S. (1998). Praise for intelligence can undermine children's motivation and performance. *Journal of Personality and Social Psychology,* 75, 33–52.

O'Brien, L., & Crandall, C. S. (2003). Stereotype threat and arousal: Effects on women's math performance. *Personality and Social Psychology Bulletin,* 29, 782–789.

Robinson, A., & Katzman, J. (1992). *Princeton Review: Cracking the GRE,* 1993. New York: Random House.

Schmader, T., Johns, M., & Forbes, C. (in press). An intregrated process model of stereotype threat effects on performance. *Psychological Review.*

Schmader, T., & Johns, M. (2003). Converging evidence that stereotype threat reduces working memory capacity. *Journal of Personality and Social Psychology,* 85, 440–452.

Shih, M., Ambady, N., Richeson, J. A., Fujita, K., & Gray, H. M. (2002). Stereotype performance boosts: The impact of self-relevance and the manner of stereotype activation. *Journal of Personality and Social Psychology,* 83, 638–647.

Shih, M., Pittinsky, T. L., & Ambady, N. (1999). Stereotype susceptibility: Identity salience and shifts in quantitative performance. *Psychological Science,* 10, 80–83.

Spencer, S. J., Steele, C. M., & Quinn, D. M. (1999). Stereotype threat and women's math performance. *Journal of Experimental Social Psychology,* 35, 4–28.

Steele, C. M. (1997). A threat in the air: How stereotypes shape intellectual identity and performance. *American Psychologist,* 52, 613–629.

Steele, C. M., & Aronson, J. (1995). Contending with a stereotype: African-American intellectual test performance and stereotype threat. *Journal of Personality and Social Psychology,* 69, 797–811.

Steele, C. M., Spencer, S. J., & Aronson, J. (2002). Contending with group image: The psychology of stereotype and social identity threat. In M. P. Zanna (Ed.). *Advances in experimental social psychology* (Vol. 34, pp. 379–440). New York: Academic Press.

Steinberg, L. (1996). Beyond the classroom: Why school reform has failed and what parents need to do. New York, NY: Simon & Schuster.

Sternberg, R. J. (1996). Myths, countermyths, and truths about intelligence. *Educational Researcher,* 25, 11–16.

Stipek, D., & Gralinski, J. H. (1996). Children's beliefs about intelligence and school performance. *Journal of Educational Psychology,* 88, 397–407.

Walton, G. M., & Cohen, G. L. (2003). Stereotype lift. *Journal of Experimental Social Psychology,* 39, 456–467.

Weinstein, R. (2005). *Reaching higher: The power of expectations in schooling.* Cambridge, MA: Harvard University Press.

Body Ritual Among the Nacirema

By Horace Miner, University of Michigan

The anthropologist has become so familiar with the diversity of ways in which different peoples behave in similar situations that he is not apt to be surprised by even the most exotic customs. In fact, if all of the logically possible combinations of behavior have not been found somewhere in the world, he is apt to suspect that they must be present in some yet undescribed tribe. This point has, in fact, been expressed with respect to clan organization by Murdock (1949: 71). In this light, the magical beliefs and practices of the Nacirema present such unusual aspects that it seems desirable to describe them as an example of the extremes to which human behavior can go.

Professor Linton first brought the ritual of the Nacirema to the attention of anthropologists twenty years ago (1936: 326), but the culture of this people is still very poorly understood. They are a North American group living in the territory between the Canadian Cree, the Yaqui and Tarahumare of Mexico, and the Carib and Arawak of the Antilles. Little is known of their origin, although tradition states that they came from the east. According to Nacirema mythology, their nation was originated by a culture hero, Notgnihsaw, who is otherwise known for two great feats of strength—the throwing of a piece of wampum across the river Pa-To-Mac and the chopping down of a cherry tree in which the Spirit of Truth resided.

Nacirema culture is characterized by a highly developed market economy which has evolved in a rich natural habitat. While much of the people's time is devoted to economic pursuits, a large part of the fruits of these labors and a considerable portion of the day are spent in ritual activity. The focus of this activity is the human body, the appearance and health of which loom as a dominant concern in the ethos of the people. While such a concern is certainly not unusual, its ceremonial aspects and associated philosophy are unique.

The fundamental belief underlying the whole system appears to be that the human body is ugly and that its natural tendency is to debility and disease. Incarcerated in such a body, man's only hope is to avert these characteristics through the use of the powerful influences of ritual and ceremony. Every household has one or more shrines devoted to this purpose. The more powerful individuals in the society have several shrines in their houses and, in fact, the opulence of a house is often referred to in terms of the number of such ritual centers it possesses. Most houses are of wattle and daub construction, but the shrine rooms of the more wealthy are walled with stone. Poorer families imitate the rich by applying pottery plaques to their shrine walls.

Horace Miner, "Body Ritual Among the Nacirema," *American Anthropologist*, vol. 58, no. 3, pp. 503–507. Copyright © 1956 by American Anthropological Association. Reprinted with permission.

While each family has at least one such shrine, the rituals associated with it are not family ceremonies but are private and secret. The rites are normally only discussed with children, and then only during the period when they are being initiated into these mysteries. I was able, however, to establish sufficient rapport with the natives to examine these shrines and to have the rituals described to me.

The focal point of the shrine is a box or chest which is built into the wall. In this chest are kept the many charms and magical potions, without which no native believes he could live. These preparations are secured from a variety of specialized practitioners. The most powerful of these are the medicine men, whose assistance must be rewarded with substantial gifts. However, the medicine men do not provide the curative potions for their clients, but decide what the ingredients should be and then write them down in an ancient and secret language. This writing is understood only by the medicine men and by the herbalists who, for another gift, provide the required charm.

The charm is not disposed of after it has served its purpose, but is placed in the charm-box of the household shrine. As these magical materials are specific for certain ills, and the real or imagined maladies of the people are many, the charm-box is usually full to overflowing. The magical packets are so numerous that people forget what their purposes were and fear to use them again. While the natives are very vague on this point, we can only assume that the idea in retaining all the old magical materials is that their presence in the charm-box, before which the body rituals are conducted, will in some way protect the worshipper.

Beneath the charm-box is a small font. Each day every member of the family, in succession, enters the shrine room, bows his head before the charmbox, mingles different sorts of holy water in the font, and proceeds with a brief rite of ablution. The holy waters are secured from the Water Temple of the community, where the priests conduct elaborate ceremonies to make the liquid ritually pure.

In the hierarchy of magical practitioners, and below the medicine men in prestige, are specialists whose designation is best translated "holy-mouthmen." The Nacirema have an almost pathological horror of and fascination with the mouth, the condition of which is believed to have a supernatural influence on all social relationships. Were it not for the rituals of the mouth, they believe that their teeth would fall out, their gums bleed, their jaws shrink, their friends desert them, and their lovers reject them. They also believe that a strong relationship exists between oral and moral characteristics. For example, there is a ritual ablution of the mouth for children which is supposed to improve their moral fiber.

The daily body ritual performed by everyone includes a mouth-rite. Despite the fact that these people are so punctilious about care of the mouth, this rite involves a practice which strikes the uninitiated stranger as revolting. It was reported to me that the ritual consists of inserting a small bundle of hog hairs into the mouth, along with certain magical powders, and then moving the bundle in a highly formalized series of gestures.

In addition to the private mouth-rite, the people seek out a holy-mouthman once or twice a year. These practitioners have an impressive set of paraphernalia, consisting of a variety of augers, awls, probes, and prods. The use of these objects in the exorcism of the evils of the mouth involves almost unbelievable ritual torture of the client. The holy-mouth-man opens the client's mouth and, using the above mentioned tools, enlarges any holes which decay may have created in the teeth. Magical materials are put into these holes. If there are no naturally occurring holes in the teeth, large sections of one or more teeth are gouged out so that the supernatural substance can be applied. In the client's view, the purpose of these ministrations is to arrest decay and to draw friends. The extremely sacred and traditional character of the rite is evident in the fact that the natives return to the holy-mouth-men year after year, despite the fact that their teeth continue to decay.

It is to be hoped that, when a thorough study of the Nacirema is made, there will be careful inquiry into the personality structure of these people. One has but to watch the gleam in the eye of a holy-mouth-man, as he jabs an awl into an exposed nerve, to suspect that a certain amount of sadism is involved. If this can be established, a very interesting pattern emerges, for most of the population shows definite masochistic tendencies. It was to these that Professor Linton referred in discussing a distinctive part of the daily body ritual which is performed only by men. This part of the rite involves scraping and lacerating the surface of the face with a sharp instrument. Special women's rites are performed only four times during each lunar month, but what they lack in frequency is made up in barbarity. As part of this ceremony, women bake their heads in small ovens for about an hour. The theoretically interesting point is that what seems to be a preponderantly masochistic people have developed sadistic specialists.

The medicine men have an imposing temple, or *latipso,* in every community of any size. The more elaborate ceremonies required to treat very sick patients can only be performed at this temple. These ceremonies involve not only the thaumaturge but a permanent group of vestal maidens who move sedately about the temple chambers in distinctive costume and headdress.

The *latipso* ceremonies are so harsh that it is phenomenal that a fair proportion of the really sick natives who enter the temple ever recover. Small children whose indoctrination is still incomplete have been known to resist attempts to take them to the temple because "that is where you go to die." Despite this fact, sick adults are not only willing but eager to undergo the protracted ritual purification, if they can afford to do so. No matter how ill the supplicant or how grave the emergency, the guardians of many temples will not admit a client if he cannot give a rich gift to the custodian. Even after one has gained admission and survived the ceremonies, the guardians will not permit the neophyte to leave until he makes still another gift.

The supplicant entering the temple is first stripped of all his or her clothes. In every-day life the Nacirema avoids exposure of his body and its natural functions. Bathing and excretory acts are performed only in the secrecy of the household shrine, where they are ritualized as part of the body-rites. Psychological shock results from the fact that body secrecy is suddenly lost upon entry into the *latipso.* A man, whose own wife has never seen him in an excretory act, suddenly finds himself naked and assisted by a vestal maiden while he performs his natural functions into a sacred vessel. This sort of ceremonial treatment is necessitated by the fact that the excreta are used by a diviner to ascertain the course and nature of the client's sickness. Female clients, on the other hand, find their naked bodies are subjected to the scrutiny, manipulation and prodding of the medicine men.

Few supplicants in the temple are well enough to do anything but lie on their hard beds. The daily ceremonies, like the rites of the holy-mouth-men, involve discomfort and torture. With ritual precision, the vestals awaken their miserable charges each dawn and roll them about on their beds of pain while performing ablutions, in the formal movements of which the maidens are highly trained. At other times they insert magic wands in the supplicant's mouth or force him to eat substances which are supposed to be healing. From time to time the medicine men come to their clients and jab magically treated needles into their flesh. The fact that these temple ceremonies may not cure, and may even kill the neophyte, in no way decreases the people's faith in the medicine men.

There remains one other kind of practitioner, known as a "listener." This witch-doctor has the power to exorcise the devils that lodge in the heads of people who have been bewitched. The Nacirema believe that parents bewitch their own children. Mothers are particularly suspected of putting a curse on children while teaching them the secret body rituals. The counter-magic of the witch-doctor is unusual in its lack of ritual. The patient simply tells the "listener" all his troubles and fears, beginning with the earliest difficulties he can remember. The memory displayed by the Nacirema in these exorcism sessions is truly remarkable. It is not uncommon for the patient to bemoan the rejection he felt upon being weaned as a babe, and a few individuals even see their troubles going back to the traumatic effects of their own birth.

In conclusion, mention must be made of certain practices which have their base in native esthetics but which depend upon the pervasive aversion to the natural body and its functions. There are ritual fasts to make fat people thin and ceremonial feasts to make thin people fat. Still other rites are used to make women's breasts larger if they are small, and smaller if they are large. General dissatisfaction with breast shape is symbolized in the fact that the ideal form is virtually outside the range of human variation. A few women afflicted with almost inhuman hypermammary development are so idolized that they make a handsome living by simply going from village to village and permitting the natives to stare at them for a fee.

Reference has already been made to the fact that excretory functions are ritualized, routinized, and relegated to secrecy. Natural reproductive functions are similarly distorted. Intercourse is taboo as a topic and scheduled as an act. Efforts are made to avoid pregnancy by the use of magical materials or by limiting intercourse to certain phases of the moon. Conception is actually very infrequent. When pregnant, women dress so as to hide their condition. Parturition takes place in secret, without friends or relatives to assist, and the majority of women do not nurse their infants.

Our review of the ritual life of the Nacirema has certainly shown them to be a magic-ridden people. It is hard to understand how they have managed to exist so long under the burdens which they have imposed upon themselves. But even such exotic customs as these take on real meaning when they are viewed with the insight provided by Malinowski when he wrote (1948: 70):

> Looking from far and above, from our high places of safety in the developed civilization, it is easy to see all the crudity and irrelevance of magic. But without its power and guidance early man could not have mastered his practical difficulties as he has done, nor could man have advanced to the higher stages of civilization.

References Cited

Linton, Ralph, 1936. *The Study of Man*. New York, D. Appleton-Century Co.

Malinowski, Bronislaw, *Magic, Science, and Religion*. Glencoe, The Free Press.

Murdock, George P., *Social Structure*. New York, The Macmillan Co.

Confronting Perpetrators of Prejudice

The Inhibitory Effects of Social Costs

By J. Nicole Shelton and Rebecca E. Stewart *Princeton University*

The purpose of this research is to investigate the extent to which social costs influence whether or not targets of prejudice confront individuals who behave in a prejudiced manner during interpersonal interactions. Consistent with our predictions, we found that although women believe they will confront perpetrators of prejudice regardless of the social costs, in reality, they are less likely to confront male perpetrators in high social cost situations. Implications for how targets cope with prejudice and discrimination are discussed.

When targets of prejudice perceive they have been discriminated against or encounter a prejudicial incident, they must decide whether to confront or to ignore the perpetrator's behavior. Empirical findings are somewhat mixed as to how targets will respond. Evidence from the sexual harassment literature suggests that the overwhelming response of women who experience sexual harassment in the real world is *not* to confront the perpetrator (e.g., Fitzgerald, Swan, & Fischer, 1995; Gruber & Bjorn, 1986; Harris & Firestone, 1997). In contrast, laboratory research suggests that women are just as likely to confront perpetrators of prejudice as they are not to confront them. Swim and Hyers (1999), for example, found that 45% of women confronted a male partner during a problem-solving task when he made sexist comments. Similarly, Woodzicka and LaFrance (2001) found that 48% of women confronted a male interviewer who asked sexually harassing questions during an interview setting. Given that these numbers hover around 50%, it seems that targets are just as likely to confront perpetrators of prejudice as they are not to.

One factor that could explain the difference in the sexual harassment findings and the laboratory findings is how researchers operationalize confrontation. In the sexual harassment literature, researchers tend to focus primarily on direct verbal comments to the perpetrator. However, in the laboratory studies, confrontation includes additional confronting styles such as nonverbal signs of disgust to express participants' displeasure. For instance, Swim and Hyers (1999) found that only 16% of the women confronted the sexist male with direct verbal comments compared to 45% who expressed some sort of displeasure in general (e.g., humor, sarcasm, or surprised exclamations). Thus, there is evidence

J. Nicole Shelton & Rebecca E. Stewart, "Confronting Perpetrators of Prejudice: The Inhibitory Effects of Social Costs," *Psychology of Women Quarterly*, vol. 28, no. 3, pp. 215–223. Copyright © 2004 by SAGE Publications, Inc. Reprinted with permission.

to support the claim that targets tend not to confront perpetrators and there is evidence to support the claim that they do confront perpetrators in their own way.

In addition to examining whether or not targets of prejudice will confront a perpetrator, some researchers have explored under what conditions targets would be likely to confront. For instance, researchers have examined the extent to which the gender composition of the group (i.e., Swim & Hyers, 1999) and presence of other ingroup members (i.e., Stangor, Swim, Van Allen, & Sechrist, 2002) influence public claims of discrimination. Consistent with this line of work, in the present research we examined a situational factor that may influence targets' of prejudice responses to prejudice. Specifically, we examined whether or not social costs inhibit women from confronting men who ask sexist questions during an interview. Furthermore, we examined the extent to which women are (in)accurate in forecasting the power of social costs when imagining how they will respond to prejudice.

The Perceived Costs of Confronting

Regardless of how appropriate it seems, informing someone that his/her behavior is prejudiced could be considered a sign of complaining. Kowalski (1996) argues that before a complaint is made a person will weigh the costs and benefits of complaining. The costs may include being disliked, being considered a complainer, being retaliated against, or having one's values dismissed. If the costs are high, the person will be less likely to make the complaint. Thus, if the perceived costs are high, targets of prejudice may be less willing to confront the perpetrator (Crosby, 1993; Haslett & Lippman, 1997).

Recent research suggests that targets of prejudice believe there are costs associated with publicly acknowledging their dissatisfaction during prejudicial encounters. This is evident by research showing that targets who believe there are costs behave differently when they encounter prejudice compared to targets who do not believe there are costs. For example, using retrospective surveys, Kaiser and Miller (2002) demonstrated that women who believed that confronting discrimination was interpersonally costly were less likely to report having confronted a perpetrator during a sexist incident in the past. Similarly, Stangor et al. (2002) found that women and African Americans who received a poor grade from a prejudiced evaluator were less likely to claim discrimination in front of men and Whites than in front of other women and African Americans. This finding suggests that targets believe that there were costs involved with claiming discrimination in the presence of outgroup members.

Although the two aforementioned studies suggest that social costs may inhibit targets of prejudice from confronting perpetrators, neither explicitly examined the causal impact of costs on confronting behavior. Stangor et al. (2002) focused on attributions to discrimination as opposed to confronting perpetrators. Making an attribution to discrimination is different from accusing a particular person of behaving in a prejudiced manner. Kaiser and Miller (2002) used a correlational design, which makes it difficult to determine the order of causality. Although the findings from these studies have been insightful, it remains unclear as to whether social costs influence targets' of prejudice confronting behavior. In the present research, we explicitly address this issue.

Actual Costs of Confronting Prejudice

Targets of prejudice may be accurate in their perception of the costs involved in expressing their displeasure with prejudicial treatment. Kaiser and Miller (2001) found that an African American student was judged less favorably and as a complainer if he attributed his failure on a test to prejudice, regardless of the likelihood that the evaluator was prejudiced. Moreover, the African American student who attributed his failure to discrimination was rated less favorably than the African American student who attributed his failure to other external (e.g., test difficulty) and internal (e.g., his ability—the quality of the answers he provided on the test) factors. This suggests that the tendency to be evaluated negatively when one attributes failure to an external cause is strong only when the cause is prejudice. That is, claiming prejudice seems to be a special case that evokes retaliatory responses that are not evoked when other claims of offense are made. Why might this be the case?

Targets may be punished for claiming discrimination because dominant group members feel threatened and anxious regarding issues of prejudice, and deal with their threat and anxiety by derogating the target (cf. Kaiser & Miller, 2003). That is, because dominant group members like to perceive themselves and other ingroup members as nonprejudiced individuals, when targets make accusations of prejudice, it threatens dominant group members' sense of self. Consequently, they respond to targets' confronting behavior by disliking the target. If the confronting behavior is not linked to prejudice, then dominant group members are less likely to feel threatened and need not derogate the target. Targets may become aware of this distinction through their experiences and thus become less likely to confront perpetrators of prejudice.

Forecasting the Power of Perceived Social Costs

There is a longstanding literature that indicates that people underestimate the power of situational forces on their behavior (Jones, 1990). As such, although social costs should inhibit targets of prejudice from confronting perpetrators, we predict that targets will not imagine that social costs will influence their responses. Targets of prejudice will not accurately forecast how they will respond to prejudice because they will not take into consideration the power of social costs in the situation. Previous researchers have also made the prediction that targets of prejudice are unable to accurately forecast their behavior in this area. However, they have not been explicit in arguing that social cost is the cause of this lack of accuracy. For example, Swim and Hyers (1999) and Woodzicka and LaFrance (2001) were interested in the unacknowledged constraining nature of the situation. In these studies, one group of participants either read scenarios in which they were exposed to a sexist individual or were instructed to imagine a sexually harassing job interview. A second group of participants was actually exposed to the sexist individual or participated in the sexually harassing interview. In both studies, the majority of participants who imagined being in the situation expected that they would confront the perpetrator, but fewer actually did. For example, 62% of women in Woodzicka and LaFrance's study predicted that they would either ask the interviewer why he asked sexist questions or inform the interviewer that the questions were inappropriate. However, only 36% of the women actually did so.

It seems that targets of prejudice are overly confident about their responses to prejudicial treatment. Woodzicka and LaFrance emphasized anticipating the wrong emotion (anger rather than anxiety) as the reason why participants were not accurate in predicting their responses. Swim and Hyers emphasized that women were less aware of the desire to appear polite in actual situations as the explanation for participants' inaccuracy. In our research, we argue, and explicitly test, that people do not anticipate the social cost of confronting the perpetrator.

Overview of Studies

We conducted two studies to investigate the role of social costs in women's responses to sexually offensive behavior. We utilized an interview paradigm in which women imagined being interviewed (Study 1) or were actually interviewed (Study 2) by a male. Because we wanted our female participants to be concerned with how they would be evaluated, we manipulated the level of social costs associated with confronting the interviewer. We either emphasized that it was essential for the woman to make a good impression and obtain the job (high cost) or we emphasized that she was simply interviewing to gain experience (low cost). The interviewer either asked offensive but nonsexist questions or sexually offensive questions. We predicted that women who imagined being in the interview would indicate they would confront the male who asked the sexist question regardless of the costs. That is, they would not forecast that social costs would influence their decision regarding how to respond to the interviewer. In contrast, women who actually participated in the interview would confront the male who asked sexist questions only when the costs of confronting were low.

Pilot Study

We conducted a pilot test to make sure that the offensive and sexist questions were seen as equally offensive. We also examined the extent to which the sexist questions were seen as more sexist than the offensive questions.

Method

Participants and Procedures

Twenty female students at Princeton University participated in the pilot study. A female experimenter approached individuals as they entered a dining hall alone. The experimenter asked each participant if she would be willing to complete a brief questionnaire in exchange for a small candy bar. If the participant agreed, then the experimenter gave her a questionnaire which asked the participant to imagine that she was in a job interview and that she received three specific interview questions. Half of the participants imagined they received three sexist questions: (a) Do you have a boyfriend?, (b) Do people find you desirable?, and (c) Do you think it is important for women to wear bras to work? The other half of the participants imagined they received three offensive but nonsexist questions: (a) Do you have a best friend?, (b) Do people find you morbid?, and (c) Do you think it is important for people to believe in God? We selected these questions from Woodzicka and LaFrance (2001) who demonstrated that the offensive questions were comparably surprising for a job interview but not perceived as being sexist. After reading each question participants indicated how offensive they thought it would be for the interviewer to ask them the question. Additionally, we asked participants, "Taken together, how offensive do you think these questions are for an interview setting?" and "Taken together, how sexist do you think these questions are for an interview setting?" Participants made all responses on a 7-point scale where higher numbers represent more offensiveness or sexist.

Results and Discussion

We created a composite score of participants' ratings of how offensive the three questions were for an interview. Results revealed that participants thought the offensive ($M = 4.63$, $SD = 1.62$) and sexist ($M = 5.20$, $SD = 1.32$) questions were equally offensive, $t(18) = .86$, $p = .40$. Similarly, when judged together as a set (i.e., taken together, how offensive are these questions), participants thought the offensive ($M = 4.90$, $SD = 1.85$) and sexist ($M = 5.10$, $SD = 1.79$) questions were equally offensive, $t(18) = .24$, $p = .81$. Finally, when judged together as a set, participants thought the sexist questions ($M = 5.50$, $SD = 1.90$) were more sexist than the offensive questions ($M = 2.30$, $SD = 2.16$), $t(18)$, 3.51, $p = .002$. These findings support our claim that both sets of interview questions were seen as offensive, but the sexist questions were seen as more sexist than the offensive questions.

Study 1

The goal of Study 1 was to show that when targets of prejudice imagine encountering someone who behaves in a sexist manner they predict that they would express their dissatisfaction to the perpetrator regardless of the social costs.

Method

Participants and Procedures

Fifty-six undergraduate women participated in this study. The sample consisted of 24 Whites, 18 African Americans, 6 Asian Americans, and 8 students who indicated that their race was not listed on the demographic form. In addition, the sample consisted mostly of first and second-year students (82%). A female experimenter approached participants as they entered the campus center. She explained to participants that she was conducting a psychology study and would greatly appreciate it if they would complete a brief questionnaire in exchange for a candy bar. She further explained that participants would read a short vignette and answers several questions. If participants agreed to participate, then the experimenter gave them the questionnaire.

Participants read a vignette in which they imagined they were being interviewed by a male interviewer. We randomly assigned participants to either a high cost or a low cost condition. In the high cost condition, participants imagined that it was important to make a good impression during the interview because it was the job of their dreams, the job market was tough, the other applicants were highly competitive, and they really needed to be offered the job. In the low cost condition, participants imagined that they had another job offer, the interview was not crucial for their future, and that they only agreed to the interview for the experience. Additionally, all participants read a list of 10 questions that the interviewer asked them. Seven were standard interview questions (e.g., How do you handle constructive criticism?) and three were sexist or offensive questions spaced throughout the list. In the sexist condition, the interviewer asked: (a) Do you have a boyfriend?, (b) Do people find you desirable?, and (c) Do you think it is important for women to wear bras to work? In the offensive condition, the interviewer asked: (a) Do you have a best friend?, (b) Do people find you morbid?, and (c) Do you think it is important for people to believe in God?

After reading the vignette, participants rated the extent to which they would: (a) ignore the person's behavior/comments, (b) question the person about his behavior/comments, (c) comment on the appropriateness of the behavior/comments, (d) use sarcasm or humor in reply, (e) hide their emotions, and (f) show signs of surprise or disgust. Participants rated all responses on 7-point scales ranging from 1 *(definitely would not)* to 7 *(definitely would)*. We combined the items (reverse-coded when necessary) to create a confronting variable such that higher numbers indicated that participants believed they definitely would confront the interviewer *(a = .67)*.

Participants rated how sexist they thought the questions were and how much they thought they had to lose by confronting the interviewer about his behavior. Participants rated both questions on 7-point scales ranging from 1 *(not at all)* to 7 *(very much)*.

Results and Discussion

Manipulation Checks

A 2 (cost: low vs. high) x 2 (type of question: offensive vs. sexist) ANOVA on how sexist participants perceived the questions to be resulted in a main effect for type of question, $F(1, 51) = 38.77$, $p < .001$. As expected, participants rated the sexist questions *(M = 5.79, SD = 1.36)* as more sexist than the offensive questions *(M = 3.29, SD = 1.52)*. No other effects were significant. A 2 (cost: low vs. high) x 2 (type of question: offensive vs. sexist) ANOVA on how much women felt was at stake if they confronted the interviewer resulted in a main effect for cost, $F(1,51) = 32.73$, $p < .001$. As expected, participants thought they had more to lose by confronting the interviewer in the high cost situation (M = 5.56, SD = 1.11) compared to the low cost situation (M = 3.17, SD = 1.79). No other effects were significant.

Confronting Behavior

As predicted, participants indicated that they would be more likely to confront the interviewer who asked sexist questions ($M = 4.29$, $SD = 1.17$) than the one who asked offensive questions ($M = 3.67$, $SD = 1.17$), $F(1,52) = 3.84$, $p = .05$ (Cohen's $d = .54$). No other effects were significant, $F(1,52) = .35$, $p = .56$ for cost main effect, $F(1,52) = .00$, $p = .99$ for interaction. This finding is consistent with previous work that shows women believe they would confront a sexist person if they were in such a situation (e.g., Swim & Hyers, 1998; Woodzicka & LaFrance, 2001). However, our findings provide clearer evidence that women believe that social costs would not influence their decision to confront the perpetrator. These findings show that women believe that regardless of how costly the situation, they would stand up to the perpetrator and express their dissatisfaction. But would women's behavior be influenced by the perceived costs of confronting in a face-to-face interview situation?

Study 2

In Study 2 we examined whether social costs inhibit women's confronting behavior during an exchange with a sexist interviewer.

Method

Participants and Design

We contacted participants by e-mail and asked them to participate in a study on first impressions. Sixty women and 16 men participated in the study. The women were predominately White (68.3%) and all of the men were White. We paid women $8 and men $20 for their participation (we paid men more because their participation involved more time).

The experimental design was a 2 (costs: low vs. high) x 2 (type of interview question: sexist vs. offensive) between subjects factorial design. Women played the role of the job applicant, and men played the interviewer. All participants read and signed a consent form which indicated that they could withdraw from the study at any time without penalty.

Procedure

Female applicant preparation. The experimenter (White female) explained to participants that she was interested in how quickly people form first impressions and how likely they are to change them during job interviews. The experimenter noted that another participant was involved in the study and that one of them would be selected to be the interviewer. She then indicated that the participant had been randomly assigned to the "interviewee" condition. The experimenter also told all interviewees that the interviewer had been told to interview them as he or she saw appropriate.

The experimenter then randomly assigned the female applicant to be in the lower high cost condition. Specifically, in the high cost condition the experimenter told participants the interview was for a prestigious investment banking company. Moreover, the experimenter informed participants that the job market is tight and the competition for this type of job is fierce. The experimenter also explained that the salary was high and that many people wanted this type of job. By contrast, in the low cost condition the experimenter told participants the interview was for a charity organization. Moreover, the experimenter informed participants that competition for these jobs is not tough. She also explained that the salary would be low and that it would be relatively easy for many people to obtain this job. After giving the participants the information regarding the perceived cost, the experimenter informed each participant that the interview would last approximately 10–15 minutes and took the participant to another room to meet the interviewer.

Male interviewer preparation. The experimenter explained to each male participant that the study examined first impressions. She told each male that he would interview four women.[1] The experimenter emphasized that it was important for them not to diverge from the script. Next, the experimenter gave the male interviewers four sheets of paper that contained interview questions. She emphasized that it was important for the interviewers to use a different sheet of questions for each interviewee, and to present the questions in the order that they appeared in the packet. Furthermore, the experimenter explained, "Some of the questions that you will have to ask the interviewees are offensive and otherwise bizarre. It is absolutely crucial that you remain straight-faced regardless of the oddity of the remarks or despite the reactions of the interviewees." The experimenter informed the interviewer how he should respond if the interviewee questioned why he was asking the questions. For example, if the interviewee says something akin to "What the heck?" or "Why do you need to know that?" respond in one of two ways:

1. *"I'm merely interested."* (Repeat the question). If she still refuses or otherwise objects, move on to the next question.
2. *"I am trying to get a look into your personality to see if you are a good fit for the job."* (Repeat the question). If she still refuses or otherwise objects, move on to the next question.

In addition, the experimenter told the interviewers not to rush through the questions, to make sure they allowed ample time for the applicant to answer the questions, not to preface the questions with his own comments, and not to make a lot of descriptive comments after the interviewee's responses. The experimenter explained that he should behave as an interviewer would in a normal interview situation. The experimenter allowed the interviewer to review all interview questions and express any concerns or questions that he had at the time. Additionally, the experimenter went over each interview question with the interviewer to make sure he felt comfortable asking the question and to make sure he could ask the question such that it seemed as if he had thought of the question. The interviewers were not aware of the cost manipulation.

Interview questions. The questions were identical to the ones used in Study 1. The key questions were numbers 2, 5, and 9. Each interviewer was assigned to ask two women the sexist questions and two women the offensive questions. The order in which the males asked the questions was counterbalanced. The experimenter was blind to the question condition.

After the interview, female participants returned to the original room and completed a questionnaire. Male participants also completed a questionnaire. Then the experimenter fully debriefed all participants and explained the necessity of deception (males were debriefed after interviewing all of the women). In addition, the experimenter informed all participants that they had been covertly videotaped during the interview, and asked them to sign a release form for our use of the tapes.[2] All participants signed the release form.

Measures

Confronting behavior. Two female coders made ratings of females' behavior during the interview. The coding scheme was based on work by Swim and Hyers (1998) and Woodzicka and LaFrance (2001). Consistent with previous laboratory research, we included a wide range of behaviors, from subtle to direct, to capture women's responses to the interview questions. Additionally, we included subtle responses because gender norms suggest that women tend not to behave in aggressive, direct, hostile ways during cross-gender interactions. The coders noted whether or not the female displayed the following behaviors during the three key questions: (a) no confrontation—ignored completely or just answered the question (k = .82), (b) negative confrontation—aggressively countering the legitimacy of the question (k = .88), (c) positive confrontation—asking why the question was asked (k = .90), (d) questioning— asking to clarify or explain the question (k = .79), exclaiming—responding in surprise or disgust (k = .89), grumbling (k = 1.0), and (g) reporting the incident to the experimenter (k = 1.0). Coders could select more than one style for each interview question. Coders were blind to the cost condition but not to the question condition.

Interviewers' ratings. Males rated the extent to which they perceived the female applicant as a complainer (argumentative, troublemaker, complainer; *a* = .69). Additionally, they rated the extent to which they perceived the applicant as being a good person (warm, would be a good friend, compassionate, and considerate; *a* = .82). Finally, they rated how hireable the applicant appeared (would be a good coworker, seems to have a strong work ethic, would hire her for the job; *a* = .80). All of these items were embedded in filler items. Participants made their ratings using 7-point scales ranging from 1 *(not at all)* to 7 *(very much)*.

Manipulation check. After completing all dependent measures, female participants completed two questions that served as manipulation checks. Specifically, they indicated whether they thought the interview was supposed to be a low-pressure or a high-pressure interview. Additionally, they indicated whether the questions they received during the interview were offensive but not sexist or offensive and sexist.

Results

Manipulation Check

All female participants correctly indicated their social cost condition. However, nine female participants incorrectly indicated which type of question they received. These participants were removed from all subsequent analyses. However, the pattern of results remains the same if we include them in the analyses.

Confronting Behavior

Below is a description of the percentage of women who used each of the confronting styles. The main style of confrontation was to question the interviewer (47.1%; e.g., "What do you mean by desirable?"). The second common style was to positively confront the interviewer (13.7%; e.g., "That is a strange question!" or, "Why is this question relevant to my employment?"). The third common style was to negatively confront the interviewer (9.8%; e.g., "That is a sexist question." or, "Why does it matter?!"). The fourth common style was to exclaim (5.9%; e.g., "Oh my God!" or, "What?!"). Similarly, few women (5.9%) refused to answer the key questions. Only one participant (2%) reported the incident to the experimenter. Finally, no participant used grumbling as a means to confront the interviewer.

A logistic regression was conducted using cost and type of interview question as the independent variables and a dichotomous confronting behavior variable as the dependent variable. The dichotomous confronting behavior variable is collapsed across all six confronting styles. (We collapsed across all six confronting styles as opposed to examining each style separately because there are not enough

Table 1. Correlations from Study 2

Variables	1	2	3	4
Sexist Condition				
Confront	—	.44*	.46*	-.22
Perceived as a complainer		—	-.73**	-.31
Perceived as a good person			—	.49*
Hireability				—
Offensive Condition				
Confront	—	.21	-.20	.18
Perceived as a complainer		—	-.12	-.10
Perceived as a good person			—	.29
Hireability				—

p < .05. **p < .01.

participants who used each confrontational style to warrant using each style as a separate dependent variable.) Results revealed a main effect for cost, $\chi^2 (1) = 7.68$, $p < .05$ (effect size = .38). Women in the low cost condition were more likely to confront the male interviewer than were women in the high cost condition. As predicted, the interaction was also significant, $\chi^2 = 2.82$, $p = .05$ (effect size = .23). Further analysis revealed that for the offensive questions, cost did not determine whether or not women confronted ($\chi^2 = 2.14$, $p = .14$; 60% and 33% in the low and high cost conditions, respectively). As predicted, for the sexist questions, participants were less likely to confront in the high cost condition (22%) than in the low cost condition (92%; $\chi^2 = 10.52$, $p < .01$, effect size = .71). Put differently, in the sexist condition, those in the low cost condition were more likely to confront (92%) than not confront (8%), whereas those in the high cost condition were less likely to confront (22%) than not (78%). Thus, anticipated costs inhibited women's confronting behavior in the sexist condition. Those who felt they had a lot to lose were less likely to confront the interviewer who asked sexist questions.

Supplementary Analyses

Previous research suggests that targets of prejudice are penalized (e.g., disliked and perceived as complainers) for challenging prejudice, but not for challenging offensive but nonprejudiced behavior (Kaiser & Miller, 2001, 2003; Shelton, Richeson, & Carranza, 2003). Consistent with previous results, we found that in the sexist question condition, the more often women confronted the interviewer about his behavior, the more she was perceived as a complainer, and the less she was perceived as a good person. By contrast, in the offensive but nonsexist condition, women's confronting behavior was unrelated to the interviewer's perceptions of her. See Table 1 for correlations. However, the correlations between the two conditions were not significantly different from one another ($Z = .815$, $p = .21$ for comparing the perceived as a complainer variables, $Z = .96$, $p = .19$ for comparing the perceived as a good person variables, and $Z = 1.35$, $p = .08$ for comparing the hireability variables).

General Discussion

Our findings show that targets of prejudice are less likely to confront individuals who behave in a prejudiced manner under high cost conditions, but that targets of prejudice believe that social costs would not influence their behavior. Specifically, when imagining the situation women believe they will be just as likely to challenge men who ask sexually offensive questions when the costs are high as when they are low (Study 1). In reality, however, the costs had a major impact on women's behavior (Study 2).

The contrast between Studies 1 and 2 is fascinating. As researchers, we like to think that having participants imagine being in a situation is equivalent to being in the real situation, or at least a simulated one in the laboratory. Perhaps, for most phenomena we are correct (see Robinson & Clore, 2001). Our findings suggest, however, that our thinking may be incorrect when it comes to confronting individuals who offend us because of our group membership. Study 1 shows that women do not consider, or at least do not want to admit to, the constraining nature of the situation when they imagine being in a sexually offensive situation. However, once in the situation, the dynamics of the situation have a major impact on their behavior. The cues in the situation (e.g., person in front of me controlling my fate) are so powerful in the face-to-face situation that it prevents women from behaving how they think they would behave. It is astonishing that we obtain these effects even with a simulated interview situation. Although the cues may have been more salient in the situation than in the vignette, the women did not have much to lose in Study 2. After all, they were simply participating in a psychology study for pay. Imagine the effect in the real world where people's careers and reputations are truly at stake. Our results suggest that the costs of not receiving a job, a promotion, or being disliked by one's colleagues will have a major impact on whether or not targets of prejudice confront their offenders. These results explain why so few people report group-based harassment in the workplace. As observers, we are likely to imagine that we would respond and thus expect others to respond as well. However, once in the situation, the social costs seem to be more salient and they prevent us from doing so.

It is important to highlight that the social costs did not have the same impact on how women responded to the offensive but nonsexist questions. As noted earlier, previous research has demonstrated that dominant group members are more likely to punish targets for confronting prejudice than for confronting offensive behavior in general (Kaiser & Miller, 2003; Shelton et al., 2003). The findings from the present research suggest that targets of prejudice may be aware of this differentiation. Targets of prejudice know that they are more likely to be punished for confronting sexist behavior compared to offensive but nonsexist behavior. As a result, they are likely to pick their battles wisely.

Consistent with previous laboratory research, we included various responses as indicators of confronting behavior. We did this in order to explore the subtle ways in which targets may confront offenders. Although some of their response may be very subtle, targets of prejudice are attempting to express to perpetrators that the behavior is unacceptable. Nevertheless, it is interesting to point out that the women in our study rarely aggressively confronted the sexist interviewer. Moreover, women generally answered every question that was posed and then proceeded to question the interviewer or comment on the appropriateness of the question. Why might this be the case? Perhaps, women are aware of the costs of different confrontational styles. For example, more serious interpersonal consequences may accrue with more aggressive confrontational styles (see Carli, 1990). The indirect confrontational style utilized by women may be an avenue by which they can confront their perpetrators while minimizing the costs associated with aggressive confrontational styles.

It is unclear whether or not social costs have the same effects on inhibiting targets other than women (e.g., Blacks) as well as nontraditional targets (e.g., Whites and men) from confronting perpetrators when they experience prejudice because of their group membership. Stangor et al. (2002) found that nontraditional targets (i.e., Whites and men) are just as likely to make an attribution to discrimination in private and in public contexts when they experience negative treatment that could be a result of prejudice toward their group membership. In addition, it is unclear whether or not social costs have the same effect on inhibiting individuals from confronting perpetrators on behalf of others who are the victims of prejudice (i.e., Whites and men confronting on behalf of Blacks and women). Czopp and Monteith (2003) found that perpetrators of prejudice experience more guilt and self-criticism when nontraditional targets (i.e., Whites and men) challenge prejudiced behavior directed at traditional targets compared to when traditional targets (i.e., Blacks and women) challenge prejudiced behavior. Taken together, these findings suggest that the social costs may be less severe for nontraditional targets of prejudice (e.g., Whites and men) who challenge prejudice, and these individuals may be aware that the costs are not high.

In Study 2, we examined perpetrators' evaluations of targets who confront them in face-to-face encounters. A shortcoming of previous published research was that vignettes were used. It is possible that individuals in the previous studies negatively evaluated targets who claimed discrimination because the target was not someone they knew. Our research suggests that even after getting to know the person in a face-to-face interaction, albeit a short one, perpetrators are just as likely to negatively evaluate targets and denigrate them when the targets point out their behavior is inappropriate. Additionally, participants who evaluated the target of prejudice in previous research represented a third party whereas the male participants in our study are the actual perpetrators, albeit they were playing a role. Thus, we have a better understanding of how perpetrators respond to targets of prejudice confronting them about their own behavior.

Several limitations of this research are important to note. First, in Study 2 several of the women in the sexist condition thought the interview questions were offensive but not sexist. This was surprising given that pilot testing demonstrated that women, on average, thought the sexist questions were not only offensive but also sexist. Nevertheless, the problem with the manipulation may have influenced women's perception of the situation and their behavior in Study 2. However, given that we excluded participants who did not get the manipulation check correct, this does not pose as a serious limitation of our work. Second, because the interviewers did not use a standardized script, their behavior could have varied across applicants. The third limitation concerns the nonsignificant difference between the low and high social cost groups for the offensive questions. It is possible that our design lacked statistical power to detect differences of moderate size for the offensive questions. A design with greater power would possibly detect differences between the low and high social cost groups for offensive questions, albeit less so than for prejudicial comments. Finally, although we have been using the term "perpetrator of prejudice" in our discussion of the findings, it is important to note that the male interviewers were instructed to behave the way they did. That is, their behavior did not reflect their own gender beliefs and sentiments about how women should be treated in interpersonal interactions. We used this methodology because, given the politically correct climate on college campuses, it would have been virtually impossible to get men to provide sexist remarks in a controlled laboratory setting where they are being observed and videotaped. Critics may argue that instructing our male participants to behave in a sexist manner could have caused them to experience anxiety that would have influenced the way they perceived the female participants. We concur with such critics that male participants' anxiety could have influenced their *perceptions* of the female (i.e., our supplementary analyses), but it could not explain why women were less likely to confront their behavior in the high cost condition.

Despite these limitations, this research has serious implications for society. Social costs may prevent targets from challenging individuals who treat them negatively because of their group membership. However, just because targets are less likely to challenge the perpetrator does not mean that targets are satisfied with the situation. Perpetrators, however, may assume that because they were not challenged, their behavior is acceptable, and they may continue to behave inappropriately. In fact, high-powered males who are sexist may never be challenged and are likely to continue to treat women in a sexist manner. It may even be difficult for perpetrators to take seriously a target who confronts them after a second incident if the target did not confront them previously. In sum, social costs prevent targets from expressing their true dissatisfaction, which could lead to the continuation of prejudicial treatment.

Confronting perpetrators in face-to-face interactions may be unpleasant for both targets and perpetrators of prejudice. Targets may risk being disliked and denigrated (Shelton et al., 2003). Perpetrators may risk being humiliated (Czopp & Monteith, 2003). Changing one perpetrator at a time through confrontation, even if the costs are high, however, may be a first step in prejudice reduction against stigmatized individuals.

Initial submission: July 5, 2003
Initial acceptance: October 3, 2003
Final acceptance: December 22, 2003

Notes

1. Due to scheduling conflicts, men interviewed between 3–5 women.
2. The Internal Review Panel for Human Subjects at Princeton University approved of the videotaping without the participants' knowledge as long as all participants were given the right to have their videotape erased at the end of the study if they desired to do so. None of the participants requested that their videotape be erased.

References

Carli, L. L. (1990). Gender, language and influence. *Journal of Personality and Social Psychology,* 59, 941–951.

Crosby, F. J. (1993). Why complain? *Journal of Social Issues,* 49, 169–184.

Czopp, A. M., & Monteith, M. J. (2003). Confronting prejudice (literally): Reactions to confrontations of racial and gender bias. *Personality and Social Psychology Bulletin,* 29, 532–544.

Fitzgerald, L. F., Swan, S., & Fischer, K. (1995). Why didn't she just report him? The psychological and legal implications of women's responses to sexual harassment. *Journal of Social Issues,* 51, 117–138.

Gruber, J., & Bjorn, L. (1986). Women's responses to sexual harassment: An analysis of sociocultural, organizational, and personal resource models. *Social Science Quarterly,* 67, 814–825.

Harris, R., & Firestone, J. (1997). Subtle sexism in the U.S. military: Individual responses to sexual harassment. In N. V. Benokraitis (Ed.), *Subtle sexism: Current practice and prospects for change* (pp. 154–171). Thousand Oaks, CA: Sage.

Haslett, B., & Lippman, S. (1997). Micro-inequities: Up close and personal. In N. V. Benokraitis (Ed.), *Subtle sexism: Current practice and prospects for change* (pp. 34–53). Thousand Oaks, CA: Sage.

Jones, E. E. (1990). *Interpersonal perception*. New York: Freeman.

Kaiser, C. R., & Miller, C. T. (2001). Stop complaining! The social costs of making attributions to discrimination. *Personality and Social Psychology Bulletin, 27*, 254–263.

Kaiser, C. R., & Miller, C. T. (2002). Silence in the face of prejudice: How interpersonal costs prevent women from confronting discrimination. Manuscript submitted for publication.

Kaiser, C. R., & Miller, C. T. (2003). Derogating the victim: The interpersonal consequences of blaming events on discrimination. *Group Processes and Intergroup Relations, 6*, 227–237.

Kowalski, R. M. (1996). Complaints and complaining: Functions, antecedents, and consequences. *Psychological Bulletin, 119*, 179–196.

Robinson, M., & Clore, G. (2001). Simulation, scenarios, and emotional appraisal: Testing the convergence of real and imagined reactions to emotional stimuli. *Personality and Social Psychology Bulletin, 27*, 1520–1532.

Shelton, J. N., Richeson, J. A., & Carranza, E. (2003). Taking a stand against prejudice: The costs and benefits for targets of prejudice. Manuscript submitted for publication.

Stangor, C., Swim, J. K., Van Allen, K. L., & Sechrist, G. B. (2002). Reporting discrimination in public and private contexts. *Journal of Personality and Social Psychology, 82*, 69–76.

Swim, J. K., & Hyers, L. L. (1999). Excuse me, what did you just say?! Women's public and private responses to sexist remarks. *Journal of Experimental Social Psychology, 35*, 68–88.

Woodzicka, J. A., & LaFrance, M. (2001). Real versus imagined gender harassment. *Journal of Social Issues, 57*, 15–30.

Concerns About Appearing Prejudiced

Implications for Anxiety During Daily Interracial Interactions

By J. Nicole Shelton, Tessa V. West, and Thomas E. Trail

Abstract

We investigated the relationship between Whites' and ethnic minorities' concerns about appearing prejudiced and anxiety during daily interracial interactions. College roommate pairs completed an individual difference measure of concerns about appearing prejudiced at the beginning of the semester. Then they completed measures of anxiety and perceptions of their roommates' anxiety-related behaviors for 15 days. Results indicated that among interracial roommate pairs, Whites' and ethnic minorities' concerns about appearing prejudiced were related to their self-reported anxiety on a daily basis; but this was not the case among same-race roommate pairs. In addition, among interracial roommate pairs, roommates who were concerned about appearing prejudiced began to "leak" their anxiety towards the end of the diary period, as indicated by their out-group roommate who perceived their anxious behaviors as increasing across time, and who consequently liked them less. The implications of these findings for intergroup relations are discussed in this article.

People often enter social encounters with concerns about how they might be evaluated by others. Students, for example, may be concerned with being perceived as unintelligent during interactions with professors. Spouses may be concerned with being perceived as unlikable during interactions with their in-laws. One specific concern that people negotiate during intergroup interactions is their concern with appearing prejudiced. This concern can serve as a lens through which people view themselves, view others, and are actually viewed by others during interpersonal interactions (Crandall & Eshleman, 2003). The goal of the present research was to illustrate the extent to which Whites' and ethnic minorities' concerns about appearing prejudiced, measured prior to intergroup contact, have implications for anxiety and perceptions of one's partner—in particular liking—during interracial interactions among college roommates.

J. Nicole Shelton, Tessa V. West & Thomas E. Trail, "Concerns About Appearing Prejudiced: Implications for Anxiety During Daily Interracial Interactions," *Group Processes & Intergroup Relations*, vol. 13, no. 3 , pp. 329–344. Copyright © 2010 by SAGE Publications, Inc. Reprinted with permission.

Interpersonal concerns about appearing prejudiced

In contemporary American society, holding or expressing prejudiced beliefs about a racial/ethnic group is not tolerated as much as it was in the past (Dovidio & Gaertner, 2004). As a result, many people have become quite concerned about appearing prejudiced towards racial out-groups. For example, as implied in a quote by George W. Bush in which he stated, "You can call me anything you want, but do not call me a racist!" (Williams, 2005), calling someone in American society racist can be quite offensive. To date, research on concerns about appearing prejudiced has focused on Whites. Undoubtedly, this is in part because, given the history of overt prejudice and discrimination by Whites against ethnic minorities as well as status and power differences between the groups, it may be more important for Whites not to express racial bias. Nonetheless, given that social norms are egalitarian, both Whites and ethnic minorities are likely to be concerned with appearing prejudiced, though Whites and minorities might differ in their mean level of concern. Moreover, these concerns may have similar consequences for the dynamics of interracial interactions, which is the focus of our research.

The perspective of Whites

Although Whites may unconsciously behave in a prejudiced manner, most Whites consciously deny any ill intent and are against unfair treatment toward minority groups (Dovidio, Kawakami, Johnson, Johnson, & Howard, 1997; Fazio, Jackson, Dunton, & Williams, 1995). Nevertheless, they are aware that their actions and inactions may be perceived as prejudiced, and thus either for internal (e.g., personal values) or external (e.g., societal norms) reasons they are motivated not to behave in a prejudiced manner in public settings (Legault, Green-Demers, Grant, & Chung, 2007; Plant & Devine, 1998). Whites' concerns about appearing prejudiced have been shown to have negative effects for the self during intergroup interactions. Specifically, Whites' concerns about appearing prejudiced are related to more self-reported anxiety (Shelton, 2003) and less enjoyment (Vorauer, Main, & O'Connell, 1998) during an interracial interaction, as well as more anxiety anticipating an upcoming interaction and the desire to avoid intergroup interactions (Plant & Butz, 2006). Disentangling internal and external sources of concerns about appearing prejudiced, Plant (2004) had non-Blacks complete measures of internal and external motivation to control prejudice, and then two weeks later, reflect upon their interracial interactions during the past two weeks. She found that, in predicting responses across the two weeks, non-Black participants high in internal motivation (i.e., motivated for personal values) consistently reported less anxiety about interracial interactions and less of a desire to avoid these interactions. However, non-Black participants high in external motivation (i.e., motivated by social norms) reported marginally more anxiety about interracial interactions. Taken together, these findings show that Whites' concerns about appearing prejudiced, especially when the motivation is external, have harmful effects for the self during interracial interactions.

The negative experiences that Whites who are concerned with appearing prejudiced have, may be a result of the pressure on Whites to monitor their thoughts, feelings, and behaviors during interracial interactions (Dovidio & Gaertner, 2004; Monteith, 1993). For example, the desire to appear unbiased is so pervasive among Whites that they report not noticing that a person is Black, even when race is the most noticeable characteristic available (Norton, Sommers, Apfelbaum, Pura, & Ariely, 2007). As Norton et al. (2007) note, it is as if Whites believe: "If I do not notice race, then I cannot be racist" (p. 949). Moreover, Whites who are at most risk of being perceived as prejudiced—i.e., those with higher levels of racial bias—control their behaviors when they are concerned about appearing biased (Richeson & Shelton, 2007). Given the dearth of research taking a dyadic approach to studying interracial interactions, it is not surprising that little research exists on how Whites' concerns about appearing prejudiced influence their partner's perceptions and experiences during the interaction. If Whites monitor their thoughts, feelings, and behaviors during interracial interactions in order to avoid being perceived as prejudiced, then their interaction partner is likely to be influenced by such self-regulatory processes. Successful self-regulation should reap positive partner effects. The only study, to our knowledge, that has explored the impact of Whites' concerns on their partners' perceptions, revealed that Blacks liked Whites who tried not to be prejudiced during an interaction more than they liked Whites who did not (Shelton, 2003). This suggests that despite feeling anxious and not enjoying the interaction, Whites who are concerned with appearing prejudiced are successful at not allowing their anxiety to leak during brief interracial interactions. However, because this process is mentally and physically exhausting (Richeson & Shelton, 2007), the self-regulatory demands of controlling one's thoughts, feelings, and behaviors are likely to break down over time, causing Whites who are concerned with appearing prejudiced to appear non-anxious during initial interactions but eventually begin to "leak" anxiety over time. Thus, we predict that when one is examining interactions over time, as in the present research, the more Whites are concerned with appearing prejudiced, the more anxious they will eventually appear to their ethnic minority partner across time. This increase in anxiety should be coupled with a decrease in liking; that is, the more Whites are concerned with appearing prejudiced, the less they will be liked by their partner.

The perpective of ethnic minorities

Because of evidence indicating that ethnic minorities have negative attitudes about Whites (Johnson & Leci, 2003; Monteith & Spicer, 2000), it is reasonable that they may be concerned with not appearing prejudiced during interactions. In the only research to our knowledge that has explored this issue, Plant (2004) suggests that, similar to Whites, Blacks are concerned with appearing prejudiced for internal reasons—they are personally against racial bias of all types—as well as for external reasons; they are sensitive to the repercussions of behaving in a biased way toward a powerful group. Furthermore, she found that the more Blacks were internally motivated to respond without prejudice at Time 1, the more they grew to expect Whites to respond without bias two weeks later (Plant, 2004). Unlike the research with Whites, however, researchers have not examined how ethnic minorities' concerns about appearing prejudiced influence their own and their partner's experiences *during* interracial interactions. Given that societal norms are against all people expressing prejudice, we predict that ethnic minorities' concerns about appearing prejudiced will operate in a similar manner as Whites' concerns.

That is, similar to Whites, the more ethnic minorities are concerned about appearing prejudiced, the more anxiety they should experience during interracial interactions because of the negative social repercussions of allowing racial biases to leak through. Moreover, the effort associated with trying to show that one is not prejudiced is likely to be exhausting and difficult to maintain over time, in the same way it is for Whites. Thus, the more ethnic minorities are concerned with appearing prejudiced, the more anxious they will eventually appear to their White partners, which will be coupled with a decrease in liking by their White partners across time. Alternatively, however, Whites' perceptions of their ethnic minority partners may not be a function of their partners' concerns about appearing prejudiced. Ethnic minorities' racial attitudes do not influence Whites' experiences in an interracial interaction (Shelton & Richeson, 2006). Thus, it is feasible that ethnic minorities' concerns about revealing those attitudes may also not be associated with Whites' experiences, in this case, the extent to which Whites like their partners. Nonetheless, we suspect that the demands associated with regulating one's thoughts, feelings, and behaviors over time are just as taxing for minorities as they are for Whites (indeed, interracial interactions are just as cognitively depleting for Blacks as they are for Whites; Richeson & Shelton, 2007). As a result, across time, the ability to regulate one's thoughts and behavior is likely to wane, leaving ethnic minorities' anxiety about how they are appearing to their partner quite discernable.

The present research

In the present research, we examined the role that concerns about appearing prejudiced plays during interracial interactions in a natural setting— between college roommates—across time. The goals of our research were twofold. First, we examined how both Whites' and ethnic minorities' concerns about appearing prejudiced influence self-reported anxiety during daily interracial interactions. We predicted that the more both groups were concerned about appearing prejudiced, the more anxiety they would experience during daily interracial interactions. Second, we examined how both Whites' and ethnic minorities' perceptions of their roommates are a function of their roommate's concerns about appearing prejudiced. That is, how much people like their roommate, for example, is a function of how much their roommate is concerned with appearing prejudiced. Based on the self-regulatory framework that it is difficult to control one's feelings and behaviors on a regular basis over an extended period of time, we predict that Whites and ethnic minorities will perceive their roommates who have high concerns about appearing prejudiced as more anxious and will like them less across time.

Method

Participants[1]

Seventy-nine same-sex freshmen roommate dyads participated in a study on roommate relationships for $50 and a chance to win monetary prizes in a lottery drawing. The sample consisted of 28 cross-race (White-ethnic minority) and 51 same race (40 White-White and 11 ethnic minority-ethnic minority) roommate dyads. Moreover, 45 were female pairs and 34 were male pairs. Gender did not moderate our effects; thus, it will not be discussed further. The students were randomly assigned by university officials to be roommates during the summer prior to their freshman year.

Procedures

We recruited students during the first week of the school year to participate in a study about freshmen roommates and their college experiences. We informed students that it was important but not essential for their roommate to be involved in the study. As a result, we obtained roommate pairs as well as participants whose roommate did not participate in the study. Given that we are interested in how participants' concerns about appearing prejudiced influenced their own *and* their roommate's experiences, we excluded participants whose roommate did not participate in the study from all analyses. All participants who agreed to participate in the study attended an orientation session where they were told that they would complete a questionnaire during the session and a daily diary questionnaire during the next three weeks. The pre-diary questionnaire included demographic questions and several individual difference measures. After completing the pre-diary questionnaire, we gave participants instructions about how to complete the daily questionnaires. Specifically, we told participants that an e-mail with the URL for the diary webpage would be sent to them at the end of the day as a reminder to complete the diary questionnaire. We urged participants to complete a diary entry every night. An automatic e-mail was delivered to all participants who had not completed the diary questionnaire by 8 a.m. the following morning. Participants completed the diary questionnaire Sunday-Thursday for three weeks for a total of 15 days.[2] At the end of the diary period, participants attended a post-diary session where they completed a final questionnaire, were informed of the purpose of the study, and received their payment.

Background measures

Race of roommate Participants indicated the race and sex of their roommate. All participants had a roommate of the same sex. In all of our analyses, we examined differences between Whites and members of ethnic minorities (i.e., Blacks and Latinos). We refer to the dichotomous variable that distinguishes individuals as a racial majority (i.e., White) member or racial minority (i.e., Black or Latino) member as *minority status*. Preliminary analyses were conducted comparing Blacks to Latinos to determine if the pattern of effects for these two groups differed. For all analyses reported herein, Blacks and Latinos demonstrated consistent effects. We did not include individuals who identified themselves as biracial or Asian because their experiences as ethnic minorities have been shown to be considerably different from those of Blacks and Latinos on college campuses (Shelton & Yip, 2007).

Concerns about appearing prejudiced We used the *concern about acting prejudiced* subscale of Dunton and Fazio's (1997) Motivation to Control Prejudice scale. Participants indicated the extent to which they agreed with items such as "It is never acceptable to express one's prejudices" and "If I have a prejudiced thought or feeling, I keep it to myself," using a scale from 1 (strongly disagree) to 7 (strongly agree). The scale was acceptably reliable for Whites (a = .86) and ethnic minorities (a = .82).

Daily level measures

Anxiety Participants completed eight items adapted from the Positive and Negative Affect Schedule and the Profile of Mood States (e.g., anxious, uncomfortable, uncertain) to assess how anxious they felt during interactions with their roommate that day using a scale from 1 (strongly disagree) to 7 (strongly agree). The items were combined to form an anxiety composite ($\alpha = .84$, at the study midpoint), where higher values indicate more anxiety.

Anxiety-related behaviors Participants made daily ratings of their roommate's anxiety-related behaviors. Schlenker and Leary (1982) noted that high levels of anxiety cause people to fidget a lot; impair their ability to communicate effectively, including speaking less often; and lead people to distance themselves from others, including avoiding eye contact and disclosing less information about themselves to others. Based on this work, we asked participants to rate the extent to which they agreed that their roommate fidgeted, avoided eye contact, smiled, and talked a lot. In addition, participants rated the extent to which their roommate "concealed his/her true opinions" and "had an easy time contributing to our conversations." They answered these questions using a scale from 1 (strongly disagree) to 7 (strongly agree). Smiled, talked a lot, and contributed to conversations were reversed coded and combined with the other three items to form an *anxious behavior* composite ($\alpha = .86$, at the study midpoint).

Liking Participants indicated the extent to which they agreed that they liked their roommate that day using a scale from 1 (strongly disagree) to 7 (strongly agree).

Data analyses strategy

Our dataset includes dyadic data from dyad members measured over time. Our hypotheses center on how changes across time are moderated by the respondent's and the roommate's concerns about appearing prejudiced, as well as the respondent's minority status and their roommate's minority status. Given the complexity of our data and hypotheses, we provide in the following lines, a general description of the analyses we conducted.

Actor—partner interdependence model

We used the actor-partner interdependence model (APIM) (Kashy & Kenny, 2000; Kenny & Acitelli, 2001) as an analytic framework. In the APIM, predictors of a respondent's outcome are examined at two levels: (1) the path from the respondent's own predictor to the respondent's outcome is termed the *actor effect;* (2) the path from the respondent's roommate's predictor to the respondent's outcome is termed the *partner* effect. There are two facets of our model that reflect an APIM approach. First, we examine how a respondent's own concerns about appearing prejudiced (the actor effect) as well as his or her roommate's concerns about appearing prejudiced (the partner effect) predicted self-feelings of anxiety, perceived roommate anxious behaviors, and liking of roommate. Second, we used a method for the analysis of minority status effects that is based on the APIM. Termed the factorial approach, West, Popp, and Kenny (2008) demonstrate a strategy whereby minority status is treated as factor in a two (status of the respondent) by two (status of the roommate) full factorial design. To examine differences between the four types of individuals in our study (i.e., White respondents with White roommates, White respondents with roommates belonging to an ethnic minority, minority respondents with White roommates, and minority respondents with minority roommates), three parameters are simultaneously estimated: the main effect of status of the respondent (the actor effect), the main effect of status of the respondent's roommate (the partner effect), and the interaction between status of the respondent and status of the roommate. The status of the respondent by status of the roommate interaction compares same-status to mixed-status dyads, and can be thought of as dyad-status. Note that if *only* an interaction between status of the respondent and status of the roommate is found (i.e, a dyad-status effect), then no difference exists between Whites and minorities within mixed-status dyads, and no difference exists between Whites and minorities within same-status dyads; only the type of dyad has an effect on the outcome (for a full explanation of this effect see West et al., 2008).

Growth curve modeling of dyadic data We estimated multilevel statistical models using a method especially designed for the analysis of overtime dyadic data (Kashy, Donnellan, Burt, & McGue, 2008; Kenny, Kashy, & Cook, 2006). Our models were complicated by the issue of *distinguishability* of dyad members; specifically, White-minority dyads had members who were distinguishable from one another based on status (i.e, one partner was White, the other partner was an ethnic minority member), and minority-minority and White-White dyads had members who were indistinguishable from one another. As such, all dyads must be treated as indistinguishable (Kenny et al., 2006). Given that members were treated as indistinguishable, we used a statistical strategy illustrated by Kashy et al. (2008) for the analysis of growth curve models with indistinguishable dyads, using the SAS mixed procedure (version 9.1). It is important to note that the procedure can yield fractional degrees of freedom. In all models, predictor variables were grand mean centered, and time was centered at the midpoint of the study. In each model, we examined the overall effects of the three status variables (i.e., respondent status, roommate status, and their interaction), the overall effects of respondent and roommate concerns about appearing prejudiced, and all possible interactions between these variables on each outcome. Given that we used a growth curve modeling approach, we also examined how all of the status and concerns effects (and their interactions) changed across time. That is, each of the above interactions also interacted with time. Analyses were complicated by the fact that we found non-linear, cubic trends for perceptions of roommate's anxious behaviors and liking. When non-linear cubic effects are found, it is necessary to also include the effects of linear and quadratic time. Although these effects were included in all of our models, we focus on reporting the non-linear effects. There were non-linear trends in how concerns about appearing prejudiced or racial status influenced perceptions. All of our models were fully saturated at the level of the fixed effects. That is, we included all possible main effects, two-, three-, and four-way interactions. Given the large number of parameters estimated in each model, we do not report every non-significant interaction, but only those that are of theoretical interest. Often in dyadic research, the random effects are of just as much theoretical interest as the fixed effects. For example, the degree to which dyad members co-vary in their day-to-day perceptions, co-vary in their perceptions at the starting point of the study, and co-vary in their changes across time, are all interesting theoretical questions. In the current study, however, we do not report the random effects (our focus is on the fixed effects), but it is important to note that they were estimated. In our models, we estimated several random effects (20 in total), including variances in the within-person linear, quadratic, and cubic slopes, variance in the intercepts, within-person covariance between the intercept and each of the three slopes. We also included the covariance between dyad members' intercepts, slopes, and intercept—slope covariance. It is important to note that because dyad members were indistinguishable, parameter constraints were set on the variance—covariance matrix to account for the arbitrary distinction between person 1 and person 2 (see Kashy et al., 2008 for a complete description of the analysis strategy).

Results

Table 1 contains the means for concerns about appearing prejudiced, self-reported anxiety, perceived roommate anxious behaviors, and liking (the latter three pooled across time points) for mixed-race dyads and same-race dyads. Correlations between outcome variables are reported at the study midpoint

Table 1. Descriptive statistics of all outcome measures. Means are averaged across time points, and correlations are reported at Time Point 8 (the study mid-point)

	Mean (SD)	Self-reported anxiety	Anxious behaviors	Liking
Self-reported anxiety				
Same-race	1.26 (.55)	—	.333**	-.327**
Mixed-race	1.32 (.54)	—	.173	-.074
Anxious behaviors				
Same-race	2.27 (1.14)	—	—	-.683**
Mixed-race	2.90 (1.05)	—	—	471**
Liking				
Same-race	5.96 (1.31)	—	—	—
Mixed-race	5.41 (1.41)	—	—	—

Note: **$p < .01$.

(i.e., time 8). Patterns of correlations between outcomes at each of the time points are consistent with those reported at the midpoint.

Given theoretical work suggesting that concerns about appearing prejudiced may be more important for Whites than for ethnic minorities, we compared the mean differences on this measure for both groups. Results indicated that although Whites reported slightly higher levels of concerns about appearing prejudiced *(M = 5.29, SD = 1.03)* than did ethnic minorities (M = 5.06, SD = 1.02), the difference between these two groups was not statistically reliable, t(156) = 1.36, *p* = .18.

Are concerns about appearing prejudiced related to anxiety in daily interracial interactions?

We examined whether respondents' and their roommates' concerns about appearing prejudiced influenced self-reported anxiety during daily interactions.

Self-reported anxiety The main effects of time, t(78.8) = -1.27, *p* = .21, and concerns about appearing prejudiced, t(145) = .52, *p* = .60, were not statistically significant. Likewise, the respondent status by roommate status interaction, t(76.8) = -1.00, *p* = .31, was not significant. However, a marginally significant respondent status by roommate status by respondent concerns about appearing prejudiced interaction was found, t(133) = -1.83, *p* = .07 (see Figure 1). As predicted, simple effects tests revealed that in the same-status dyads, concerns about appearing prejudiced were not related to anxiety, t(141) = -.37, *p* = .71. However, in the mixed-status dyads, Whites and members of ethnic minorities who were more concerned about appearing prejudiced felt more anxious than those who were less concerned,

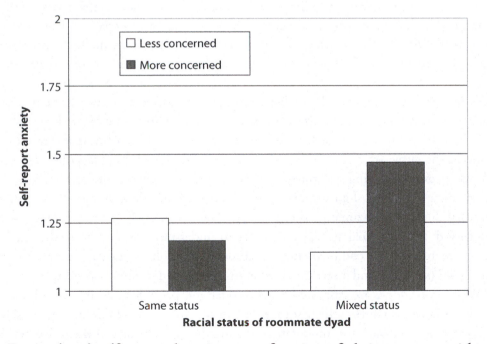

Figure 1. Respondents' self-reported anxiety as a function of their concerns with appearing prejudiced.

t(123) = 2.23, *p* = .03. Note that this effect did not interact with time, indicating that minorities and Whites who were more concerned about appearing prejudiced felt consistently more anxious overall than did Whites and minorities who were less concerned about appearing prejudiced. In addition, no main effects were found for respondent or roommate minority status, indicating that the dyad-status effect was consistent for minorities and Whites in mixed and same-status dyads.

Are concerns with appearing prejudiced related to partner's perceptions?

We examined the extent to which respondent's perceptions of their roommate are a function of how much their roommate is concerned about appearing prejudiced.

Anxious behaviors As described above, given that a large number of parameters are estimated in each model, we do not report all non-significant effects, but only those are that are theoretically relevant. The overall effect of time was not significant, t(72.2) = 1.48, *p* = .14, nor was the overall effect of roommate concerns about appearing prejudiced, t(117) = -.47, *p* = .64. A statistically significant respondent status by roommate status interaction was found, t(69.5) = -2.13, *p* = .001, indicating that Whites and ethnic minorities in mixed-status dyads perceived their roommates as engaging in more anxious behaviors than did Whites and ethnic minorities in same-status dyads. The two-way respondent status by roommate status interaction was qualified by a respondent status by roommate status by roommate concerns about appearing prejudiced by cubic time interaction, t(147) = -2.58, *p* = .01. Simple effects tests reveal that the effect of roommate concerns about appearing prejudiced on the cubic growth trajectory was significant for respondents in mixed-status dyads, t(138) = 2.63, *p* = .01, yet the effect was not significant for respondents in same-status dyads, t(154) = -1.05, *p* = .26 (see Figure 2a). Figure 2b demonstrates the pattern of results for individuals in mixed-status dyads whose roommates are one standard deviation above and below the mean on concerns about appearing prejudiced.

As shown in Figure 2b, the majority of the change in the trajectory appears to be in approximately the last six days of the study; in contrast, there is little change across time in the first nine days of the trajectory. This non-linear pattern of little to no change followed by a linear increase or decrease is characteristic of the cubic trajectory. When data are best fitted with a cubic slope, it is very difficult to identify when exactly during the trajectory meaningful differences emerge between the groups. In the present data, the cubic slope appears to be picking up on two different linear trajectories: one linear trajectory during approximately the first nine days (or lack of a linear change), and a second linear trajectory during the final six days. In order to understand the nature of the cubic effect, we used piecewise regression as a complementary method. We simultaneously estimated one linear slope during days 1—9 (slope 1), and a second variable that estimated the linear trajectory of days 10—15 (slope 2).[3] When both slopes are estimated in one model, it is possible to examine the linear slope (and what variables moderate it) during the first nine days of the trajectory, while simultaneously examining the linear slope (and what variables moderate it) during the final six days of the trajectory. Essentially, piecewise regression examines the extent to which the cubic trajectory for mixed-status dyads is actually characterized by two linear slopes.[4]

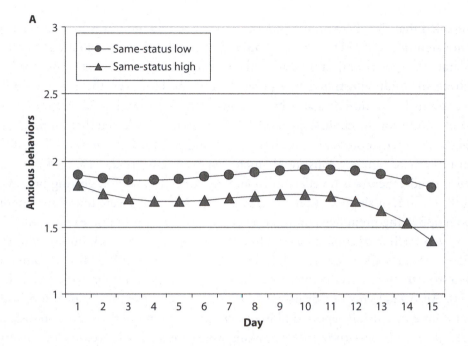

Figure 2a. Respondents' perceptions of their roommates' anxious behaviors as a function of their roommate's concerns with appearing prejudiced for same-status dyads.

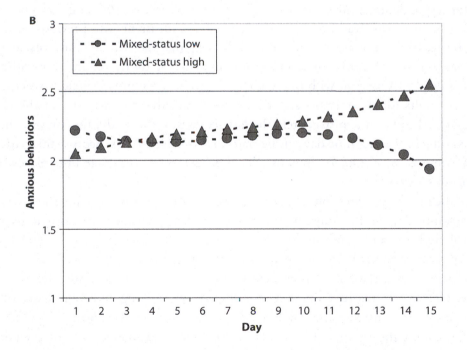

Figure 2b. Respondents' perceptions of their roommates' anxious behaviors as a function of their roommate's concerns about appearing prejudiced for mixed-status dyads.

Results revealed that the effect of respondent status by roommate status by roommate concerns by slope 1 was not significant, $t(271) = -.55$, $p = .58$, indicating that concerns about appearing prejudiced did not moderate the growth trajectory during the first nine days of the study. This result is consistent with the pattern of results illustrated in Figures 2a and 2b. However, there was a significant effect of respondent status by roommate status by roommate concerns by slope 2, $t(267) = -2.78$, $p < .01$. Consistent with results for the cubic slope model, follow-up tests indicated that for mixed-status dyads, the more concerned their roommate was about appearing prejudiced, the more respondent's perceptions of their roommate's anxiety consistently increased from day 9 to day 15, $t(245) = 3.21$, $p = .002$. For same-status dyads, there was no effect of roommate concerns about appearing prejudiced on slope 1, $t(298) = .78$, $p = .44$, or slope 2, $t(286) = -.79$, $p = .43$. No effects were found for respondents' own concerns about appearing prejudiced on their perceptions of their roommate's anxious behaviors.

Liking. No main effect of cubic time was found, $t(77.8) = .64$, $p = .53$, but a main effect of linear time, $t(75.5) = -3.57$, $p = .001$, was found, indicating that people's liking of their roommate declined over time. No overall effect of concerns about the roommate appearing prejudiced was found, $t(130) = .39$, $p = .70$. An overall effect of dyad-status, $t(77.9) = 2.78$, $p = .007$ was found, indicating that respondents in same-race dyads reported liking their roommate more than did respondents in mixed-race dyads. Results for the over-time effects of liking were consistent with results for anxious roommate behaviors. Specifically, a respondent status by roommate status by roommate concern's about appearing prejudiced by cubic time interaction was found, $t(138) = 2.93$, $p = .004$. Simple effects tests revealed that the effect of roommate concerns about appearing prejudiced on the cubic growth trajectory was significant for respondents in mixed-status dyads, $t(133) = -2.07$, $p = .04$, and was also significant for respondents in same-status dyads, $t(138) = 2.17$, $p = .04$. Consistent with previous results, no effects were found for respondent or roommate status, indicating that the effect of concerns about appearing prejudiced was consistent for minorities and Whites in mixed-status dyads, and minorities and Whites in same-status dyads. Consistent with the results for perceived roommate anxiety, when we examined the pattern of results for the mixed-status dyads, we found that the majority of the change in the trajectory appeared to be in approximately the last six days of the study; in contrast, there was little change across time in the first nine days of the trajectory (see Figure 3a). Because this pattern of results appeared the same as the results for anxious-related behaviors, we conducted the piecewise regression as in our previous analyses.

Results of the piecewise regression revealed that the cubic effect was not primarily driven by changes during the first nine days of the study; the effect of respondent status by roommate status by roommate concerns on slope 1 was not significant, $t(286) = 1.36$, $p = .18$. However, there was an effect of respondent status by roommate status by roommate concerns on slope 2, $t(240) = 2.55$, $p = .01$. Consistent with results for the cubic slope model (and consistent with results for anxious roommate behaviors), follow-up tests revealed a negative linear relationship between liking and roommate concerns about appearing prejudiced for mixed-status dyads, $t(237) = -2.00$, $p = .04$. As shown in Figure 3a, for mixed-status dyads, the more the respondent's roommate was concerned about appearing prejudiced, the less the respondent reported liking his or her roommate from day 9 to day 15. For same-status dyads, there

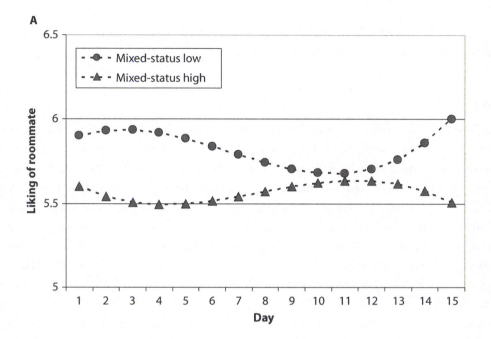

Figure 3a. Respondents' liking of their roommate as a function of their roommate's concerns with appearing prejudiced for mixed-status dyads.

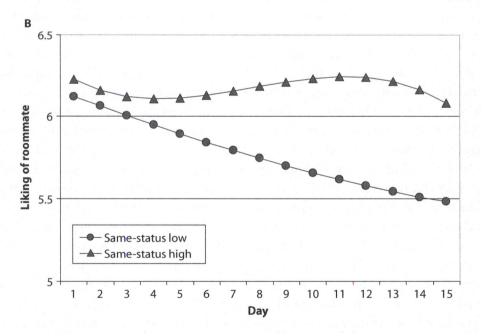

Figure 3b. Respondents' liking of their roommate as a function of their roommate's concerns with appearing prejudiced for same-status dyads.

was no consistent pattern of effects; that is, there was no effect of roommate concerns about appearing prejudiced on slope 1, t(275) = .58, p = .56, or slope 2, t(242) = 1.61, p = .11 (see Figure 3b).

Discussion

Intergroup interactions can be difficult. People try to manage their biases, expectations, and concerns during these interactions, sometimes with success whereas other times without it. Our results reveal that concerns about appearing prejudiced have serious implications for the dynamics of interracial interactions over time. The long-term picture is quite bleak from the perspective of the person who is concerned about appearing prejudiced. The more concerned they are, the more anxiety they experience during the interactions. Fortunately, they do not appear anxious to their out-group partner during the initial interactions. However, eventually their partner is able to pick up on their anxiety; perceived partner anxiety increased over time after the first nine days. Coupled with this increase in perceived anxiety is a decrease in liking for out-group members who are concerned about appearing prejudiced. We suggest that our effects are a result of a break down in self-regulatory processes. That is, people who are concerned about appearing prejudiced are on guard for what they say and how they behave during the interaction. They are nervous about how they appear to their partner. Fortunately, they are able to "hide" their anxiety during initial interactions; in laboratory studies they are perceived as likeable during a brief interaction (Shelton, 2003). However, their attempt to control their feelings and behaviors begins to take a toll, such that they are no longer able to do so successfully; the current findings show that their partner perceives them as being more anxious and likes them less after multiple interactions across time. We do not suspect that the roommates in our study actually began to behave in a prejudiced manner across time, though that is certainly possible. Instead, we suspect that it was difficult to control their fears about how they were coming across in their interactions, and this started to leak out over time. Alternatively, our effects may not be related to self-regulatory processes per se. Instead, is possible that as the roommates became used to living together, the social pressure to appear unprejudiced became less of an issue. However, a one-item daily measure of how concerned people were about appearing prejudiced that day, revealed that respondents who were concerned about appearing prejudiced (i.e., dispositional level of concern) remained concerned about appearing prejudiced on a daily basis across time: they did not show a decline in their concerns. An additional alternative explanation is that individuals become better able to perceive their roommates' anxiety over time, thus accounting for increased perceptions in anxious behaviors. Although there is evidence to indicate that perceivers are more able to accurately detect emotions felt by in-group members than by out-group members (Elfenbein & Ambady, 2002; Gray, Mendes, & Denny-Brown, 2008), there is also evidence indicating that perceptions of anxiety are more accurate when the partner is an out-group member than an in-group member (Pearson et al., 2008), and that ethnic minorities are able to accurately assess Whites' prejudice level based on non-verbal cues (Richeson & Shelton, 2005). To date, however, the majority of research examining accuracy for perceptions of in-group and out-group members' emotions has only examined brief interactions in the laboratory. Future research is needed to examine this issue in diary methodologies as used in this research. The present findings contribute to the existing literature in several ways. First, our findings illustrate the importance of taking a dyadic approach to examining interracial interactions. They highlight that people's experiences and perceptions in interactions are not solely about the concerns they bring to the interaction but are also about the concerns their partner brings to the interaction. For instance, we found that the level of roommates' concerns about appearing prejudiced, but not participants' own concerns about appearing prejudiced, influences how much participants like their roommate. These results are only obtainable taking a dyadic approach where the concerns of both people in the interaction are examined. From an actor's perspective, we found that Whites' and members of ethnic minorities' own concerns about appearing prejudiced were related to their own anxiety level during daily interracial interactions. Related work has shown that Whites' concerns about appearing prejudiced lead them to automatically perceive Black people as threatening (Richeson & Trawalter, 2008). Perhaps both Whites and minorities who are concerned about appearing prejudiced perceive interracial interactions as threatening and thus, they experience anxiety. From a partner's perspective, we found that respondents who were paired with an out-group roommate who had high concerns about appearing prejudiced perceived that roommate as being more anxious and liked them less, compared to respondents paired with roommates who were less concerned, after approximately nine days of interacting. Together, these findings highlight the importance of examining dyadic interactions from the perspective of both individuals in the interaction, something that seems rather natural but is often not addressed in intergroup contact research.

Second, our effects are consistent with and extend laboratory research on Whites' concerns about appearing prejudiced. Previous research revealed that the more Whites were concerned about appearing prejudiced, the less they expected to enjoy an interracial interaction (Vorauer et al., 1998) and the more anxiety they reported when experiencing an interracial interaction (Plant & Butz, 2006; Shelton, 2003). This previous work was conducted in the laboratory with brief (15 minutes) or anticipated interactions. In contrast, we used a natural context where the stakes are higher for getting along, and thus the interactions are likely to be more important. Our work revealed a similar effect as the laboratory studies: people who were concerned about appearing prejudiced reported being more anxious than those who were less concerned. This is quite disturbing when considered against the backdrop that these individuals may avoid future intergroup contact because of their anxiety. Their avoidance is likely to prevent intergroup friendships from developing as well as prevent fears about interacting with out-group members to be reduced. It is people who are most concerned about appearing prejudiced who are likely to be more open to diversity and to improve intergroup relations. If they are anxious, however, they may be less willing to work with out-group members to facilitate harmonious intergroup relationships. With respect to extending the literature, our data suggest that Whites and ethnic minorities who are concerned about appearing prejudiced are able to regulate their anxiety so that it does not leak out during initial interactions with their partner, but with repeated contact with the same person this regulation breaks down. Our partner effect suggests that with repeated contact over time, Whites' and ethnic minorities' anxiety begins to leak and can be picked up by their out-group partner. It would be difficult for data from one-shot, short interactions in the laboratory to have revealed this pattern.

At first, it may appear that our findings contradict research using the same population—college roommates—that has shown that Whites' concerns about appearing prejudiced do not influence outcomes during interracial interactions. Specifically, Towles-Schwen and Fazio (2006) studied Whites who had been randomly assigned to have a Black roommate during their freshman year of college. They examined the extent to which Whites' implicit racial attitudes and concerns about acting prejudiced predicted the longevity of their relationship with their roommate and how satisfied Whites were with it. Results revealed that Whites' implicit racial attitudes predicted the longevity of the relationship, such that the more negative their attitudes, the more likely the relationship would dissolve by the end of the year. More relevant to the present research, Whites' concerns about acting prejudiced, however, did not have a direct impact on the relationship's longevity, nor did it moderate the implicit attitude and relationship's longevity effect. That is, Whites who were concerned about appearing prejudiced were not more likely to stay together or be satisfied with their roommate than Whites who were less concerned about appearing prejudiced. Although Towles-Schwen and Fazio (2006) examined concerns about appearing prejudiced in a context in which Whites had the opportunity to interact with Blacks on a repeated basis, unfortunately, they did not assess Whites' experiences and behaviors on a daily basis; instead they focused on what might be called the ultimate behavior in a relationship: dissolution. Future research should explore the outcomes we examined in the present research as well as dissolution as Towles-Schwen and Fazio (2006) explored in their work, making sure that both Whites and ethnic minorities are examined.

A third contribution of our research to the literature is made by our inclusion of ethnic minorities. The majority of research on intergroup contact has ignored studying contact from the perspective of ethnic minorities (cf. Shelton, 2000). For example, research on prejudice reduction strategies typically targets Whites; in Pettigrew and Tropp's (2006) meta-analysis of intergroup contact, over 70% of the research solely examined Whites. We included both Whites and ethnic minorities as respondents in our study and, as a result, we were able to assess both of the groups' concerns about appearing prejudiced. Our results revealed that ethnic minorities' concerns about appearing prejudiced are not completely irrelevant for dyadic interactions. In fact, ethnic minorities' concerns about appearing prejudiced have parallel effects for interracial interactions as do Whites' concerns. The more ethnic minorities were concerned about appearing prejudiced, the more anxiety they experienced during daily interactions with a White roommate, the more anxious they came across, and the less liked they were by their White roommates, during the final six days of the study. Therefore, in future research it would be useful for researchers to study ethnic minorities' concerns about appearing prejudiced (not just their concerns about being the target of prejudice) because they are quite important for the dynamics of interracial interactions. Finally, by studying interracial dyads across three weeks we were able to discover specific time points that are likely to be pivotal in terms of when people's experiences are apt to change during interracial interactions. We did not predict the specific day in which people's experience would change; thus, more work is needed to understand why these relationships start to break down after approximately the first week. Understanding why the first week is crucial is important because it may help university policy makers as they make decisions about interventions that could improve housing arrangements, or it may be useful for any organization in which people have contact with the same out-group members on a daily basis.

Limitations and future research

There are several limitations in the present research that should be addressed in the future. First, we did not distinguish between people's internal and external concerns about appearing prejudiced. Plant and colleagues (Plant, 2004; Plant & Devine, 1998) have suggested that the reason underlying people's desire to respond without prejudice has different implications for their behavior toward out-group members. Future work is needed to explore the extent to which internal and external pressures not to be prejudiced influence daily interracial interactions in which people have sustained contact over time with an out-group member. Based on Plant's theorizing, we predict that internal motivations would be associated with positive outcomes, whereas external motivations would be associated with negative outcomes.

A second limitation of our study is that we relied on respondents' perceptions of their roommates' anxiety-related behaviors instead of on a direct assessment of how anxious their roommate appeared. This is problematic because we may have inadvertently trained participants to focus on their own and their roommate's behaviors across time. Specifically, we could have made participants pay more attention to their own anxiety, making them more anxious over time. Although this is a problem, it might be offset by some of the advantages of using respondents' perceptions of their roommates' behaviors. Recent work suggests that perceived partner anxiety might be more influential in interracial interactions than actual partner anxiety. Pearson et al. (2008) had strangers in intergroup and intra-group dyads interact over a closed-circuit monitor either in real time or with a subtle temporal disruption (a one-second delay) in audiovisual feedback. People in intergroup dyads reported more anxiety and less interest in contact; they also perceived their partner as being more anxious, under temporal delay compared to the real-time condition. Furthermore, perceived partner anxiety but not actual partner anxiety influenced respondent's interest in having another conversation with their partner. Also, focusing on non-verbal behaviors as opposed to self-report ratings of anxiety (e.g., "How anxious does your roommate appear?") is a strength, because nonverbal behaviors have been shown to be instrumental in the communication process during interpersonal interactions (Patterson, 1982), especially intergroup interactions (Dovidio, Hebl, Richeson, & Shelton, 2006; Malloy & Ristikari, 2006; Miller & Malloy, 2003). Thus, people's perceptions of their partner's behaviors shed light on the interpersonal processes that occur during interracial interactions.

A third limitation is that our results do not address the direction of causation between liking and perceptions of roommate's anxious behaviors. It is possible that the more respondents disliked their roommates, the more anxiety-related behaviors they perceived. Recall, however, that Whites and minorities in mixed-status dyads reported feeling more anxious the more concerned they were about appearing prejudiced. It is likely that the roommates of concerned individuals picked up on behaviors that reflected concerned individuals' anxiety, which played a role in them liking their roommate less. This argument is consistent with work showing that anxiety has detrimental effects on intergroup interactions, including decreased desire to engage in intergroup contact in the future (Pearson et al., 2008). Nevertheless, our findings are correlational in nature, and need to be interpreted as such.

Moving beyond racial attitudes

The degree to which intergroup contact effectively leads to prejudice reduction has been a topic of interest among social scientists for over 50 years (see Pettigrew & Tropp, 2006). Interest continues to grow as scholars focus on specific factors that moderate the effectiveness of intergroup contact; for example, examining how power and status moderate the successfulness of intergroup contact (Saguy, Dovidio, & Pratto, 2008). We believe the interplay between people's concerns about appearing prejudiced and their actual experiences during interracial interactions may be important to examine with respect to prejudice reduction. If people feel more anxious and, over time, are liked less in interracial interactions because of concerns about appearing prejudiced, they may abandon these concerns and develop negative attitudes about out-groups. This would be quite ironic, of course, because concerns about appearing prejudiced, which on the surface seems like a healthy concern, may create hostility and prejudiced beliefs that undermine intergroup relations in a manner similar to actually being prejudiced against out-groups.

Concluding thoughts

Social norms in contemporary American society set the stage for people to be worried about making a social faux pas that could signal they are (sometimes erroneously) prejudiced. Our research highlights that people's concerns about committing a social blunder have serious implications for their experiences and how they are perceived by their interaction partner. Perhaps making people aware that being concerned about appearing prejudiced is a step in the right direction to reducing prejudice, and that it is initially perceived positively by outgroup members (Shelton, 2003) will help reduce the anxiety people experience, thereby opening doors to more harmonious intergroup relations.

Notes

1. This dataset was used by West, Shelton, and Trail (2009); the research questions and results presented in this manuscript, however, do not overlap with those in the paper by these authors.
2. A session with a small sample of students revealed that the weekend was not ideal to collect data because students often go home, resulting in no contact with their roommates, or their being engaged in too many parties to complete the questionnaire in a way that would produce usable data.
3. Slope 1 is coded as follows: days 1—9 are coded as 1, 2, 3, 4 ... 9 and days 10—15 are all coded as zero. Slope 2 is coded as follows: days 1—9 are all coded as zero, and days 10—15 are coded as 1, 2, 3 ... 6. Although two slopes were estimated, the intercept was always time 1. Re-centering the intercept to be the midpoint does not change the results.
4. We chose day 9 because that is where the slope appears to change. Choosing day 10 revealed the same results.

Acknowledgments

The Russell Sage Foundation (Grant #87-02-04) and the National Institute of Mental Health (1 R03MH06912101) provided funding for this research. We are indebted to David Kenny for his invaluable statistical help on this manuscript, and to Lisa Pugh and Bonnie Burlingham for their assistance with data collection.

References

Crandall, C. S., & Eshleman, A. (2003). A justification/suppression model of the expression and experience of prejudice. *PsychologicalBulletin*, 129, 414–446.

Dovidio, J. F., & Gaertner, S. L. (2004). Aversive racism. In M. Zanna (Ed.), *Advances in experimental social psychology* (Vol. 36, pp. 1–52). San Diego, CA: Elsevier Academic Press.

Dovidio, J. F., Hebl, M., Richeson, J. A, & Shelton, J. N.(2006). Nonverbal communication, race, and intergroup interaction. In V. Manusov & M. L. Patterson (Eds.), *The Sage handbook of nonverbal communication.* Thousand Oaks, CA: Sage.

Dovidio, J. F., Kawakami, K., Johnson, C., Johnson, B., & Howard, A. (1997). On the nature of prejudice: Automatic and controlled processes. *Journal of Experimental Social Psychology*, 33, 510–540.

Dunton, B. C., & Fazio, R. H. (1997). An individual difference measure of motivation to control prejudiced reactions. *Personality and Social Psychology Bulletin*, 23, 316–326.

Elfenbein, H. A., & Ambady, N. (2002). On the universality and cultural specificity of emotion recognition: A meta-analysis. *Psychological Bulletin*, 128, 203–235.

Fazio, R. H., Jackson, J. R., Dunton, B. C., & Williams, C. J. (1995). Variability in automatic activation as an unobtrusive measure of racial attitudes: A bona fide pipeline? *Journal of Personality and Social Psychology*, 69, 1013–1027.

Gray, H. M., Mendes, W. B., & Denny-Brown, C. (2008). An in-group advantage in detecting intergroup anxiety. *Psychological Science*, 19, 1233–1237.

Johnson, J. D., & Leci, L. (2003). Assessing anti-White attitudes and predicting perceived racism: The JohnsonLeci scale. *Personality and Social Bulletin*, 29, 299–312.

Kashy, D. A., Donnellan, B. M., Burt, A. S., & McGue, M. (2008). Growth curve modeling for indistinguishable dyads using multilevel modeling and structural equation modeling: The case of adolescent twins' conflict with their mothers. *Developmental Psychology*, 44, 316–329.

Kashy, D. A., & Kenny, D. A. (2000). The analysis of data from dyads and groups. In H. T. Reis & C. M. Judd (Eds.), *Handbook of research methods in social and personality psychology* (pp. 451–477). New York: Cambridge University Press.

Kenny, D. A., & Acitelli, L. K. (2001). Accuracy and bias in the perception of the partner in a close relationship. *Journal of Personality and Social Psychology*, 80, 439–448.

Kenny, D. A., Kashy, D. A., & Cook, W. L. (2006). *Dyadic data analysis.* New York: Guilford.

Legault, L., Green-Demers, I., Grant, P., & Chung, J. (2007). On the self-regulation of implicit and explicit prejudice: A self-determination theory perspective. *Personality and Social Psychology Bulletin*, 33, 732–749.

Malloy, T. E., & Ristikari, T. (2006). *Cognitive, affective, and behavioral responses in interracial dyads.* Unpublished manuscript.

Miller, S., & Malloy, T. E. (2003). Interpersonal behavior, perception, and affect in status-discrepant dyads: Social interaction of gay and heterosexual men. *Psychology of Men and Masculinity,* 4, 121–135.

Monteith, M. J. (1993). Self-regulation of prejudiced responses: Implications for progress in prejudice reduction efforts. *Journal of Personality and Social Psychology,* 65, 469–485.

Monteith, M. J., & Spicer, C. V. (2000). Contents and correlates of Whites' and Blacks' racial attitudes. *Journal of Experimental Social Psychology,* 36, 125–154.

Norton, M. I., Sommers, S. R., Apfelbaum, E. P., Pura, N., & Ariely, D. (2007). Color blindness and interracial interaction: Playing the political correctness game. *Psychological Science,* 17, 949–953.

Patterson, M. L. (1982). A sequential functional-model of nonverbal exchange. *Psychological Review,* 89, 231–249.

Pearson, A. R., West, T. V, Dovidio, J. F., Powers, S., Buck, R., & Henning, R. (2008). The fragility of intergroup relations: Divergent effects of delayed audio-visual feedback in intergroup and intragroup interactions. *Psychological Science,* 19, 1272–1279.

Pettigrew, T. F., & Tropp, L. R. (2006). A metaanalytic test of intergroup contact theory. *Journal of Personality and Social Psychology,* 90, 751–783.

Plant, E. A. (2004). Responses to interracial interactions over time. *Personality and Social Psychology Bulletin,* 30, 1458–1471.

Plant, E. A., & Butz, D. A. (2006). The causes and consequences of an avoidance-focus for interracial interactions. *Personality and Social Psychology Bulletin,* 32, 83–846.

Plant, E. A., & Devine, P. (1998). Internal and external motivation to respond without prejudice. *Journal of Personality and Social Psychology,* 75, 811–832.

Richeson, J. A., & Shelton, J .N. (2005). Thin slices of racial bias. *Journal of Nonverbal Behavior,* 29, 75–86.

Richeson, J. A., & Shelton, J. N. (2007). Negotiating interracial interactions: Costs, consequences, and possibilities. *Current Directions in Psychological Science,* 16, 316–320.

Richeson, J. A., & Trawalter, S. (2008). The threat of appearing prejudiced and race-based attentional biases. *Psychological Science,* 19, 98–102.

Saguy, T., Dovidio, J. F., & Pratto, F. (2008). Beyond contact: Intergroup contact in the context of power relations. *Personality and Social Psychology Bulletin,* 34, 432–445.

Schlenker, B. R., & Leary, M. R. (1982). Social anxiety and self-presentation: A conceptualization and model. *Psychological Bulletin,* 92, 641–669.

Shelton, J. N. (2000). A reconceptualization of how we study issues of racial prejudice. *Personality and Social Psychology Review,* 4, 374–390.

Shelton, J. N. (2003). Interpersonal concerns in social encounters between majority and minority group members. *Group Processes & Intergroup Relations,* 6, 171–185.

Shelton, J. N., & Richeson, J. A. (2006). Ethnic minorities' racial attitudes and contact experiences with White people. *Cultural Diversity and Ethnic Minority Psychology,* 12, 149–164.

Shelton, J. N., & Yip, T. (2007). *Not fitting in: Predictors and consequences of intragroup and intergroup alienation.* Unpublished manuscript.

Towles-Schwen, T., & Fazio, R. H. (2006). Automatically activated racial attitudes as predictors of the success of interracial roommate relationships. *Journal of Experimental Social Psychology,* 42, 698–705.

Vorauer, J., Main, K., & O'Connell, G. (1998). How do individuals expect to be viewed by members of lower status groups?: Content and implications of meta-stereotypes. *Journal of Personality and Social Psychology*, 75, 917–937.

West, T. V, Popp, D., & Kenny, D. A. (2008). A guide for the estimation of gender and sexual orientation effects in dyadic data: An actor-partner interdependence model approach. *Personality and Social Psychology Bulletin*, 34, 321–336.

West, T. V, Shelton, J. N., & Trail, T. E. (2009). Relational anxiety in interracial interactions. *Psychological Science*, 20(3), 289–292.

Williams, B. (Anchor). (2005). *Nightly news* [Television broadcast]. New York: NBC.

Biographical notes

J. NICOLE SHELTON is an associate professor of Psychology at Princeton University. She earned her BA in psychology from the College of William and Mary in 1993 and her PhD in psychology from the University of Virginia in 1998. She was a postdoctoral fellow at the University of Michigan from 1998 to 2000. Her primary research focuses on how Whites and ethnic minorities navigate issues of prejudice in interracial interactions. She is also interested in the consequences of confronting perpetrators of prejudice.

TESSA WEST is an assistant professor of social psychology at New York University. Broadly speaking, her work focuses on understanding the dynamics of person perception during dyadic and grouplevel interactions. Her work focuses specifically on the interplay between Whites' and ethnic minorities' own and their partners' perceptions and behaviors, and how these perceptions and behaviors influence rapport building in the short term, and relationship building in the long term.

THOMAS E. TRAIL is a graduate student in social psychology at Princeton University. His research interests include the role of emotions in inter- and intra-group processes, interracial friendships, and affective reactions to norm violations.

Automatic Activation of Stereotypes

The Role of Self-Image Threat

By Steven J. Spencer, University of Waterloo; Steven Fein, Williams College; Connie T. Wolfe, University of Michigan; Christina Fong, Williams College; Meghan A. Dunn, Yale University

Does self-image threatening feedback make perceivers more likely to activate stereotypes when confronted by members of a minority group? Participants in Study 1 saw an Asian American or European American woman for several minutes, and participants in Studies 2 and 3 were exposed to drawings of an African American or European American male face for fractions of a second. These experiments found no evidence of automatic stereotype activation when perceivers were cognitively busy and when they had not received negative feedback. When perceivers had received negative feedback, however, evidence of stereotype activation emerged even when perceivers were cognitively busy. The theoretical implications of these results for stereotype activation and the relationship of motivation, affect, and cognition are discussed.

When we see a red-breasted bird, we say to ourselves "robin." When we see a crazily swaying automobile, we think, "drunken driver." ... A person with dark brown skin will activate whatever concept of Negro is dominant in our mind.

— Allport (1954, p. 20)

When we confront members of a stereotyped group, do we automatically stereotype them? As Allport (1954) might have put it, is prejudgment not only normal but unavoidable? The question of whether stereotype activation occurs spontaneously and is inevitable on mere exposure to members of stereotyped groups is critical to our understanding of stereotyping and prejudice. If particular environmental cues automatically activate stereotypes regardless of individual differences in personality, motivation, and norms, then such stereotype activation can be seen as a consummate illustration of the role of cognitive processes in stereotyping and prejudice, and it would suggest the difficulty of reducing the incidence and consequences of stereotypes. As a growing literature has demonstrated, perceivers are often unaware of the subtle but significant influences that stereotype activation can have on their subsequent perceptions, judgments, and behaviors (e.g., Bargh, 1994, 1997; Bargh, Chen, & Burrows, 1996; Devine, 1989; Dovidio & Gaertner, 1991; Greenwald & Banaji, 1995).

Steven J. Spencer, Steven Fein, Connie T. Wolfe, Christina Fong & Meghan A. Dunn, "Automatic Activation of Stereotypes: The Role of Self-Image Threat," *Personality and Social Psychology Bulletin*, vol. 24, no. 11, pp. 1139–1152. Copyright © 1998 by SAGE Publications, Inc. Reprinted with permission.

An important question addressed in recent research is whether stereotype activation occurs spontaneously and inevitably. The answer to this question remains open to debate. Some theory and research indicate that when individuals perceive members of groups for which there are well-known stereotypes or when they are exposed to group or stereotype labels, stereotypes may be activated spontaneously and often without awareness (Bargh, 1997; Bargh et al., 1996; Devine, 1989; Fiske & Neuberg, 1990; Macrae, Bodenhausen, & Milne, 1995; Macrae, Milne, & Bodenhausen, 1994; Winter & Uleman, 1984). Moreover, Devine (1989) proposed that although perceivers who are motivated to refrain from stereotyping may be able to suppress their application of stereotypes, they cannot avoid the automatic activation of the stereotypes.

Other research, however, suggests that although stereotypes can be activated unintentionally and outside of awareness, stereotype activation is not a fully automatic process in that other factors can inhibit it. More specifically, stereotype activation may depend on the availability of sufficient cognitive resources (Gilbert & Hixon, 1991), the strength and accessibility of the stereotype (Fazio, 1990, 1995; Fazio, Jackson, Dunton, & Williams, 1995; Lepore & Brown, 1997; Wittenbrink, Judd, & Park, 1997), and the absence of counter-stereotypic expectations (Blair & Banzyi, 1996). Gilbert & Hixon (1991), for example, found that although participants who had available cognitive resources did exhibit activation of the well-known Asian stereotype when exposed to a member of this stereotyped group, participants did not exhibit stereotype activation if their cognitive resources were taxed by simultaneous performance of some other cognitive task. In other words, these latter participants were too busy cognitively to activate their stereotype despite recognizing the target's group membership. Gilbert and Hixon argued that this disruption of stereotype activation demonstrates that stereotype activation is not automatic.

In the present research, we examine whether motivation can also affect the automatic activation of stereotypes. In particular, we examine whether the goal of self-image maintenance can lead to efficient activation of stereotypes. In previous research (Fein & Spencer, 1997), we have shown that self-image threat made participants more likely to evaluate a stereotyped target negatively, and this negative evaluation, in turn, raised the participants' state self-esteem. This research suggested that when people experience self-image threat, they may often stereotype others to restore their own threatened self-image. Fein and Spencer (1997) argued that because stereotypes are likely to be a salient and particularly effective means for people to restore a threatened self-image, stereotyping others may be a common way for people to seek to maintain a positive image of themselves.

But can a self-image maintenance goal lead to the automatic activation of stereotypes? We reason that it can. One model that provides a useful perspective concerning this issue is Bargh's automotive model (Bargh, 1997; Bargh & Gollwitzer, 1994). This model proposes that motives or goals that are repeatedly paired with an environmental cue can become automatically activated when that environmental cue is encountered. Bargh and his colleagues have demonstrated that these automatically activated goals can operate at the preconscious level. Goals that are primed outside of awareness can lead to plans to achieve the goal that interacts with the information available in the environment. These nonconscious goals can have the same effects that consciously activated goals have on perceivers' evaluations of a target (Chartrand & Bargh, 1996). Thus, environmental cues can automatically trigger goals that can be achieved preconsciously without need of attentional resources.

We argue that threats to one's self-image trigger the goal of restoring the threatened self-image, and one mechanism by which individuals often restore their self-images is to activate and apply negative stereotypes of particular groups when they encounter members of these groups. Based on the reasoning underlying the auto-motive model, we argue that to the extent that the motivation to restore one's threatened self-image frequently and consistently leads to the use of stereotypes on exposure to members of particular stereotyped groups, the link between self-image threat and activation of available stereotypes may become automatic.

The present research examined whether self-image maintenance goals in the context of environmental cues relevant to stereotyping (e.g., the presence of a member of a stereotyped group) can automatically activate stereotypes. If, as Fein and Spencer (1997) suggest, self-image maintenance goals lead people frequently and consistently to use stereotypes when they encounter members of particular stereotyped groups, then in the presence of these group members (or related goal-relevant cues in the environment), the representation of the goal of self-image maintenance may form an automatic link with the representation of the cued stereotypes. Thus, we argue that when people experience self-image threat, they will have the goal to restore their self-image, and if they encounter a member of a group for which there is a readily available stereotype, they will be likely to stereotype that person even if this stereotyping occurs outside of their conscious awareness.

In the current studies, we investigated whether the presence of an Asian American or African American target would cause perceivers to automatically activate their stereotypes about these groups. We predicted that in the presence of cues about a stereotyped group, participants who experienced self-image threat, which should have primed a self-image maintenance goal, would be more likely to automatically activate their stereotype about this group than perceivers who did not experience self-image threat. To test for the automaticity of the stereotype activation, we examined whether cognitive load would disrupt the activation of the stereotype in the presence of the stereotyped group member (Gilbert & Hixon, 1991). If self-image threat makes people more likely to automatically activate stereotypes in the presence of stereotype-relevant information in the environment, then the stereotype should be activated even in the face of cognitive load. In contrast, in the absence of self-image threat, cognitive load should interfere with stereotype activation.

Experiment 1

To test this prediction, Study 1 used some of the procedures and materials from Gilbert and Hixon (1991). Gilbert and Hixon exposed their primarily European American sample of participants to a videotape of a woman who appeared to be either of Asian or European descent The videotape featured the woman— ostensibly an experimental assistant—holding a series of cards to the camera. Each card contained a word fragment, such as "s_y." For each word fragment shown on the videotape, participants indicated the first words that came to mind to complete the fragment (e.g., "say"). Some of these word fragments could be completed with words that are consistent with Asian American stereotypes (e.g., "shy" for "s_y"); other fragments were irrelevant to the stereotype (e.g., "p_st") and were included as fillers. Stereotype activation was measured by examining the extent to which perceivers were more likely to complete the relevant fragments with words consistent with the Asian American stereotype if the experimental assistant on the videotape was Asian American than if she was European American.

In addition to varying the race of the female assistant, Gilbert and Hixon (1991) also manipulated whether participants were under cognitive load. While attending to the videotape, some of the participants were distracted by having to perform another cognitive task (remembering an eight-digit number), whereas others were not given this distracting task. Gilbert and his colleagues have found that this and similar tasks are quite successful in depleting participants' cognitive resources necessary for various social judgment tasks (e.g., Gilbert, Pelham, & Krull, 1988).

Gilbert and Hixon (1991) found evidence for stereotype activation only among participants who were not under cognitive load. Even though participants in the Asian American condition saw the target person for several minutes and did successfully categorize her as Asian American, their word completions suggested that they did not activate the Asian American stereotype if they were cognitively busy with an unrelated task. These results suggested that stereotype activation required the allocation of sufficient cognitive resources.

The current study used a variant of this paradigm. The participants saw the same stimulus materials—that is, word fragments and an Asian American or European American woman—as seen by the participants in Gilbert & Hixon's (1991) study.[1] However, in the present study all of the participants were under cognitive load. In addition, half of the participants received negative, self-image threatening feedback just prior to the word-completion procedure, and half received positive, nonthreatening feedback. This manipulation was identical to that used in Fein and Spencer (1997, Study 3). Fein and Spencer found that this manipulation had a significant effect on participants' state self-esteem (Heatherton & Polivy, 1991).

If factors such as self-image threat lead to stereotype activation, then the participants who received negative feedback in the present study should have exhibited more stereotype activation than the participants who received positive feedback. That is, in the absence of negative feedback, the cognitive demands of the distracter task should have prevented participants from activating the Asian American stereotype when exposed to the Asian American woman. If the negative feedback leads to automatic stereotype activation, however, then participants who had just received such feedback should have been more likely to activate the stereotype despite the cognitive load.

Method

Participants And Design

Participating in the study for partial fulfillment of course credit were 62 undergraduate students (36 men and 26 women; 51 identifying themselves as European American, 3 as Asian American, 4 as

African American, and 4 as Latino) from the University of Michigan. Because this study involved stereotypes about Asian Americans, and we were unable to recruit enough Asian Americans to include them as a factor in the design, we did not include the Asian American students in the analyses for this study. Nonetheless, the results are similar if these students are included. The experiment used a 2 (feedback condition: positive or negative) x 2 (race of assistant: European American or Asian American) factorial design. Participants were assigned randomly to experimental conditions.

Procedure

Participants reported to the lab in groups of 2 to 4 to participate in two (ostensibly) different studies—one involving an intelligence test and one involving a word completion task. Each participant completed the first experiment together in a room with the other participants, after which he or she entered an individual cubicle and completed the second experiment alone.

Feedback manipulation. In the first experiment, the experimenter explained to the participants that the study concerned a new intelligence test that the researchers were using across a large sample of university students. The test and procedure were identical to those used in Fein and Spencer (1997, Study 3). The test consisted of matching vocabulary words to various pictures.

Half of the participants received positive false feedback about their test performance (i.e., a score of 26 out of 30 that ostensibly put them in the 89th percentile for the university), whereas the other half received negative false feedback (i.e., a score of 15 out of 30 that ostensibly put them in the 47th percentile—which participants in Fein & Spencer, 1997, and Stein, 1994, found to be quite negative). Fein and Spencer (1997) found that participants believed the feedback and that it significantly affected their state self-esteem.

After participants received their feedback, the experimenter thanked them for their participation and directed them to the word completion experiment, which was located in a separate lab room on the same floor.

Word completion task. When participants arrived at the word completion experiment, they were greeted by a different experimenter and escorted to individual cubicles. The European American male experimenter explained that the study concerned cognitive psychological processes. The experimenter told the participants, "We are interested in left and right brain functions and whether left and right brain tasks interfere with one another. Therefore, in this study you will be doing both verbal and nonverbal tasks simultaneously." The experimenter explained that the verbal task consisted of a word completion task, and he explained the procedure to the participants. The experimenter told the participants that the nonverbal task required them to try to remember an eight-digit number throughout the experiment. He then read the eight-digit number to each participant and rehearsed the number with the participants until they could remember it.

When each participant understood the instructions, the experimenter started the videotape and left the participant's cubicle. The two videotapes used in this study were copies of those used by Gilbert and Hixon (1991). Each videotape featured a series of 19 word fragments presented on posterboard cards that were held by a female assistant. The two videotapes were identical except that in one videotape the assistant who held the cards was Asian American and in the other she was European American. Participants were given 15 seconds to generate completions for each word fragment.

The participants stated their completions into an audiotape recorder. Gilbert and Hixon (1991) designated five completions as stereotypic in their experiment: s_y (shy), s_ort (short), ri_e (rice), poli_e (polite), and n_p (nip). They designated the rest of the word fragments as fillers.

It should be noted that the manipulation of feedback concerning the intelligence test should not have been related semantically to the stereotype examined in this study. Learning that they scored above or below average on an intelligence test should not have primed participants through any semantic links to increase significantly the accessibility of words such as *shy, short, rice, polite*, and *nip*.

After the word completion task, participants were asked to recall the eight-digit number and to indicate the race of the experimental assistant shown on the videotape. Participants were then probed for suspicion about the feedback on the intelligence test, debriefed thoroughly, and dismissed. The debriefing used in the studies reported in this article, similar to those in Fein and Spencer (1997), used a process debriefing procedure that emphasized the random nature of assignment to feedback conditions, the details that the experimenters created to make the testing procedure and feedback seem as believable and plausible as possible, and the possibility of belief perseverance (e.g., Ross, Lepper, & Hubbard, 1975) and why such beliefs are erroneous.

Results and Discussion

Manipulation Checks

All but 4 participants reported that they believed the feedback from the intelligence test. Each of these 4 participants had received positive feedback—2 in the Asian American assistant condition and 2 in the European American assistant condition. To be conservative, we included the data from these 4 participants in the analyses reported below. However, the analyses yield similar results if their data are excluded. Participants' ability to recall correctly the eight-digit number or to recall the race of the assistant did not vary by condition, $Fs < 1$. Five of the participants incorrectly recalled more than half of the items in the eight-digit number. Following Gilbert and Hixon (1991), we excluded the data from these 5 participants in subsequent analyses. Also following Gilbert and Hixon (1991), we included the data from the participants who did not recall correctly the race of the assistant.[2] Finally, the data from 3 participants were dropped from subsequent analyses because the tape recorder that recorded their responses malfunctioned. Thus, the subsequent analyses include data from 51 participants.

Stereotypic Completions

Gilbert and Hixon (1991) found no difference in the number of stereotypic completions made as a function of the race of the experimental assistant seen on the videotape when participants were cognitively busy. In our study, all of the participants were cognitively busy. We predicted that the

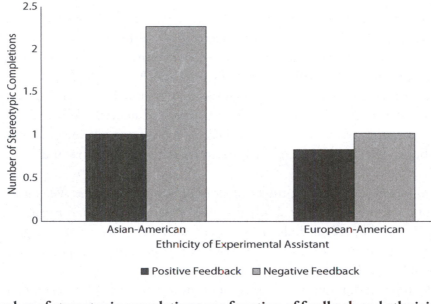

Figure 1. Number of stereotypic completions as a function of feedback and ethnicity of the experimental assistant.

participants in the present study who had just received positive feedback on the intelligence test would similarly show no evidence of stereotype activation. In contrast, for the participants who had just received negative feedback, we predicted that the race of the assistant would have an effect; that is, these participants would make more stereotypic completions if they were exposed to the Asian American rather than the European American woman. Figure 1 illustrates that the results conformed to this prediction.

A 2 (feedback condition: positive or negative) x 2 (race of assistant: European American or Asian American) analysis of variance (ANOVA) was conducted on the number of stereotypic completions made by the participants in their first completions of the relevant fragments.[3] The ANOVA revealed significant main effects for the manipulations of feedback, $F(1, 47) = 7.38$, $p < .01$, and the race of the assistant, $F(1, 47) = 7.38$, $p < .01$. More important, these main effects were qualified by a significant interaction, $F(1, 47) = 4.11$, $p < .05$. As can be seen in Figure 1, participants who received negative feedback and saw the Asian American assistant were particularly likely to indicate stereotypic completions relative to all other conditions. A planned contrast revealed that the predicted difference between this cell and all others was significant, $t(49) = 4.67$, $p < .01$. Simple-effects analyses showed further that the race of the assistant had a significant effect on participants' stereotypic completions if they had received negative feedback, $F(1, 47) = 11.09$, $p < .01$, but not if they had received positive feedback, $F < 1$, and the manipulation of feedback had a significant effect on participants' stereotypic completions if they saw the Asian American assistant, $F(1, 47) = 12.68$, $p < .01$, but not if they saw the European American assistant, $F < 1$.

Separating positive and negative stereotypic completions. Stereotyping others to restore a threatened self-image is most likely to be effective if the stereotype of another group is negative. Therefore, our account implies that activation of a negative stereotype should be more likely to be triggered by self-image threat than activation of positive stereotypes, although it certainly is possible that even positive stereotypes typically have negative connotations (such as the negative, antisocial connotations of *smart* as a stereotypic attribute of Jews and Asians) or that they at least serve to help discriminate against an outgroup. The stereotypic completions examined in the present study consisted of words that were relatively positive, negative, and neutral. To test the prediction that negative stereotypic attributes would be more likely to result from self-image threat than positive stereotypic attributes, we ran a series of analyses to examine the positive and negative attributes separately.

Of the five stereotypic completions, the most clearly positive was *polite*. We considered *rice* to be neutral. *Short* and *nip* seemed the most clearly negative. *Shy* could be seen as negative or neutral;[4] we ran analyses with and without *shy* included as a negative attribute. There were no significant effects of our manipulations on participants' likelihood of completing the word *polite*; participants who received self-image threat and saw the Asian American assistant were no more likely to say "polite" than were the participants in the other conditions, $t < 1$. In contrast, however, participants who received self-image threat and saw the Asian American assistant were significantly more likely to say "short" or "nip," or "shy," "short," or "nip," than were participants in the other conditions, $t(49) = 2.84$, $p < .01$, and $*(49) = 2.82$, $p < .01$, respectively.

Summary

The results for the participants who had received positive feedback on the intelligence test replicated the results of Gilbert and Hixon (1991): While cognitively busy, participants showed no evidence of stereotype activation on exposure to an Asian American target person. Among the participants who had received negative feedback, however, evidence for stereotype activation did emerge. Thus, after negative feedback, stereotype activation occurred automatically on exposure to a member of a stereotyped minority group. Moreover, this stereotype activation could not be explained by the semantic content of the feedback because the stereotypic words were unrelated to the feedback.

These results demonstrate that self-image maintenance goals can lead perceivers to activate stereotypes when they encounter members of a stereotyped group even under conditions that otherwise make stereotype activation unlikely.

Experiment 2

Consistent with the findings of Gilbert and Hixon (1991), the results of Study 1 support the idea that cognitive load can influence whether a stereotype is activated by exposure to a member of the stereotyped group. More noteworthy, however, these results demonstrate that the consequences of receiving self-image threatening feedback can also play an important role in stereotype activation, leading perceivers to activate a stereotype despite being under cognitive constraints that would otherwise inhibit such activation.

The next pair of studies investigated these issues further by examining activation of a stereotype that may be stronger and more chronically accessible to participants and by making participants' exposure to the member of the stereotyped group much more subtle.

Some reviews of the relevant literature (e.g., Bargh, 1994; Hamilton & Sherman, 1994; von Hippel, Sekaquaptewa, & Vargas, 1995) have questioned whether Gilbert & Hixon's (1991) participants exhibited no stereotype activation under cognitive load because the stereotype used was relatively weak, particularly compared to the African American stereotype—which Devine's (1989) research suggested was likely to be automatically activated. Of course, the relative strength of the stereotype is likely to depend on a number of factors, including the participant population (cf. Lepore & Brown, 1997). In any case, we felt it was important to examine the African American stereotype, which might provide a stronger test of whether the activation of overlearned stereotypes can be moderated. Studies 2 and 3, therefore, examined this stereotype.

A second goal of Studies 2 and 3 was to examine stereotype activation in a more subtle context—one in which participants would have little or no idea that they were even exposed to a member of a stereotyped group. Devine (1989) found that exposing participants to subliminal presentations of words relevant to the African American stereotype caused the perceivers to activate the stereotype despite their lack of awareness of either the exposure itself or the effects of the exposure. Other research has also demonstrated automatic activation of concepts due to exposure to subliminally presented primes (e.g., Bargh, Chen, & Burrows, 1996; Chen & Bargh, 1997; Perdue, Dovidio, Gurtman, & Tyler, 1990; for reviews, see Bargh, 1994; Greenwald, 1992). In addition to subliminal presentations, stereotypes and stereotype-relevant concepts have been primed through subtle procedures, such as having participants unscramble sentences that contain words relevant to a stereotype or concept (e.g., Banaji, Hardin, & Rothman, 1993; Bargh, 1997; Srull & Wyer, 1979).

Although the stereotype or concept activation in these studies typically is unintentional and occurs outside of participants' awareness, it is not clear if the activation is truly automatic in the sense that it is inevitable and efficient enough not to be inhibited by competing cognitive demands. One question raised by the results of Study 1 and by the results of Gilbert and Hixon's (1991) research is whether cognitive load would interfere with stereotype activation in response to very subtle priming cues that typically lead to such activation. If this unintended and primarily nonconscious stereotype activation depends on the availability of sufficient attentional resources, then cognitive busyness should moderate stereotype activation. A second question, then, would be whether self-image threat can moderate this stereotype activation as well.

Study 2, therefore, examined whether participants would be more likely to show stereotype activation after very brief exposure to an African American face than to a European American face and whether cognitive busyness would inhibit this effect. The moderating effects of self-image threat would be tested in Study 3.

Method

Participants And Design

Volunteering for this study were 65 undergraduate students (37 men and 28 women; 50 identifying themselves as European American, 9 as Asian American, 2 as African American, and 2 as Latino, plus 2 who did not identify their race) from Williams College. Because this study involved stereotypes about African Americans, and we were unable to recruit enough African Americans to include them as a factor in the design, we did not include the African American students in the analyses for this study. Nonetheless, the results are similar if these students are included. The experiment used a 2 (cognitive busyness: busy or not busy) x 2 (race of prime: African American or European American) factorial design. Participants were assigned randomly to the conditions.

Procedure

Participants were run individually in small cubicles. One of two female European American experimenters met each participant and seated him or her in front of a Macintosh computer. Participants read the experimental instructions, which presented a similar cover story as that used in Study 1. Participants read that the study concerned left- and right-brain functioning and that they would have to do both left- and right-brain tasks in the experiment. The participants in the cognitive-busy condition read that one such task would require them to try to remember a 10-item alphanumeric string.[5] Participants in the not-busy condition did not receive this task. All participants were then given instructions for the word-stem completion task. They learned that the word-stem completion task would begin with the presentation of an asterisk in the center of the computer screen, which would be followed by a visual distracter presented somewhere on the screen, which in turn would be followed by a word stem—that is, a few letters and a blank line to indicate the beginning of an uncompleted word—presented in the center of the screen. The instructions emphasized that participants should focus their gaze on the center of the screen at all times during the task. In addition, participants learned that they should complete each word stem as quickly as possible by saying as many different English words as they could generate from the stem until they saw the asterisk again in the center of the screen, which signaled that the next trial was about to begin.

When participants understood the instructions, those in the not-busy condition began the word completion task. In the busy condition, the experimenter gave the participants the 10-item alphanumeric string, rehearsed it with them until they could remember it, and then presented the word-stem completion task.

Word-Stem Completion Task

The word-stem completion task was developed using materials and a computer program developed by Dovidio and his colleagues (e.g., Dovidio &Fazio, 1991).[6] This task consisted of 20 trials. It was presented on a Macintosh computer set at the standard 640 x 480 dots per inch resolution and that had a refresh rate of 67 hertz. The color depth of the monitor was set to monochrome, and the background was set to white.

Participants sat approximately 20 centimeters from the computer screen. Each trial began with a 1-second presentation of an asterisk on which participants were instructed to focus. In the next screen refresh after the presentation of the asterisk, a European American or African American male face or a nonsense prime (scribbled lines) flashed briefly in the parafoveal field for approximately 17 milliseconds. The primes were presented in one of eight randomly selected areas that were 7.6 centimeters from the fixation point. This should have placed each face entirely outside of the foveal visual field and within the parafoveal visual field (Bargh et al., 1986; Nelson & Loftus, 1980; Rayner, 1978). The prime was followed by a set of nonsense scribbles that masked the prime. This mask appeared for 102 milliseconds in the exact spot where the prime had been presented. Following the mask, the word stem appeared foveally for 7 seconds. Each trial presented a different word stem.

Half of the participants were primed with either of two African American male faces, and the other half were primed with either of two European American male faces. The faces were created using a computer graphics program, which allowed the creation of two pairs of nearly identical African American and European American faces. Each African American face was darker than the corresponding European American face, and the noses and brows of the faces were varied to better simulate African American and European American features. Each face was otherwise identical to the corresponding face.[7]

Six of the 20 word stems were chosen because they could be completed with words relevant to the African American stereotype but that would be unlikely to result in ceiling effects (i.e., due to the large majority of participants saying these words first). The African American or European American face prime appeared before each of these word stems. In addition to these 6 word stems, 14 irrelevant word stems were included as fillers. The African American or European American face prime appeared before half of these filler stems, and the nonsense prime appeared before the other half.

The relevant stems were presented in the following order (separated from one another by two irrelevant, filler stems): hos——(hostile), dan——(dangerous), wel——(welfare), jan——(janitor), ste——(steal), and stu——(stupid).

After finishing the 20 trials, participants in the cognitive-busy condition were asked to recall the alphanumeric string. All participants then completed a questionnaire designed to check for suspicion or awareness of the primes. Participants were then debriefed thoroughly and thanked for their participation.

Results and Discussion

Manipulation Checks

We were interested in examining the effects of very subtle exposure to stereotype-relevant cues in this study; the issue of whether the presentation of the faces was truly subliminal or merely suboptimal (see

Murphy & Zajonc, 1993) was not very important to us in this context. We therefore did not conduct the entire set of tests needed to determine the subliminality of the presentations. Nevertheless, we did recruit separate groups of participants from the same population for some relatively conservative tests of our priming procedure.

We exposed 30 participants to the primes used in this study and asked them to make on-line guesses about what was flashed before the masks. Only 3 of these participants made a correct guess in any of the 20 trials (2 for the African American face prime and 1 for the European American face prime). In addition, we randomly assigned another group of 80 participants to be exposed to one of the four faces used in this study for 20 trials. We then told them that we may have flashed an object before the mask and asked them to make a series of guesses about what the object might have been. On the critical question, we told them that a face may have flashed before the prime. We then asked the participants to guess which of the four faces they thought was presented before the prime. Participants exposed to an African American face guessed one of the European American faces 56.8% of the time. Participants exposed to one of the European American faces guessed one of the European American faces 57.4% of the time. This difference is not statistically significant, $t < 1$. These two results provide at least some evidence that the prime was outside of participants' awareness.

At the conclusion of the study, none of the participants in the study itself could identify the primes that appeared just before the masks. In addition to checking the manipulation of prime, we also checked to see if participants who were given the alphanumeric string to rehearse remembered the string at the conclusion of the word-stem completion task. Three of the participants incorrectly recalled more than half of the items. Following Gilbert & Hixon (1991), the analyses reported below excluded the data from these participants, but the results are very similar if they are included. Thus, the subsequent analyses include data from 60 participants.

Stereotypic Completions

The principal questions addressed in this study were (a) whether participants' word-stem completions would reveal activation of the African American stereotype if they had been exposed very briefly to African American faces, even if the participants were not consciously aware of this exposure, and (b) whether cognitive busyness would reduce or eliminate this effect. To the extent that activation of the African American stereotype requires conscious awareness, then there should have been little or no stereotype activation. To the extent that it is automatic and inevitable on exposure to cues relevant to the category or stereotype, then stereotype activation should have been evident whether participants were cognitively busy. To the extent that it can be spontaneous and nonconscious but requires sufficient attentional resources, then stereotype activation should have been evident primarily among participants who were not cognitively busy. The results supported this latter hypothesis.

As in Study 1, we examined the first words indicated by the participants to complete the word stems. Based on the criteria used by Gilbert and Hixon (1991), we dropped two of the six stereotype-relevant word stems from the analyses because virtually none of the participants indicated the stereotypic response. Only 3 participants said "hostile" in response to "hos—" (almost all of the participants in the

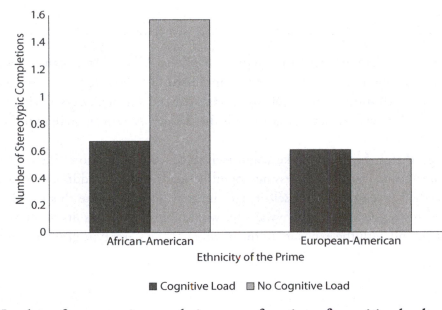

Figure 2. Number of stereotypic completions as a function of cognitive load and ethnicity of prime.

study added only one letter to the stem and said "host" or "hose"), and only 1 participant said "welfare" in response to "wel—" (almost all participants said "well" or "welcome"). This left four relevant stems and their stereotypic completions: dan—(dangerous), jan—(janitor), ste—(steal), and stu—(stupid).

A 2 (cognitive busyness: busy or not busy) x 2 (race of prime: African American or European American) ANOVA was conducted on the number of stereotypic completions made by the participants in their first completions of the relevant fragments. The ANOVA revealed a significant main effect for the manipulation of race, $F(1,56) = 4.97$, $p < .05$, and a marginally significant main effect for the manipulation of cognitive busyness, $F(l, 56) = 3.14$, $p < .10$. More important, both of these main effects were qualified by a significant interaction, $F(l, 56) = 4.20$, $p < .05$. As can be seen in Figure 2, activation of the African American stereotype in response to the brief exposures to the African American face primes was evident only if the participants were not cognitively busy. A planned contrast revealed that the predicted difference between this cell and all others was significant, $£(58) = 3.57$, $£ <.01$.

Simple-effects analyses revealed that participants who were not cognitively busy with the task of rehearsing the alphanumeric string were more likely to indicate stereotypic completions if they were exposed to the African American face primes than if they were exposed to the European American face primes, $F(1, 56) = 9.47$, $p < .01$, but this difference did not emerge if the participants were cognitively busy, $F <1$. Simple-effects analyses also showed that the manipulation of cognitive busyness affected the completions made by the participants exposed to the African American face primes, $F(1, 56) = 7.29$, $p < .01$, but not by the participants exposed to the European American face primes, $F < 1$.

Experiment 3

The results of Study 2 demonstrated that activation of the African American stereotype can be spontaneous and nonconscious but that it can be inhibited by cognitive load. In other words, the automaticity of the activation of this stereotype may depend on perceivers having sufficient attentional resources. This was evident even though the African American stereotype is particularly strong and well-known.

Can self-image threat, however, make cognitively busy perceivers more likely to activate this stereotype despite the activation-suppressing cognitive load? Study 3 addressed this question. If participants who had just experienced self-image threat would overcome this cognitive load and show evidence of stereotype activation anyway, this would replicate the results of Study 1 but with a different stereotype and with the exposure to the member of the stereotype group occurring without perceivers' awareness.

Method

Participants And Design

Participating in this study to receive credit for their introductory psychology class were 110 under-graduate students (79 men and 31 women; 61 identifying themselves as European American, 32 as Asian American, 11 as African American, 4 as Latino, and 2 as other) from the State University of New York at Buffalo. Because this study involved stereotypes about African Americans, and we were unable to recruit enough African Americans to include them as a factor in the design, we did not include the African American students in the analyses for this study. Nonetheless, the results are similar if these students are included. The experiment used a 2 (feedback: positive or negative) x 2 (race of prime: African American or European American) factorial design. Participants were assigned randomly to the conditions.

Procedure

As in Study 1, participants learned that they would be participating in two different experiments. As in Study 1, participants first took the bogus intelligence test and received false feedback—half receiving positive feedback and half receiving negative feedback. Participants then went to the ostensibly unrelated second experiment. From this point, the procedures and materials were identical to those used in Study 2, with the following exceptions. First, in the present study all participants were made cognitively busy by rehearsing an eight-digit number. Second, on the basis of pretesting conducted on participants from the population used in Study 3, we used a slightly different set of word stems, which is described below.

Word Stems

Because so few participants gave stereotypic completions to hos—(hostile) and wel—(welfare) in Study 2, we did not include these stems in the present study but instead replaced them with neutral stems designed to be fillers. In addition, pretesting indicated that participants in the population used in Study 3 were much more likely to indicate the stereotypic completion to ste—(steal) than the alternative completions and so we replaced this stem with one that pretesting suggested would better satisfy the criteria used by Gilbert and Hixon (1991): du—(dumb). Thus, the present study used four word stems that had stereotypic completions: dan—(dangerous), jan—(janitor), du—(dumb), and stu—(stupid), and 10 word stems served as fillers.

As in Study 2, a drawing of an African American or European American male face flashed briefly before the (four) stereotype-relevant stems and before half of the irrelevant stems, and a nonsense prime flashed before the remaining half of the irrelevant stems.

Results and Discussion

Manipulation Checks

None of the participants could identify the primes that appeared just before the masks. Furthermore, all but 6 of the participants reported that they believed the feedback from the intelligence test. Two of these 6 participants received positive feedback and were exposed to the Black face prime, 2 received positive feedback and were exposed to the White face prime, and 2 received negative feedback and were exposed to the Black face prime. To be conservative, we included the data from these 6 participants in the analyses reported below. However, the analyses yield similar results if their data are excluded. Twelve of the participants incorrectly recalled more than half of the items in the eight-digit number. Following Gilbert & Hixon (1991), the analyses reported below excluded the data from these participants, but the results are very similar if they are included. The subsequent analyses, therefore, include data from 87 participants.

Stereotypic Completions

The principal question addressed in this study was whether participants' word-stem completions would be more or less likely to indicate activation of the African American stereotype as a function of the manipulation of feedback on the intelligence test. We predicted that given the cognitive load, the participants who had just received positive feedback on the intelligence test would show no evidence of stereotype activation. For the participants who had just received negative feedback, in contrast, we predicted that the race of the prime would have an effect despite the cognitive load; that is, these participants would make more stereotypic completions if they were exposed to the African American rather than to the European American face. Figure 3 illustrates that the results conformed to this prediction.

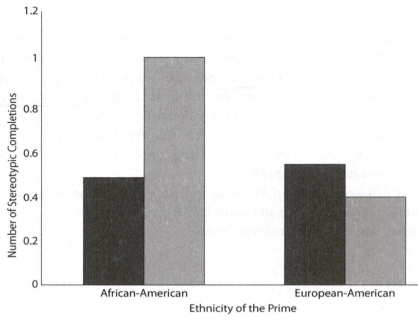

Figure 3. Number of stereotypic completions as a function of feedback and ethnicity of the prime.

As in Studies 1 and 2, we examined the first words indicated by the participants to complete the word stems. A 2 (feedback: positive or negative) x 2 (race of prime: African American or European American) ANOVA on this measure revealed a significant interaction between the manipulation of feedback and the race of the prime, $F(1, 83) = 3.91$, $p = .05$. No other effects obtained significance, $Fs < 1.6$, $ps > .20$. As can be seen in Figure 3, participants who received negative feedback and were exposed to the African American face were particularly likely to indicate stereotypic completions relative to all other conditions. A planned contrast revealed that the predicted difference between this cell and all others was significant, $J(85) = 2.69$, $p < .01$. Simple-effects analyses showed further that the race of the prime had a significant effect on participants' stereotypic completions if they had received negative feedback, $F(1, 83) = 5.35$, $p < .05$, but not if they had received positive feedback, $F < 1$, and the manipulation of feedback had a significant effect on participants' stereotypic completions if they were exposed to the African American face, $F(1, 83) = 5.18$, $p < .05$, but not if they were exposed to the European American face, $F < 1$.

To ensure that the negative feedback in the Black prime condition activated negative stereotypes about African Americans and not simply negative words in general, we conducted a series of analyses on participants' completions of the filler fragments. These analyses revealed that the total number of negative completions and the ratio of negative completions to positive completions did not differ as a function of feedback or prime condition, $Fs < 1$. These results suggest that self-image threat led to activation of stereotypes about African Americans on exposure to the African American face but did not increase the overall negativity of participants' responses.

General Discussion

The results of the three experiments demonstrate that the activation of stereotypes about minority groups in the presence of minority group members occurs automatically when people experience self-image threat but is not fully automatic when people do not experience self-image threat.

More specifically, Study 1 replicated Gilbert and Hixon's (1991) finding that cognitively busy participants who were exposed incidentally to an Asian American woman showed no evidence of activation of the Asian American stereotype. More important, however, Study 1 also demonstrated that if the participants had just received bogus, self-image threatening negative feedback, they did show evidence of stereotype activation despite the cognitive load. Moreover and consistent with our emphasis on self-image maintenance process, this effect occurred exclusively with the negative stereotypic words. These words should have been more likely to be activated automatically than positive stereotypic words because they would better satisfy the self-image maintenance goal of restoring the participants' threatened self-image. It is also worth noting that this stereotype activation could not be explained by the semantic content of the feedback because the stereotypic words were unrelated to the feedback.

Studies 2 and 3 extended the first study by testing activation of the African American rather than Asian American stereotype. In addition, Studies 2 and 3 examined the effects of cognitive load and self-image threat on stereotype activation in a much more subtle situation—in which the perceivers were not even aware that they were exposed to a cue that could activate the African American stereotype. Study 2 demonstrated that participants did activate this stereotype but only if they were not cognitively busy. Participants who were cognitively busy showed no evidence of stereotype activation. This finding suggests that cognitive busyness can moderate the activation of stereotypes about African Americans. Study 3 replicated this effect of cognitive load inhibiting stereotype activation among participants who did not experience self-image threat. Study 3 extended previous research, however, by demonstrating that self-image threat facilitated activation of the African American stereotype despite the cognitive load.

Taken together, this research provides strong evidence that self-image maintenance goals can lead to the automatic activation of stereotypes about minority group members in response to stereotype-relevant cues in perceivers' environments. These findings suggest that people's motivations can affect the activation of stereotypes even when this stereotypic activation occurs automatically. Specifically, these results provide evidence of a new route to automatic stereotype activation: stereotyping in the service of self-image maintenance. We believe that these findings suggest that motivation can play a more central role in stereotype activation than has been previously acknowledged.

Self-Image Maintenance Goals and the Automatic Activation of Stereotypes

The findings reported in this article support our contention (Fein & Spencer, 1997) that when people experience self-image threat, one powerful and widely available strategy to restore their self-image is to stereotype others. As discussed before, Bargh's (1997) automotive model posits that any two mental representations that are repeatedly paired with one another will form an automatic link. In light of this model and the research that supports it, the stereotype activation demonstrated in the present studies suggests the presence of a strong link between the goal to restore one's self-image in the face of self-image threat and the activation of stereotypes in the presence of stereotype-relevant albeit very subtle cues in the environment. This link between threat and stereotype activation was demonstrated in the present studies under conditions that otherwise inhibit stereotype activation. These findings imply, therefore, that the processes of self-image maintenance can play a critically important role in moderating the activation of stereotypes when individuals encounter a member of a stereotyped group.

In addition to highlighting the role of self-image maintenance processes, the current research also highlights the power of the situation to provoke both particular goals and participants' goal-relevant responses. Information available in the participants' environment triggered self-image maintenance threat, thereby inducing the affect and motivation prompted by the threat. Participants' responses to this threat were, in turn, shaped by the goal-relevant information in the environment—the presence or absence of stereotype-relevant cues. Participants who had received self-image threatening information did not simply become more negative in their responses. Rather, they were negative selectively in response to the cues present in the situation. If cues associated with stereotypes that people frequently use in response to a threatened self-image were available, then the participants used the cues and exhibited stereotype activation. In the absence of these cues, neither specific stereotype activation nor general negativity was evident.

Sinclair and Kunda (1997) recently reported evidence that adds support to this account. They found that when an African American in the role of a manager evaluated participants negatively, the participants automatically activated negative stereotypes about African Americans. This automatic activation did not occur when the manager was European American or when the African American manager provided positive feedback. Their results, similar to ours, illustrate the interaction of the self and the information available in the environment in moderating stereotype activation.

Another contribution of the current research is that it shows that this interaction can affect not only conscious but preconscious processes. The goal of self-image maintenance has been shown to have strong effects on a number of conscious processes (e.g., Spencer, Josephs, & Steele, 1993; Steele, 1988; Tesser, 1988; Tesser & Cornell, 1991), and in Study 1 of this article, this goal facilitated stereotype activation in response to a stereotype-relevant cue of which participants were aware. In Study 3, however, this goal interacted with a preconscious stereotype-relevant cue to produce stereotype activation. An intriguing question raised by these results concerns whether goals affect preconscious and conscious processes in the same or contrasting ways. Self-image maintenance goals in the current research had similar effects on stereotype activation whether the stereotypic cues were at the preconscious or conscious levels. On the other hand, some goals, such as the goal to be egalitarian and not to stereotype or discriminate (e.g., Blair & Banaji, 1996; Devine, 1989; Dovidio & Gaertner, 1991; Fazio et al., 1995; Monteith, Zuwerink, & Devine, 1994), might have independent or even opposing effects as a function of awareness.

The role of conscious awareness in stereotype activation is not limited to awareness of stereotype-relevant cues in the environment. Even if the cue is there to be seen clearly by the perceivers, such as the race of the person with whom they are interacting, the perceivers may be unaware of the connection between that person's race and their own word-fragment completions or even their own evaluations of that person on a number of dimensions. If activation of even very well-known and strong stereotypes is not always fully automatic, as the present research suggests, perceivers' goals may have important and very different moderating effects on stereotype activation as a function of this kind of awareness. For example, if perceivers are made aware of the link between a target person's race and their word-stem completions, the potentially self-image restoring effect of stereotype activation may be subverted. For some people, believing that they easily activate stereotypes about other groups would be at least as threatening as receiving negative performance feedback. Can the motivation not to stereotype interfere with the strong link between self-image threat and stereotype activation in the presence of stereotype-relevant cues? Addressing this kind of question in future research could provide important insights into the relationships among motivation, preconscious, and conscious processes relevant to stereotyping.

The relationships among motivation, affect, and cognition are also clearly implicated as an important set of issues to be pursued in extensions of the present research. Previous research has focused primarily on how these factors affect the application of stereotypes to impression formation, judgments, or behavior. The present research suggests that more basic processing of information may be affected by such factors as well. More specifically, self-image threat in the current studies affected perceivers' activation of stereotypes under circumstances in which the perceivers were cognitively busy and in which their exposure to stereotype-relevant information was quite minimal. These findings suggest that the activation of stereotypes may be a more complex process and may include more factors, such as motivation and affect, than has previously been acknowledged.

Mediational Accounts

A question that needs to be addressed by future research is how such effects are mediated. We have emphasized the processes relevant to the auto-motive model of Bargh and his colleagues (e.g., Bargh, 1997). In conjunction with Fein and Spencer (1997), we argue that it is common for self-image threats to lead perceivers to derogate members of stereotyped groups when the environment provides readily available stereotype-relevant cues. Perceivers may learn to activate these stereotypes spontaneously, efficiently, unintentionally, and without awareness when their self-image has been threatened and when they are exposed to cues identifying a stereotyped group.

A second mediational account is that motivation and affect may prime the content or valence of perceivers' thoughts, and this may, in turn, facilitate activation of stereotypes that are consistent with these thoughts. Forgas and Fiedler (1996), for example, discuss how mood can affect cognition through selective priming of information that is similar in valence (Bower, 1991; Clark & Isen, 1982; Forgas & Bower, 1988; Isen, 1984) or through the use of heuristic strategies to infer one's thoughts (Forgas, 1995; Schwarz & Clore, 1983). Thus, mood and affect and perhaps motivation as well may lead to the activation of thought processes that are congruent with the content of the stereotypes about certain groups. For example, when people are in a negative mood, this negative mood may facilitate the activation of negative aspects of certain stereotypes.

A third account is that motivation and affect moderate the cognitive resources that perceivers dedicate to a task. Research has suggested that individuals try to regulate their moods by engaging in more or less processing of information. People in a good mood, for example, may exhibit more stereotyping and intergroup discrimination because they process information more heuristically to maintain their positive mood (Bodenhausen, 1993; Clark & Isen, 1982; Forgas & Fiedler, 1996). People in a negative mood may exhibit more stereotyping and intergroup discrimination because they engage in highly motivated processing in an attempt to repair their affective state (Forgas & Fiedler, 1996). Thus, motivation and affect may lead individuals to deploy attentional resources that facilitate stereotype activation.

These various accounts suggest some potentially exciting questions for future research to address. It is plausible that each of these accounts explains some of the ways in which motivation and affect mediate stereotype activation. At a broader level, the present research is part of a growing body of recent research that reflects a fuller integration of sociocultural, motivational, and cognitive factors in stereotyping and prejudice (Devine, 1989; Dovidio & Gaertner, 1991; Esses & Zanna, 1995; Mackie & Hamilton, 1993).

The Relevance of Stereotype Activation

But why study stereotype activation in the first place? It may seem that activation of stereotypes, especially the activation of stereotypes outside of perceivers' awareness, is a far cry from discrimination and prejudice against the targets of these stereotypes. However, a considerable literature suggests that when stereotypes are activated, they often become the lens through which targets of stereotypes are perceived and the catalyst by which targets are discriminated against. When stereotypes are activated outside of people's awareness, they can bias judgment and lead to action without the perceiver acknowledging or censoring their impact. For example, Bargh and his colleagues (Bargh et al., 1996; Chen & Bargh, 1997) have shown that even preconsciously activated stereotypes can have profound effects on social interactions. This work finds that preconsciously activated stereotypes can cause perceivers to act in ways that elicit confirmation of the stereotype when interacting with members of stereotyped groups. Because these perceivers do not see the influence they had on the interaction, the target's behavior is seen as unambiguously confirming the stereotype.

In addition, the current research demonstrates that stereotype activation may be influenced by some of the same factors that influence stereotype application. More specifically, this research suggests that stereotype activation can be affected by motivational factors, whereas previous analyses of stereotype activation have focused solely on cognitive factors. Thus, a more complex set of factors may influence stereotype activation than has been acknowledged previously. This raises the question of whether there are additional factors that not only can facilitate stereotype activation but also can inhibit it. Motivational factors therefore may play a critical and heretofore unexamined role in determining when stereotypes are more or less likely to be activated. How these factors affect stereotype activation, application, and the interaction between them should be a provocative question for further research.

Notes

1. We thank Daniel Gilbert and Gregory Hixon for their generosity in sharing their stimulus materials with us.
2. A higher percentage of participants failed to correctly recall the assistant's ethnicity in our study (26%) compared to Gilbert and Hixon's (1991) studies (6% and 11% in their two studies). In any event, we obtained similar results—the two-way interaction and the contrast and simple-effects comparisons remained statistically significant— when participants who could not identify the experimental assistant's ethnicity were excluded from the analyses. Furthermore, we obtained similar results if we included the data from the participants who incorrecdy recalled more than half of the items in the eight-digit number.
3. We analyzed the completions in a slightly different manner than did Gilbert and Hixon (1991). Instead of analyzing the total number of stereotypic completions that participants generated, we analyzed the number of times that participants said the stereotypic word as their first completion. Given that some of the stereotypic words were generated by almost all participants in every condition, this seemed to us to be a more valid and precise measure of stereotype activation. Moreover, it would allow us to be more consistent with the procedures used in the subsequent studies reported in this article. Nevertheless, we obtained similar results (i.e., the two-way interaction and the contrast and simple-effects comparisons remained statistically significant) when we used the same measure that Gilbert and Hixon (1991) used.
4. Research by Bargh et al. (1986) tested the affective valence of shyness and found evidence that it was judged to be affectively neutral. Thus, *nip* and *short* are the completions that probably are best represented as negative in valence. Nevertheless, we reported both analyses to show that the inclusion of *shy* as a negatively valenced word does not alter the results.
5. Pilot testing revealed that the task used in Study 1 and in Gilbert and Hixon (1991) of asking participants to remember an eight-digit number was not taxing enough for the participants in this population.
6. We thank John Dovidio for his generosity in providing the computer program used in this experiment.
7. A separate group of 23 participants used 7-point scales to rate the attractiveness and likeability of either the two African American faces or the two European American faces, which were each presented on a computer screen for 15 seconds, and they also indicated the race of the individuals depicted. There were no differences in the ratings as a function of race, and all participants identified the race of the individuals consistent with the intent of the manipulation.

References

Allport, G. W. (1954). *The nature of prejudice.* Cambridge, MA: AddisonWesley.

Banaji, M. R., Hardin, C., & Rothman, A. J. (1993). Implicit stereotyping in person judgment. *Journal of Personality and Social Psychology, 65,* 272–281.

Bargh, J. A. (1994). The four horsemen of automaticity: Awareness, intention, efficiency, and control in social cognition. In R. S. Wyer & T. K. Srull (Eds.), *Handbook of social cognition: Vol 1. Basic processes* (pp. 1–40). Hillsdale, NJ: Lawrence Erlbaum.

Bargh, J. A. (1997). The automaticity of everyday life. In R. S. Wyer Jr. (Ed.), *Advances in social cognition* (Vol. 10). Mahwah, NJ: Erlbaum.

Bargh, J. A., Bond, R. N., Lombardi, W. J., & Tota, M. E. (1986). The additive nature of chronic and temporary sources of construct accessibility. *Journal of Personality and Social Psychology, 50,* 869–878.

Bargh, J. A., Chen, M., & Burrows, L. (1996). Automaticity of social behavior: Direct effects of trait construct and stereotype activation. *Journal of Personality and Social Psychology, 71,* 230–244.

Bargh, J. A., & Gollwitzer, P. M. (1994). Environmental control of goal-directed action: Automatic and strategic contingencies between situations and behavior. *Nebraska Symposium on Motivation, 41,* 71–124.

Blair, I. V., & Banaji, M. R. (1996). Automatic and controlled processes in stereotype priming. *Journal of Personality and Social Psychology, 70,* 1142–1163.

Bodenhausen, G. V. (1993). Emotion, arousal, and stereotypic judgment: A heuristic model of affect and stereotyping. In D. M. Mackie & D. L. Hamilton (Eds.), *Affect, cognition, and stereotyping: Interactive processes in group perception* (pp. 13–37). New York: Academic Press.

Bower, G. H. (1991). Mood congruity of social judgments. In J. P. Forgas (Ed.), *Emotion and social judgments* (pp. 31–54). Oxford, UK: Pergamon.

Brewer, M. B. (1988). A dual process model of impression formation. In R. S. Wyer Jr. & T. K. Srull (Eds.), *Handbook of social cognition* (Vol. 1, pp. 1–36). Hillsdale, NJ: Lawrence Erlbaum.

Chartrand, T., & Bargh, J. A. (1996). Automatic activation of impression formation and memorization goals: Nonconscious goal priming reproduces effects of explicit task instructions. *Journal of Personality and Social Psychology, 71,* 464–478.

Chen, M., & Bargh, J. A. (1997). Nonconscious behavioral confirmation processes: The self-fulfilling consequences of automatic stereotype activation, *Journal of Experimental Social Psychology, 33,* 541–560.

Clark, M. S., & Isen, A. M. (1982). Towards understanding the relationship between feeling states and social behavior. In A. H. Hastorf & A. M. Isen (Eds.), *Cognitive social psychology* (pp. 73–108). New York: Elsevier-North Holland.

Devine, P. G. (1989). Stereotypes and prejudice: Their automatic and controlled components. *Journal of Personality and Social Psychology, 56,* 5–18.

Dovidio, J. F., & Fazio, R. H. (1991). New technologies for the direct and indirect assessment of attitudes. In J. M. Tanur (Ed.), *Questions about questions: Inquiries into the cognitive bases of surveys* (pp. 204–237). New York: Russell Sage.

Dovidio, J. F., & Gaertner, S. L. (1991). Changes in the nature and assessment of racial prejudice. In H. Knopke J. Norrell, & R. Rogers (Eds.), *Opening doors: An appraisal of race relations in contemporary America* (pp. 201–241). Tuscaloosa: University of Alabama Press.

Esses, V. M., & Zanna, M. P. (1995). Mood and expression of ethnic stereotypes. *Journal of Personality and Social Psychology, 69,* 1052–1068.

Fazio, R. H. (1990). Multiple process by which attitudes guide behavior: The MODE model as an integrative framework. In M. P. Zanna (Ed.), *Advances in experimental social psychology* (Vol. 23, pp. 75–109). New York: Academic Press.

Fazio, R. H. (1995). Attitudes as object-evaluation associations: Determinants, consequences, and correlates of attitude accessibility. In R. E. Petty & J. A. Krosnick (Eds.), *Attitude strength: Antecedents and consequences* (pp. 247–282). Hillsdale, NJ: Lawrence Erlbaum.

Fazio, R. H., Jackson, J. R., Dunton, B. C., & Williams, C. J. (1995). Variability in automatic activation as an unobtrusive measure of racial attitudes: A bona fide pipeline? *Journal of Personality and Social Psychology, 69,* 1013–1027.

Fein, S., & Spencer, S.J. (1997). Prejudice as self-image maintenance: Affirming the self through negative evaluations of others. *Journal of Personality and Social Psychology, 73,* 31–44.

Fiske, S. T., & Neuberg, S. L. (1990). A continuum of impression formation, from category-based to individuating processes. Influences of information and motivation on attention and interpretation. In M. P. Zanna (Ed.), *Advances in experimental social psychology* (Vol. 23, pp. 1–74). New York: Academic Press.

Forgas, J. P. (1995). Mood and judgment: The affect infusion model (AIM). *Psychological Bulletin, 116,* 39–66.

Forgas, J. P., & Bower, G. H. (1988). Affect in social and personal judgments. In K. Fiedler & J. Forgas (Eds.), *Affect, cognition and social behavior* (pp. 183–208). Toronto, Canada: Hogrefe.

Forgas, J. P., & Fiedler, K. (1996). Us and them: Mood effects on intergroup discrimination. *Journal of Personality and Social Psychology, 70,* 28–40.

Gilbert, D. T., & Hixon, J. G. (1991). The trouble of thinking: Activation and application of stereotypic beliefs. *Journal of Personality and Social Psychology, 60,* 509–517.

Gilbert, D. T., Pelham, B. W., & Krull, D. S. (1988). On cognitive busyness: When person perceivers meet persons perceived. *Journal of Personality and Social Psychology, 54,* 733–740.

Greenwald, A. G. (1992). New Look 3: Unconscious cognition reclaimed. *American Psychologist, 47,* 766–779.

Greenwald, A. G., & Banaji, M. R. (1995). Implicit social cognition: Attitudes, self-esteem, and stereotypes. *Psychological Review, 102,* 4–27.

Hamilton, D. L., & Sherman, J. W. (1994). Stereotypes. In R. S. Wyer & T. K. Srull (Eds.), *Handbook of social cognition* (Vol. 2, pp. 1–68). Hillsdale, NJ: Lawrence Erlbaum.

Heatherton, T. F., & Polivy, J. (1991). Development and validation of a scale for measuring state self-esteem. *Journal of Personality and Social Psychology, 60,* 895–910.

Isen, A. M. (1984). Toward understanding the role of affect in cognition. In R. S. Wyer & T. K. Srull (Eds.), *Handbook of social cognition* (Vol. 3, pp. 179–236). Hillsdale, NJ: Lawrence Erlbaum.

Lepore, L., & Brown, R. (1997). Category and stereotype activation: Is prejudice inevitable? *Journal of Personality and Social Psychology, 72,* 275–287.

Mackie, D. M., & Hamilton, D. L. (Eds.). (1993). *Affect, cognition, and stereotyping: Interactive processes in group perception.* New York: Academic Press.

Macrae, C. N., Bodenhausen, G. V., & Milne, A. B. (1995). The dissection of selection in person perception: Inhibitory processes in social stereotyping. *Journal of Personality and Social Psychology, 69,* 397–407.

Macrae, C. N., Milne, A. B., & Bodenhausen, G. V. (1994). Stereotypes as energy-saving devices: A peek inside the cognitive toolbox. *Journal oj Personality and Social Psychology, 66,* 37–47.

Monteith, M.J., Zuwerink, J. R., & Devine, P. G. (1994). Prejudice and prejudice reduction: Classic challenges, contemporary approaches. In P. G. Devine, D. L. Hamilton, & T. M. Ostrom (Eds.), *Social cognition: Impact on social psychology* (pp. 324–346). San Diego, CA: Academic Press.

Murphy, S. T., & Zajonc, R. B. (1993). Affect, cognition, and awareness: Affective priming with optimal and subop-timal exposures. *Journal of Personality and Social Psychology, 64*, 723–739.

Nelson, W. W., & Loftus, G. R. (1980). The functional visual field dining picture viewing. *Journal of Experimental Psychology: Human Learning and Memory, 6*, 391–399.

Perdue, C. W., Dovidio, J. F., Gurtman, M. B., & Tyler, R. B. (1990). Us and them: Social categorization and the process of intergroup bias. *Journal of Personality and Social Psychology, 59*, 475–486.

Rayner, K. (1978). Foveal and parafoveal cues in reading. In J. Requin (Ed.), *Attention and performance VIII* (pp. 149–461). Hillsdale, NJ: Lawrence Erlbaum.

Ross, L., Lepper, M. R., & Hubbard, M. (1975). Perseverance in self-perception and social perception: Biased attribu-tion processes in the debriefing paradigm. *Journal of Personality and Social Psychology, 32*, 880–892.

Schwarz, N., & Clore, G. L. (1983). Mood, misattribution, and judgments of well-being: Informative and directive functions of affective states. *Journal of Personality arid Social Psychology, 45*, 513–523.

Sinclair, L., & Kunda, Z. (1997). Feedback-dependent evaluation of evaluators: Motivated application and inhibition of stereotypes. *Unpublished manuscript,* University of Waterloo, Ontario.

Spencer, S. J., Josephs, R. A., & Steele, C. M. (1993). Low self-esteem: The uphill struggle for self-integrity. In R. Baumeister (Ed.), *Self-esteem and the puzzle of low self-regard* (pp. 21–36). New York: Plenum.

Srull, T. K., & Wyer, R. S. (1979). The role of category accessibility in the interpretation of information about persons: Some determinants and *implications. Journal of Personality and Social Psychology, 37*, 1660–1672.

Steele, C. M. (1988). The psychology of self-affirmation: Sustaining the integrity of the self. In L. Berkowitz (Ed.), *Advances in experimental social psychology* (Vol. 21, pp. 261–302). New York: Academic Press.

Stein, K. F. (1994). Complexity of the self-schema and responses to discontinuing feedback. *Cognitive Therapy and Research, 18*, 161–178.

Tesser, A. (1988). Toward a self-evaluation maintenance model of social behavior. In L. Berkowitz (Ed.), *Advances in experimental social psychology* (Vol. 21, pp. 181–227). New York: Academic Press.

Tesser, A., & Cornell, D. P. (1991). On the confluence of self processes. *Journal of Experimental Social Psychology, 27*, 501–526.

von Hippel, W. H., Sekaquaptewa, D., & Vargas, P. (1995). On the role of encoding processes in stereotype main-tenance. In M. R. Zanna (Ed.), *Advances in experimental social psychology* (Vol. 27, pp. 177–254). New York: Academic Press.

Winter, L., & Uleman, J. S. (1984). When are social judgments made? Evidence for the spontaneousness of trait inferences. *Journal of Personality and Social Psychology, 47*, 237–252.

Wittenbrink, B., Judd, C. M., & Park, B. (1997). Evidence for racial prejudice at the implicit level and its relationship with questionnaire measures, *Journal of Personality and Social Psychology, 72*, 262–274.

I Thought We Could Be Friends, but …

Systematic Miscommunication and Defensive Distancing as Obstacles to Cross-Group Friendship Formation

By Jacquie D. Vorauer and Yumiko Sakamoto, University of Manitoba, Winnipeg, Manitoba, Canada

Abstract

This study examined the precursors and consequences of systematic miscommunications regarding relationship interest during intergroup interaction. Pairs of previously unacquainted same-sex students (White-White, White-Chinese, or Chinese-Chinese) engaged in a relatively intimate controlled interaction. White participants who had had little prior contact with Chinese persons were more apt to exhibit a signal-amplification bias (i.e., to perceive that their overtures had conveyed more interest than was actually the case) in intergroup as compared with intragroup exchanges. In contrast, White participants with high levels of prior contact with Chinese persons and Chinese participants did not show enhanced signal amplification in intergroup relative to intragroup exchanges. These results support our hypothesis that lack of intergroup contact experience sets the stage for miscommunications regarding friendship interest. White participants' tendency to feel that they had initially communicated more interest in being friends than their Chinese partner mediated a downward shift in their actual friendship interest over time, suggesting that signal amplification triggers defensive distancing and ultimately lowers the likelihood of cross-group friendship formation.

The benefits of cross-group friendships for both majority and minority group members, such as more positive intergroup attitudes, reduced intergroup anxiety, and enhanced personal development, are widely acknowledged (e.g., Levin, van Laar, & Sidanius, 2003; Pettigrew, 1998; see also Steele, Spencer, & Aronson, 2002). However, current understanding of the dynamics surrounding the formation of such friendships remains quite limited. Research on friendship development—and, indeed, on relationship development in general—has placed much more emphasis on predicting initial interpersonal attraction than on other factors that also determine whether a relationship actually forms.

In particular, relationship development depends on the effective communication of positive regard and interest. Individuals' overtures need to be perceived as such by their intended recipients. Moreover, individuals are well served by an awareness of the effectiveness of their efforts. If they fail to realize that

Jacquie D. Vorauer & Yumiko Sakamoto, "I Thought We Could Be Friends, but … Systematic Miscommunication and Defensive Distancing as Obstacles to Cross-Group Friendship Formation," *Psychological Science*, vol. 17, no. 4, pp. 326–331.

their overtures toward relationship development have gone undetected by their potential partner, they may be left waiting for reciprocation that is not forthcoming. Ultimately, they may feel rejected and withdraw their efforts and interest prematurely.

The present research was designed to examine the precursors and consequences of systematic miscommunications regarding relationship interest that may be especially likely to occur when an individual's potential friend is an out-group member. Our first goal was to demonstrate that individuals are more likely to show a signal-amplification bias, that is, to perceive that their overtures have conveyed more interest than is actually the case, in the context of intergroup rather than intragroup interactions. We expected this pattern to be most evident for those individuals with little prior contact with the out-group. Our second goal was to demonstrate that signal amplification has important negative interpersonal consequences, in that it leads to decreased interest in intergroup friendship over time.

Signal Amplification

Vorauer, Cameron, Holmes, and Pearce (2003) first provided evidence for the signal-amplification bias in a series of studies focusing on communications between potential romantic partners. Participants in these studies consistently perceived that their overtures communicated more relationship interest to a potential romantic partner than was the case. More recently, Vorauer (2005) found that White Canadians who were similarly interested in First Nations Canadians and White Canadians as potential friends were more likely to evidence signal amplification when making friendship overtures to First Nations Canadians; that is, signal amplification was more likely across than within ethnic-group boundaries. Consistent with previous research and theory suggesting that individuals may experience heightened self-awareness in intergroup interaction as a function of the relative novelty of such exchanges (see, e.g., Blair, Park, & Bachelor, 2003; Buss, 1980) and that self-awareness is linked to the sense that one's feelings are transparent to others (e.g., Vorauer & Ross, 1999), Vorauer's results indicated that greater signal amplification with respect to intergroup communications was mediated by heightened feelings of transparency in these contexts. That is, her findings suggested that individuals made especially egocentric judgments in intergroup interaction, assuming that their inner feelings of interest were easily detectable by their potential friend, because of self-awareness triggered by the novelty of the social situation.

In the present study, we sought to examine the role of novelty more directly by testing how individuals' propensity to exhibit signal amplification is affected by the amount of prior contact they have had with the out-group. Interactions between majority group members (White Canadians) and minority group members (Chinese Canadians) were the focus of our research. We predicted that majority group members who had lower levels of prior contact with the out-group would exhibit more signal amplification than those with higher levels of prior contact, because of the greater novelty of the interaction situation: Uncertainty experienced in an unfamiliar situation should foster self-focus and hence more egocentric judgments. We assessed potential correlates of White individuals' prior contact with the out-group, namely, prejudice and in-group identification, so as to be able to test the effects of contact per se with maximum precision.

By virtue of their numerical representation in the population, minority group members are apt to have much more contact with majority group members than vice versa. We predicted that this prior intergroup experience might essentially protect Chinese individuals against greater signal amplification in intergroup as compared with intragroup interaction. In examining the implications of previous intergroup contact for signal amplification, a bias in social perception, we sought to answer the call, made by numerous investigators, for research assessing the effects of intergroup contact on outcomes other than attitudes (e.g., Devine, Evett, & Vasquez-Suson, 1996).

Defensive Distancing

Although it is not difficult to imagine a variety of negative interpersonal consequences attached to egocentric biases in individuals' beliefs about the attributes and feelings they have communicated to others (see, e.g., Gilovich, Kruger, & Savitsky, 1999), in fact there have been few empirical demonstrations of the social costs of such biases. In the present study, we sought to show that signal amplification can hinder the development of cross-group friendships. The specific possibility that we investigated was connected to the fact that signal amplification, when in evidence, should often lead individuals to feel that they have communicated more interest than their interaction partner— that they have shown themselves to be more enthusiastic than the other person about a possible relationship. We hypothesized that this potentially embarrassing perception would lead individuals to engage in defensive distancing, so that they would decide they were not interested in the potential friend after all. We tested this hypothesis by assessing participants' interest in pursuing a friendship with their partner at different points in their interaction with the partner, so that we could look at changes in interest over time. We also assessed participants' general liking for and sense that they shared things in common with their partner, so as to ensure that the discovery of interpersonal differences could not account for any changes in friendship interest that were evident.

Method

Participants

One hundred twelve introductory psychology students (56 same-sex pairs) participated in the study in exchange for partial course credit. There were 22 White-White pairs, 19 White-Chinese pairs, and 15 Chinese-Chinese pairs. The ratio of male to female pairs was approximately the same across the three pair types. All of these students had taken part in a mass testing session in which they provided demographic information and indicated the amount of direct personal contact they had had with Chinese persons (1 = *none at all*, 10 = *a great deal*; for White participants, $M = 4.41$, $SD = 2.35$). They also completed McConahay, Hardee, and Batts's (1981) Modern Racism Scale adapted for a Canadian context and the measure of in-group identification included in the race-specific version of Luhtanen and Crocker's (1992) Collective Self-Esteem scale (for White participants, M = 4.22, SD = 1.30, α = .72, and M = 4.43, SD = 2.05, α = .69, respectively, on 10-point scales). Students were assigned to pairs on the basis of scheduling convenience, with the constraint that the age difference between members of a pair could not exceed 10 years. The experimenter ascertained that participants who were paired together were unacquainted prior to their session.

Procedure

Participants arrived in the laboratory for a study of "social perception in a first-meeting situation." Each pair member was assigned to a different location to wait for the Asian female experimenter. She greeted each participant individually, escorting him or her to a separate room, where she provided an overview of the study procedures. The overview included an explanation that the participant's communication with his or her partner would be restricted, generally involving the exchange of written and audiotaped responses, but that the pair could have a more extensive face-to-face meeting at the end of the study if both members were interested. Participants' first task was to spend 10 min. writing answers to four questions about themselves. Each pair member started with four different questions, which were taken from Aron, Melinat, Aron, Vallone, and Bator's (1997) closeness-generating procedure (e.g., "What would constitute a 'perfect' day for you?"). After answering the questions, partners were introduced briefly, ostensibly to exchange their answers, but also so that they would learn each other's ethnicity (i.e., White or Asian).

After being separated once again and spending a few minutes reading their partner's answers, participants provided their own answers to the four questions first answered by their partner. This time, they spoke their answers into a tape recorder rather than writing them down. The experimenter instructed participants that "this is the part of the study that is meant to be more like a real conversation, in that you can respond to things that the other person said and you will be talking rather than writing." Hence, participants had the opportunity to make social overtures at this point, if they so desired. They were left alone to make their recording. The experimenter then gave participants the first questionnaire, which focused on the interest they believed they had conveyed with their audiotaped message. Finally, participants listened to their partner's recording and filled out the second questionnaire, which focused on their impressions of their partner's interest in them. In each case, participants were assured that their questionnaire responses were confidential. Participants were then fully debriefed.

Dependent Measures

Metaperceptions and Initial Feelings

Participants completed the first questionnaire immediately after recording their audiotaped message. The questionnaire began by asking them to indicate their metaperceptions regarding what their audiotaped comments would convey to their partner about their feelings toward him or her. There were six closed-ended items (α = .86), three of which addressed interest in developing a friendship or pursuing further contact (e.g., "After listening to my tape-recorded comments, my partner will probably think that I am—interested in pursuing a friendship with him/her"), and three of which addressed liking (e.g., "After listening to my tape-recorded comments, my partner will probably think that I feel we have __ in common"). In all cases (for these and all subsequent scale items), participants responded by circling the appropriate number on a 9-point scale, with higher numbers reflecting greater endorsement. An open-ended item asked participants to indicate whether they had, at any point, explicitly tried to communicate to their partner that they were interested in getting to know him or her better or that they wanted to be friends. If so, they were asked to describe what they said or did, listing each overture on a separate numbered line. This item was scored by counting the number of overtures listed. Scores for these closed and open-ended items were standardized and averaged together to obtain an index of *metaperceptions regarding feelings conveyed.*

The first questionnaire also contained six closed-ended items (α = .90) assessing participants' *initial feelings* toward their partner. These items were directly parallel to the closed-ended metaperception items (e.g., "I am __ interested in pursuing a friendship with my partner").

Impressions and Final Feelings

Participants completed the second questionnaire immediately after listening to their partner's audiotaped message. This questionnaire assessed their *impressions of their partner's feelings* toward them with six closed-ended items (e.g., "I think that my partner is __ interested in pursuing a friendship with me;" α = .94) and an open-ended item that were directly parallel to those assessing metaperceptions in the first questionnaire. As for the metaperception scores, scores on these items were standardized and combined to form an index. Participants were then asked to make a comparative judgment regarding whose tape-recorded comments communicated more interest in the other person, choosing "my partner's comments" or "my comments." After indicating their *final feelings* toward their partner by answering the same six items used to assess initial feelings in the first questionnaire (α = .92), participants were asked to estimate the ethnicity of their partner using a checklist.

Behavior

In order to achieve a more complete understanding of differences between intergroup and intragroup communications in this study, we arranged for outside coders to assess participants' behavior. Two White and two Chinese coders listened to the tapes and indicated the impression they would have formed of each participant's interest in them had they been the intended target of the message. They responded to closed- and open-ended items directly parallel to those completed by study participants when judging their partner's tape. Agreement across coders was acceptable, αs = .81 and .86 for scale ratings and specific overtures detected, respectively. Coders' judgments were standardized and combined to form a behavior index.[1] Notably, the correlations between ratings made by different coders were similar regardless of ethnicity, average rs = .59 for same-ethnicity coders and .60 for different-ethnicity coders.

Results

We report results from the perspective of White and Chinese participants in turn.

White Participants' Perspective

Our analyses from White participants' perspective involved only White-White and White-Chinese pairs. In the White-Chinese pairs, the White pair member was designated as the participant, and the Chinese pair member was designated as the partner. In the White-White pairs, we randomly selected one pair member to be the participant and the other to be the partner (see Vorauer & Kumhyr, 2001). Two pairs (one White-White and one White-Chinese) in which White participants misperceived their partner's ethnicity were excluded from all analyses. A White-Chinese pair in which the partner misperceived the participant's ethnicity and a White-Chinese pair in which the partner did not successfully audiotape responses to the questions were dropped from analyses involving the partner's impressions and audiotaped responses, respectively.

Preliminary Analyses

We first tested whether White participants' initial feelings and behavior toward their partner varied according to the predictor variables. White participants' initial feelings toward their partner were entered into a regression with partner ethnicity (White = 0, Chinese = 1), previous contact with Chinese persons (centered), and the interaction between these variables as predictors. The main effects were entered on the first step, and the interaction on the second step. There were no significant or marginal

---

[1]Across metaperceptions, impressions, and behavior, the average correlation between scores on the closed-ended items regarding feelings conveyed and responses to the open-ended item regarding specific overtures was .44.

effects, overall $M = 4.61$, $SD = 1.52$. A parallel analysis of participants' scores on the behavior index also revealed no significant effects.[2]

Signal Amplification

Signal amplification was computed in terms of the discrepancy between participants' metaperceptions regarding the feelings they had conveyed and the impressions that their partners actually formed. In line with our hypotheses, a regression analysis of these discrepancy scores revealed a main effect for partner ethnicity; discrepancies were higher when participants were paired with a Chinese compared with a White partner, $b = 0.65$, $\beta = .35$, $t(35) = 2.20$, $p < .05$, $d = 0.73$. The analysis also yielded a Partner Ethnicity x Prior Contact interaction, $b = -0.25$, $\beta = -.47$, $t(34) = 2.00$, $p = .05$, $d = 0.66$. Simple effects analyses indicated that participants with lower levels of previous contact with Chinese persons showed greater signal amplification when interacting with a Chinese partner than when interacting with a White partner, $b = 1.23$, $t(34) = 3.04$, $p < .01$, $d = 1.00$, whereas participants with higher levels of previous contact did not, $b = 0.07$, $t < 1$. The predicted values are presented in Table 1. The effects of partner ethnicity and the Partner Ethnicity x Prior Contact interaction were similar or stronger when participants' initial feelings toward their partners were controlled, $b = 0.62$, $\beta = .34$, $t(34) = 2.11$, $p < .05$, and $b = -0.32$, $\beta = -.60$, $t(33) = 2.53$, $p < .025$, respectively. There was no effect for scores on the behavior index when they were entered into the regression analysis of signal amplification, $t < 1$.

TABLE 1. Predicted Values From Regression Analyses of Participants' Metaperceptions Regarding Feelings Conveyed and of Their Partners' Actual Impressions as a Function of Partner Ethnicity and Prior Contact

Prior contact	Partners' metaperceptions	Participants' impressions	Discrepancy (metaperceptions — impressions)
High			
White partner	-0.05	-0.34	0.29
Chinese partner	0.21	-0.15	0.36
Low			
White partner	-0.36	0.12	-0.48
Chinese partner	0.56	-0.19	0.75

Note: Simple effects for high and low prior contact were conducted at 1 standard deviation above and below the mean on this variable.

---

[2]Further analyses revealed no overall mean difference between participants' metaperceptions and their partners' actual impressions on either the closed-ended or open-ended measure, $ts < 1.23$, n.s.

Supplemental analyses confirmed that previous contact with Chinese persons was unrelated to participants' prejudice and ingroup identification, rs(37) = .02 and .15, n.s., respectively. Moreover, the Partner Ethnicity **X** Prior Contact interaction that was evident for metaperception-impression discrepancies remained significant in a further analysis in which prejudice and its interaction with partner ethnicity were controlled, as well as in a parallel analysis in which in-group identification and its interaction with partner ethnicity were controlled.

Implications of Signal Amplification

We began our examination of the implications of signal amplification by confirming that White participants were in fact more likely to think that they had communicated more interest than their partner in the mixed- rather than same-ethnicity pairs. As expected in light of White participants' propensity toward signal amplification, their responses to the dichotomous question regarding which person's audiotape communicated more interest in the other revealed an effect for partner ethnicity, $b = 0.40$, $\beta = .40$, t(34) = 2.55, $p < .025$, $d = 0.87$; participants were more likely to indicate that they had communicated more interest than their partner when their partner was Chinese (10/16, 63%) rather than White (5/21, 24%). Analyses of partners' responses to this question confirmed that they did not corroborate participants' judgments, $t < 1$.

Next, we assessed changes in participants' interest in becoming friends with their partner over the course of the interaction. Because our predictions centered on the defensive distancing that might occur in response to feeling rejected, rather than on the discovery of interpersonal differences that detract from liking, we examined changes in interest in pursuing a friendship separately from changes in liking and the feeling of sharing things in common. That is, the three items assessing initial and final friendship interest were analyzed separately from the three items assessing initial and final liking. In line with predictions, regression analyses revealed that participants' reported interest in pursuing a friendship decreased over time to a greater extent when their partner was Chinese rather than White, $b = 0.66$, $\beta = .36$, t(34) = 2.26, $p < .05$, $d = 0.75$, and that there was no such change for liking, $t < 1$.

To provide more direct support for the defensive-distancing account, we examined whether participants' perceptions regarding whose audiotaped message communicated more interest mediated decreases in friendship interest over time. Because there were no effects involving the contact variable to this point, they were not included in the mediation analyses. When participants' judgments regarding who had communicated more interest were entered into the regression predicting change in interest over time, there was a significant effect for these judgments, $b = 0.62$, $\beta = .33$, t(34) = 2.00, $p = .05$, $d = 0.66$, and the effect for partner ethnicity was no longer significant ($p = .25$). Analyses revealed a significant mediation effect, Sobel's $Z = 1.64$, $p = .05$ (one-tailed). The results for the mediation analysis were somewhat stronger when we instead entered the discrepancy between participants' metaperceptions and their impression of the interest that their partner had conveyed as the mediator, $Z = 1.70$, $p < .05$ (one-tailed). Thus, White participants' sense that they had gone out on a limb and their partner had not done the same in turn appeared to account for their eventual withdrawal of interest and engagement from Chinese partners.

Chinese Participants' Perspective

Our analyses from Chinese participants' perspective involved only Chinese-Chinese and White-Chinese pairs. In the White-Chinese pairs, the Chinese pair member was designated as the participant, and the White pair member was designated as the partner. In the Chinese-Chinese pairs, we randomly selected one pair member to be the participant and the other to be the partner. Two White-Chinese pairs in which Chinese participants misperceived their partner's ethnicity or did not successfully audiotape responses were excluded from all analyses. One White-Chinese pair in which the partner misperceived the participant's ethnicity was dropped from analyses involving the partner's impressions.

Preliminary Analyses

We first tested whether Chinese participants' initial feelings and behavior toward their partner varied according to their partner's ethnicity. Chinese participants' initial feelings toward their partner were entered into a regression with partner ethnicity (White = 0, Chinese = 1) as a predictor. There was no significant or marginal effect, overall $M = 5.56$, $SD = 1.50$. A parallel analysis of participants' scores on the behavior index also revealed no significant effect.

Signal Amplification

A regression analysis of the discrepancies between participants' metaperceptions regarding the feelings they had conveyed and the impressions that their partners actually formed revealed no effect for partner ethnicity, $t < 1$.

Implications of Signal Amplification

In view of the fact that there was no evidence of signal amplification by Chinese participants, it was not surprising that analyses of their responses to the question regarding which person's audiotape communicated more interest and of changes in their friendship interest over time yielded no effects for partner ethnicity.

Discussion

This study sheds new light on the precursors and consequences of systematic miscommunications regarding relationship interest that can occur during intergroup interaction. Consistent with our hypothesis that low levels of intergroup contact set the stage for signal amplification in intergroup interaction, individuals' propensity to exhibit heightened bias with respect to intergroup as compared with intragroup overtures was most evident for those with little prior experience with the out-group. These results suggest a positive consequence of intergroup contact that is not centered on individuals' intergroup attitudes. Contact with the out-group may, by making intergroup interaction more familiar and less anxiety provoking, reduce individuals' propensity to exhibit egocentric social perception biases such as signal amplification.

Our results also illuminate, in turn, the mechanism through which signal amplification might hinder relationship development. White participants' perception of having initially communicated more interest than their Chinese partner mediated subsequent decreases in their interest in pursuing a friendship with him or her. This pattern, which was specific to intergroup communications, likely reflects that the sense of having communicated more enthusiasm than the other person fostered dismay and defensive distancing. In essence, White participants decided—in a self-protective fashion—that they were not interested in their Chinese partner after all. The plausibility of this account is enhanced by the fact that there were no parallel changes in White participants' perceptions of how much they shared in common with their partner, and hence no evidence that the discovery of interpersonal differences played a role. These results highlight the interpersonal costs attached to egocentric biases in individuals' beliefs about the attributes and feelings they have communicated to others, and illustrate that such biases can be particularly problematic in intergroup interaction.

Finally, an important limitation of the present research needs to be acknowledged. Our results regarding the effects of prior intergroup contact are correlational. The distinct results for White versus Chinese participants clearly could be attributable to a wide variety of factors aside from prior intergroup experience, such as group status, collectivism, or other cultural differences. However, our confidence in the role of prior intergroup experience per se is bolstered by the fact that we did obtain the expected effects for this variable when it was directly measured across majority group members.

Conclusion

The present findings complement recent research by Shelton and Richeson (2005) and Vorauer (2005) revealing misunderstandings surrounding communications across group boundaries. One important implication of our results is that contact with the out-group may have subtle positive effects on intergroup relations by reducing individuals' propensity to exhibit egocentric social perception biases in the context of intergroup interaction. Another key implication is that efforts to "save face" contribute to the robust tendency for individuals to form social bonds primarily within their own ethnic group. In particular, our findings underscore that miscommunications regarding relationship interest constitute a significant potential barrier—beyond prejudice and lack of opportunity—to the formation of cross-group friendships.

Acknowledgments

This article is based on a premaster's thesis submitted by Yumiko Sakamoto to the Department of Psychology at the University of Manitoba. The research was facilitated by a grant from the Social Sciences and Humanities Research Council of Canada to Jacquie Vorauer. We thank Richard Elias, Gabrielle Gosselin, Kristin Stevens, Jennifer Tan, and Pek Har Yee for their assistance with coding and data entry, and Dan Bailis and Jessica Cameron for their comments on a previous version of the article.

References

Aron, A., Melinat, E., Aron, E., Vallone, R.D., & Bator, R.J. (1997). The experimental generation of interpersonal closeness: A procedure and some preliminary findings. *Personality and Social Psychology Bulletin, 23*, 363–377.

Blair, I.V., Park, B., & Bachelor, J. (2003). Understanding intergroup anxiety: Are some people more anxious than others? *Group Processes and Intergroup Relations, 6*, 151–169.

Buss, A.H. (1980). *Self-consciousness and social anxiety.* San Francisco: Freeman.

Devine, P.G., Evett, S.R., & Vasquez-Suson, K.A. (1996). Exploring the interpersonal dynamics of intergroup contact. In R. Sorrentino & E.T. Higgins (Eds.), *Handbook of motivation and cognition:* Vol. 3. *The interpersonal context* (pp. 423–464). New York: Guilford Press.

Gilovich, T., Kruger, J., & Savitsky, K. (1999). Everyday egocentrism and everyday interpersonal problems. In R.M. Kowalski & M.R. Leary (Eds.), *The social psychology of emotional and behavioral problems: Interfaces of social and clinical psychology* (pp. 69–95). Washington, DC: American Psychological Association.

Levin, S., van Laar, C., & Sidanius, J. (2003). The effects of ingroup and outgroup friendship on ethnic attitudes in college: A longitudinal study. *Group Processes and Intergroup Relations, 6*, 76–92.

Luhtanen, R., & Crocker, J. (1992). A collective self-esteem scale: Self-evaluation of one's social identity. *Personality and Social Psychology Bulletin, 18*, 302–318.

McConahay, J.G., Hardee, B.B., & Batts, V. (1981). Has racism declined? It depends on who's asking and what is asked. *Journal of Conflict Resolution, 25*, 563–579.

Pettigrew, T.F. (1998). Intergroup contact theory. *Annual Review of Psychology, 49*, 65–85.

Shelton, J.N., & Richeson, J.A. (2005). Intergroup contact and pluralistic ignorance. *Journal of Personality and Social Psychology, 88*, 91–107.

Steele, C.M., Spencer, S.J., & Aronson, J. (2002). Contending with group image: The psychology of stereotype and social identity threat. In M.P. Zanna (Ed.), *Advances in experimental social psychology* (Vol. 34, pp. 379–440). San Diego, CA: Academic Press.

Vorauer, J.D. (2005). Miscommunications surrounding efforts to reach out across group boundaries. *Personality and Social Psychology Bulletin, 31*, 1653–1664.

Vorauer, J.D., Cameron, J.J., Holmes, J.G., & Pearce, D.G. (2003). Invisible overtures: Fears of rejection and the signal amplification bias. *Journal of Personality and Social Psychology, 84*, 793–812.

Vorauer, J.D., & Kumhyr, S.M. (2001). Is this about you or me? Self- versus other-directed judgments and feelings in response to intergroup interaction. *Personality and Social Psychology Bulletin, 27*, 706–719.

Vorauer, J.D., & Ross, M. (1999). Self-awareness and feeling transparent: Failing to suppress one's self. *Journal of Experimental Social Psychology, 35*, 415–440.

The Nonverbal Mediation of Self-Fulfilling Prophecies in Interracial Interaction

By Carl O. Word, Mark P. Zanna, and Joel Cooper, Princeton University

Two experiments were designed to demonstrate the existence of a self-fulfilling prophecy mediated by nonverbal behavior in an interracial interaction. The results of Experiment 1, which employed naive, white job interviewers and trained white and black job applicants, demonstrated that black applicants received (a) less immediacy, (b) higher rates of speech errors, and (c) shorter amounts of interview time. Experiment 2 employed naive, white applicants and trained white interviewers. In this experiment subject-applicants received behaviors that approximated those given either the black or white applicants in Experiment 1. The main results indicated that subjects treated like the blacks of Experiment 1 were judged to perform less adequately and to be more nervous in the interview situation than subjects treated like the whites. The former subjects also reciprocated with less proximate positions and rated the interviewers as being less adequate and friendly. The implications of these findings for black unemployment were discussed.

Sociologist Robert Merton (1957), by suggesting that an originally false definition of a situation can influence the believer to act in such a way as to bring about that situation, is generally credited with focusing attention on the phenomenon of the self-fulfilling prophecy. The present investigation is concerned with such a phenomenon in face-to-face, dyadic interactions. In this context it is hypothesized that one person's attitudes and expectations about the other person may influence the believer's actions, which in turn, may induce the other person to behave in a way that confirms the original false definition. Interpersonally, this phenomenon has been documented in schools, with teachers' expectations influencing students' performances, and in psychology laboratories, with experimenters' expectations influencing subjects' responses (cf. Rosenthal, 1971). In the present study attention will be directed toward (1) possible nonverbal mediators of this effect, and (2) the reciprocal performances of the interactants. The focus, in addition, will be on the interaction of black and white Americans with a view toward examining the employment outcomes of black job applicants interviewed by whites.

Carl O. Word, Mark P. Zanna & Joel Cooper, "The Nonverbal Mediation of Self-Fulfilling Prophecies in Interracial Interaction," *Journal of Experimental Social Psychology*, vol. 10, no. 2, pp. 109–120. Copyright © 1974 by Elsevier Science & Technology Journals. Reprinted with permission.

Attitudes and Immediacy

Mehrabian (1968) has recently reported a series of studies linking attitudes toward a target person and the concomitant nonverbal behavior directed toward that person. The results of these studies have consistently found that closer interpersonal distances, more eye contact, more direct shoulder orientation, and more forward lean are a consequence of more positive attitudes toward an addressee. Mehrabian (1969) has considered such nonverbal behaviors in terms of "immediacy" and has defined immediacy "as the extent to which communication behaviors enhance closeness to and nonverbal interaction with another … greater immediacy is due to increasing degrees of physical proximity and/or increasing perceptual availability of the communicator to the addressee" (p. 203).

A related series of studies has been conducted by Kleck and his associates (Kleck, 1968; Kleck, Buck, Goller, London, Pfeiffer & Vukcevic, 1968; Kleck, Ono & Hastorf, 1966) pursuing Goffman's (1963) observation that normals tend to avoid stigmatized persons. They have begun to document what might be called a nonverbal stigma effect. For example, normal interactants were found to terminate interviews sooner (Kleck et al., 1966) and to exhibit greater motoric inhibition (Kleck, 1968) with a handicapped person (i.e., leg amputee), and to employ greater interaction distances with an epileptic stranger (Kleck et al., 1968). This set of studies, then, also suggests that those persons who possess a personal characteristic which is discrediting in the eyes of others are treated with less immediate behaviors. In addition to such discrediting characteristics as a physical disability or a criminal record, Goffman (1963) includes blackness in a white society as a stigmatizing trait.

Thus, a body of data suggests that (1) attitudes toward an individual are linked with nonverbal behavior emitted toward that individual, and (2) positive attitudes lead to more immediate nonverbal behaviors. Two questions that now arise are concerned with whether such behaviors are (1) decoded or understood by the target and (2) reciprocated.

Decoding and Reciprocating Immediacy

Recent studies suggest that such evaluative, nonverbal behaviors are both decoded and reciprocated. Mehrabian (1967) found friendliness ratings of an interviewer varied as a function of the physical interaction distance, and the immediacy of head and body positions given subjects. Eye contact has been extensively investigated. Both Kleck and Nuessle (1968) and Jones and Cooper (1971) found that a high degree of eye contact produced higher evaluations of the communicator and produced more positive evaluations on the part of the subjects than did low eye contact. Since individuals apparently are able to decode affective components of communications from variations in immediacy behavior, it seems reasonable to expect they would reciprocate such variations. This proposition also has received support, Rosenfeld (1967), for example, found that subjects treated to more smiles and positive head nods did reciprocate with more of each.

Thus individuals apparently decode less immediacy as indicating less friendly behavior and reciprocate with less friendly (i.e., less immediate) behavior of their own. Since individuals seldom are able to monitor their own nonverbal behaviors, they are more likely to attribute the reciprocated immediacy, not to their own, original nonverbal behavior, but instead to some disposition inherent in their cointeractant (cf. Jones & Nisbett, 1971). With this nonverbal reciprocation, then, a self-fulfilling prophecy is born.

White-Black Interaction in a Job Interview Setting

So far we have been concerned with describing possible mechanisms of interpersonal, self-fulfilling prophecies. The discussion now turns to consider such a process in black-white, dyadic interactions. It has been demonstrated time and again that white Americans have generalized, negative evaluations (e.g., stereotypes) of black Americans. This has been shown most recently in our own subject population by Darley, Lewis, and Glucksberg (1972). Such negative evaluations, of course, represent the kind of attitudes that can initiate an interpersonal, self-fulfilling prophecy. The general hypothesis that the present study sought to investigate, therefore, was that whites interacting with blacks will emit nonverbal behaviors corresponding to negative evaluations and that blacks, in turn, will reciprocate with less immediate behaviors. If the context in which the interaction occurs involves a job interview, with the white interviewing the black, such reciprocated behavior may be interpreted as less adequate performance, thus confirming, in part, the interviewer's original attitude.

These general expectations are operationalized by two subhypotheses: First, black, as compared to white, job applicants will receive less immediate nonverbal communications from white job interviewers; second, recipients of less immediate nonverbal communications, whether black or white, will reciprocate these communications and be judged to perform less adequately in the job interview situation than recipients of more positive nonverbal communications. The first hypothesis was tested in Experiment 1, which employed naive, white job interviewers and trained white and black job applicants; the second in Experiment 2, which used naive, white job applicants and trained white job interviewers who were instructed to emit either immediate or nonimmediate cues.

Experiment 1

Method

Overview

In the context of a study on group decision-making white subjects, as representatives of a team in competition with other teams, interviewed both white and black job applicants. The applicants were trained to respond similarly in both the verbal and nonverbal channels. The interview situation itself was arranged to give the subject-interviewers the opportunity to treat their applicants differentially without the knowledge (1) that their own behavior was being monitored, or (2) that race of the applicants was the experimental variable.

Subjects (Interviewers) and Confederates (Applicants and Team Members)

Subject-interviewers were 15 white, Princeton males recruited to participate in a study of group decision-making conducted by Career Services and the Psychology Department. They were informed that the study would last approximately one hour and a half and that they would be paid $2.00 and possibly $5.00 more. One of the subjects was eliminated when he indicated that he was aware of the purpose of the study before the debriefing period. No other subject volunteered this sort of information after intensive probing, leaving an *n* of 14.

Confederate-applicants were two black and three white high school student volunteers referred by their high school counselor. Each was told that the study was concerned with cognitive functioning and that the experimenter was interested in finding out how subjects made up their minds when forced to choose between nearly identical job applicants. All confederates in both experiments were naive with respect to the hypotheses. Intensive probing following the experiment indicated that they did not become aware. The three confederates who served as the subject's "team members" and the experimenter were male Princeton volunteers.

Procedure

Upon arrival the subjects entered a room containing two confederate team members, who introduced themselves and acted friendly. Another confederate entered and acted friendly, as well. Then the experimenter entered, handed out written instructions and answered any questions.

The instructions informed subjects that the four people in the room constituted a team; that they were to compete with four other teams in planning a marketing campaign; and that they needed to select another member from four high school applicants. In order to increase incentive and concern, an additional $5.00 was promised to the team which performed best in the competition. Using a supposedly random draw, the subject was chosen to interview the applicants. He was then handed a list of 15 questions which was to serve as the interview material, told he had 45 minutes to interview all four high school students and taken to the interview room where the first confederate-applicant was already seated. In order to measure the physical distance that the interviewer placed himself from the applicant, the experimenter upon entering the interview room, feigned to discover that there was no chair for the interviewer. Subjects were then asked to wheel in a chair from an adjoining room.

Subjects were led to believe that there would be four interviews so that the race variable would be less apparent to them. In addition, to eliminate any special effect that might occur in the first and last interview, an a priori decision was made not to analyze the data from the first "warm-up" interview and not to have a fourth interview. The "warm-up" job candidate was always white. Half the subjects then interviewed a black followed by a white applicant; the other half interviewed a white then a black candidate. After completion of the third interview, subjects were told that the fourth applicant had called to cancel his appointment. After the third interview, subjects were paid and debriefed.

Applicant Performance

Confederate-applicants were trained to act in a standard way to all interviewers. First, they devised answers to the 15 questions such that their answers, though not identical, would represent equally qualifying answers. Confederates then rehearsed these answers until two judges rated their performances to be equal. Confederates were also trained to seat themselves, shoulders parallel to the backs of their chairs (10° from vertical) and to make eye contact with the interviewer 50% of the time. A code was devised to signal confederates during their interviews if they deviated from the pose or began to reciprocate the gestures or head nods given them.

Dependent Measures

Immediacy behaviors. Following Mehrabian (1968, 1969), four indices of psychological immediacy were assessed: (1) Physical Distance between interviewer and interviewee, measured in inches; (2) Forward Lean, scored in 10° units, with zero representing the vertical position and positive scores representing the torso leaning toward the confederate; (3) Eye Contact, defined as the proportion of time the subject looked directly at the confederate's eyes; and (4) Shoulder Orientation, scored in units of 10° with zero representing the subject's shoulders parallel to those of the confederate and positive scores indicating a shift in either direction. Two judges,[1] placed behind one-way mirrors, scored the immediacy behaviors.

More distance and shoulder angle represent less immediate behaviors while more forward lean and more eye contact represent more immediate behaviors. An index of total immediacy was constructed by summing the four measures, standardized, and weighted according to the regression equation beta weights established by Mehrabian (1969). Final scores of this index represent (-.6) distance + (.3) forward lean + (.3) eye contact + (- .1) shoulder orientation. Positive scores represent more immediate performances.

Related Behaviors. Two related behaviors, which indicate differential evaluations of the applicants (cf. Mehrabian, 1969), were also assessed: (1) Interview length indicates the amount of time from the point the subject entered the interview room until he announced the interview was over, in minutes. This measure was taken by the experimenter. (2) Speech Error Rate, scored by two additional judges from audiotapes, represents the sum of (a) sentence changes, (b) repetitions, (c) stutters, (d) sentence incompletions, and (e) intruding, incoherent sounds divided by the length of the interview and averaged over the two judges. Higher scores represent more speech errors per minute.

Results

Reliabilities and Order Effects

Reliabilities, obtained by correlating the judges' ratings, ranged from .60 to .90 (see Table 1). Preliminary analyses also indicated that there were no effects for the order in which confederate-applicants appeared, so that the results are based on data collapsed across this variable.

---

[3]All judges employed in the present research were Princeton undergraduates. Each worked independently and was naive concerning the hypothesis under investigation. Intensive probing indicated that they did not become aware of the hypothesis.

Immediacy Behaviors

The results, presented in Table 1, indicate that, overall, black job candidates received less immediate behaviors than white applicants ($t = 2.79$; $df = 13$; $p < .02$). On the average, blacks received a negative total immediacy score; whites received a positive one. This overall difference is primarily due to the fact that the white interviewers physically placed themselves further from black than white applicants ($t = 2.36$; $df = 13$; $p < .05$). None of the other indices of immediacy showed reliable differences when considered separately.

Related Behaviors

The results for interview length and speech error rate are also presented in Table 1. Here it can be seen that blacks also received less immediate behaviors. White interviewers spent 25% less time ($t = 3.22$; $df = 13$; $p < .01$) and had higher rates of speech errors ($t = 2.43$; $df = 13$; $p < .05$) with black as compared to white job candidates.

The results of the first experiment provide support for the hypothesis that black, as compared to white, job applicants receive less immediate nonverbal communications from white job interviewers. Indirectly the results also provide support for the conceptualization of blackness as a stigmatizing trait. The differences in time (evidenced by 12 of 14 interviewers), in total immediacy (evidenced by 10 of 14 interviewers), and in speech error rate (evidenced by 11 of 14 interviewers) argues for an extension of the stigma effect obtained by Kleck and his associates to include black Americans.

TABLE 1. Mean Interviewer Behavior as a Function of Race of Job Applicant; Experiment 1

Behavior	Reliability	Blacks	Whites	t^b	P
Total immediacy[1]	——	-.11	.38	2.79	<.02
Distance	.90	62.29 inches	58.43 inches	2.36	<.05
Forward lean	.68	-8.76 degrees	-6.12 degrees	1.09	n.s.
Eye contact	.80	62.71%	61.46%	<1	n.s.
Shoulder orientation	.60	22.46 degrees	23.08 degrees	<1	n.s.
Related behaviors					
Interview length	—	9.42 min.	12.77 min.	3.22	<.01
Speech error rate	.88	3.54 errors/min.	2.37 errors/min.	2.43	<05

[a] See text for weighting formula, from Mehrabian (1969).

[b] t test for correlated samples was employed.

Experiment 2

Method

Overview

A second experiment was conducted to ascertain what effect the differences black and white applicants received in Experiment 1 would have on an applicant's job interview performance. In the context of training job interviewers, subject-applicants were interviewed by confederate-interviewers under one of two conditions. In the Immediate condition, as compared to the Nonimmediate condition, interviewers (1) sat closer to the applicant, (2) made fewer speech errors per minute, and (3) actually took longer to give their interviews. The main dependent measures were concerned with the interview performance of the applicant, both in terms of its judged adequacy for obtaining the job and in terms of its reciprocation of immediacy behaviors.

Subjects (Job Applicants) and Confederates (Interviewers)

Thirty white male Princeton University students were recruited ostensibly to help Career Services train interviewers for an upcoming summer job operation. No subjects were eliminated from the study, leaving an n of 15 in each condition. The two confederate-interviewers were also white male Princeton students.

Procedure

Upon arrival each subject was given an instruction sheet which informed him that Career Services had contracted with the Psychology Department to train Princeton juniors and seniors in the techniques of job interviewing and that one of the techniques chosen included videotaping inter-viewers with job applicants for feedback purposes. The subject was then asked to simulate a job applicant, to be honest, and to really compete for the job, so as to give the interviewer real, lifelike practice. To make the simulation more meaningful, subjects were also informed that the applicant chosen from five interviewed that evening would receive an additional $1.50. Subjects were taken to the interview room and asked to be seated in a large swivel chair, while the Experimenter turned on the camera. The confederate-interviewer then entered, and assumed either an immediate or nonimmediate position which will be described in more detail below. Exactly five minutes into the interviewing in both conditions, a guise was developed whose result was that the experimenter had to reclaim the chair in which the subject was sitting. The subject was then asked to take a folding chair leaning against the wall and to continue the interview. The distance from the interviewer which the subject placed his new chair was one of the study's dependent measures designed to assess reciprocated immediacy.

When the interview ended, the experimenter took the subject to another room where a second investigator, blind as to the condition of the subject, administered self-report scales and answered any questions. Subject was then paid and debriefed.

Immediacy Manipulation

As in the Kleck and Nuessle (1968) and the Jones and Cooper (1971) studies, systematic nonverbal variations were introduced by specifically training confederates. Two confederate-interviewers alternated in the two conditions. In the Immediate condition, confederates sat at a chair on the side of a table. In the Nonimmediate condition, confederates sat fully behind the table. The difference in distance from the subject's chair was about four inches, representing the mean difference in distance white interviewers gave black and white applicants in Experiment 1.[2]

In addition, the confederate-interviewers in the Immediate condition were trained to behave as precisely as possible like the subject-interviewers in Experiment 1 had acted toward white applicants. In the Nonimmediate condition, interviewers were trained to act as subject-interviewers had acted toward Blacks in Experiment 1. The factors used to simulate the immediacy behaviors found in the first experiment were speech error rate, length of interview and, as has been previously mentioned, physical distance. Eye contact, shoulder orientation and forward lean did not show significant differences in Experiment 1 and thus were held constant in Experiment 2 (with levels set at 50% eye contact, 0° shoulder orientation and 20° forward lean).

Dependent Measures

Three classes of dependent variables were collected: (1) judges' ratings of interview performance; (2) judges' ratings of reciprocated immediacy behaviors; and (3) subjects' ratings of their post-interview mood state and attitudes toward the interviewer.

Applicant performance. Applicant interview performance and demeanor were rated by a panel of two judges from videotapes of the interviews. The videotapes were recorded at such an angle that judges viewed only the applicant, not the confederate- interviewer. The judges were merely instructed about the type of job subjects were applying for, and were asked to rate (1) the overall adequacy of each subject's performance and (2) each subject's composure on five (0–4) point scales. High scores, averaged over the judges, represent more adequate and more calm, relaxed performances, respectively.

Reciprocated immediacy behaviors. Two additional judges, placed behind one-way mirrors as in Experiment 1, recorded subjects' forward lean, eye contact, and shoulder orientation in accordance with the procedures established by Mehrabian (1969). Distance was directly measured after each interview, and represents the distance, in inches, from the middle of the interviewer-confederate's chair to the middle of the subject's chair, after the interruption. Speech errors were scored by another panel of

---

[4]By having the interviewer sit either behind or at the side of the table, the impact of the four inch difference in distance was intentionally maximized in terms of psychological immediacy.

two judges from audiotapes of the interviews, also according to Mehrabian's (1969) procedures. High scores represent more speech errors per minute.

Applicant mood and attitude toward the interviewer. After the interview, subjects filled out a series of questionnaires designed to assess their mood state and their attitudes toward the interviewer. Following Jones and Cooper (1971), subjects' moods were expected to vary as a function of immediacy conditions. The mood scale adapted from that study was employed. It consisted of six polar adjectives (e.g., happy-sad) separated by seven-point scales. Subjects were asked to respond to each pair according to "the way you feel about yourself."

Two measures of subjects' attitudes toward the interviewer were collected. First, subjects were asked to rate the friendliness of the interviewer on an 11-point scale, with zero representing an "unfriendly" and 10 representing a "friendly" interviewer, respectively. Second, in order to assess subjects' attitudes concerning the adequacy of the interviewer as an individual, they were asked to check the six adjectives best describing their interviewer from a list of 16 drawn from Gough's Adjective Checklist. Final scores represent the number of positive adjectives chosen minus the number of negative adjectives checked.

Results

Reliabilities and Interviewer Effects

Reliabilities, obtained by correlating judges' ratings, ranged from .66 to .86 (see Table 2). Preliminary analyses also indicated that there were no effects for interviewers, so that the results presented are based on data collapsed across this variable.

Applicant Performance

It was predicted from an analysis of the communicative functions of nonimmediacy that applicants would be adversely affected by the receipt of nonimmediate communications. Those effects were expected to manifest themselves in less adequate job-interview performances.

Subjects in the two conditions were rated by two judges from videotapes. The main dependent measure, applicant adequacy for the job, showed striking differences as a function of immediacy conditions (see Table 2). Subjects in the Nonimmediate condition were judged significantly less adequate for the job (F = 7.96; *df* = 1/28; *p* < .01). Subjects in the Nonimmediate condition were also judged to be reliably less calm and composed (F = 16.96; *df* = 1/28; *p* < .001).

Reciprocated Immediacy Behaviors

Following Rosenfeld (1967) among others, it was expected that subjects encountering less immediate communications would reciprocate with less immediate behaviors of their own. This expectation was supported by both the measures of physical distance and speech error rate (see Table 2).

TABLE 2. Mean Applicant Responses Under Two Conditions of Interviewer Immediacy; Experiment 2

Response	Reliability	Nonimmediate	Immediate	F	P
Applicant performance					
Rated performance	.66	1.44	2.22	7.96	<.01
Rated demeanor	.86	1.62	3.02	16.46	<.001
Immediacy behaviors					
Distance	—	72.73 inches	56.93 inches	9.19	<.01
Speech error rate	.74	5.01 errors/min.	3.33 errors/min.	3.40	<.10
Self reported mood and attitudes					
Mood	—	3.77	5.97	1.34	n.s
Interviewer friendliness	—	4.33	6.60	22.91	<.001
Interviewer adequacy	—	-1.07	1.53	8.64	<.01

Subjects in the Immediate condition, on the average, placed their chairs eight inches closer to the interviewer after their initial chair was removed; subjects in the Nonimmediate conditions placed their chairs four inches further away from their interviewer. The mean difference between the two groups was highly significant ($F = 9.19$; $df = 1/28$; $P < .01$).

As in Experiment 1 mean comparisons for the forward lean, eye contact, and shoulder orientation measures of immediacy did not reach significance. The combination of these measures, using the weighting formula devised by Mehrabian (1969), however, was reliably different (means of — .29 and .29 in the Nonimmediate and Immediate conditions, respectively; $F = 5.44$; $df = 1/28$; $P < .05$).

The rate at which subjects made speech errors also tended to be reciprocated with subjects in the Nonimmediate condition exhibiting a higher rate than subjects in the Immediate condition ($F = 3.40$; $df = 1/28$; $P < .10$).

Applicant Mood and Attitude Toward the Interviewer

It was expected that subjects receiving less immediate (i.e., less positive) communication would (1) feel less positively after their interviews, and (2) hold less positive attitudes toward the interviewer himself. These expectations were only partially supported (see Table 2). Although subjects in the Nonimmediate condition reported less positive moods than subjects in the Immediate condition, this difference was not statistically reliable.

Subjects in the less immediate condition did, however, rate their interviewers to be less friendly ($F = 22.91$; $df = 1/28$; $P < .001$) and less adequate overall ($F = 8.64$; $df = 1/28$; $P < .01$) than subjects in the more immediate condition.

Discussion

Results from the two experiments provide clear support for the two subhypotheses, and offer inferential evidence for the general notion that self-fulfilling prophecies can and do occur in interracial interactions.

The results of Experiment 1 indicated that black applicants were, in fact, treated to less immediacy than their white counterparts. Goffman's (1963) conception of blackness as a stigmatizing trait in Anglo-American society is, thus, given experimental support—insofar as that classification predicts avoidance behaviors in interactions with normals. These results may also be viewed as extending the stigma effect documented by Kleck and his associates with handicapped persons.

That the differential treatment black and white applicants received in Experiment 1 can influence the performance and attitudes of job candidates was clearly demonstrated in Experiment 2. In that experiment those applicants, treated similarly to the way Blacks were treated in Experiment 1, performed less well, reciprocated less immediacy, and found their interviewers to be less adequate. Taken together the two experiments provide evidence for the assertion that nonverbal, immediacy cues mediate, in part, the performance of an applicant in a job- interview situation. Further, the experiments suggest that the model of a self-fulfilling prophecy, mediated by nonverbal cues, (1) is applicable to this setting, and (2) can account, in part, for the less adequate performances of black applicants (cf. Sattler, 1970).

Social scientists have often tended to focus their attention for such phenomena as unemployment in black communities on the dispositions of the disinherited. Such an approach has been termed "victim analysis" for its preoccupation with the wounds, defects and personalities of the victimized as an explanation for social problems (Ryan, 1971). The present results suggest that analyses of black-white interactions, particularly in the area of job-seeking Blacks in white society, might profit if it were assumed that the "problem" of black performance resides not entirely within the Blacks, but rather within the interaction setting itself.

References

Darley, J. M., Lewis, L. D., & Glucksberg., S. *Stereotype persistence and change among college students: one more time.* Unpublished Manuscript, Princeton University, 1972.

Goffman, E. Stigma: notes on the management of spoiled identity. *Englewood Cliffs,* New Jersey: Prentice-Hall, 1963.

Jones, R. E., & Cooper, J. Mediation of experimenter effects. *Journal of Personality and Social Psychology*, 1971, 20, 70–74.

Jones, E. E., & Nisbett, R. E. The actor and the observer: divergent perceptions of the causes of behavior. In E. E. Jones, D. E. Kanouse, H. H. Kelley, R. E. Nisbett, S. Valins and B. Weiner (Eds.), *Attribution; perceiving the causes of behavior.* New York: General Learning Press, 1971.

Kleck, R. E. Physical stigma and nonverbal cues emitted in face-to-face interactions. *Human Relations,* 1968, 21, 19–28.

Kleck, R., Buck, P. L., Goller, W. L., London, R. S., Pfeiffer, J. R., & Vukcevic, D. P. Effects of stigmatizing conditions on the use of personal space. *Psychological Reports*, 1968, *23*, 111–118.

Kleck, R. E., & Nuessle, W. Congruence between indicative and communicative functions of eye contact in interpersonal relations. *British Journal of Social and Clinical Psychology*, 1968, *7*, 241–246.

Kleck, R. E., Ono, H., & Hastorf, A. H. The effects of physical deviance upon face-to-face interaction. *Human Relations*, 1966, 19, 425-436.

Mehrabian, A. Orientation behaviors and nonverbal attitude communication. *Journal of Communication*, 1967, 17, 324–332.

Mehrabian, A. Inference of attitudes from the posture, orientation, and distance of a communicator. *Journal of Consulting and Clinical Psychology*, 1968, 32, 296–308.

Mehrabian, A. Some referents and measures of nonverbal behavior. *Behavior Research Methods and Instrumentation*, 1969, 1, 203–207. MERTON, R. K. *Social theory and social structure.* New York: Free Press, 1957.

Rosenfeld, H. M. Nonverbal reciprocation of approval: an experimental analysis. *Journal of Experimental and Social Psychology*, 1967, 3, 102–111.

Rosenthal, R. Teacher expectations. In G. S. Lesser (Ed.), *Psychology and the educational process.* Glenview, Illinois:

Ryan, W., Scott, Foresman. *Blaming the victim.* New York: Pantheon, 1971.

SATTLER, J. Racial "experimenter effects" in experimentation, testing, interviewing and psychotherapy. *Psychological Bulletin*, 1970, 73, 136–160.

CPSIA information can be obtained
at www.ICGtesting.com
Printed in the USA
FSOW03n1044030915
10687FS